CCNA Security
Lab Manual
Version 1.2

Cisco Networking Academy

Cisco Press
800 East 96th Street
Indianapolis, Indiana 46240 USA

CCNA Security Lab Manual
Version 1.2

Cisco Networking Academy

Copyright© 2015 Cisco Systems, Inc.

Published by:
Cisco Press
800 East 96th Street
Indianapolis, IN 46240 USA

Printed in the United States of America

First Printing September 2014

Library of Congress Control Number: 2014948812

ISBN-13: 978-1-58713-347-3
ISBN-10: 1-58713-347-4

Warning and Disclaimer

This book is designed to provide information about networking. Every effort has been made to make this book as complete and as accurate as possible, but no warranty or fitness is implied.

The information is provided on an "as is" basis. The authors, Cisco Press, and Cisco Systems, Inc. shall have neither liability nor responsibility to any person or entity with respect to any loss or damages arising from the information contained in this book or from the use of the discs or programs that may accompany it.

The opinions expressed in this book belong to the author and are not necessarily those of Cisco Systems, Inc.

Trademark Acknowledgments

All terms mentioned in this book that are known to be trademarks or service marks have been appropriately capitalized. Cisco Press or Cisco Systems, Inc., cannot attest to the accuracy of this information. Use of a term in this book should not be regarded as affecting the validity of any trademark or service mark.

This book is part of the Cisco Networking Academy® series from Cisco Press. The products in this series support and complement the Cisco Networking Academy curriculum. If you are using this book outside the Networking Academy, then you are not preparing with a Cisco trained and authorized Networking Academy provider.

For more information on the Cisco Networking Academy or to locate a Networking Academy, please visit www.cisco.com/edu.

CISCO

Feedback Information

At Cisco Press, our goal is to create in-depth technical books of the highest quality and value. Each book is crafted with care and precision, undergoing rigorous development that involves the unique expertise of members from the professional technical community.

Readers' feedback is a natural continuation of this process. If you have any comments regarding how we could improve the quality of this book, or otherwise alter it to better suit your needs, you can contact us through email at feedback@ciscopress.com. Please make sure to include the book title and ISBN in your message.

We greatly appreciate your assistance.

Publisher	Paul Boger
Associate Publisher	Dave Dusthimer
Business Operation Manager, Cisco Press	Jan Cornelssen
Executive Editor	Mary Beth Ray
Managing Editor	Sandra Schroeder
Project Editor	Mandie Frank
Proofreader	Sarah Kearns
Editorial Assistant	Vanessa Evans
Cover Designer	Mark Shirar

Americas Headquarters
Cisco Systems, Inc.
170 West Tasman Drive
San Jose, CA 95134-1706
USA
www.cisco.com
Tel: 408 526-4000
800 553-NETS (6387)
Fax: 408 527-0883

Asia Pacific Headquarters
Cisco Systems, Inc.
168 Robinson Road
#28-01 Capital Tower
Singapore 068912
www.cisco.com
Tel: +65 6317 7777
Fax: +65 6317 7799

Europe Headquarters
Cisco Systems International BV
Haarlerbergpark
Haarlerbergweg 13-19
1101 CH Amsterdam
The Netherlands
www-europe.cisco.com
Tel: +31 0 800 020 0791
Fax: +31 0 20 357 1100

Cisco has more than 200 offices worldwide. Addresses, phone numbers, and fax numbers are listed on the Cisco Website at **www.cisco.com/go/offices**.

Contents

About This Lab Manual

The only authorized Lab Manual for the Cisco Networking Academy CCNA Security Version 1.2 course.

The Cisco® Networking Academy® course on CCNA® Security provides a next step for students who want to expand their CCNA-level skill set to prepare for a career in network security. The CCNA Security course also prepares students for the Implementing Cisco IOS® Network Security (IINS) certification exam (640-554), which leads to the CCNA Security certification.

The *CCNA Security Lab Manual* provides you with all 15 labs from the course designed as hands-on practice to master the knowledge and skills needed to prepare for entry-level security specialist careers.

All the hands-on labs in the course can be completed on actual physical equipment or in conjunction with the NDG NETLAB+® solution. For current information on labs compatible with NETLAB+® go to http://www.netdevgroup.com/content/cnap/.

Through procedural, skills integration challenges, troubleshooting, and model building labs, this CCNA Security course aims to develop your in-depth understanding of network security principles as well as the tools and configurations used.

Command Syntax Conventions

The conventions used to present command syntax in this book are the same conventions used in the IOS Command Reference. The Command Reference describes these conventions as follows:

- **Boldface** indicates commands and keywords that are entered literally as shown. In actual configuration examples and output (not general command syntax), boldface indicates commands that are manually input by the user (such as a **show** command).

- *Italic* indicates arguments for which you supply actual values.

- Vertical bars (|) separate alternative, mutually exclusive elements.

- Square brackets ([ ]) indicate an optional element.

- Braces ({ }) indicate a required choice.

- Braces within brackets ([{ }]) indicate a required choice within an optional element.

Chapter 1: Modern Network Security Threats

Lab 1.5.1.1 - Researching Network Attacks and Security Audit Tools

Objectives

Part 1: Researching Network Attacks

- Research network attacks that have occurred.
- Select a network attack and develop a report for presentation to the class.

Part 2: Researching Security Audit Tools

- Research network security audit tools.
- Select a tool and develop a report for presentation to the class.

Background / Scenario

Attackers have developed many tools over the years to attack and compromise networks. These attacks take many forms, but in most cases, they seek to obtain sensitive information, destroy resources, or deny legitimate users access to resources. When network resources are inaccessible, worker productivity can suffer, and business income may be lost.

To understand how to defend a network against attacks, an administrator must identify network vulnerabilities. Specialized security audit software, developed by equipment and software manufacturers, can be used to help identify potential weaknesses. Additionally, the same tools used by individuals to attack networks can also be used by network professionals to test the ability of a network to mitigate an attack. After the vulnerabilities are known, steps can be taken to help protect the network.

This lab provides a structured research project that is divided into two parts: Researching Network Attacks and Researching Security Audit Tools. You can elect to perform Part 1, Part 2, or both. Let your instructor know what you plan to do. This will ensure that a variety of network attacks and vulnerability tools are reported on by the members of the class.

In Part 1, research various network attacks that have actually occurred. Select one of these attacks and describe how the attack was perpetrated and how extensive the network outage or damage was. Next, investigate how the attack could have been mitigated or what mitigation techniques might have been implemented to prevent future attacks. Finally, prepare a report based on the predefined form included within this lab.

In Part 2, research network security audit tools and investigate one that can be used to identify host or network device vulnerabilities. Create a one-page summary of the tool based on a predefined form included within this lab. Prepare a short (5–10 minute) presentation to present to the class.

You may work in teams of two, with one person reporting on the network attack and the other reporting on the security audit tools. All team members deliver a short overview of their findings. You can use live demonstrations or PowerPoint to summarize your findings.

Required Resources

- Computer with Internet access for research
- Presentation computer with PowerPoint or other presentation software installed
- Video projector and screen for demonstrations and presentations

Part 1: Researching Network Attacks

In Part 1 of this lab, research various network attacks that have actually occurred and select one on which to report on. Fill in the form below based on your findings.

Step 1: Research various network attacks.

List some of the attacks you identified in your search.

_____

_____

_____

_____

Step 2: Fill in the following form for the network attack selected.

Name of attack:	
Type of attack:	
Dates of attacks:	
Computers / Organizations affected:	
How it works and what it did:	

Mitigation options:
References and info links:
Presentation support graphics (include PowerPoint filename or web links):

Part 2: Researching Security Audit Tools

In Part 2 of this lab, research network security audit and attacker tools. Investigate one that can be used to identify host or network device vulnerabilities. Fill in the report below based on your findings.

Step 1: Research various security audit and network attack tools.

List some of the tools that you identified in your search.

_____

_____

_____

_____

_____

_____

_____

Step 2: Fill in the following form for the security audit or network attack tool selected.

Name of tool:	
Developer:	
Type of tool (character-based or GUI):	
Used on (network device or computer host):	
Cost:	
Description of key features and capabilities of product or tool:	

References and info links:

Reflection

1. What is the prevalence of network attacks and what is their impact on the operation of an organization? What are some key steps organizations can take to help protect their networks and resources?

    _____

    _____

    _____

    _____

    _____

    _____

2. Have you actually worked for an organization or know of one where the network was compromised? If so, what was the impact to the organization and what did it do about it?

    _____

    _____

    _____

    _____

    _____

    _____

3. What steps can you take to protect your own PC or laptop computer?

    _____

    _____

    _____

    _____

    _____

    _____

Chapter 2: Securing Network Devices

Lab 2.5.1.1 - Securing the Router for Administrative Access

Topology

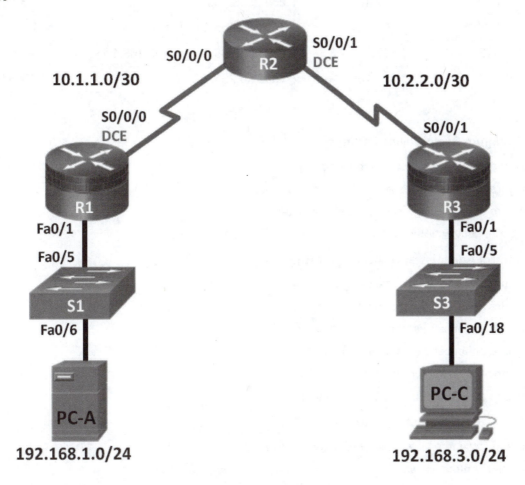

Note: ISR G2 devices use GigabitEthernet interfaces instead of FastEthernet interfaces.

IP Addressing Table

Device	Interface	IP Address	Subnet Mask	Default Gateway	Switch Port
R1	Fa0/1	192.168.1.1	255.255.255.0	N/A	S1 Fa0/5
	S0/0/0 (DCE)	10.1.1.1	255.255.255.252	N/A	N/A
R2	S0/0/0	10.1.1.2	255.255.255.252	N/A	N/A
	S0/0/1 (DCE)	10.2.2.2	255.255.255.252	N/A	N/A
R3	Fa0/1	192.168.3.1	255.255.255.0	N/A	S3 Fa0/5
	S0/0/1	10.2.2.1	255.255.255.252	N/A	N/A
PC-A	NIC	192.168.1.3	255.255.255.0	192.168.1.1	S1 Fa0/6
PC-C	NIC	192.168.3.3	255.255.255.0	192.168.3.1	S3 Fa0/18

Objectives

Part 1: Configure Basic Device Settings

- Cable the network as shown in the topology.
- Configure basic IP addressing for routers and PCs.
- Configure static routing, including default routes.
- Verify connectivity between hosts and routers.

Part 2: Control Administrative Access for Routers

- Configure and encrypt all passwords.
- Configure a login warning banner.
- Configure enhanced username password security.
- Configure enhanced virtual login security.
- Configure an SSH server on a router.
- Configure an SSH client and verify connectivity.

Part 3: Configure Administrative Roles

- Create multiple role views and grant varying privileges.
- Verify and contrast views.

Part 4: Configure Cisco IOS Resilience and Management Reporting

- Secure the Cisco IOS image and configuration files.
- Configure a router as a synchronized time source for other devices using NTP.
- Configure Syslog support on a router.
- Install a Syslog server on a PC and enable it.
- Configure trap reporting on a router using SNMP.
- Make changes to the router and monitor syslog results on the PC.

Part 5: Configure Automated Security Features

- Lock down a router using AutoSecure and verify the configuration.
- Use the CCP Security Audit tool to identify vulnerabilities and to lock down services.
- Contrast the AutoSecure configuration with CCP.

Background / Scenario

The router is a key component that controls the movement of data into and out of the network and between devices within the network. It is particularly important to protect network routers because the failure of a routing device could make sections of the network, or the entire network, inaccessible. Controlling access to routers and enabling reporting on routers are critical to network security and should be part of a comprehensive security policy.

In this lab, you build a multi-router network and configure the routers and hosts. Use various CLI and CCP tools to secure local and remote access to the routers, analyze potential vulnerabilities, and take steps to mitigate them. Enable management reporting to monitor router configuration changes.

The router commands and output in this lab are from a Cisco 1841 router using Cisco IOS software, release 15.1(4)M8 (Advanced IP Services image). Other routers and Cisco IOS versions can be used. See the Router Interface Summary Table at the end of the lab to determine which interface identifiers to use based on the equipment in the lab. Depending on the model of the router, the commands available and output produced may vary from what is shown in this lab.

Note: Make sure that the routers and the switches have been erased and have no startup configurations.

Required Resources

- 3 Routers (Cisco 1841 with Cisco IOS Release 15.1(4)M8 Advanced IP Services image or comparable)
- 2 Switches (Cisco 2960 or comparable)
- 2 PCs (Windows Vista or Windows 7 with CCP 2.5, SSH Client, Kiwi or Tftpd32 Syslog server, latest version of Java, Internet Explorer, and Flash Player)
- Serial and Ethernet cables as shown in the topology
- Console cables to configure Cisco networking devices

CCP Notes:

- If the PC on which CCP is installed is running Windows Vista or Windows 7, it may be necessary to right-click on the CCP icon or menu item, and choose **Run as administrator**.
- In order to run CCP, it may be necessary to temporarily disable antivirus programs and O/S firewalls. Make sure that all pop-up blockers are turned off in the browser.

Part 1: Configure Basic Device Settings

In Part 1, set up the network topology and configure basic settings such as interface IP addresses and static routing.

Step 1: Cable the network.

Attach the devices, as shown in the topology diagram, and cable as necessary.

Step 2: Configure basic settings for each router.

a. Configure host names as shown in the topology.

b. Configure interface IP addresses as shown in the IP Addressing Table.

c. Configure a clock rate for routers with a DCE serial cable attached to their serial interface. R1 is shown here as an example:

```
R1(config)# interface S0/0/0
R1(config-if)# clock rate 64000
```

d. To prevent1 the router from attempting to translate incorrectly entered commands as though they were host names, disable DNS lookup. R1 is shown here as an example:

```
R1(config)# no ip domain-lookup
```

Step 3: Configure static routing on the routers.

a. Configure a static default route from R1 to R2 and from R3 to R2.

b. Configure a static route from R2 to the R1 LAN and from R2 to the R3 LAN.

Step 4: Configure PC host IP settings.

Configure a static IP address, subnet mask, and default gateway for PC-A and PC-C as shown in the IP Addressing Table.

Step 5: Verify connectivity between PC-A and R3.

a. Ping from R1 to R3.

If the pings are not successful, troubleshoot the basic device configurations before continuing.

b. Ping from PC-A, on the R1 LAN, to PC-C, on the R3 LAN.

If the pings are not successful, troubleshoot the basic device configurations before continuing.

Note: If you can ping from PC-A to PC-C, you have demonstrated that static routing is configured and functioning correctly. If you cannot ping but the device interfaces are up and IP addresses are correct, use the **show run** and **show ip route** commands to help identify routing protocol-related problems.

Step 6: Save the basic running configuration for each router.

Save the basic running configuration for the routers as text files on your PC so that they can be used to restore configurations later in the lab.

Part 2: Control Administrative Access for Routers

In Part 2, you will:

• Configure and encrypt passwords.

• Configure a login warning banner.

- Configure enhanced username password security.
- Configure enhanced virtual login security.
- Configure an SSH server on R1 using the CLI.
- Research terminal emulation client software and configure the SSH client.

Note: Perform all tasks, on both R1 and R3. The procedures and output for R1 are shown here.

Task 1: Configure and Encrypt Passwords on Routers R1 and R3.

Step 1: Configure a minimum password length for all router passwords.

Use the **security passwords** command to set a minimum password length of 10 characters.

```
R1(config)# security passwords min-length 10
```

Step 2: Configure the enable secret password.

Configure the enable secret encrypted password on both routers.

```
R1(config)# enable secret cisco12345
```

How does configuring an enable secret password help protect a router from being compromised by an attack?

_____

_____

_____

_____

_____

_____

Step 3: Configure basic console, auxiliary port, and virtual access lines.

Note: Passwords in this task are set to a minimum of 10 characters but are relatively simple for the benefit of performing the lab. More complex passwords are recommended in a production network.

a. Configure a console password and enable login for routers. For additional security, the **exec-timeout** command causes the line to log out after 5 minutes of inactivity. The **logging synchronous** command prevents console messages from interrupting command entry.

   Note: To avoid repetitive logins during this lab, the **exec-timeout** command can be set to 0 0, which prevents it from expiring. However, this is not considered a good security practice.

```
R1(config)# line console 0
R1(config-line)# password ciscocon
R1(config-line)# exec-timeout 5 0
R1(config-line)# login
R1(config-line)# logging synchronous
```

   When you configured the password for the console line, what message was displayed?

_____

_____

b. Configure a new password of **ciscoconpass** for the console.

c. Configure a password for the AUX port for router R1.

```
R1(config)# line aux 0
R1(config-line)# password ciscoauxpass
R1(config-line)# exec-timeout 5 0
R1(config-line)# login
```

d. Telnet from R2 to R1.

```
R2> telnet 10.1.1.1
```

Were you able to login? Why or why not?

_____

_____

What messages were displayed?

_____

_____

_____

_____

e. Configure the password on the vty lines for router R1.

```
R1(config)# line vty 0 4
R1(config-line)# password ciscovtypass
R1(config-line)# exec-timeout 5 0
R1(config-line)# login
```

f. Telnet from R2 to R1 again. Were you able to login this time?

_____

g. Enter privileged EXEC mode and issue the **show run** command. Can you read the enable secret password? Why or why not?

_____

_____

Can you read the console, aux, and vty passwords? Why or why not?

_____

_____

h. Repeat the configuration portion of steps 3a through 3g on router R3.

Step 4: Encrypt clear text passwords.

a. Use the **service password-encryption** command to encrypt the console, aux, and vty passwords.

```
R1(config)# service password-encryption
```

b. Issue the **show run** command. Can you read the console, aux, and vty passwords? Why or why not?

_____

_____

At what level (number) is the enable secret password encrypted? _____

At what level (number) are the other passwords encrypted? _____

Which level of encryption is harder to crack and why?

_____

_____

Task 2: Configure a Login Warning Banner on Routers R1 and R3.

Step 1: Configure a warning message to display prior to login.

a. Configure a warning to unauthorized users with a message-of-the-day (MOTD) banner using the **banner motd** command. When a user connects to one of the routers, the MOTD banner appears before the login prompt. In this example, the dollar sign ($) is used to start and end the message.

```
R1(config)# banner motd $Unauthorized access strictly prohibited!$
R1(config)# exit
```

b. Issue the **show run** command. What does the $ convert to in the output?

_____

_____

c. Exit privileged EXEC mode using the **disable** or **exit** command and press **Enter** to get started. Does the MOTD banner look like what you created with the **banner motd** command?

If the MOTD banner is not as you wanted it, recreate it using the **banner motd** command.

Task 3: Configure Enhanced Username Password Security on Routers R1 and R3.

Step 1: Investigate the options for the username command.

In global configuration mode, enter the following command:

```
R1(config)# username user01 password ?
```

What options are available?

_____

_____

_____

Step 2: Create a new user account using the username command.

a. Create the user01 account, specifying the password with no encryption.

```
R1(config)# username user01 password 0 user01pass
```

b. Use the **show run** command to display the running configuration and check the password that is enabled.

Even though unencrypted (0) was specified, you still cannot read the password for the new user account, because the **service password-encryption** command is in effect.

Step 3: Create a new user account with a secret password.

a. Create a new user account with MD5 hashing to encrypt the password.

```
R1(config)# username user02 secret user02pass
```

b. Exit global configuration mode and save your configuration.

c. Display the running configuration. Which hashing method is used for the password?

_____

_____

Step 4: Test the new account by logging in to the console.

a. Set the console line to use the locally defined login accounts.

```
R1(config)# line console 0
R1(config-line)# login local
R1(config-line)# end
R1# exit
```

b. Exit to the initial router screen which displays: R1 con0 is now available; press RETURN to get started.

c. Log in using the username **user01** and the password **user01pass**, previously defined.

What is the difference between logging in at the console now and previously?

_____

_____

d. After logging in, issue the **show run** command. Were you able to issue the command? Explain.

_____

_____

e. Enter privileged EXEC mode using the **enable** command. Were you prompted for a password? Explain.

_____

_____

Step 5: Test the new account by logging in from a Telnet session.

a. From PC-A, establish a Telnet session with R1.

```
PC-A> telnet 192.168.1.1
```

Were you prompted for a user account? Why or why not?

_____

_____

b. Set the vty lines to use the locally defined login accounts.

```
R1(config)# line vty 0 4
R1(config-line)# login local
```

c. From PC-A, telnet to R1 again.

```
PC-A> telnet 192.168.1.1
```

Were you prompted for a user account? Explain.

_____

_____

d. Log in as **user01** with a password of **user01pass**.

e. During the Telnet session to R1, access privileged EXEC mode with the **enable** command.

What password did you use?

_____

f. For added security, set the AUX port to use the locally defined login accounts.

```
R1(config)# line aux 0
R1(config-line)# login local
```

g. End the Telnet session with the **exit** command.

Task 4: Configure Enhanced Virtual Login Security on Routers R1 and R3.

Step 1: Configure the router to protect against login attacks.

Use the **login block-for** command to help prevent brute-force login attempts from a virtual connection, such as Telnet, SSH, or HTTP. This can help slow down dictionary attacks and help protect the router from a possible DoS attack.

a. From the user EXEC or privileged EXEC prompt, issue the **show login** command to see the current router login attack settings.

```
R1# show login
    No login delay has been applied.
    No Quiet-Mode access list has been configured.

    Router NOT enabled to watch for login Attacks
```

b. Use the **login block-for** command to configure a 60-second login shutdown (quiet mode timer) if two failed login attempts are made within 30 seconds.

```
R1(config)# login block-for 60 attempts 2 within 30
```

c. Exit global configuration mode and issue the **show login** command.

```
R1# show login
```

Is the router enabled to watch for login attacks? _____

What is the default login delay?

_____

_____

Step 2: Configure the router to log login activity.

a. Configure the router to generate system logging messages for both successful and failed login attempts. The following commands log every successful login and log failed login attempts after every second failed login.

```
R1(config)# login on-success log
R1(config)# login on-failure log every 2
R1(config)# exit
```

b. Issue the **show login** command. What additional information is displayed?

_____

_____

Step 3: Test the enhanced login security login configuration.

a. From PC-A, establish a Telnet session with R1.

    PC-A> **telnet 10.1.1.1**

b. Attempt to log in with the wrong user ID or password two times. What message was displayed on PC-A after the second failed attempt?

    _____

    _____

    What message was displayed on the router R1 console after the second failed login attempt?

    _____

    _____

    _____

c. From PC-A, attempt to establish another Telnet session to R1 within 60 seconds. What message was displayed on PC-A after the attempted Telnet connection?

    _____

    _____

    What message was displayed on router R1 after the attempted Telnet connection?

    _____

    _____

d. Issue the **show login** command within 60 seconds. What additional information is displayed?

    _____

    _____

Task 5: Configure the SSH Server on Router R1 and R3 Using the CLI.

In this task, use the CLI to configure the router to be managed securely using SSH instead of Telnet. Secure Shell (SSH) is a network protocol that establishes a secure terminal emulation connection to a router or other networking device. SSH encrypts all information that passes over the network link and provides authentication of the remote computer. SSH is rapidly replacing Telnet as the remote login tool of choice for network professionals.

Note: For a router to support SSH, it must be configured with local authentication (AAA services, or username) or password authentication. In this task, you configure an SSH username and local authentication.

Step 1: Configure a domain name.

Enter global configuration mode and set the domain name.

    R1# **conf t**
    R1(config)# **ip domain-name ccnasecurity.com**

Step 2: Configure a privileged user for login from the SSH client.

a. Use the **username** command to create the user ID with the highest possible privilege level and a secret password.

```
R1(config)# username admin privilege 15 secret cisco12345
```

b. Exit to the initial router login screen. Log in with the username admin and the associated password. What was the router prompt after you entered the password?

_____

_____

Step 3: Configure the incoming vty lines.

Specify a privilege level of **15** so that a user with the highest privilege level (15) will default to privileged EXEC mode when accessing the vty lines. Other users will default to user EXEC mode. Use the local user accounts for mandatory login and validation, and accept only SSH connections.

```
R1(config)# line vty 0 4
R1(config-line)# privilege level 15
R1(config-line)# login local
R1(config-line)# transport input ssh
R1(config-line)# exit
```

Note: The **login local** command should already be configured in a previous step. It is included here to provide all commands if you were doing this for the first time.

Note: If you add the keyword **telnet** to the **transport input** command, users can log in using Telnet as well as SSH, however, the router will be less secure. If only SSH is specified, the connecting host must have an SSH client installed.

Step 4: Erase existing key pairs on the router.

```
R1(config)# crypto key zeroize rsa
```

Note: If no keys exist, you might receive this message: `% No Signature RSA Keys found in configuration.`

Step 5: Generate the RSA encryption key pair for the router.

The router uses the RSA key pair for authentication and encryption of transmitted SSH data.

Configure the RSA keys with **1024** for the number of modulus bits. The default is 512, and the range is from 360 to 2048.

```
R1(config)# crypto key generate rsa general-keys modulus 1024
The name for the keys will be: R1.ccnasecurity.com

% The key modulus size is 1024 bits
% Generating 1024 bit RSA keys, keys will be non-exportable...[OK]

R1(config)#
*Dec 16 21:24:16.175: %SSH-5-ENABLED: SSH 1.99 has been enabled
R1(config)# exit
```

Note: The details of encryption methods are covered in Chapter 7.

Step 6: Verify the SSH configuration.

a. Use the **show ip ssh** command to see the current settings.

    R1# **show ip ssh**

b. Fill in the following information based on the output of the **show ip ssh** command.

    SSH version enabled: _____

    Authentication timeout: _____

    Authentication retries: _____

Step 7: Configure SSH timeouts and authentication parameters.

The default SSH timeouts and authentication parameters can be altered to be more restrictive using the following commands:

    R1(config)# **ip ssh time-out 90**
    R1(config)# **ip ssh authentication-retries 2**

Step 8: Save the running-config to the startup-config.

    R1# **copy running-config startup-config**

Task 6: Research Terminal Emulation Client Software and Configure the SSH Client.

Step 1: Research terminal emulation client software.

Conduct a web search for freeware terminal emulation client software, such as TeraTerm or PuTTy. What are some capabilities of each?

_____

_____

_____

_____

_____

_____

_____

_____

Step 2: Install an SSH client on PC-A and PC-C.

a. If the SSH client is not already installed, download either TeraTerm or PuTTY.

b. Save the application to the desktop.

Note: The procedure described here is for PuTTY and pertains to PC-A.

Step 3: Verify SSH connectivity to R1 from PC-A.

a. Launch PuTTY by double-clicking the putty.exe icon.

b. Input the R1 Fa0/1 IP address **192.168.1.1** in the **Host Name (or IP address)** field.

c. Verify that the **SSH** radio button is selected.

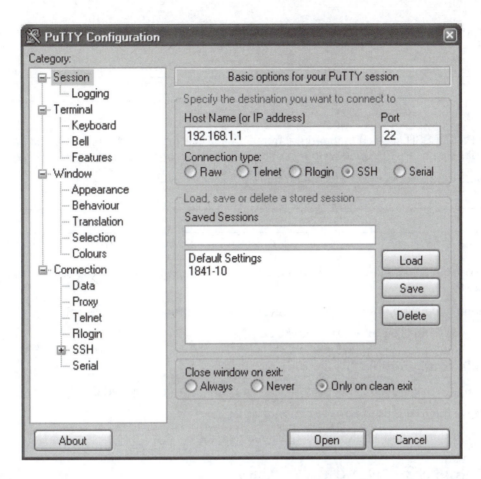

d. Click **Open**.

e. In the PuTTY Security Alert window, click **Yes**.

f. Enter the **admin** username and password **cisco12345** in the PuTTY window.

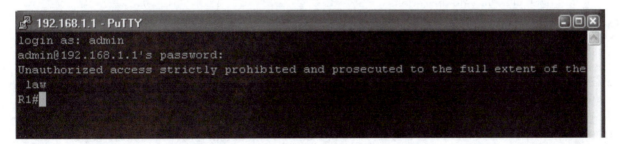

g. At the R1 privileged EXEC prompt, enter the **show users** command.

    R1# **show users**

What users are connected to router R1 at this time?

_____

_____

_____

h. Close the PuTTY SSH session window.

i.   Try to open a Telnet session to your router from PC-A. Were you able to open the Telnet session? Explain.

_____

_____

j.   Open a PuTTY SSH session to the router from PC-A. Enter the **user01** username and password **user01pass** in the PuTTY window to try connecting for user who does not have privilege level of 15.

If you were able to login, what was the prompt?

_____

_____

k.   Use the **enable** command to enter privilege EXEC mode and enter the enable secret password **cisco12345**.

l.   Disable the generation of system logging messages for successful login attempts.

```
R1(config)# no login on-success log
```

Step 4: Save the configuration.

Save the running configuration to the startup configuration from the privileged EXEC prompt.

```
R1# copy running-config startup-config
```

Note: Complete steps 3 and 4 between PC-C and router R3.

Part 3: Configure Administrative Roles

In Part 3 of this lab, you will:

*   Create multiple administrative roles or views on routers R1 and R3.
*   Grant each view varying privileges.
*   Verify and contrast the views.

The role-based CLI access feature allows the network administrator to define views, which are a set of operational commands and configuration capabilities that provide selective or partial access to Cisco IOS EXEC and configuration (config) mode commands. Views restrict user access to the Cisco IOS CLI and configuration information. A view can define which commands are accepted and what configuration information is visible.

Note: Perform all tasks on both R1 and R3. The procedures and output for R1 are shown here.

Task 1: Enable Root View on R1 and R3.

If an administrator wants to configure another view to the system, the system must be in root view. When a system is in root view, the user has the same access privileges as a user who has level-15 privileges, but the root view user can also configure a new view and add or remove commands from the view. When you are in a CLI view, you have access only to the commands that have been added to that view by the root view user.

Step 1: Enable AAA on router R1.

To define views, AAA must be enabled.

```
R1# config t
```

```
R1(config)# aaa new-model
R1(config)# exit
```

Note: AAA is covered in Chapter 3.

Step 2: Enable the root view.

Use the command **enable view** to enable the root view. Use the **enable secret password cisco12345**. If the router does not have an enable secret password, create one now.

```
R1# enable view
Password: cisco12345
*Dec 16 22:41:17.483: %PARSER-6-VIEW_SWITCH: user unknown successfully set to view
'root'.
```

Task 2: Create New Views for the Admin1, Admin2, and Tech Roles on R1 and R3.

Step 1: Create the admin1 view, establish a password, and assign privileges.

a. The admin1 user is the top-level user below root that is allowed to access this router. It has the most authority. The admin1 user can use all **show**, **config**, and **debug** commands. Use the following command to create the admin1 view while in the root view:

```
R1(config)# parser view admin1
R1(config-view)#
```

Note: To delete a view, use the command **no parser view** *viewname*.

b. Associate the admin1 view with an encrypted password.

```
R1(config-view)# secret admin1pass
R1(config-view)#
```

c. Review the commands that can be configured in the admin1 view. Use the **commands ?** command to see available commands. The following is a partial listing of the available commands:

```
R1(config-view)# commands ?
  RITE-profile          Router IP traffic export profile command mode
  RMI Node Config       Resource Policy Node Config mode
  RMI Resource Group    Resource Group Config mode
  RMI Resource Manager  Resource Manager Config mode
  RMI Resource Policy   Resource Policy Config mode
  SASL-profile          SASL profile configuration mode
  aaa-attr-list         AAA attribute list config mode
  aaa-user              AAA user definition
  accept-dialin         VPDN group accept dialin configuration mode
  accept-dialout        VPDN group accept dialout configuration mode
  address-family        Address Family configuration mode
<output omitted>
```

d. Add all **config**, **show**, and **debug** commands to the admin1 view and then exit from view configuration mode.

```
R1(config-view)# commands exec include all show
R1(config-view)# commands exec include all config terminal
R1(config-view)# commands exec include all debug
R1(config-view)# end
```

e. Verify the admin1 view.

```
R1# enable view admin1
Password: admin1pass
*Dec 16 22:56:46.971: %PARSER-6-VIEW_SWITCH: user unknown successfully set to
view 'admin1'.

R1# show parser view
Current view is 'admin1'
```

f. Examine the commands available in the admin1 view.

```
R1# ?
Exec commands:
   configure  Enter configuration mode
   debug      Debugging functions (see also 'undebug')
   enable     Turn on privileged commands
   exit       Exit from the EXEC
   show       Show running system information
```

Note: There can be more EXEC commands available than displayed depending on your device and IOS image used.

g. Examine the **show** commands available in the admin1 view.

```
R1# show ?
   aaa                  Show AAA values
   access-expression    List access expression
   access-lists         List access lists
   acircuit             Access circuit info
   adjacency            Adjacent nodes
   aliases              Display alias commands
   alignment            Show alignment information
   appfw                Application Firewall information
   archive              Archive functions
   arp                  ARP table
<output omitted>
```

Step 2: Create the admin2 view, establish a password, and assign privileges.

a. The admin2 user is a junior administrator in training who is allowed to view all configurations but is not allowed to configure the routers or use debug commands.

b. Use the **enable view** command to enable the root view, and enter the enable secret password **cisco12345**.

```
R1# enable view
Password:cisco12345
```

c. Use the following command to create the admin2 view:

```
R1(config)# parser view admin2
R1(config-view)#
```

d. Associate the admin2 view with a password.

```
R1(config-view)# secret admin2pass
R1(config-view)#
```

e. Add all **show** commands to the view, and then exit from view configuration mode.

```
R1(config-view)# commands exec include all show
R1(config-view)# end
```

f. Verify the admin2 view.

```
R1# enable view admin2
Password: admin2pass

*Dec 16 23:05:46.971: %PARSER-6-VIEW_SWITCH: user unknown successfully set to
view 'admin2'.
R1# show parser view
Current view is 'admin2'
```

g. Examine the commands available in the admin2 view.

```
R1# ?
Exec commands:
   enable      Turn on privileged commands
   exit        Exit from the EXEC
   show        Show running system information
```

Note: There can be more EXEC commands available than displayed depending on your device and IOS image used.

What is missing from the list of admin2 commands that is present in the admin1 commands?

_____

Step 3: Create the tech view, establish a password, and assign privileges.

a. The tech user typically installs end-user devices and cabling. Tech users are only allowed to use selected **show** commands.

b. Use the enable **view** command to enable the root view, and enter the enable secret password **cisco12345**.

```
R1# enable view
Password:cisco12345
```

c. Use the following command to create the tech view:

```
R1(config)# parser view tech
R1(config-view)#
```

d. Associate the tech view with a password.

```
R1(config-view)# secret techpasswd
R1(config-view)#
```

e. Add the following **show** commands to the view and then exit from view configuration mode:

```
R1(config-view)# commands exec include show version
R1(config-view)# commands exec include show interfaces
R1(config-view)# commands exec include show ip interface brief
```

```
R1(config-view)# commands exec include show parser view
R1(config-view)# end
```

f. Verify the tech view.

```
R1# enable view tech
Password:techpasswd
*Dec 16 23:13:46.971: %PARSER-6-VIEW_SWITCH: user unknown successfully set to
view 'tech'.

R1# show parser view
Current view is 'tech'
```

g. Examine the commands available in the tech view.

```
R1# ?
Exec commands:
    enable      Turn on privileged commands
    exit        Exit from the EXEC
    show        Show running system information
```

Note: There can be more EXEC commands available than displayed depending on your device and IOS image used.

h. Examine the **show** commands available in the tech view.

```
R1# show ?
    flash:      display information about flash: file system
    interfaces  Interface status and configuration
    ip          IP information
    parser      Show parser commands
    version     System hardware and software status
```

Note: There can be more EXEC commands available than displayed depending on your device and IOS image used.

i. Issue the **show ip interface brief** command. Were you able to do it as the tech user? Why or why not?

_____

_____

j. Issue the **show ip route** command. Were you able to do it as the tech user?

_____

_____

k. Return to root view with the **enable view** command.

```
R1# enable view
Password: cisco12345
```

l. Issue the **show run** command to see the views you created. For tech view, why are the **show** and **show ip** commands listed as well as **show ip interface** and **show ip interface brief**?

_____

_____

Step 4: Save the configuration on routers R1 and R3.

Save the running configuration to the startup configuration from the privileged EXEC prompt.

Part 4: Configure IOS Resilience and Management Reporting

In Part 4 of this lab, you will:

- Secure the Cisco IOS image and configuration files.

- Using NTP, configure a router as a synchronized time source for other devices.

- Configure syslog support on a router.

- Install a syslog server on a PC and enable it.

- Configure the logging trap level on a router.

- Make changes to the router and monitor syslog results on the PC.

Note: Perform all tasks on both R1 and R3. The procedure and output for R1 is shown here.

Task 1: Secure Cisco IOS Image and Configuration Files on R1 and R3.

The Cisco IOS resilient configuration feature enables a router to secure the running image and maintain a working copy of the configuration. This ensures that those files can withstand malicious attempts to erase the contents of persistent storage (NVRAM and flash). This feature secures the smallest working set of files to preserve persistent storage space. No extra space is required to secure the primary Cisco IOS image file. In this task, you configure the Cisco IOS Resilient Configuration feature.

Note: Cisco IOS resilient configuration feature is not available on the Cisco 1921 router.

Step 1: Display the files in flash memory for R1.

The show flash: command displays the contents of sub-directories. The **dir** command only displays contents of the current directory.

```
R1# show flash:
-#- --length-- -----date/time------ path
1     45756600 Apr 30 2014 13:40:20 +00:00 c1841-advipservicesk9-mz.151-4.M8.bin
2            0 Jan 6 2009 01:28:44 +00:00 ipsdir
3       334531 Jan 6 2009 01:35:40 +00:00 ipsdir/R1-sigdef-default.xml
4          461 Jan 6 2009 01:37:42 +00:00 ipsdir/R1-sigdef-delta.xml
5         8509 Jan 6 2009 01:33:42 +00:00 ipsdir/R1-sigdef-typedef.xml
6        38523 Jan 6 2009 01:33:46 +00:00 ipsdir/R1-sigdef-category.xml
7          304 Jan 6 2009 01:31:48 +00:00 ipsdir/R1-seap-delta.xml
8          491 Jan 6 2009 01:31:48 +00:00 ipsdir/R1-seap-typedef.xml
9         1410 Oct 26 2014 04:44:08 +00:00 pre_autosec.cfg

5840896 bytes available (58171392 bytes used)


R1# dir
Directory of flash:/

     1 -rw-     45756600   Apr 30 2014 13:40:20 +00:00   c1841-advipservicesk9-mz.151-
4.M8.bin
```

```
2    drw-              0    Jan 6 2009 01:28:44 +00:00   ipsdir
9    -rw-           1410    Oct 26 2014 04:44:08 +00:00   pre_autosec.cfg

65126400 bytes total (18952192 bytes free)
```

Step 2: Secure the Cisco IOS image and archive a copy of the running configuration.

a. The **secure boot-image** command enables Cisco IOS image resilience, which hides the file from the **dir** command and **show** commands. The file cannot be viewed, copied, modified, or removed using EXEC mode commands. (It can be viewed in ROMMON mode.) When turned on for the first time, the running image is secured.

```
R1(config)# secure boot-image
.Dec 17 25:40:13.170: %IOS_RESILIENCE-5-IMAGE_RESIL_ACTIVE: Successfully secured
running image
```

b. The **secure boot-config** command takes a snapshot of the router running configuration and securely archives it in persistent storage (flash).

```
R1(config)# secure boot-config
.Dec 17 25:42:18.691: %IOS_RESILIENCE-5-CONFIG_RESIL_ACTIVE: Successfully secured
config archive [flash:.runcfg-20081219-224218.ar]
```

Step 3: Verify that your image and configuration are secured.

You can use only the **show secure bootset** command to display the archived filename. Display the status of configuration resilience and the primary bootset filename.

```
R1# show secure bootset
IOS resilience router id FTX1111W0QF

IOS image resilience version 15.1 activated at 25:40:13 UTC Wed Dec 17 2008
Secure archive flash: c1841-advipservicesk9-mz.151-4.M8.bin type is image (elf)
[]
    file size is 37081324 bytes, run size is 37247008 bytes
    Runnable image, entry point 0x8000F000, run from ram

IOS configuration resilience version 15.1 activated at 25:42:18 UTC Wed Dec 17 2008
Secure archive flash:.runcfg-20081219-224218.ar type is config
configuration archive size 1986 bytes
```

What is the name of the archived running config file and on what is the name based?

_____

_____

Step 4: Display the files in flash memory for R1.

a. Display the contents of flash using the **show flash** command.

```
R1# show flash:
-#- --length-- -----date/time------ path
2              0 Jan 6 2009 01:28:44 +00:00 ipsdir
3         334531 Jan 6 2009 01:35:40 +00:00 ipsdir/R1-sigdef-default.xml
4            461 Jan 6 2009 01:37:42 +00:00 ipsdir/R1-sigdef-delta.xml
```

```
5            8509 Jan 6 2009 01:33:42 +00:00 ipsdir/R1-sigdef-typedef.xml
6           38523 Jan 6 2009 01:33:46 +00:00 ipsdir/R1-sigdef-category.xml
7             304 Jan 6 2009 01:31:48 +00:00 ipsdir/R1-seap-delta.xml
8             491 Jan 6 2009 01:31:48 +00:00 ipsdir/R1-seap-typedef.xml
9            1410 Oct 26 2014 .04:44:08 +00:00 pre_autosec.cfg


18944000 bytes available (46182400 bytes used)
```

Is the Cisco IOS image or the archived running config file listed?

_____

_____

b.   How can you tell that the Cisco IOS image is still there?

_____

_____

Step 5: Disable the IOS Resilient Configuration feature.

a.   Disable the Resilient Configuration feature for the Cisco IOS image.

```
R1# config t
R1(config)# no secure boot-image
.Dec 17 25:48:23.009: %IOS_RESILIENCE-5-IMAGE_RESIL_INACTIVE: Disabled secure
image archival
```

b.   Disable the Resilient Configuration feature for the running config file.

```
R1(config)# no secure boot-config
.Dec 17 25:48:47.972: %IOS_RESILIENCE-5-CONFIG_RESIL_INACTIVE: Disabled
secure config archival [removed flash:.runcfg-20081219-224218.ar]
```

Step 6: Verify that the Cisco IOS image is now visible in flash.

Use the **show flash:** command to display the files in flash.

```
R1# show flash:
-#- --length-- -----date/time------ path
1     45756600 Apr 30 2014 13:40:20 +00:00 c1841-advipservicesk9-mz.151-4.M8.bin
2            0 Jan 6 2009 01:28:44 +00:00 ipsdir
3       334531 Jan 6 2009 01:35:40 +00:00 ipsdir/R1-sigdef-default.xml
4          461 Jan 6 2009 01:37:42 +00:00 ipsdir/R1-sigdef-delta.xml
5         8509 Jan 6 2009 01:33:42 +00:00 ipsdir/R1-sigdef-typedef.xml
6        38523 Jan 6 2009 01:33:46 +00:00 ipsdir/R1-sigdef-category.xml
7          304 Jan 6 2009 01:31:48 +00:00 ipsdir/R1-seap-delta.xml
8          491 Jan 6 2009 01:31:48 +00:00 ipsdir/R1-seap-typedef.xml
9         1410 Oct 26 2014 04:44:08 +00:00 pre_autosec.cfg


18952192 bytes available (46174208 bytes used)
```

Step 7: Save the configuration on both routers.

Save the running configuration to the startup configuration from the privileged EXEC prompt.

Task 2: Configure a Synchronized Time Source Using NTP.

R2 will be the master NTP clock source for routers R1 and R3.

Note: R2 could also be the master clock source for switches S1 and S3, but it is not necessary to configure them for this lab.

Step 1: Set Up the NTP Master using Cisco IOS commands.

R2 is the master NTP server in this lab. All other routers and switches learn the time from it, either directly or indirectly. For this reason, you must ensure that R2 has the correct Coordinated Universal Time set.

Note: If you are using CCP to configure R2 to support NTP, skip this step and go to Step 2.

a. Use the **show clock** command to display the current time set on the router.

```
R2# show clock
*01:19:02.331 UTC Mon Dec 15 2008
```

b. To set the time on the router, use the **clock set** *time* command.

```
R2# clock set 20:12:00 Dec 17 2008
R2#
*Dec 17 20:12:18.000: %SYS-6-CLOCKUPDATE: System clock has been updated from
01:20:26 UTC Mon Dec 15 2008 to 20:12:00 UTC Wed Dec 17 2008, configured from
console by admin on console.
```

c. Configure R2 as the NTP master using the **ntp master** *stratum-number* command in global configuration mode. The stratum number indicates the distance from the original source. For this lab, use a stratum number of **3** on R2. When a device learns the time from an NTP source, its stratum number becomes one greater than the stratum number of its source.

```
R2(config)# ntp master 3
```

Step 2: Configure R1 and R3 as NTP clients using the CLI.

a. R1 and R3 will become NTP clients of R2. To configure R1, use the global configuration command **ntp server** *hostname*. The host name can also be an IP address. The command **ntp update-calendar** periodically updates the calendar with the NTP time.

```
R1(config)# ntp server 10.1.1.2
R1(config)# ntp update-calendar
```

b. Verify that R1 has made an association with R2 with the **show ntp associations** command. You can also use the more verbose version of the command by adding the **detail** argument. It might take some time for the NTP association to form.

```
R1# show ntp associations

address      ref clock    st  when  poll reach  delay  offset    disp
~10.1.1.2   127.127.1.1    3    14    64     3  0.000  -280073   3939.7
*sys.peer, # selected, +candidate, -outlyer, x falseticker, ~ configured
```

c. Issue the **debug ntp all** command to see NTP activity on R1 as it synchronizes with R2.

```
R1# debug ntp all
NTP events debugging is on
NTP core messages debugging is on
NTP clock adjustments debugging is on
NTP reference clocks debugging is on
NTP packets debugging is on
```

```
Dec 17 20.12:18.554: NTP message sent to 10.1.1.2, from interface 'Serial0/0/0'
(10.1.1.1).
Dec 17 20.12:18.574: NTP message received from 10.1.1.2 on interface 'Serial0/0/0'
(10.1.1.1).
Dec 17 20:12:18.574: NTP Core(DEBUG): ntp_receive: message received
Dec 17 20:12:18.574: NTP Core(DEBUG): ntp_receive: peer is 0x645A3120, next action is
1.
Dec 17 20:12:18.574: NTP Core(DEBUG): receive: packet given to process_packet
Dec 17 20:12:18.578: NTP Core(INFO): system event 'event_peer/strat_chg' (0x04)
status 'sync_alarm, sync_ntp, 5 events, event_clock_reset' (0xC655)
Dec 17 20:12:18.578: NTP Core(INFO): synchronized to 10.1.1.2, stratum 3
Dec 17 20:12:18.578: NTP Core(INFO): system event 'event_sync_chg' (0x03) status
 'leap_none, sync_ntp, 6 events, event_peer/strat_chg' (0x664)
Dec 17 20:12:18.578: NTP Core(NOTICE): Clock is synchronized.
Dec 17 20:12:18.578: NTP Core(INFO): system event 'event_peer/strat_chg' (0x04)
status 'leap_none, sync_ntp, 7 events, event_sync_chg' (0x673)
Dec 17 20:12:23.554: NTP: Calendar updated.
```

d.   Issue the **undebug all** or the **no debug ntp all** command to turn off debugging.

```
R1# undebug all
```

e.   Verify the time on R1 after it has made an association with R2.

```
R1# show clock
*20:12:24.859 UTC Wed Dec 17 2008
```

Step 3: (Optional) Configure R1 and R3 as NTP clients using CCP.

CCP can be used to configure the router to support NTP. If you configured R1 as an NTP client using Cisco IOS commands in Step 2, you can skip this step. However, read through it to become familiar with the process. If you configured R1 and R3 as NTP clients using Cisco IOS commands in Step 2, you can still perform this step, but you need to issue the following commands first on each router:

```
R1(config)# no ntp server 10.1.1.2
R1(config)# no ntp update-calendar
```

a.   Enable HTTP server.

```
R1(config)# ip http server
```

b.   For a secure connection, enable the secure HTTP server.

```
R1(config)# ip http secure-server
% Generating 1024 bit RSA keys, keys will be non-exportable...
[OK] (elapsed time was 3 seconds)

R1(config)#
*Jan 1 17:23:44.103: %SSH-5-ENABLED: SSH 1.99 has been enabled
*Jan 1 17:23:44.215: %PKI-4-NOAUTOSAVE: Configuration was modified. Issue "write
memory" to save new certificate
R1(config)# username admin privilege 15 secret cisco12345
R1(config)# ip http authentication local
```

c. Start CCP on PC-A. In the Manage Devices window, add the R1 IP address **192.168.1.1** in the first IP address field. Enter **admin** in the Username field, and **cisco12345** in the Password field. Click the **OK** button.

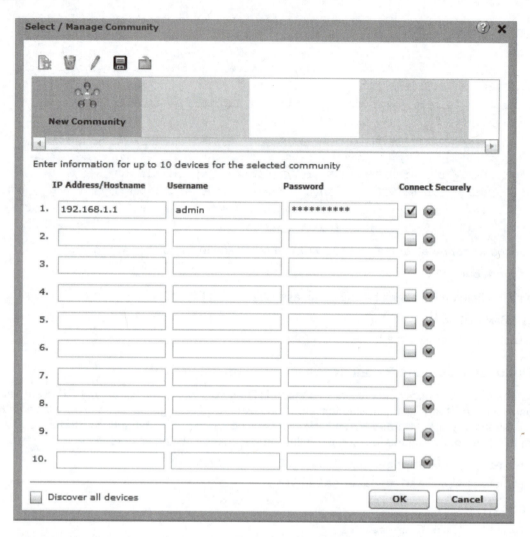

d. At the CCP Dashboard, click the **Discover** button to discover and connect to R1. If discovery fails, use the **Discovery Details** button to troubleshoot the problem and resolve it.

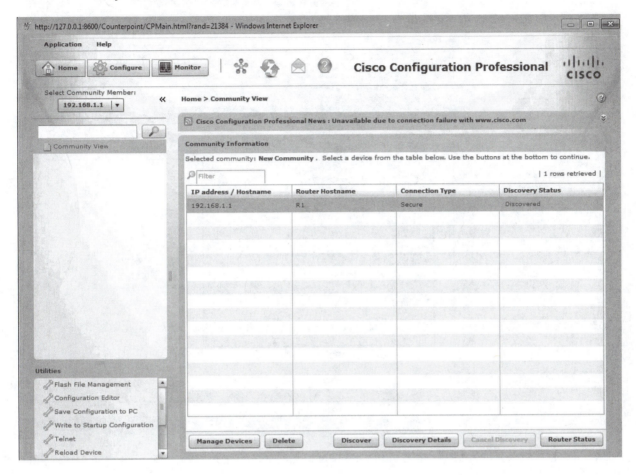

e. To configure an NTP server, click the **Configure** button and choose **Router** > **Time** > **NTP and SNTP**. Click **Add**.

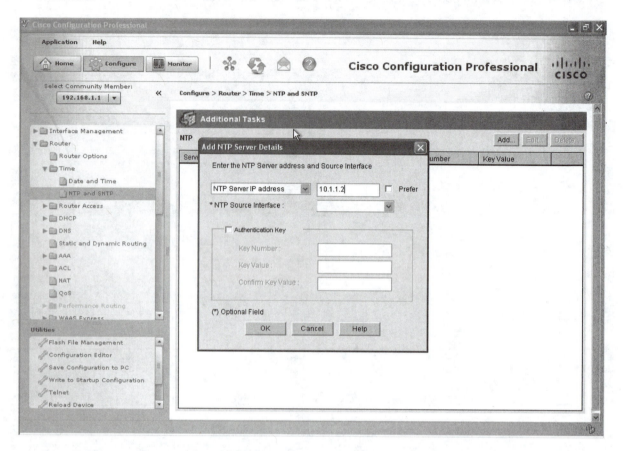

f. In the NTP Server IP Address field, enter the IP address of the R2 master NTP router (**10.1.1.2**) and click **OK**.

g. In the Deliver Configuration to Router window, click **Deliver**.

h. Click **OK** in the Commands Delivery Status window.

i. Open a console connection to the router, and verify the associations and time on R1 after it has made an association with R2. It might take some time for the NTP association to form.

```
R1# show ntp associations

address     ref clock     st   when  poll reach  delay  offset    disp
~10.1.1.2   127.127.1.1    3    14    64     3   0.000  -280073   3939.7
*sys.peer, # selected, +candidate, -outlyer, x falseticker, ~ configured


R1# show clock
*20:12:24.859 UTC Wed Dec 17 2008
```

Task 3: Configure syslog Support on R1 and PC-A.

Step 1: Install the syslog server.

Tftpd32 includes a TFTP server, TFTP client, and a syslog server and viewer. The Kiwi Syslog Daemon is only a dedicated syslog server. You can use either with this lab. Both are available as a free version and run with Microsoft Windows.

If a syslog server is not currently installed on the host, download the latest version of Tftpd32 from http://tftpd32.jounin.net or Kiwi from http://www.kiwisyslog.com and install it on your desktop. If it is already installed, go to Step 2.

Note: This lab uses the Ttftpd32 application for the syslog server functionality.

Step 2: Configure R1 to log messages to the syslog server using the CLI.

a. Verify that you have connectivity between R1 and PC-A by pinging the R1 Fa0/1 interface IP address 192.168.1.1. If it is not successful, troubleshoot as necessary before continuing.

b. NTP was configured in Task 2 to synchronize the time on the network. Displaying the correct time and date in syslog messages is vital when using syslog to monitor a network. If the correct time and date of a message is not known, it can be difficult to determine what network event caused the message.

Verify that the timestamp service for logging is enabled on the router using the **show run** command. Use the following command if the timestamp service is not enabled:

```
R1(config)# service timestamps log datetime msec
```

c. Configure the syslog service on the router to send syslog messages to the syslog server.

```
R1(config)# logging host 192.168.1.3
```

Step 3: Configure the logging severity level on R1.

Logging traps can be set to support the logging function. A trap is a threshold that when reached, triggers a log message. The level of logging messages can be adjusted to allow the administrator to determine what kinds of messages are sent to the syslog server. Routers support different levels of logging. The eight levels range from 0 (emergencies), indicating that the system is unstable, to 7 (debugging), which sends messages that include router information.

Note: The default level for syslog is 6, informational logging. The default for console and monitor logging is 7, debugging.

a. Use the **logging trap** command to determine the options for the command and the various trap levels available.

```
R1(config)# logging trap ?
<0-7>          Logging severity level
alerts         Immediate action needed              (severity=1)
critical       Critical conditions                  (severity=2)
debugging      Debugging messages                   (severity=7)
emergencies    System is unusable                   (severity=0)
errors         Error conditions                     (severity=3)
informational  Informational messages               (severity=6)
notifications  Normal but significant conditions    (severity=5)
warnings       Warning conditions                   (severity=4)
<cr>
```

b. Define the level of severity for messages sent to the syslog server. To configure the severity levels, use either the keyword or the severity level number (0–7).

Severity Level	Keyword	Meaning
0	emergencies	System is unusable
1	alerts	Immediate action required
2	critical	Critical conditions
3	errors	Error conditions
4	warnings	Warning conditions
5	notifications	Normal but significant condition
6	informational	Informational messages
7	debugging	Debugging messages

Note: The severity level includes the level specified and anything with a lower severity number. For example, if you set the level to 4, or use the keyword **warnings**, you capture messages with severity level 4, 3, 2, 1, and 0.

c. Use the **logging trap** command to set the severity level for R1.

```
R1(config)# logging trap warnings
```

d. What is the problem with setting the level of severity too high or too low?

_____

_____

e. If the command **logging trap critical** were issued, which severity levels of messages would be logged?

_____

_____

Step 4: Display the current status of logging for R1.

Use the **show logging** command to see the type and level of logging enabled.

```
R1# show logging
Syslog logging: enabled (0 messages dropped, 3 messages rate-limited, 0 flushes, 0
overruns, xml disabled, filtering disabled)

No Active Message Discriminator.



No Inactive Message Discriminator.


    Console logging: level debugging, 72 messages logged, xml disabled,
                     filtering disabled
    Monitor logging: level debugging, 0 messages logged, xml disabled,
                     filtering disabled
     Buffer logging:  level debugging, 72 messages logged, xml disabled,
                     filtering disabled
```

```
          Exception Logging: size (4096 bytes)
          Count and timestamp logging messages: disabled
          Persistent logging: disabled

    No active filter modules.

          Trap logging: level warnings, 54 message lines logged
              Logging to 192.168.1.13   (udp port 514, audit disabled,
                  link up),
                  3 message lines logged,
                  0 message lines rate-limited,
                  0 message lines dropped-by-MD,
                  xml disabled, sequence number disabled
                  filtering disabled
              Logging to 192.168.1.3   (udp port 514, audit disabled,
                  link up),
                  3 message lines logged,
                  0 message lines rate-limited,
                  0 message lines dropped-by-MD,
                  xml disabled, sequence number disabled
                  filtering disabled
              Logging Source-Interface:       VRF Name:
```

At what level is console logging enabled?

_____

At what level is trap logging enabled?

_____

What is the IP address of the syslog server?

_____

What port is syslog using?

_____

Step 5: (Optional) Use CCP to configure R1 to log messages to the syslog server.

You can also use CCP to configure the router for syslog support. If you previously configured R1 for syslog and trap levels, you can skip this step. If you used Cisco IOS commands in Step 4 to configure R1 syslog and trap levels, you can still perform this step, but you need to issue the following commands on the router first:

```
R1(config)# no logging 192.168.1.3
R1(config)# no logging trap warnings
```

a. Open CCP and discover R1 by entering the R1 IP address **192.168.1.1** in the Address field. Use **admin** for the username and **cisco12345** for the password.

b. Choose **Configure** > **Router** > **Logging**, and double-click **Syslog**.

c. In the Logging window, click **Add** and enter the IP address of the syslog server, PC-A (**192.168.1.3**). Click **OK**.

d. From the Logging Level drop-down menu, select the logging level of **Warnings (4)**.

e. Deselect **Logging Buffer**, and then click **OK**.

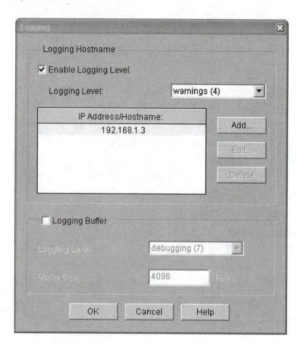

f. Click **Yes** in the CCP Warning dialog box.

g. In the Deliver Configuration to Router window, click **Deliver**. Click **OK** in the Commands Delivery Status window.

Step 6: Start the Ttftpd32 Syslog Server.

a. Open the Tftpd32 application icon on your desktop or click the **Start** button and choose **All Programs > Tftpd32 > Tftpd32**.

b. Select the **Syslog server** tab.

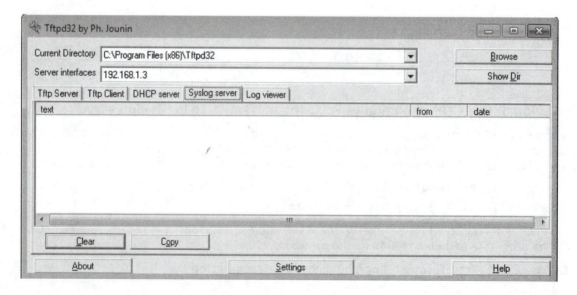

Step 7: Verify that logging to the syslog server is occurring.

On the syslog server host PC-A, observe messages as they are sent from R1 to the syslog server.

Generate a logging message by shutting down the Serial0/0/0 interface on R1 or R2 and then re-enabling it.

```
R2(config)# interface S0/0/0
R2(config-if)# shutdown
R2(config-if)# no shutdown
```

The Tftpd32 screen should look similar to the one below.

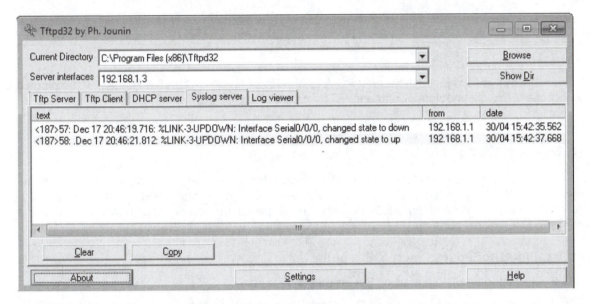

What would happen if you shut down the Fa0/1 interface on R1 (do not actually perform this action)?

_____

_____

Part 5: Configure Automated Security Features

In Part 5 of this lab, you will do as follows:

- Restore routers R1 and R3 to their basic configuration.
- Use AutoSecure to secure R3.
- Use the CCP Security Audit tool on R1 to identify security risks.
- Fix security problems on R1 using the Security Audit tool.
- Review router security configurations with CCP and the CLI.

Task 1: Restore Router R3 to Its Basic Configuration.

To avoid confusion as to what was already entered and what AutoSecure provides for the router configuration, start by restoring router R3 to its basic configuration.

Step 1: Erase and reload the router.

a. Connect to the R3 console and log in as admin.

b.   Enter privileged EXEC mode.

c.   Erase the startup config and then reload the router.

Step 2: Restore the basic configuration.

a.   When the router restarts, restore the basic configuration for R3 that was created and saved in Part 1 of this lab.

b.   Issue the **show run** command to view the current running configuration. Are there any security related commands?

_____

_____

c.   Test connectivity by pinging from host PC-A on the R1 LAN to PC-C on the R3 LAN. If the pings are not successful, troubleshoot the router and PC configurations until they are.

d.   Save the running config to the startup config using the **copy run start** command.

Task 2: Use AutoSecure to Secure R3.

By using a single command in CLI mode, the AutoSecure feature allows you to disable common IP services that can be exploited for network attacks. It can also enable IP services and features that can aid in the defense of a network when under attack. AutoSecure simplifies the security configuration of a router and hardens the router configuration.

Step 1: Use the AutoSecure Cisco IOS feature.

a.   Enter privileged EXEC mode using the **enable** command.

b.   Issue the **auto secure** command on R3 to lock down the router. R2 represents an ISP router, so assume that R3 S0/0/1 is connected to the Internet when prompted by the AutoSecure questions. Respond to the AutoSecure questions as shown in the following output. The responses are bolded.

```
R3# auto secure

            --- AutoSecure Configuration ---


*** AutoSecure configuration enhances the security of
the router, but it will not make it absolutely resistant
to all security attacks ***


AutoSecure will modify the configuration of your device.
All configuration changes will be shown. For a detailed
explanation of how the configuration changes enhance security
and any possible side effects, please refer to Cisco.com for
Autosecure documentation.
At any prompt you may enter '?' for help.
Use ctrl-c to abort this session at any prompt.


Gathering information about the router for AutoSecure

Is this router connected to internet? [no]:  yes
```

Enter the number of interfaces facing the internet [1]: Press **ENTER** to
accept the default of 1 in square brackets.

Interface	IP-Address	OK?	Method	Status	Protocol
FastEthernet0/0	unassigned	YES	NVRAM	administratively down	down
FastEthernet0/1	192.168.3.1	YES	NVRAM	up	up
Serial0/0/0	unassigned	YES	NVRAM	administratively down	down
Serial0/0/1	10.2.2.1	YES	NVRAM	up	up

Enter the interface name that is facing the internet: **serial0/0/1**

Securing Management plane services...

Disabling service finger
Disabling service pad
Disabling udp & tcp small servers
Enabling service password encryption
Enabling service tcp-keepalives-in
Enabling service tcp-keepalives-out
Disabling the cdp protocol

Disabling the bootp server
Disabling the http server
Disabling the finger service
Disabling source routing
Disabling gratuitous arp

Here is a sample Security Banner to be shown
at every access to device. Modify it to suit your
enterprise requirements.

Authorized Access only
   This system is the property of So-&-So-Enterprise.
   UNAUTHORIZED ACCESS TO THIS DEVICE IS PROHIBITED.
   You must have explicit permission to access this
   device. All activities performed on this device
   are logged. Any violations of access policy will result
   in disciplinary action.

Enter the security banner {Put the banner between
k and k, where k is any character}:

 # Unauthorized Access Prohibited #

Enable secret is either not configured or

```
 is the same as enable password
Enter the new enable secret: cisco12345
Confirm the enable secret : cisco12345
Enter the new enable password: cisco67890
Confirm the enable password: cisco67890


Configuration of local user database
Enter the username: admin
Enter the password: cisco12345
Confirm the password: cisco12345
Configuring AAA local authentication
Configuring Console, Aux and VTY lines for
local authentication, exec-timeout, and transport
Securing device against Login Attacks
Configure the following parameters


Blocking Period when Login Attack detected: 60


Maximum Login failures with the device: 2


Maximum time period for crossing the failed login attempts: 30


Configure SSH server? [yes]: Press ENTER to accept the default of yes


Enter the domain-name: ccnasecurity.com


Configuring interface specific AutoSecure services
Disabling the following ip services on all interfaces:

 no ip redirects
 no ip proxy-arp
 no ip unreachables
 no ip directed-broadcast
 no ip mask-reply
Disabling mop on Ethernet interfaces


Securing Forwarding plane services...


Enabling CEF (This might impact the memory requirements for your platform)
Enabling unicast rpf on all interfaces connected
to internet


Configure CBAC Firewall feature? [yes/no]: no
Tcp intercept feature is used prevent tcp syn attack
on the servers in the network. Create autosec_tcp_intercept_list
```

to form the list of servers to which the tcp traffic is to be observed

Enable tcp intercept feature? [yes/no]: **yes**

This is the configuration generated:

```
no service finger
no service pad
no service udp-small-servers
no service tcp-small-servers
service password-encryption
service tcp-keepalives-in
service tcp-keepalives-out
no cdp run
no ip bootp server
no ip http server
no ip finger
no ip source-route
no ip gratuitous-arps
no ip identd
banner motd ^C Unauthorized Access Prohibited ^C
security passwords min-length 6
security authentication failure rate 10 log
enable secret 5 $1$FmV1$.xZUegmNYFJwJv/oFwwvG1
enable password 7 045802150C2E181B5F
username admin password 7 01100F175804575D72
aaa new-model
aaa authentication login local_auth local
line con 0
 login authentication local_auth
 exec-timeout 5 0
 transport output telnet
line aux 0
 login authentication local_auth
 exec-timeout 10 0
 transport output telnet
line vty 0 4
 login authentication local_auth
 transport input telnet
line tty 1
 login authentication local_auth
 exec-timeout 15 0
login block-for 60 attempts 2 within 30
ip domain-name ccnasecurity.com
crypto key generate rsa general-keys modulus 1024
```

```
    ip ssh time-out 60
    ip ssh authentication-retries 2
    line vty 0 4
     transport input ssh telnet
    service timestamps debug datetime msec localtime show-timezone
    service timestamps log datetime msec localtime show-timezone
    logging facility local2
    logging trap debugging
    service sequence-numbers
    logging console critical
    logging buffered
    interface FastEthernet0/0
     no ip redirects
     no ip proxy-arp
     no ip unreachables
     no ip directed-broadcast
     no ip mask-reply
     no mop enabled
    interface FastEthernet0/1
     no ip redirects
     no ip proxy-arp
     no ip unreachables
     no ip directed-broadcast
     no ip mask-reply
     no mop enabled
    interface Serial0/0/0
     no ip redirects
     no ip proxy-arp
     no ip unreachables
     no ip directed-broadcast
     no ip mask-reply
    interface Serial0/0/1
     no ip redirects
     no ip proxy-arp
     no ip unreachables
     no ip directed-broadcast
     no ip mask-reply
    interface Vlan1
     no ip redirects
     no ip proxy-arp
     no ip unreachables
     no ip directed-broadcast
     no ip mask-reply
     no mop enabled
    ip cef
```

```
access-list 100 permit udp any any eq bootpc
interface Serial0/0/1
 ip verify unicast source reachable-via rx allow-default 100
ip tcp intercept list autosec_tcp_intercept_list
ip tcp intercept drop-mode random
ip tcp intercept watch-timeout 15
ip tcp intercept connection-timeout 3600
ip tcp intercept max-incomplete low 450
ip tcp intercept max-incomplete high 550
!
end

Apply this configuration to running-config? [yes]: <ENTER>

Applying the config generated to running-config
The name for the keys will be: R3.ccnasecurity.com

% The key modulus size is 1024 bits
% Generating 1024 bit RSA keys, keys will be non-exportable...
[OK] (elapsed time was 3 seconds)

"ip tcp intercept max-incomplete low <val>" is deprecated
Please use "ip tcp intercept max-incomplete low <val> high <val>"
"ip tcp intercept max-incomplete high <val>" is deprecated
Please use "ip tcp intercept max-incomplete low <val> high <val>"
R3#
000037: *Dec 19 21:18:52.495 UTC: %AUTOSEC-1-MODIFIED: AutoSecure
configuration
has been Modified on this device
```

Note: The questions asked and the output may vary depend on the features on the IOS image and device.

Step 2: Establish an SSH connection from PC-C to R3.

a. Start PuTTy or another SSH client, and log in with the **admin** account and password **cisco12345** created when AutoSecure was run. Enter the IP address of the R3 Fa0/1 interface **192.168.3.1**.

b. Because SSH was configured using AutoSecure on R3, you will receive a PuTTY security warning. Click **Yes** to connect anyway.

c. Enter privileged EXEC mode, and verify the R3 configuration using the **show run** command.

d. Issue the **show flash** command. Is there a file that might be related to AutoSecure, and if so, what is its name and when was it created?

_____

_____

e. Issue the command **more flash:pre_autosec.cfg**. What are the contents of this file, and what is its purpose?

_____

_____

f. How would you restore this file if AutoSecure did not produce the desired results?

_____

_____

Step 3: Contrast the AutoSecure-generated configuration of R3 with the manual configuration of R1.

a. What security-related configuration changes were performed on R3 by AutoSecure that were not performed in previous sections of the lab on R1?

_____

_____

_____

_____

_____

_____

_____

_____

_____

b. What security-related configuration changes were performed in previous sections of the lab that were not performed by AutoSecure?

_____

_____

_____

_____

_____

_____

c. Identify at least five unneeded services that were locked down by AutoSecure and at least three security measures applied to each interface.

Note: Some of the services listed as being disabled in the AutoSecure output above might not appear in the **show running-config** output because they are already disabled by default for this router and Cisco IOS version.

Services disabled include:

_____

_____

For each interface, the following were disabled:

_____

_____

_____

_____

_____

Step 4: Test connectivity.

Ping from PC-A on the R1 LAN to PC-C on the router R3 LAN. If pings from PC-A to PC-C are not successful, troubleshoot before continuing.

Task 3: Restore R1 to Its Basic Configuration.

To avoid confusion as to what was previously configured, and what CCP Security Audit tool provides for the router configuration, start by restoring router R1 to its basic configuration.

Step 1: Erase and reload the router.

a. Connect to the R1 console and log in as admin.

b. Enter privileged EXEC mode.

c. Erase the startup config and then reload the router.

Step 2: Restore the basic config.

a. When the router restarts, cut and paste the basic startup config for R1 that was created and saved in Part 1 of this lab.

b. Test connectivity by pinging from host PC-A to R1. If the pings are not successful, troubleshoot the router and PC configurations to verify connectivity before continuing.

c. Save the running config to the startup config using the **copy run start** command.

Task 4: Use the CCP Security Audit Tool on R1 to Identify Security Risks.

In this task, use the CCP graphical user interface to analyze security vulnerabilities on router R1. CCP is faster than typing each command and provides greater control than the AutoSecure feature.

Step 1: Verify that CCP is installed on Host PC.

Note: If CCP is not installed on the PC-A, consult your instructor for directions.

Step 2: Create a CCP user and enable the HTTP server on R1.

a. Create a privilege level 15 username and password on R1.

```
R1(config)# username admin privilege 15 secret cisco12345
```

b. Enable HTTP server.

```
R1(config)# ip http server
```

c. For a secure connection, enable the secure HTTP server on R1.

```
R1(config)# ip http secure-server
% Generating 1024 bit RSA keys, keys will be non-exportable...[OK]
R1(config)#
*Dec 19 17:01:07.763: %SSH-5-ENABLED: SSH 1.99 has been enabled
*Dec 19 17:01:08.731: %PKI-4-NOAUTOSAVE: Configuration was modified. Issue
"write memory" to save new certificate
```

d. Enable local HTTP authentication on R1.

```
R1(config)# ip http authentication local
R1(config)# end
```

e. Save the running config to the startup config.

```
R1# copy run start
```

Step 3: Start CCP.

a. From PC-A, run the CCP application.

Note: Make sure that all pop-up blockers are turned off in the browser, and make sure that Java is installed and updated.

b. In the Manage Devices window, add R1 IP address 192.168.1.1 in the first IP address field. Enter **admin** in the username field, and **cisco12345** in the password field. Click the **Connect Securely** check box to use secure-server for your connection. Check the **Discover All Devices** check box, and click on the **OK** button.

c. When the Security Certification Alert is displayed, click **Yes**.

If the Discovery fails, use the **Discovery Details** button to determine the problem and resolve it.

Step 4: Back up the current router configuration using CCP.

a. Back up the router configuration from within CCP by choosing **Utilities** > **Save Configuration to PC**.

b. Save the configuration on the desktop using the default name of **RunningConfig_192.168.1.1.txt**.

Step 5: Begin the security audit.

a. Choose **Configure** > **Security** > **Security Audit**.

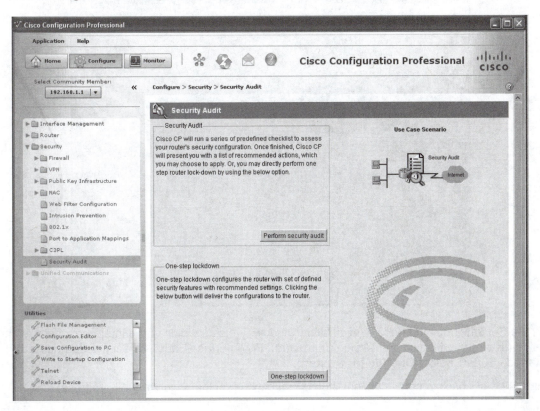

b. Click the **Perform security audit** button to start the Security Audit wizard, which analyzes potential vulnerabilities. This helps you become familiar with the types of vulnerabilities that Security Audit can identify. You will be given an opportunity to fix all or selected security problems after the audit finishes.

Note: The Security Audit tool also provides a **One-step lockdown** option that performs a function similar to AutoSecure but does not prompt the user for input.

c.   After you have familiarized yourself with the wizard instructions, click **Next**.

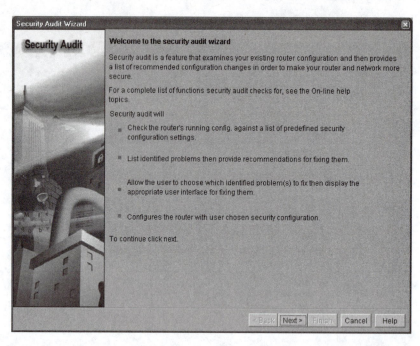

d.   On the Security audit interface configuration window, indicate which of the interfaces that are shown are inside (trusted) and which are outside (untrusted). For interface Fa0/1, select **Inside (trusted)**. For interface S0/0/0, select **Outside (untrusted)**.

e.   Click **Next** to check security configurations. You can watch the security audit progress.

Step 6: Review Security Audit unneeded services list and recommended configurations.

a.   Scroll through the Security Audit results screen. What are some of the major vulnerabilities listed as Not Passed?

_____

_____

_____

_____

b. After reviewing the Security Audit report, click **Save Report**. Save the report to the desktop using the default name CPSecurityAuditReportCard.html.

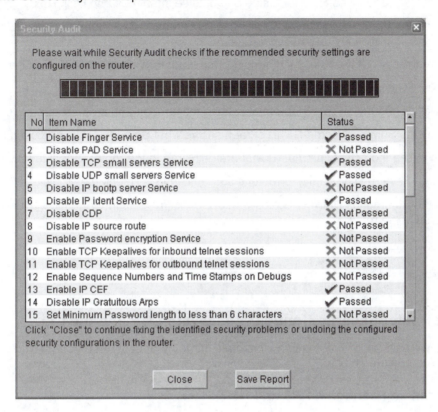

c. Open the report card HTML document you saved on the desktop to view the contents and then close it.

Task 5: Fix Security Problems on R1 Using the Security Audit Tool.

In this task, you will use the Security Audit wizard to make the necessary changes to the router configuration.

Step 1: Review the Security Problems Identified window for potential items to fix.

a. In the Security Audit window, click **Close**.

b. A window appears listing the items that did not pass the security audit. Click **Next** without choosing any items. What message did you get?

_____

_____

c. Click **OK** to remove the message.

Step 2: Fix security problems.

With the Security Audit tool, you can fix selected problems or all security problems identified.

a. Click **Fix All** and then click **Next** to fix all security problems.

b. When prompted, enter an enable secret password of **cisco12345** and confirm it.

c. Enter the text for the login banner: **Unauthorized Access Prohibited**. Click **Next**.

d. Add the logging host IP address **192.168.1.3** and click **OK**. Click **Next** to accept the logging defaults.

e. The Advanced Firewall Configuration Wizard window appears; click **Next**.

f. Accept the default security settings for inside and outside interfaces and click **Next**.

g. Click **OK** to accept the warning regarding the inability to launch CCP from the serial0/0/0 interface after finishing the configuration in Firewall Wizard.

   Note: If CCP detected CME, you can choose if voice traffic is allowed through the firewall.

h. For the security level, select **Low Security** and click **Next**.

i. At the Firewall Configuration Summary, review the configuration and click **Finish**.

j. Scroll through the Summary screen. This screen shows what Security Audit will configure for the router.

k. Click **Finish** to see the actual commands that are delivered to the router. Scroll to review the commands.

l. Make sure that Save running config to router's startup config is selected and click **Deliver**.

m. Click **OK** in the Commands Delivery Status window to exit the Security Audit tool. How many commands were delivered to the router?

_____

_____

Task 6: Review Router Security Configurations with CCP and the CLI.

In this task, you will use Cisco CCP to review changes made by Security Audit on R1 and compare them to those made by AutoSecure on R3.

Step 1: View the running configs for R1 and R3.

a. From the PC-A CCP session with R1, in the utilities area at the bottom-left corner, click the **View > Running Configuration**.

b. Using PuTTY, open an SSH connection to router R3, and log in as **admin**.

c. Enter privileged EXEC mode, and issue the **show run** command.

Step 2: Contrast AutoSecure with CCP Security Audit.

a. Compare the function and ease of use between AutoSecure and CCP Security Audit. What are some similarities and differences?

_____

_____

_____

_____

_____

_____

b. Refer to the AutoSecure configuration on R3 and the CCP Security Audit configuration on R1. What are some similarities and differences between the configurations that are generated by AutoSecure and Security Audit?

_____

_____

_____

_____

_____

_____

Step 3: Test connectivity.

a. Ping from router R1 to the router R3 S0/0/1 interface (**10.2.2.1**). Were the pings successful? Explain.

_____

_____

Note: Firewalls are covered in detail in Chapter 4.

b. Ping from PC-A on the R1 LAN to PC-C on the router R3 LAN. Were the pings successful? Explain.

_____

_____

c. Ping from router R3 to the router R2 S0/0/0 interface (**10.1.1.2**). Were the pings successful? Explain.

_____

_____

d. Ping from router R3 to the router R1 S0/0/0 interface (**10.1.1.1**). Were the pings successful? Explain.

_____

_____

e. Ping from PC-C on the R3 LAN to PC-A on the router R1 LAN. Were the pings successful? Explain.

_____

_____

Reflection

1. Explain the importance of securing router access and monitoring network devices.

_____

_____

_____

_____

_____

_____

2. What advantages does SSH have over Telnet?

_____

_____

3. How scalable is setting up usernames and using the local database for authentication?

_____

_____

_____

_____

_____

_____

4. Why it is better to have centralized logging servers rather than only have the routers log locally?

_____

_____

_____

_____

_____

_____

5. What are some advantages to using automated security mechanisms like AutoSecure and CCP Security Audit?

_____

_____

_____

_____

_____

_____

Router Interface Summary Table

Router Interface Summary				
Router Model	Ethernet Interface #1	Ethernet Interface #2	Serial Interface #1	Serial Interface #2
1800	Fast Ethernet 0/0 (Fa0/0)	Fast Ethernet 0/1 (Fa0/1)	Serial 0/0/0 (S0/0/0)	Serial 0/0/1 (S0/0/1)
1900	Gigabit Ethernet 0/0 (G0/0)	Gigabit Ethernet 0/1 (G0/1)	Serial 0/0/0 (S0/0/0)	Serial 0/0/1 (S0/0/1)
2801	Fast Ethernet 0/0 (Fa0/0)	Fast Ethernet 0/1 (Fa0/1)	Serial 0/1/0 (S0/1/0)	Serial 0/1/1 (S0/1/1)
2811	Fast Ethernet 0/0 (Fa0/0)	Fast Ethernet 0/1 (Fa0/1)	Serial 0/0/0 (S0/0/0)	Serial 0/0/1 (S0/0/1)
2900	Gigabit Ethernet 0/0 (G0/0)	Gigabit Ethernet 0/1 (G0/1)	Serial 0/0/0 (S0/0/0)	Serial 0/0/1 (S0/0/1)

Note: To find out how the router is configured, look at the interfaces to identify the type of router and how many interfaces the router has. There is no way to effectively list all the combinations of configurations for each router class. This table includes identifiers for the possible combinations of Ethernet and Serial interfaces in the device. The table does not include any other type of interface, even though a specific router may contain one. An example of this might be an ISDN BRI interface. The string in parenthesis is the legal abbreviation that can be used in Cisco IOS commands to represent the interface.

Chapter 3: Authentication, Authorization, and Accounting

Lab 3.6.1.1 - Securing Administrative Access Using AAA and RADIUS

Topology

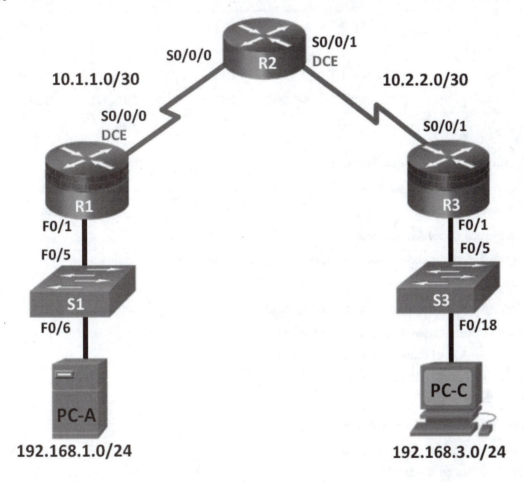

Note: ISR G2 devices use GigabitEthernet interfaces instead of FastEthernet interfaces.

Addressing Table

Device	Interface	IP Address	Subnet Mask	Default Gateway	Switch Port
R1	Fa0/1	192.168.1.1	255.255.255.0	N/A	S1 Fa0/5
R1	S0/0/0 (DCE)	10.1.1.1	255.255.255.252	N/A	N/A
R2	S0/0/0	10.1.1.2	255.255.255.252	N/A	N/A
R2	S0/0/1 (DCE)	10.2.2.2	255.255.255.252	N/A	N/A
R3	Fa0/1	192.168.3.1	255.255.255.0	N/A	S3 Fa0/5
R3	S0/0/1	10.2.2.1	255.255.255.252	N/A	N/A
PC-A	NIC	192.168.1.3	255.255.255.0	192.168.1.1	S1 Fa0/6
PC-C	NIC	192.168.3.3	255.255.255.0	192.168.3.1	S3 Fa0/18

Objectives

Part 1: Configure Basic Device Settings

- Configure basic settings such as host name, interface IP addresses, and access passwords.
- Configure static routing.

Part 2: Configure Local Authentication

- Configure a local database user and local access for the console, vty, and aux lines.
- Test the configuration.

Part 3: Configure Local Authentication Using AAA

- Configure the local user database using Cisco IOS.
- Configure AAA local authentication using Cisco IOS.
- Configure AAA local authentication using CCP.
- Test the configuration.

Part 4: Configure Centralized Authentication Using AAA and RADIUS

- Install a RADIUS server on a computer.
- Configure users on the RADIUS server.
- Use Cisco IOS to configure AAA services on a router to access the RADIUS server for authentication.
- Use CCP to configure AAA services on a router to access the RADIUS server for authentication.
- Test the AAA RADIUS configuration.

Background / Scenario

The most basic form of router access security is to create passwords for the console, vty, and aux lines. A user is prompted for only a password when accessing the router. Configuring a privileged EXEC mode enable secret password further improves security, but still only a basic password is required for each mode of access.

In addition to basic passwords, specific usernames or accounts with varying privilege levels can be defined in the local router database that can apply to the router as a whole. When the console, vty, or aux lines are configured to refer to this local database, the user is prompted for a username and a password when using any of these lines to access the router.

Additional control over the login process can be achieved using authentication, authorization, and accounting (AAA). For basic authentication, AAA can be configured to access the local database for user logins, and fallback procedures can also be defined. However, this approach is not very scalable because it must be configured on every router. To take full advantage of AAA and achieve maximum scalability, AAA is used in conjunction with an external TACACS+ or RADIUS server database. When a user attempts to log in, the router references the external server database to verify that the user is logging in with a valid username and password.

In this lab, you build a multi-router network and configure the routers and hosts. You will then use CLI commands and CCP tools to configure routers with basic local authentication by means of AAA. You will install RADIUS software on an external computer and use AAA to authenticate users with the RADIUS server.

Note: The router commands and output in this lab are from a Cisco 1841 router with Cisco IOS Release 15.1(4)M8 (Advanced IP Services image). Other routers and Cisco IOS versions can be used. See the Router Interface Summary Table at the end of the lab to determine which interface identifiers to use based on the equipment in the lab. Depending on the router model and Cisco IOS version, the commands available and output produced might vary from what is shown in this lab.

Note: Make sure that the routers and switches have been erased and have no startup configurations.

Required Resources

- 3 routers (Cisco 1841 with Cisco IOS Release 15.1(4)M8 advanced IP services image or comparable)
- 2 switches (Cisco 2960 or comparable)
- 2 PCs (Windows Vista or Windows 7 with CCP 2.5, latest version of Java, Internet Explorer, and Flash Player and RADIUS server)
- Serial and Ethernet cables, as shown in the topology
- Console cables to configure Cisco networking devices

CCP Notes:

- If the PC on which CCP is installed is running Windows Vista or Windows 7, it may be necessary to right-click on the CCP icon or menu item, and choose **Run as administrator**.
- In order to run CCP, it may be necessary to temporarily disable antivirus programs and O/S firewalls. Make sure that all pop-up blockers are turned off in the browser.

Part 1: Configure Basic Device Settings

In Part 1 of this lab, you set up the network topology and configure basic settings, such as the interface IP addresses, static routing, device access, and passwords.

All steps should be performed on routers R1 and R3. Only steps 1, 2, 3, and 6 need to be performed on R2. The procedure for R1 is shown here as an example.

Step 1: Cable the network as shown in the topology.

Attach the devices as shown in the topology diagram, and cable as necessary.

Step 2: Configure basic settings for each router.

a. Configure host names as shown in the topology.

b. Configure the interface IP addresses as shown in the IP addressing table.

c. Configure a clock rate for the routers with a DCE serial cable attached to their serial interface.

```
R1(config)# interface S0/0/0
R1(config-if)# clock rate 64000
```

d. To prevent the router from attempting to translate incorrectly entered commands as though they were host names, disable DNS lookup.

```
R1(config)# no ip domain-lookup
```

Step 3: Configure static routing on the routers.

a. Configure a static default route from R1 to R2 and from R3 to R2.

b. Configure a static route from R2 to the R1 LAN and from R2 to the R3 LAN.

Step 4: Configure PC host IP settings.

Configure a static IP address, subnet mask, and default gateway for PC-A and PC-C, as shown in the IP addressing table.

Step 5: Verify connectivity between PC-A and R3.

a. Ping from R1 to R3.

If the pings are not successful, troubleshoot the basic device configurations before continuing.

b. Ping from PC-A on the R1 LAN to PC-C on the R3 LAN.

If the pings are not successful, troubleshoot the basic device configurations before continuing.

Note: If you can ping from PC-A to PC-C, you have demonstrated that static routing is configured and functioning correctly. If you cannot ping but the device interfaces are up and IP addresses are correct, use the **show run** and **show ip route** commands to help identify routing protocol-related problems.

Step 6: Save the basic running configuration for each router.

Step 7: Configure and encrypt passwords on R1 and R3.

Note: Passwords in this task are set to a minimum of 10 characters but are relatively simple for the benefit of performing the lab. More complex passwords are recommended in a production network.

For this step, configure the same settings for R1 and R3. Router R1 is shown here as an example.

a. Configure a minimum password length.

Use the **security passwords** command to set a minimum password length of 10 characters.

```
R1(config)# security passwords min-length 10
```

b. Configure the enable secret password on both routers.

```
R1(config)# enable secret cisco12345
```

c. Configure the basic console, auxiliary port, and vty lines.

d. Configure a console password and enable login for router R1. For additional security, the **exec-timeout** command causes the line to log out after **5** minutes of inactivity. The **logging synchronous** command prevents console messages from interrupting command entry.

Note: To avoid repetitive logins during this lab, the exec timeout can be set to 0 0, which prevents it from expiring. However, this is not considered a good security practice.

```
R1(config)# line console 0
R1(config-line)# password ciscoconpass
R1(config-line)# exec-timeout 5 0
R1(config-line)# login
R1(config-line)# logging synchronous
```

e. Configure a password for the aux port for router R1.

```
R1(config)# line aux 0
```

```
R1(config-line)# password ciscoauxpass
R1(config-line)# exec-timeout 5 0
R1(config-line)# login
```

f. Configure the password on the vty lines for router R1.

```
R1(config)# line vty 0 4
R1(config-line)# password ciscovtypass
R1(config-line)# exec-timeout 5 0
R1(config-line)# login
```

g. Encrypt the console, aux, and vty passwords.

```
R1(config)# service password-encryption
```

h. Issue the **show run** command. Can you read the console, aux, and vty passwords? Explain.

_____

_____

Step 8: Configure a login warning banner on routers R1 and R3.

a. Configure a warning to unauthorized users using a message-of-the-day (MOTD) banner with the **banner motd** command. When a user connects to the router, the MOTD banner appears before the login prompt. In this example, the dollar sign ($) is used to start and end the message.

```
R1(config)# banner motd $Unauthorized access strictly prohibited!$
R1(config)# exit
```

b. Exit privileged EXEC mode by using the **disable** or **exit** command and press **Enter** to get started.

If the banner does not appear correctly, re-create it using the **banner motd** command.

Step 9: Save the basic configurations on all routers.

Save the running configuration to the startup configuration from the privileged EXEC prompt.

```
R1# copy running-config startup-config
```

Part 2: Configure Local Authentication

In Part 2 of this lab, you configure a local username and password and change the access for the console, aux, and vty lines to reference the router's local database for valid usernames and passwords. Perform all steps on R1 and R3. The procedure for R1 is shown here.

Step 1: Configure the local user database.

a. Create a local user account with MD5 hashing to encrypt the password.

```
R1(config)# username user01 secret user01pass
```

b. Exit global configuration mode and display the running configuration. Can you read the user's password?

_____

_____

Step 2: Configure local authentication for the console line and login.

a. Set the console line to use the locally defined login usernames and passwords.

```
R1(config)# line console 0
R1(config-line)# login local
```

b. Exit to the initial router screen that displays:

```
R1 con0 is now available. Press RETURN to get started.
```

c. Log in using the **user01** account and password previously defined.

What is the difference between logging in at the console now and previously?

_____

_____

d. After logging in, issue the **show run** command. Were you able to issue the command? Explain.

_____

_____

Enter privileged EXEC mode using the **enable** command. Were you prompted for a password? Explain.

_____

_____

Step 3: Test the new account by logging in from a Telnet session.

a. From PC-A, establish a Telnet session with R1.

```
PC-A> telnet 192.168.1.1
```

b. Were you prompted for a user account? Explain.

_____

_____

c. What password did you use to login? _____

d. Set the vty lines to use the locally defined login accounts.

```
R1(config)# line vty 0 4
R1(config-line)# login local
```

e. From PC-A, telnet R1 to R1 again.

```
PC-A> telnet 192.168.1.1
```

Were you prompted for a user account? Explain.

_____

_____

f. Log in as **user01** with a password of **user01pass**.

g. While connected to R1 via Telnet, access privileged EXEC mode with the **enable** command.

What password did you use?

_____

h. For added security, set the aux port to use the locally defined login accounts.

```
R1(config)# line aux 0
R1(config-line)# login local
```

i. End the Telnet session with the **exit** command.

Step 4: Save the configuration on R1.

Save the running configuration to the startup configuration from the privileged EXEC prompt.

```
R1# copy running-config startup-config
```

Step 5: Perform steps 1 through 4 on R3 and save the configuration.

Save the running configuration to the startup configuration from the privileged EXEC prompt.

Part 3: Configure Local Authentication Using AAA on R3

Task 1: Configure the Local User Database Using Cisco IOS.

Note: To configure AAA using CCP, skip to Task 3.

Step 1: Configure the local user database.

a. Create a local user account with MD5 hashing to encrypt the password.

```
R3(config)# username Admin01 privilege 15 secret Admin01pass
```

b. Exit global configuration mode and display the running configuration. Can you read the user's password?

_____

_____

Task 2: Configure AAA Local Authentication Using Cisco IOS.

On R3, enable services with the global configuration **aaa new-model** command. Because you are implementing local authentication, use local authentication as the first method, and no authentication as the secondary method.

If you were using an authentication method with a remote server, such as TACACS+ or RADIUS, you would configure a secondary authentication method for fallback if the server is unreachable. Normally, the secondary method is the local database. In this case, if no usernames are configured in the local database, the router allows all users login access to the device.

Step 1: Enable AAA services.

```
R3(config)# aaa new-model
```

Step 2: Implement AAA services for console access using the local database.

a. Create the default login authentication list by issuing the **aaa authentication login default** *method1[method2][method3]* command with a method list using the **local** and **none** keywords.

```
R3(config)# aaa authentication login default local none
```

Note: If you do not set up a default login authentication list, you could get locked out of the router and be forced to use the password recovery procedure for your specific router.

b. Exit to the initial router screen that displays:

```
R3 con0 is now available

Press RETURN to get started.
```

Log in to the console as **Admin01** with a password of **Admin01pass**. Remember that passwords are case-sensitive. Were you able to log in? Explain.

_____

_____

Note: If your session with the console port of the router times out, you might have to log in using the default authentication list.

c. Exit to the initial router screen that displays:

```
R3 con0 is now available

Press RETURN to get started.
```

d. Attempt to log in to the console as **baduser** with any password. Were you able to log in? Explain.

_____

_____

e. If no user accounts are configured in the local database, which users are permitted to access the device?

_____

_____

Step 3: Create an AAA authentication profile for Telnet using the local database.

a. Create a unique authentication list for Telnet access to the router. This does not have the fallback of no authentication, so if there are no usernames in the local database, Telnet access is disabled. To create an authentication profile that is not the default, specify a list name of TELNET_LINES and apply it to the vty lines.

```
R3(config)# aaa authentication login TELNET_LINES local
R3(config)# line vty 0 4
R3(config-line)# login authentication TELNET_LINES
```

b. Verify that this authentication profile is used by opening a Telnet session from PC-C to R3.

```
PC-C> telnet 192.168.3.1
Trying 192.168.3.1 ... Open
```

c. Log in as **Admin01** with a password of **Admin01pass**. Were you able to login? Explain.

_____

_____

d. Exit the Telnet session with the **exit** command, and Telnet to R3 again.

e. Attempt to log in as **baduser** with any password. Were you able to login? Explain.

_____

_____

Task 3: (Optional) Configure AAA Local Authentication Using Cisco CCP.

You can also use CCP to configure the router to support AAA. Even if you do not perform this task, read through the steps to become familiar with the CCP process.

Step 1: Erase and reload the router.

In this step, restore the router back to the basic configuration saved in Parts 1 and 2.

a. Connect to the R3 console, and log in with the username **Admin01** and password **Admin01pass**.

b. Enter privileged EXEC mode with the password **cisco12345**.

c. Reload the router.

```
R3# reload

System configuration has been modified. Save? [yes/no]: no
Proceed with reload? [confirm]
```

Step 2: Implement AAA services and HTTP router access prior to starting CCP.

a. From the CLI global config mode, enable a new AAA model.

```
R3(config)# aaa new-model
```

b. Enable the HTTP server on R3 for CCP access.

```
R3(config)# ip http server
```

Note: For maximum security, enable secure http server by using the **ip http secure-server** command.

c. Add a user named admin to the local database.

```
R3(config)# username admin privilege 15 secret cisco12345
```

d. Configure CCP to use the local database to authenticate web sessions.

```
R3(config)# ip http authentication local
```

Step 3: Access CCP and discover R3.

a. Start CCP on PC-C. In the Manage Devices window, add R3 IP address 192.168.3.1 in the first IP address field. Enter **admin** in the Username field, and **cisco12345** in the Password field.

b. At the CCP Dashboard, click the **Discover** button to discover and connect to R3. If discovery fails, click the **Discovery Details** button to determine the problem.

Step 4: Use CCP to create an administrative user.

a. Click the **Configure** button at the top of the screen.

b. Choose **Router > Router Access > User Accounts/View**.

c. In the User Accounts/View window, click **Add**.

d. In the Add an Account window, enter **Admin01** in the Username field.

e. Enter the password **Admin01pass** in the New Password and Confirm New Password fields. (Remember, passwords are case-sensitive.)

f. Confirm that the Encrypt password using MD5 hash algorithm check box is checked.

g. Select **15** from the Privilege Level drop-down list and click **OK**.

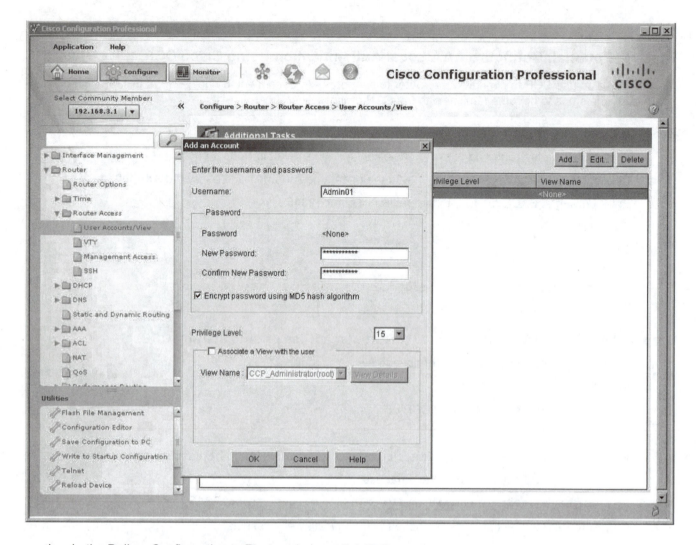

h. In the Deliver Configuration to Router window, click **Deliver**.

i. In the Commands Delivery Status window, click **OK**.

Step 5: Create AAA method list for login.

a. Click the **Configure** button at the top of the screen.

b. Choose **Router** > **AAA** > **Authentication Policies > Login**.

c. In the Authentication Login window, click **Add**.

d. In the Add a Method List for Authentication Login window, verify that **Default** is in the Name field.

e. Click **Add** in the Methods section.

f. In the Select Method List(s) for Authentication Login window, choose **local** and click **OK**. Take note of the other methods listed, which include RADIUS (group radius) and TACACS+ (group tacacs+).

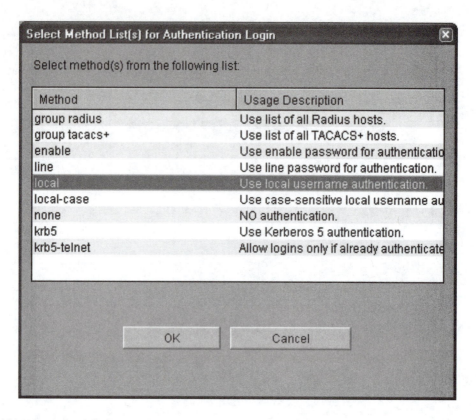

g. Click **OK** to close the window.

h. Repeat steps 4f and 4g. Choose **none** as a second authentication method and click the **OK** button when done.

i. In the Deliver Configuration to Router window, click **Deliver**. In the Commands Delivery Status window, click **OK**.

j. What command was delivered to the router?

_____

_____

Step 6: Verify the AAA username and profile for console login.

a. Exit to the initial router screen that displays:

    R3 con0 is now available

    Press RETURN to get started.

b. Log in to the console as **Admin01** with a password of **Admin01pass**. Were you able to login? Explain.

_____

_____

c. Exit to the initial router screen that displays:

    R3 con0 is now available

    Press RETURN to get started.

d. Attempt to log in to the console as **baduser**. Were you able to login? Explain.

_____

_____

If no user accounts are configured in the local database, which users are permitted to access the device?

_____

_____

e. Log in to the console as **Admin01** with a password of **Admin01pass**. Access privileged EXEC mode using the enable secret password **cisco12345** and then use **show the run** command to display the running configuration. What commands are associated with the CCP session?

_____

_____

Task 4: Observe AAA Authentication Using Cisco IOS Debug.

In this task, you use the **debug** command to observe successful and unsuccessful authentication attempts.

Step 1: Verify that the system clock and debug time stamps are configured correctly.

a. From the R3 user or privileged EXEC mode prompt, use the **show clock** command to determine what the current time is for the router. If the time and date are incorrect, set the time from privileged EXEC mode with the command **clock set HH:MM:SS DD month YYYY.** An example is provided here for R3.

```
R3# clock set 14:15:00 26 December 2008
```

b. Verify that detailed time-stamp information is available for your debug output using the **show run** command. This command displays all lines in the running config that include the text "timestamps".

```
R3# show run | include timestamps

service timestamps debug datetime msec
service timestamps log datetime msec
```

c. If the **service timestamps debug** command is not present, enter it in global config mode.

```
R3(config)# service timestamps debug datetime msec
R3(config)# exit
```

d. Save the running configuration to the startup configuration from the privileged EXEC prompt.

```
R3# copy running-config startup-config
```

Step 2: Use debug to verify user access.

a. Activate debugging for AAA authentication.

```
R3# debug aaa authentication
AAA Authentication debugging is on
```

b. Start a Telnet session from PC-C to R3.

c. Log in with username **Admin01** and password **Admin01pass**. Observe the AAA authentication events in the console session window. Debug messages similar to the following should be displayed.

```
R3#
```

```
Dec 26 14:36:42.323: AAA/BIND(000000A5): Bind i/f
Dec 26 14:36:42.323: AAA/AUTHEN/LOGIN (000000A5): Pick method list 'default'
```

d. From the Telnet window, enter privileged EXEC mode. Use the enable secret password of **cisco12345**. Debug messages similar to the following should be displayed. In the third entry, note the username (Admin01), virtual port number (tty194), and remote Telnet client address (192.168.3.3). Also note that the last status entry is "PASS."

```
R3#
Dec 26 14:40:54.431: AAA: parse name=tty194 idb type=-1 tty=-1
Dec 26 14:40:54.431: AAA: name=tty194 flags=0x11 type=5 shelf=0 slot=0 adapter=0
port=194 channel=0
Dec 26 14:40:54.431: AAA/MEMORY: create_user (0x64BB5510) user='Admin01' ruser=' NULL'
ds0=0 port='tty194' rem_addr='192.168.3.3' authen_type=ASCII service=ENABLE priv=15
initial_task_id='0', vrf= (id=0)
Dec 26 14:40:54.431: AAA/AUTHEN/START (2467624222): port='tty194' list='' action=LOGIN
service=ENABLE
Dec 26 14:40:54.431: AAA/AUTHEN/START (2467624222): non-console enable - default to
enable password
Dec 26 14:40:54.431: AAA/AUTHEN/START (2467624222): Method=ENABLE
R3#
Dec 26 14:40:54.435: AAA/AUTHEN(2467624222): Status=GETPASS
R3#
Dec 26 14:40:59.275: AAA/AUTHEN/CONT (2467624222): continue_login (user='(undef)')
Dec 26 14:40:59.275: AAA/AUTHEN(2467624222): Status=GETPASS
Dec 26 14:40:59.275: AAA/AUTHEN/CONT (2467624222): Method=ENABLE
Dec 26 14:40:59.287: AAA/AUTHEN(2467624222): Status=PASS
Dec 26 14:40:59.287: AAA/MEMORY: free_user (0x64BB5510) user='NULL' ruser='NULL'
port='tty194' rem_addr='192.168.3.3' authen_type=ASCII service=ENABLE priv=15 vrf=
(id=0)
```

e. From the Telnet window, exit privileged EXEC mode using the **disable** command. Try to enter privileged EXEC mode again, but use a bad password this time. Observe the debug output on R3, noting that the status is "FAIL" this time.

```
Dec 26 15:46:54.027: AAA/AUTHEN(2175919868): Status=GETPASS
Dec 26 15:46:54.027: AAA/AUTHEN/CONT (2175919868): Method=ENABLE
Dec 26 15:46:54.039: AAA/AUTHEN(2175919868): password incorrect
Dec 26 15:46:54.039: AAA/AUTHEN(2175919868): Status=FAIL
Dec 26 15:46:54.039: AAA/MEMORY: free_user (0x6615BFE4) user='NULL' ruser='NULL'
port='tty194' rem_addr='192.168.3.3' authen_type=ASCII service=ENABLE priv=15 vrf=
(id=0)
```

f. From the Telnet window, exit the Telnet session to the router. Then try to open a Telnet session to the router again, but this time try to log in with the username **Admin01** and a bad password. From the console window, the debug output should look similar to the following.

```
Dec 26 15:49:32.339: AAA/AUTHEN/LOGIN (000000AA): Pick method list 'default'
```

What message was displayed on the Telnet client screen?

_____

_____

g. Turn off all debugging using the **undebug all** command at the privileged EXEC prompt.

Part 4: Configure Centralized Authentication Using AAA and RADIUS

In Part 4 of the lab, you install RADIUS server software on PC-A. You then configure R1 to access the external RADIUS server for user authentication. The freeware server WinRadius is used for this section of the lab.

Task 1: Restore R1 to the Basic Configuration.

To avoid confusion as to what was already entered and the AAA RADIUS configuration, start by restoring router R1 to its basic configuration as performed in Parts 1 and 2 of this lab.

Step 1: Reload and restore saved configuration on R1.

In this step, restore the router back to the basic configuration saved in Parts 1 and 2.

a. Connect to the R1 console, and log in with the username **Admin01** and password **Admin01pass**.

b. Enter privileged EXEC mode with the password **cisco12345**.

c. Reload the router and enter **no** when prompted to save the configuration.

```
R1# reload

System configuration has been modified. Save? [yes/no]: no
Proceed with reload? [confirm]
```

Step 2: Verify connectivity.

a. Test connectivity by pinging from host PC-A to PC-C. If the pings are not successful, troubleshoot the router and PC configurations until they are.

b. If you are logged out of the console, log in again as **user01** with password **user01pass**, and access privileged EXEC mode with the password **cisco12345**.

Task 2: Download and Install a RADIUS Server on PC-A.

There are a number of RADIUS servers available, both freeware and for cost. This lab uses WinRadius, a freeware standards-based RADIUS server that runs on Windows operating systems. The free version of the software can support only five usernames.

Note: A zipped file containing the WinRadius software can be obtained from your instructor.

Step 1: Download the WinRadius software.

a. Create a folder named **WinRadius** on your desktop or other location in which to store the files.

b. Extract the WinRadius zipped files to the folder you created in Step 1a. There is no installation setup. The extracted **WinRadius.exe** file is executable.

c. You may create a shortcut on your desktop for WinRadius.exe.

Note: If WinRadius is used on a PC that uses the Microsoft Windows Vista operating system or the Microsoft Windows 7 operating system, ODBC may fail to create successfully because it cannot write to the registry.

Possible solutions:

a. Compatibility settings:

1) Right click on the **WinRadius.exe** icon and select **Properties**.

2) While in the **Properties** dialog box, select the **Compatibility** tab. In this tab, select the checkbox for **Run this program in compatibility mode for**. Then in the drop-down menu below, choose **Windows XP (Service Pack 3),** for example, if it is appropriate for your system.

3) Click **OK**.

b. Run as Administrator settings:

1) Right click on the WinRadius.exe icon and select **Properties**.

2) While in the **Properties** dialog box, select the **Compatibility** tab. In this tab, select the checkbox for **Run this program as administrator** in the Privilege Level section.

3) Click **OK**.

c. Run as Administration for each launch:

1) Right click on the WinRadius.exe icon and select **Run as Administrator**.

2) When WinRadius launches, click **Yes** in the User Account Control dialog box.

Step 2: Configure the WinRadius server database.

a. Start the WinRadius.exe application. WinRadius uses a local database in which it stores user information. When the application is started for the first time, the following messages are displayed:

```
Please go to Settings/Database and create the ODBC for your RADIUS database.
Launch ODBC failed.
```

b. Choose **Settings > Database** from the main menu. The following screen is displayed. Click the **Configure ODBC Automatically** button and then click **OK**. You should see a message that the ODBC was created successfully. Exit WinRadius and restart the application for the changes to take effect.

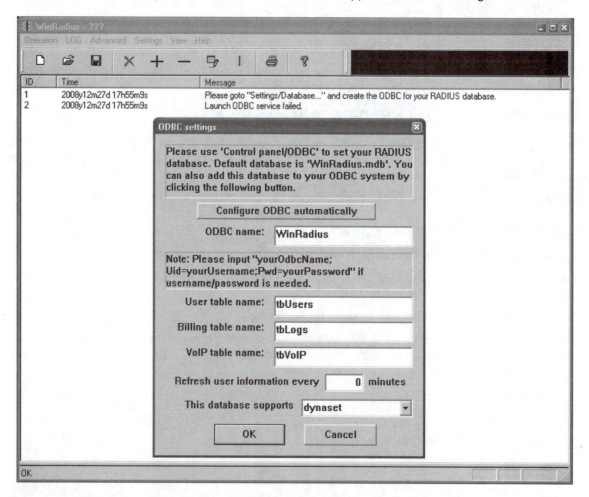

c. When WinRadius starts again, you should see messages similar to the following displayed.

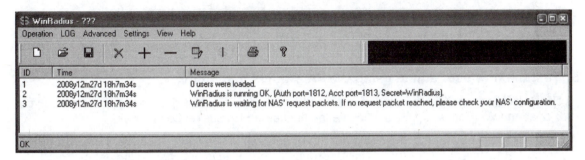

Note about WinRadius Server:

The free version of WinRadius only supports five usernames. If the first message in the above screen shows something other than 0 users were loaded, then you will need to remove the previously added users from the WinRadius database.

To determine what usernames are in the database, click on **Operation** > **Query**, and then click **OK**. A list of usernames contained in the database is displayed in the bottom section of the WinRadius window.

To delete a user, click **Operation** > **Delete User**, and then enter the username exactly as listed. Usernames are case sensitive.

d. On which ports is WinRadius listening for authentication and accounting?

_____

_____

Step 3: Configure users and passwords on the WinRadius server.

a. From the main menu, select **Operation** > **Add User**.

b. Enter the username **RadUser** with a password of **RadUserpass**. Remember that passwords are case-sensitive.

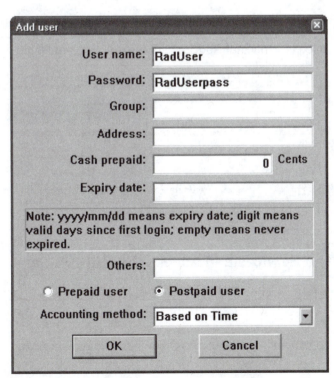

c. Click **OK**. You should see a message on the log screen that the user was added successfully.

Step 4: Clear the log display.

From the main menu, choose **Log** > **Clear**.

Step 5: Test the new user added using the WinRadius test utility.

a. A WinRadius testing utility is included in the downloaded zip file. Navigate to the folder where you unzipped the WinRadius.zip file and locate the file named RadiusTest.exe.

b. Start the RadiusTest application, and enter the IP address of this RADIUS server (**192.168.1.3**), username **RadUser**, and password **RadUserpass** as shown. Do not change the default RADIUS port number of 1813 and the RADIUS password of WinRadius.

c. Click **Send** and you should see a Send Access_Request message indicating the server at 192.168.1.3, port number 1813, received 44 hexadecimal characters.

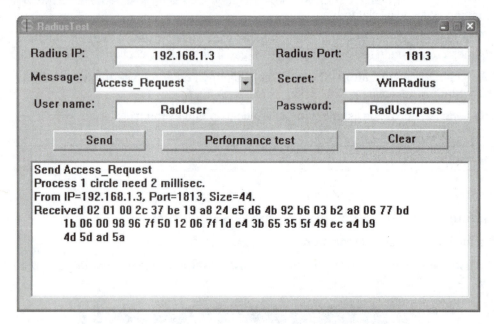

d. Review the WinRadius log to verify that RadUser successfully authenticated.

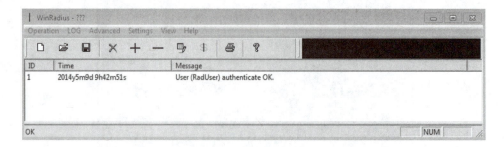

e. Close the RadiusTest application.

Task 3: Configure R1 AAA Services and Access the RADIUS Server Using Cisco IOS.

Note: To configure AAA using CCP, proceed to Task 5.

Step 1: Enable AAA on R1.

Use the **aaa new-model** command in global configuration mode to enable AAA.

```
R1(config)# aaa new-model
```

Step 2: Configure the default login authentication list.

a. Configure the list to first use RADIUS for the authentication service, and then none. If no RADIUS server can be reached and authentication cannot be performed, the router globally allows access without authentication. This is a safeguard measure in case the router starts up without connectivity to an active RADIUS server.

```
R1(config)# aaa authentication login default group radius none
```

b. You could alternatively configure local authentication as the backup authentication method instead.

Note: If you do not set up a default login authentication list, you could get locked out of the router and need to use the password recovery procedure for your specific router.

Step 3: Specify a RADIUS server.

a. Use the **radius-server host** *hostname* **key** *key* command to point to the RADIUS server. The *hostname* argument accepts either a host name or an IP address. Use the IP address of the RADIUS server, PC-A (**192.168.1.3**). The key is a secret password shared between the RADIUS server and the RADIUS client (R1 in this case) and used to authenticate the connection between the router and the server before the user authentication process takes place. The RADIUS client may be a Network Access Server (NAS), but router R1 plays that role in this lab. Use the default NAS secret password of **WinRadius** specified on the RADIUS server (see Task 2, Step 5). Remember that passwords are case-sensitive.

```
R1(config)# radius-server host 192.168.1.3 key WinRadius
```

Task 4: Test the AAA RADIUS Configuration.

Step 1: Verify connectivity between R1 and the computer running the RADIUS server.

Ping from R1 to PC-A.

```
R1# ping 192.168.1.3
```

If the pings were not successful, troubleshoot the PC and router configuration before continuing.

Step 2: Test your configuration.

a. If you restarted the WinRadius server, you must re-create the user **RadUser** with a password of **RadUserpass** by choosing **Operation** > **Add User**.

b. Clear the log on the WinRadius server by choosing **Log** > **Clear** from the main menu.

c. On R1, exit to the initial router screen that displays:

```
R1 con0 is now available

Press RETURN to get started.
```

d. Test your configuration by logging in to the console on R1 using the username **RadUser** and the password of **RadUserpass**. Were you able to gain access to the user EXEC prompt and, if so, was there any delay?

_____

_____

e. Exit to the initial router screen that displays:

```
R1 con0 is now available

Press RETURN to get started.
```

f. Test your configuration again by logging in to the console on R1 using the nonexistent username of **Userxxx** and the password of **Userxxxpass**. Were you able to gain access to the user EXEC prompt? Explain.

_____

_____

_____

_____

g. Were any messages displayed on the RADIUS server log for either login? _____

h. Why was a nonexistent username able to access the router and no messages are displayed on the RADIUS server log screen?

_____

_____

i. When the RADIUS server is unavailable, messages similar to the following are typically displayed after attempted logins.

```
*Dec 26 16:46:54.039: %RADIUS-4-RADIUS_DEAD: RADIUS server 192.168.1.3:1645,1646 is
not responding.
*Dec 26 15:46:54.039: %RADIUS-4-RADIUS_ALIVE: RADIUS server 192.168.1.3:1645,1646 is
being marked alive.
```

Step 3: Troubleshoot router-to-RADIUS server communication.

a. Check the default Cisco IOS RADIUS UDP port numbers used on R1 with the **radius-server host** command and the Cisco IOS Help function.

```
R1(config)# radius-server host 192.168.1.3 ?
  acct-port   UDP port for RADIUS acco/unting server (default is 1646)
  alias       1-8 aliases for this server (max. 8)
  auth-port   UDP port for RADIUS authentication server (default is 1645)
<Output omitted>
```

b. Check the R1 running configuration for lines containing the command **radius**.

```
R1# show run | include radius
aaa authentication login default group radius none
radius-server host 192.168.1.3 auth-port 1645 acct-port 1646 key 7
097B47072B04131B1E1F
<Output omitted>
```

What are the default R1 Cisco IOS UDP port numbers for the RADIUS server?

_____

Step 4: Check the default port numbers on the WinRadius server on PC-A.

From the WinRadius main menu, choose **Settings** > **System**.

System settings

NAS Secret: WinRadius

Authorization port: 1812

Accounting port: 1813

☐ Launch when system startups

☐ Minimize the application when startups

OK   Cancel

What are the default WinRadius UDP port numbers? _____

Note: RFC 2865 officially assigned port numbers 1812 and 1813 for RADIUS.

Step 5: Change the RADIUS port numbers on R1 to match the WinRadius server.

Unless specified otherwise, the Cisco IOS RADIUS configuration defaults to UDP port numbers 1645 and 1646. Either the router Cisco IOS port numbers must be changed to match the port number of the RADIUS server or the RADIUS server port numbers must be changed to match the port numbers of the Cisco IOS router.

a. Remove the previous configuration using the following command:

    R1(config)# **no radius-server host 192.168.1.3 auth-port 1645 acct-port 1646**

b. Issue the **radius-server host** command again and this time specify port numbers **1812** and **1813**, along with the IP address and secret key for the RADIUS server.

    R1(config)# **radius-server host 192.168.1.3 auth-port 1812 acct-port 1813 key WinRadius**

Step 6: Test your configuration by logging into the console on R1.

a. Exit to the initial router screen that displays: R1 con0 is now available; press **RETURN** to get started.

b. Log in again with the username of **RadUser** and password of **RadUserpass**. Were you able to login? Was there any delay this time?

    _____

    _____

    _____

    _____

c. The following message should display on the RADIUS server log.

    User (RadUser) authenticate OK.

d. Exit to the initial router screen that displays:

    R1 con0 is now available, Press RETURN to get started.

e. Log in again using an invalid username of **Userxxx** and the password of **Userxxxpass**. Were you able to login?

_____

_____

What message was displayed on the router?

_____

The following messages should display on the RADIUS server log:

```
Reason: Unknown username
User (Userxxx) authenticate failed
```

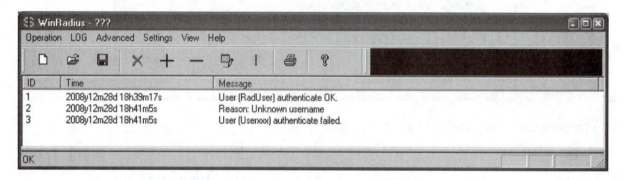

Step 7: Create an authentication method list for Telnet and test it.

a. Create a unique authentication method list for Telnet access to the router. This does not have the fallback of no authentication, so if there is no access to the RADIUS server, Telnet access is disabled. Name the authentication method list **TELNET_LINES**.

```
R1(config)# aaa authentication login TELNET_LINES group radius
```

b. Apply the list to the vty lines on the router using the login authentication command.

```
R1(config)# line vty 0 4
R1(config-line)# login authentication TELNET_LINES
```

c. Telnet from PC-A to R1, and log in with the username **RadUser** and the password of **RadUserpass**. Were you able to gain access to log in? Explain.

_____

_____

d. Exit the Telnet session, and telnet from PC-A to R1 again. Log in with the username **Userxxx** and the password of **Userxxxpass**. Were you able to log in? Explain.

_____

_____

Task 5: (Optional) Configure R1 AAA Services and Access the RADIUS Server Using CCP.

You can also use CCP to configure the router to access the external RADIUS server.

Note: If you configured R1 to access the external RADIUS server using Cisco IOS in Task 3, you can skip this task. If you performed Task 3 and you want to perform this task, restore the router to its basic configuration as described Task 1 of this part, except log in initially as **RadUser** with the password **RadUserpass.** If the RADIUS server is unavailable at this time, you will still be able to log in to the console.

If you do not perform this task, read through the steps to become familiar with the CCP process.

Step 1: Implement AAA services and HTTP router access prior to starting CCP.

a. From the CLI global config mode, enable a new AAA model.

```
R1(config)# aaa new-model
```

b. Enable the HTTP server on R1.

```
R1(config)# ip http server
```

c. Add a user named **admin** to the local database.

```
R1(config)# username admin privilege 15 secret cisco12345
```

d. Configure CCP to use the local database to authenticate web sessions.

```
R1(config)# ip http authentication local
```

Step 2: Access CCP and discover R1.

a. Start CCP on PC-C. In the Manage Devices window, add R1 IP address **192.168.1.1** in the first IP address field. Enter **admin** in the Username field, and **cisco12345** in the Password field.

b. At the CCP Dashboard, click the **Discover** button to discover and connect to R3. If discovery fails, click the **Discovery Details** button to determine the problem.

Step 3: Configure R1 AAA to access the WinRADIUS server.

a.   Click the **Configure** button at the top of the screen.

b.   Choose **Router** > **AAA** > **AAA Servers and Groups** > **Servers**.

c.   In the AAA Servers window, click **Add**.

d.   In the Add AAA Server window, verify that **RADIUS** is in the Server Type field.

e.   In the Server IP or Host field, enter the IP address of PC-A, **192.168.1.3**.

f.   Change the **Authorization Port** from 1645 to **1812**, and change the **Accounting Port** from 1646 to **1813** to match the RADIUS server port number settings.

g.   Check the **Configure Key** check box.

h.   Enter **WinRadius** in both the New Key and Confirm Key fields.

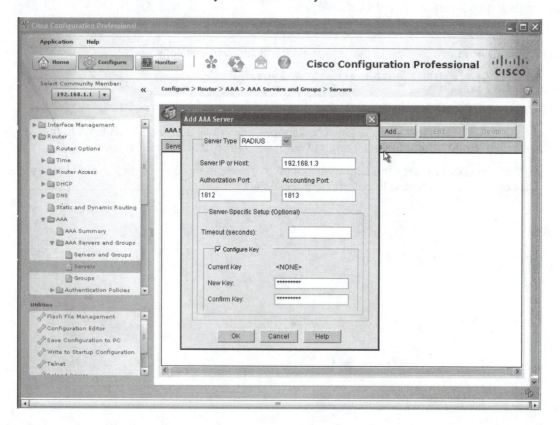

i.   In the Deliver Configuration to Router window, click **Deliver**, and in the Commands Delivery Status window, click **OK**.

j.   What command was delivered to the router?

_____

_____

Step 4: Configure the R1 AAA login method list for RADIUS.

a. Click the **Configure** button at the top of the screen.

b. Choose **Router** > **AAA** > **Authentication Policies** > **Login**.

c. In the Authentication Login window, click **Add**.

d. In the Select Method List(s) for Authentication Login window, choose **group radius** and click **OK**.

e. In the Select Method List(s) for Authentication Login window, choose **local** as a second method and click **OK**.

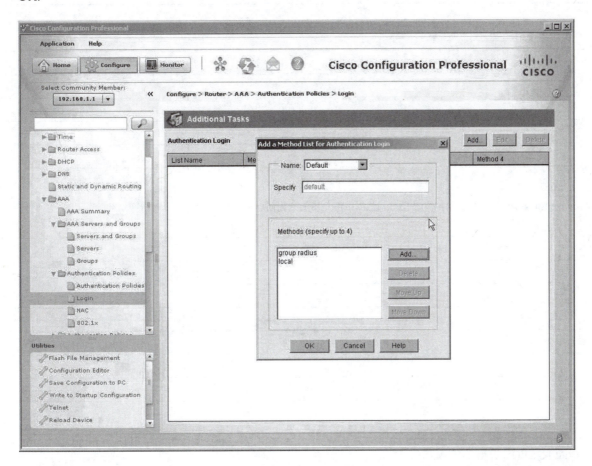

f. In the Deliver Configuration to Router window, click **Deliver** and in the Commands Delivery Status window, click **OK**.

g. What command(s) were delivered to the router?

_____

_____

_____

Step 5: Test your configuration.

a. If you restarted the RADIUS server, you must re-create the user **RadUser** with a password of **RadUserpass** by choosing **Operation** > **Add User**.

b. Clear the log on the WinRadius server by choosing **Log** > **Clear**.

c. Test your configuration by opening a Telnet session from PC-A to R1.

```
C:> telnet 192.168.1.1
```

    d. At the login prompt, enter the username **RadUser** defined on the RADIUS server and a password of **RadUserpass**.

        Were you able to login to R1? _____

Reflection

1. Why would an organization want to use a centralized authentication server rather than configuring users and passwords on each individual router?

_____

_____

_____

_____

_____

_____

_____

_____

2. Contrast local authentication and local authentication with AAA.

_____

_____

_____

_____

_____

_____

_____

_____

3. Based on the Academy online course content, web research, and the use of RADIUS in this lab, compare and contrast RADIUS with TACACS+.

_____

_____

_____

_____

_____

_____

Router Interface Summary Table

Router Interface Summary				
Router Model	Ethernet Interface #1	Ethernet Interface #2	Serial Interface #1	Serial Interface #2
1800	Fast Ethernet 0/0 (Fa0/0)	Fast Ethernet 0/1 (Fa0/1)	Serial 0/0/0 (S0/0/0)	Serial 0/0/1 (S0/0/1)
1900	Gigabit Ethernet 0/0 (G0/0)	Gigabit Ethernet 0/1 (G0/1)	Serial 0/0/0 (S0/0/0)	Serial 0/0/1 (S0/0/1)
2801	Fast Ethernet 0/0 (Fa0/0)	Fast Ethernet 0/1 (Fa0/1)	Serial 0/1/0 (S0/1/0)	Serial 0/1/1 (S0/1/1)
2811	Fast Ethernet 0/0 (Fa0/0)	Fast Ethernet 0/1 (Fa0/1)	Serial 0/0/0 (S0/0/0)	Serial 0/0/1 (S0/0/1)
2900	Gigabit Ethernet 0/0 (G0/0)	Gigabit Ethernet 0/1 (G0/1)	Serial 0/0/0 (S0/0/0)	Serial 0/0/1 (S0/0/1)

Note: To find out how the router is configured, look at the interfaces to identify the type of router and how many interfaces the router has. There is no way to effectively list all the combinations of configurations for each router class. This table includes identifiers for the possible combinations of Ethernet and Serial interfaces in the device. The table does not include any other type of interface, even though a specific router may contain one. An example of this might be an ISDN BRI interface. The string in parenthesis is the legal abbreviation that can be used in Cisco IOS commands to represent the interface.

Chapter 4: Implementing Firewall Technologies

Lab 4.4.1.1 - Configuring Zone-Based Policy Firewalls

Topology

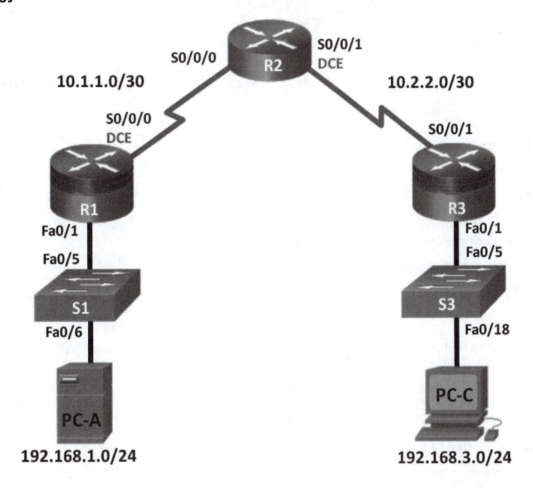

Note: ISR G2 devices have Gigabit Ethernet interfaces instead of Fast Ethernet interfaces.

IP Addressing Table

Device	Interface	IP Address	Subnet Mask	Default Gateway	Switch Port
R1	Fa0/1	192.168.1.1	255.255.255.0	N/A	S1 Fa0/5
	S0/0/0 (DCE)	10.1.1.1	255.255.255.252	N/A	N/A
R2	S0/0/0	10.1.1.2	255.255.255.252	N/A	N/A
	S0/0/1 (DCE)	10.2.2.2	255.255.255.252	N/A	N/A
R3	Fa0/1	192.168.3.1	255.255.255.0	N/A	S3 Fa0/5
	S0/0/1	10.2.2.1	255.255.255.252	N/A	N/A
PC-A	NIC	192.168.1.3	255.255.255.0	192.168.1.1	S1 Fa0/6
PC-C	NIC	192.168.3.3	255.255.255.0	192.168.3.1	S3 Fa0/18

Objectives

Part 1: Basic Router Configuration

- Configure host names, interface IP addresses, and access passwords.
- Configure the OSPF dynamic routing protocol.
- Use the Nmap port scanner to test for router vulnerabilities.

Part 2: Configuring a Zone-Based Policy Firewall (ZBF)

- Use CCP to configure a Zone-Based Policy Firewall.
- Use CCP Monitor to verify configuration.

Background

The most basic form of a Cisco IOS firewall uses access control lists (ACLs) to filter IP traffic and monitor established traffic patterns. This is referred to as a traditional Cisco IOS firewall.

The newer Cisco IOS Firewall implementation uses a zone-based approach that operates as a function of interfaces instead of access control list. A Zone-Based Policy Firewall (ZBF) allows different inspection policies to be applied to multiple host groups connected to the same router interface. It also has the ability to prohibit traffic via a default deny-all policy between firewall zones. ZBF is suited for multiple interfaces that have similar or varying security requirements. CCP generates a ZBF firewall by default.

In this lab, you build a multi-router network and configure the routers and hosts. You use CCP to configure a Zone-Based Policy Firewall.

Note: The router commands and output in this lab are from a Cisco 1841 with Cisco IOS Release 15.1(4)M8 (Advanced IP Services image). Other routers and Cisco IOS versions can be used. See the Router Interface Summary Table at the end of the lab to determine which interface identifiers to use based on the equipment in the lab. Depending on the router model and Cisco IOS version, the commands available and output produced might vary from what is shown in this lab.

Note: Make sure that the routers and switches have been erased and have no startup configurations.

Required Resources

- 3 Routers (Cisco 1841 with Cisco IOS Release 15.1(4)M8 Advanced IP Services image or comparable)

- 2 Switches (Cisco 2960 or comparable)

- 2 PCs (Windows Vista or Windows 7 with CCP 2.5, latest version of Java, Internet Explorer, and Flash Player)

- Serial and Ethernet cables, as shown in the topology

- Console cables to configure Cisco networking devices

CCP Notes:

- If the PC on which CCP is installed is running Windows Vista or Windows 7, it may be necessary to right-click on the CCP icon or menu item, and choose **Run as administrator**.

- In order to run CCP, it may be necessary to temporarily disable antivirus programs and O/S firewalls. Make sure that all pop-up blockers are turned off in the browser.

Part 1: Basic Router Configuration

In Part 1 of this lab, you set up the network topology and configure basic settings, such as the interface IP addresses, dynamic routing, device access, and passwords.

Note: All tasks should be performed on routers R1, R2, and R3. The procedure for R1 is shown here as an example.

Task 1: Configure Basic Router Settings.

Step 1: Cable the network as shown in the topology.

Attach the devices as shown in the topology diagram, and cable as necessary.

Step 2: Configure basic settings for each router.

a. Configure host names as shown in the topology.

b. Configure the interface IP addresses as shown in the IP addressing table.

c. Configure a clock rate for the serial router interfaces with a DCE serial cable attached.

```
R1(config)# interface S0/0/0
R1(config-if)# clock rate 64000
```

Step 3: Disable DNS lookup.

To prevent the router from attempting to translate incorrectly entered commands, disable DNS lookup.

```
R1(config)# no ip domain-lookup
```

Step 4: Configure the OSPF routing protocol on R1, R2, and R3.

a. On R1, use the following commands:

```
R1(config)# router ospf 1
R1(config-router)# network 192.168.1.0 0.0.0.255 area 0
R1(config-router)# network 10.1.1.0 0.0.0.3 area 0
```

b. On R2, use the following commands:

```
R2(config)# router ospf 1
R2(config-router)# network 10.1.1.0 0.0.0.3 area 0
R2(config-router)# network 10.2.2.0 0.0.0.3 area 0
```

c. On R3, use the following commands:

```
R3(config)# router ospf 1
R3(config-router)# network 192.168.3.0 0.0.0.255 area 0
R3(config-router)# network 10.2.2.0 0.0.0.3 area 0
```

Step 5: Configure PC host IP settings.

a. Configure a static IP address, subnet mask, and default gateway for PC-A, as shown in the IP addressing table.

b. Configure a static IP address, subnet mask, and default gateway for PC-C, as shown in the IP addressing table.

Step 6: Verify basic network connectivity.

a. Ping from R1 to R3.

If the pings are not successful, troubleshoot the basic device configurations before continuing.

b. Ping from PC-A on the R1 LAN to PC-C on the R3 LAN.

If the pings are not successful, troubleshoot the basic device configurations before continuing.

Note: If you can ping from PC-A to PC-C, you have demonstrated that the OSPF routing protocol is configured and functioning correctly. If you cannot ping but the device interfaces are up and IP addresses are correct, use the **show run** and **show ip route** commands to help identify routing protocol-related problems.

Step 7: Configure a minimum password length.

Note: Passwords in this lab are set to a minimum of 10 characters but are relatively simple for the benefit of performing the lab. More complex passwords are recommended in a production network.

Use the **security passwords** command to set a minimum password length of 10 characters.

```
R1(config)# security passwords min-length 10
```

Step 8: Configure basic console, auxiliary port, and vty lines.

a. Configure a console password and enable login for router R1. For additional security, the exec-timeout command causes the line to log out after **5** minutes of inactivity. The logging synchronous command prevents console messages from interrupting command entry.

Note: To avoid repetitive logins during this lab, the **exec-timeout** can be set to 0 0, which prevents it from expiring. However, this is not considered a good security practice.

```
R1(config)# line console 0
R1(config-line)# password ciscoconpass
R1(config-line)# exec-timeout 5 0
R1(config-line)# login
R1(config-line)# logging synchronous
```

b.   Configure a password for the aux port for router R1.

```
R1(config)# line aux 0
R1(config-line)# password ciscoauxpass
R1(config-line)# exec-timeout 5 0
R1(config-line)# login
```

c.   Configure the password on the vty lines for router R1.

```
R1(config)# line vty 0 4
R1(config-line)# password ciscovtypass
R1(config-line)# exec-timeout 5 0
R1(config-line)# login
```

d.   Repeat these configurations on both R2 and R3.

Step 9: Enable HTTP server.

Enabling these services allows the router to be managed using the GUI and a web browser.

```
R1(config)# ip http server
R1(config)# ip http secure-server
```

Step 10: Encrypt clear text passwords.

a.   Use the **service password-encryption** command to encrypt the console, aux, and vty passwords.

```
R1(config)# service password-encryption
```

b.   Issue the **show run** command. Can you read the console, aux, and vty passwords? Explain.

_____

_____

c.   Repeat this configuration on both R2 and R3.

Step 11: Save the basic running configuration for all three routers.

Save the running configuration to the startup configuration from the privileged EXEC prompt.

```
R1# copy running-config startup-config
```

Task 2: Use the Nmap Port Scanner to Determine Router Vulnerabilities.

In this task, you determine open ports or services running on R1 using Nmap, before configuring a firewall.

Step 1: (Optional) Download and install Nmap and the Zenmap GUI front-end.

Nmap ("Network Mapper") is a free and open source utility for network exploration or security auditing.

a.   If Nmap is already installed on PC-A and PC-C, go to Step 2. Otherwise, download the latest Windows version from http://nmap.org/download.html.

b. On PC-A and PC-C, run the Nmap setup utility and install all components listed, including the Zenmap GUI front-end. Click **Next** to accept the defaults when prompted.

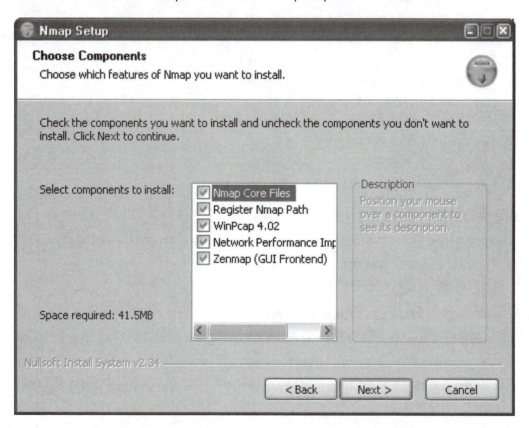

Step 2: Scan for open ports on R1 using Nmap from internal host PC-A.

a. From internal host PC-A, start the Nmap-Zenmap application and enter the IP address of the default gateway, R1 Fa0/1 (**192.168.1.1**), as the Target. Accept the default Nmap command entered for you in the Command window and use the **Intense scan** profile.

Note: If the PC is running a personal firewall, it may be necessary to turn it off temporarily to obtain accurate test results.

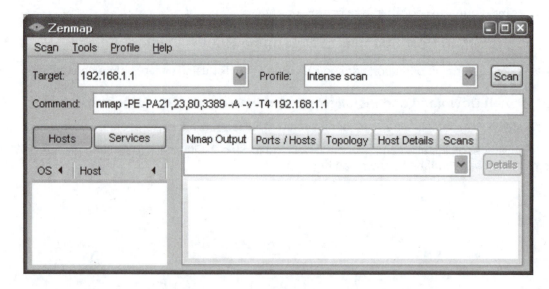

b. Click the **Scan** button to begin the scan of R1 from internal host PC-A. Allow some time for the scan to complete. The next two screens show the entire output of the scan after scrolling.

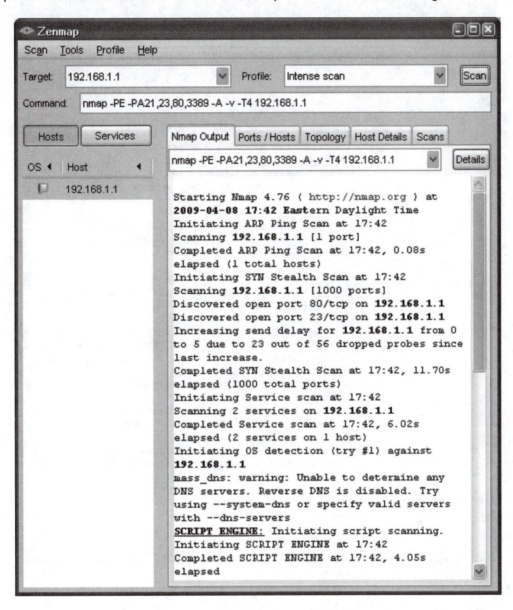

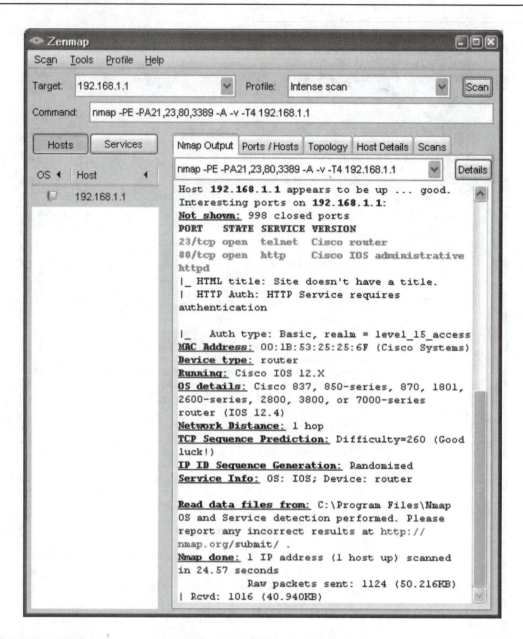

IOS 15 Note: Nmap/Zenmap may not detect the correct IOS image version.

c.   Click the **Service** button in the upper-left side of the screen. What ports are open on R1 Fa0/1 from the perspective of internal host PC-A?

_____

_____

What is the MAC address of the R1 Fa0/1 interface?

_____

_____

For R1, what type of device and what OS version does Nmap detect?

_____

_____

Step 3: Scan for open ports on R1 using Nmap from external host PC-C.

a. From external host PC-C, start the Nmap-Zenmap application and enter the IP address of R1 S0/0/0 (**10.1.1.1**) as the Target. Accept the default Nmap command entered for you in the Command window and use the **Intense scan** profile.

b. Click the **Scan** button. Allow some time for the scan to complete. The next two screens show the entire output of the scan after scrolling.

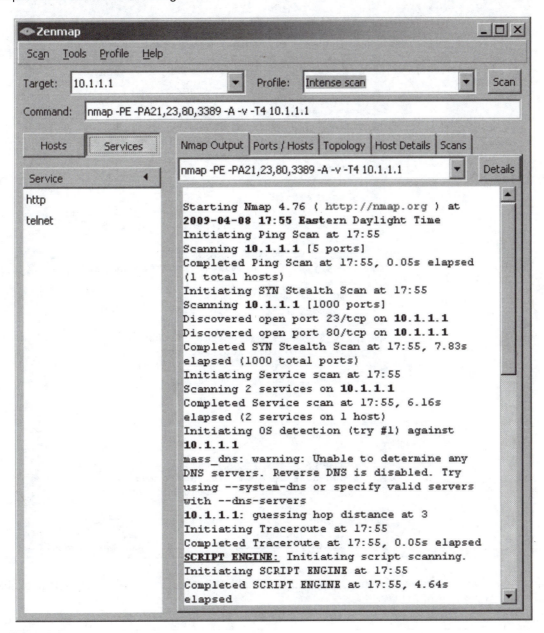

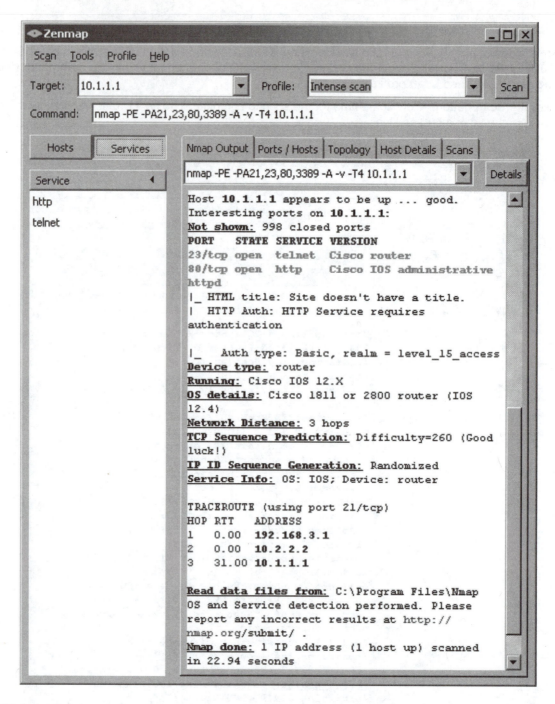

c. Click the Services button below the Command entry field. What services are running and available on R1 from the perspective of PC-C?

_____

_____

d. In the Nmap scan output, refer to the TRACEROUTE information. How many hops are between PC-C and R1 and through what IP addresses did the scan have to go to reach R1?

_____

_____

Part 2: Configuring a Zone-Based Policy Firewall (ZBF) Using CCP

In Part 2 of this lab, you configure a zone-based firewall (ZBF) on R3 by using CCP.

Task 1: Verify Current Router Configurations.

In this task, you will verify end-to-end network connectivity, and R3 is configured correctly before implementing ZBF.

Step 1: Verify end-to-end network connectivity.

a. Ping from R1 to R3.

If the pings are not successful, troubleshoot the basic device configurations before continuing.

b. Ping from PC-A on the R1 LAN to PC-C on the R3 LAN.

If the pings are not successful, troubleshoot the basic device configurations before continuing.

Step 2: Display the R3 running configurations prior to starting CCP.

a. Issue the **show run** command to review the current basic configuration on R3.

b. Verify the R3 basic configuration as performed in Part 1 of the lab. Are there any security commands related to access control?

_____

_____

Task 2: Create a Zone-Based Policy Firewall.

In this task, you use CCP to create a zone-based policy firewall on R3.

Step 1: Configure the enable secret password and HTTP router access prior to starting CCP.

a. From the CLI, configure the enable secret password for use with CCP on R3.

```
R3(config)# enable secret cisco12345
```

b. Enable the HTTP server on R3.

```
R3(config)# ip http server
R3(config)# ip http secure-server
```

c. Add admin user to the local database.

```
R3(config)# username admin privilege 15 secret cisco12345
```

d. Have CCP use the local database to authenticate web sessions.

```
R3(config)# ip http authentication local
```

Step 2: Access CCP and discover R3.

a. Start CCP on PC-C. In the Manage Devices window, add R3 IP address **192.168.3.1** in the first IP address field. Enter **admin** in the Username field, and **cisco12345** in the Password field.

b. At the CCP Dashboard, click the **Discover** button to discover and connect to R3. If discovery fails, click the **Discovery Details** button to determine the problem.

Step 3: Use the CCP Firewall wizard to configure a zone-based firewall.

a. Click **Monitor** > **Security** > **Firewall Status**. What is the state of the Firewall Policies?

_____

_____

b. Click **Configure** > **Security** > **Firewall** > **Firewall** and read through the overview descriptions for the Basic and Advanced Firewall options. What are some of the key differences?

_____

_____

_____

_____

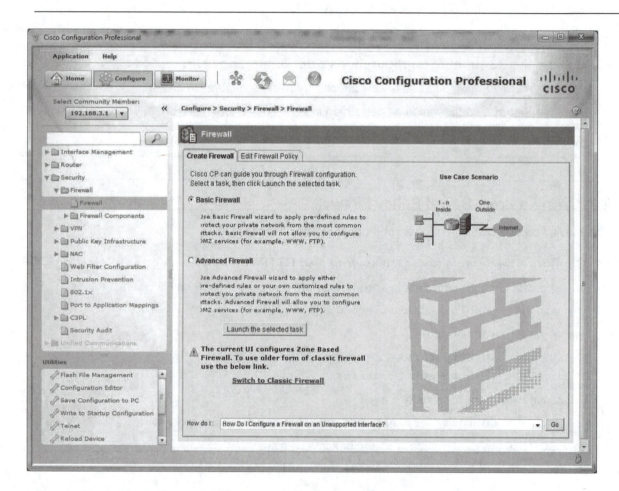

c. Choose **Basic Firewall** and click the **Launch the selected task** button.

In the Basic Firewall Configuration Wizard window, familiarize yourself with what the Basic Firewall does. What does the Basic Firewall do with traffic from outside zones to inside zones?

_____

d. Click **Next** to continue.

e. Check the **inside (trusted)** check box for **Fast Ethernet0/1** and the **outside (untrusted)** check box for **Serial0/0/1**. Click **Next**.

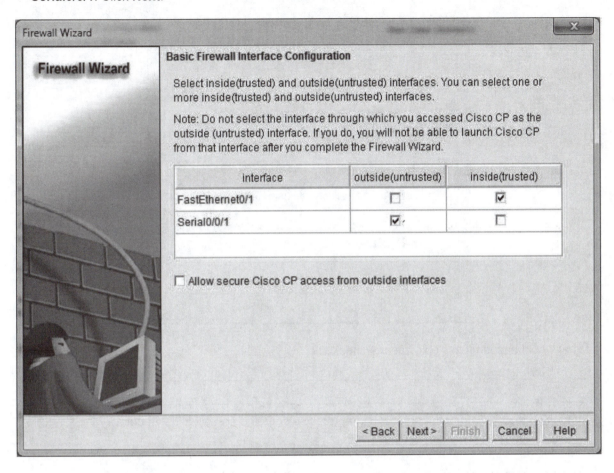

f. Click **OK** when the warning is displayed informing you that you cannot launch CCP from the S0/0/1 interface after the Firewall wizard completes.

g. Move the slider between High, Medium, and Low security to familiarize yourself with what each provides. What is the main difference between High security and Medium or Low security?

_____

_____

_____

_____

_____

h. Move the slider to **Low Security** and click the **Preview Commands** button to preview the commands that are delivered to the router. When you are finished reviewing the commands, click **Close** and then click **Next**.

i. Review the Firewall Configuration Summary. What does this display provide?

_____

_____

j. Click **Finish** to complete the Firewall wizard.

k. When the Routing traffic configuration window displays, ensure that the check box **Allow OSPF updates come through the firewall** is checked and click **OK**.

   Note: This screen only displays if a dynamic routing protocol is configured.

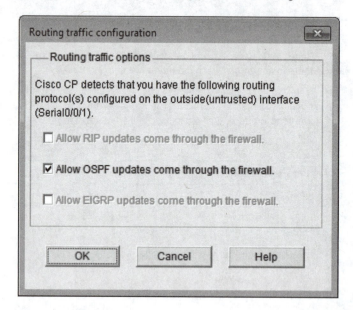

   What would happen if this box was not checked?

   _____

   _____

l. In addition to OSPF, for what other routing protocols does the firewall allow updates?

   _____

   _____

m. In the Deliver Configuration to Router window, click **Deliver**.

n. Click **OK** in the Commands Delivery Status window. How many commands were generated by the Firewall wizard?

   _____

   _____

o. Click **OK** to display the message that you have successfully configured a firewall on the router. Click **OK** to close the message window.

p. The Edit Firewall Policy window displays with the Rule Diagram.

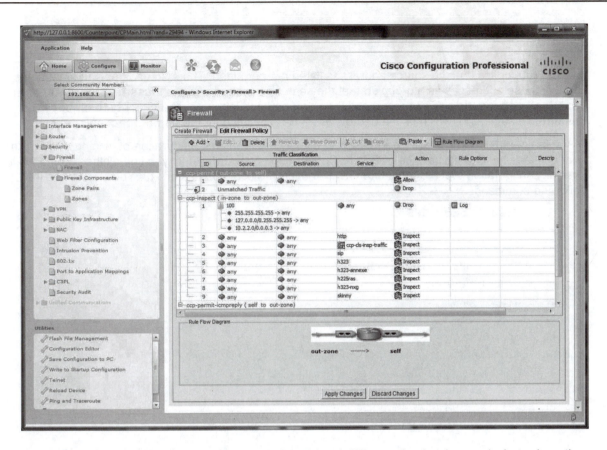

In the Rule Diagram, locate access list 100 (folder icon). What action is taken and what rule options are applied for traffic with an invalid source address in the 127.0.0.0/8 address range?

Task 3: Review the Zone-Based Firewall Configuration.

Step 1: Examine the R3 running configuration with the CLI.

a. From the R3 CLI, display the running configuration to view the changes that the CCP Basic Firewall wizard made to the router.

b. The following commands are related to ACL 100 and class-map ccp-invalid-source:

```
class-map type inspect match-all ccp-invalid-src
 match access-group 100
<output omitted>

policy-map type inspect ccp-inspect
 class type inspect ccp-invalid-src
  drop log
<output omitted>

access-list 100 remark CCP_ACL Category=128
access-list 100 permit ip host 255.255.255.255 any
access-list 100 permit ip 127.0.0.0 0.255.255.255 any
```

```
access-list 100 permit ip 10.2.2.0 0.0.0.3 any
<output omitted>
```

c. In ACL 100, notice that the source addresses listed are permitted. The ACL uses **permit** statements to identify these addresses as a group so that they can be matched with the **class-map type inspect match-all ccp-invalid-src** command and then dropped and logged by the **class type inspect ccp-invalid-src** command, which is one of the class types specified for the **ccp-inspect** policy-map.

d. Issue the command **show run | beg OSPF** to display the running configuration beginning with the line that contains the first occurrence of OSPF. Continue to press **Enter** until you see all the commands in the firewall configuration that are related to OSPF routing protocol updates on R3. You should see the following commands:

```
R3# show run | beg OSPF
class-map type inspect match-any SDM_OSPF
 match access-group name SDM_OSPF
class-map type inspect match-any ccp-cls-insp-traffic
 match protocol cuseeme
 match protocol dns
 match protocol ftp
 match protocol https
<output omitted>

class-map type inspect match-all SDM_OSPF_PT
 match class-map SDM_OSPF_TRAFFIC
class-map type inspect match-any ccp-h323-inspect
 match protocol h323
class-map type inspect match-all ccp-invalid-src
 match access-group 100
class-map type inspect match-all ccp-icmp-access
 match class-map ccp-cls-icmp-access
class-map type inspect match-any ccp-sip-inspect
 match protocol sip
class-map type inspect match-all ccp-protocol-http
 match protocol http
<output omitted>

policy-map type inspect ccp-permit
 class type inspect SDM_OSPF_PT
  pass
 class class-default
  drop
<output omitted>
```

Step 2: Use CCP to examine the R3 firewall configuration.

a. Click the **Configure** button and choose **Router > ACL > Firewall Rules**. There should be an ACL that lists fake source addresses, such as the broadcast address of 255.255.255.255 and the 127.0.0.0/8 network. These were identified in the running configuration output in Task 3, Step 1b.

b. Click the **Configure** button and choose **Security** > **Firewall** > **Firewall Components** > **Zones** to verify the zones configuration. What interfaces are listed and with which zones are they associated?

_____

_____

c. Click **Configure** and choose **Security** > **Firewall** > **Firewall Components** > **Zones Pairs** to verify the zone pairs configuration. Fill in the following information.

Zone Pair	Source	Destination	Policy

d. What is C3PL short for?

_____

_____

e. Click **Configure** and choose **Security** > **C3PL** > **Class Map** > **Inspection**. How many class maps were created by the CCP Firewall wizard?

_____

f. Choose **Security** > **C3PL** > **Policy Map** > **Protocol Inspection**. How many policy maps were created by the CCP Firewall wizard?

_____

g. Examine the details for the policy map ccp-permit that is applied to the ccp-zp-out-self zone pair. Fill in the information below. List the action for the traffic matching each of the class maps referenced within the ccp-permit policy map.

Match Class Name:_____   **Action:** _____

Match Class Name:_____   **Action:** _____

Task 4: Verify OSPF Routing Functionality on R3.

Step 1: Display the R3 routing table using the CLI.

In Task 2, Step 3, the Firewall wizard configured the router to allow OSPF updates. Verify that OSPF messages are still being exchanged using the **show ip route** command and verify that there are still OSPF learned routes in the routing table.

```
R3# show ip route
Codes: C - connected, S - static, R - RIP, M - mobile, B - BGP
       D - EIGRP, EX - EIGRP external, O - OSPF, IA - OSPF inter area
       N1 - OSPF NSSA external type 1, N2 - OSPF NSSA external type 2
       E1 - OSPF external type 1, E2 - OSPF external type 2
       i - IS-IS, su - IS-IS summary, L1 - IS-IS level-1, L2 - IS-IS level-2
       ia - IS-IS inter area, * - candidate default, U - per-user static route
       o - ODR, P - periodic downloaded static route

Gateway of last resort is not set

     10.0.0.0/30 is subnetted, 2 subnets
C       10.2.2.0 is directly connected, Serial0/0/1
O       10.1.1.0 [110/128] via 10.2.2.2, 01:55:30, Serial0/0/1
O    192.168.1.0/24 [110/129] via 10.2.2.2, 01:54:53, Serial0/0/1
```

```
C    192.168.3.0/24 is directly connected, FastEthernet0/1
```

What are the networks on R3 that were learned via the OSPF routing protocol?

_____

_____

Task 5: Verify Zone-Based Firewall Functionality.

Step 1: From PC-C, ping the R3 internal LAN interface.

From PC-C, ping the R3 interface Fa0/1 at IP address 192.168.3.1.

```
C:\> ping 192.168.3.1
```

Were the pings successful? Explain.

_____

_____

Step 2: From PC-C, ping the R2 external WAN interface.

From PC-C, ping the R2 interface S0/0/1 at IP address 10.2.2.2.

```
C:\> ping 10.2.2.2
```

Were the pings successful? Explain.

_____

_____

Step 3: From R2, ping PC-C.

a.   From external router R2, ping PC-C at IP address 192.168.3.3.

```
R2# ping 192.168.3.3
```

b.   Were the pings successful? Explain.

_____

_____

Step 4: Telnet from R2 to R3.

From router R2, telnet to R3 at IP address 10.2.2.1.

```
R2# telnet 10.2.2.1
Trying 10.2.2.1 ... Open

Trying 10.2.2.1 ...
% Connection timed out; remote host not responding
```

Why was Telnet unsuccessful?

_____

_____

Step 5: Telnet from internal PC-C to external router R2.

a.   From PC-C on the R3 internal LAN, telnet to R2 at IP address 10.2.2.2 and log in.

```
C:\> telnet 10.2.2.2
```

```
User Access verification
```
```
Password: ciscovtypass
```

b. Issue the **show policy-map type inspect zone-pair sessions** command on R3. Continue pressing
Enter until you see an Inspect Established Session section toward the end. Your output should look
similar to the following:

```
R3# show policy-map type inspect zone-pair sessions
<output omitted>
Inspect

  Number of Established Sessions = 1
  Established Sessions
    Session 657344C0 (192.168.3.3:1274)=>(10.2.2.2:23) tacacs:tcp SIS_OPEN
      Created 00:01:20, Last heard 00:01:13
      Bytes sent (initiator:responder) [45:65]
<output omitted>
```

c. In the Established Sessions in the output, what is the source IP address and port number for your
Established Sessions?

_____

_____

d. What is the destination IP address and port number for your established sessions?

_____

_____

Step 6: Use CCP Monitor to verify the ZBF function.

a. From CCP, click the **Monitor** button at the top of the screen and choose **Security** > **Firewall Status**.

b. Choose the **ccp-zp-out-self** policy from the list of policies. This policy applies to traffic from the outside
zone to the router (self) zone.

c. Verify that **Active Sessions** is selected and that the view interval is set to **Real-time data every 10 sec**.
Click the **Monitor Policy** button to start monitoring traffic from outside the zone to inside the zone.

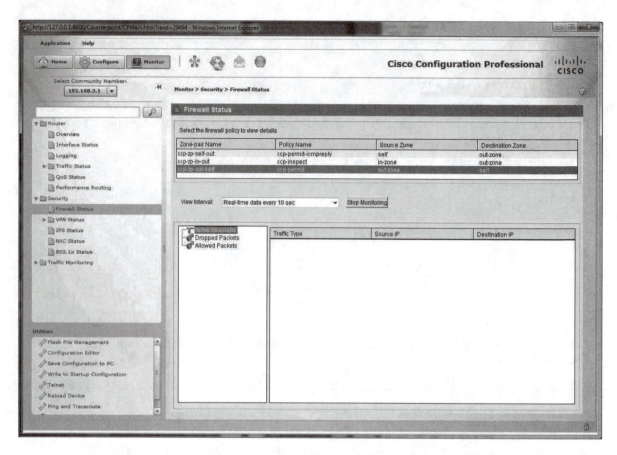

d. From the R2 CLI, ping the R3 S0/0/1 interface at IP address **10.2.2.1**. The pings should fail.

e. From the R2 CLI, telnet to the R3 S0/0/1 interface at IP address **10.2.2.1**. The Telnet attempt should fail.

f. Click the **Dropped Packets** option and observe the graph showing the number of dropped packets resulting from the failed ping and Telnet attempts. Your screen should look similar to the one below.

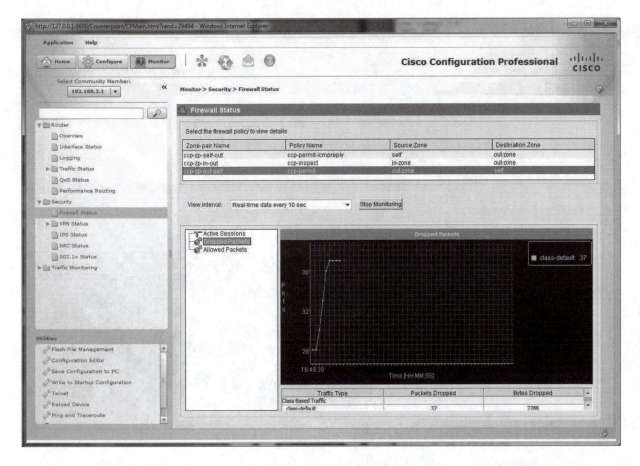

g. Click the **Allowed Packets** option and observe the graph showing the number of OSPF packets received from router R3. This number will continue to grow at a steady pace as OSPF updates are received from R2.

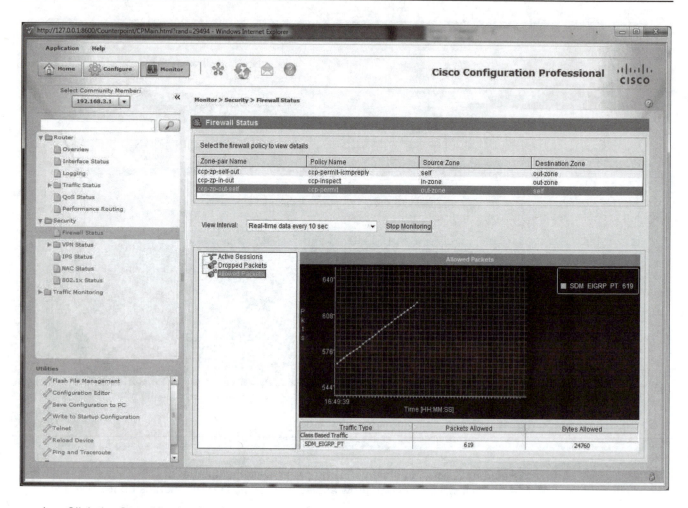

h.   Click the **Stop Monitoring** button and close CCP.

Reflection

What are some factors to consider when configuring firewalls using traditional manual CLI methods compared to using the CCP Firewall wizard GUI methods?

_____

_____

_____

_____

_____

_____

Router Interface Summary Table

Router Interface Summary				
Router Model	Ethernet Interface #1	Ethernet Interface #2	Serial Interface #1	Serial Interface #2
1800	Fast Ethernet 0/0 (F0/0)	Fast Ethernet 0/1 (F0/1)	Serial 0/0/0 (S0/0/0)	Serial 0/0/1 (S0/0/1)
1900	Gigabit Ethernet 0/0 (G0/0)	Gigabit Ethernet 0/1 (G0/1)	Serial 0/0/0 (S0/0/0)	Serial 0/0/1 (S0/0/1)
2801	Fast Ethernet 0/0 (F0/0)	Fast Ethernet 0/1 (F0/1)	Serial 0/1/0 (S0/1/0)	Serial 0/1/1 (S0/1/1)
2811	Fast Ethernet 0/0 (F0/0)	Fast Ethernet 0/1 (F0/1)	Serial 0/0/0 (S0/0/0)	Serial 0/0/1 (S0/0/1)
2900	Gigabit Ethernet 0/0 (G0/0)	Gigabit Ethernet 0/1 (G0/1)	Serial 0/0/0 (S0/0/0)	Serial 0/0/1 (S0/0/1)

Note: To find out how the router is configured, look at the interfaces to identify the type of router and how many interfaces the router has. There is no way to effectively list all the combinations of configurations for each router class. This table includes identifiers for the possible combinations of Ethernet and Serial interfaces in the device. The table does not include any other type of interface, even though a specific router may contain one. An example of this might be an ISDN BRI interface. The string in parenthesis is the legal abbreviation that can be used in Cisco IOS commands to represent the interface.

Chapter 5: Implementing Intrusion Prevention

Lab 5.5.1.1 - Configuring an Intrusion Prevention System (IPS) Using the CLI and CCP

Topology

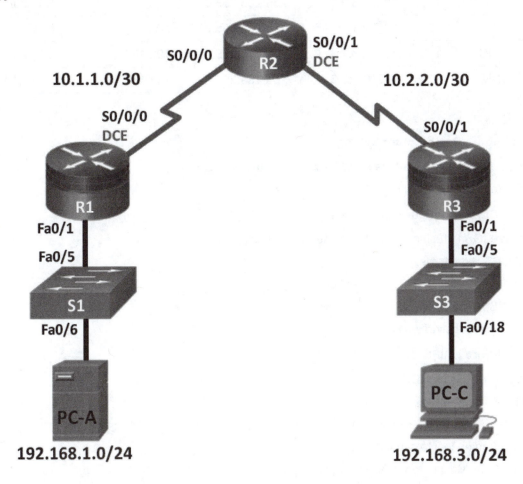

Note: ISR G2 devices use GigabitEthernet interfaces instead of FastEthernet interfaces.

IP Addressing Table

Device	Interface	IP Address	Subnet Mask	Default Gateway	Switch Port
R1	Fa0/1	192.168.1.1	255.255.255.0	N/A	S1 Fa0/5
	S0/0/0 (DCE)	10.1.1.1	255.255.255.252	N/A	N/A
R2	S0/0/0	10.1.1.2	255.255.255.252	N/A	N/A
	S0/0/1 (DCE)	10.2.2.2	255.255.255.252	N/A	N/A
R3	Fa0/1	192.168.3.1	255.255.255.0	N/A	S3 Fa0/5
	S0/0/1	10.2.2.1	255.255.255.252	N/A	N/A
PC-A	NIC	192.168.1.3	255.255.255.0	192.168.1.1	S1 Fa0/6
PC-C	NIC	192.168.3.3	255.255.255.0	192.168.3.1	S3 Fa0/18

Objectives

Part 1: Configure Basic Router Settings

- Configure hostname, interface IP addresses, and access passwords.
- Configure the static routing.

Part 2: Use CLI to Configure an IOS IPS

- Configure IOS Intrusion Prevention System (IPS) using CLI.
- Modify IPS Signatures.
- Examine the resulting IPS configuration.
- Verify IPS functionality.
- Log IPS messages to a syslog server.

Part 3: Configure an IPS Using CCP

- Configure IPS using CCP.
- Modify IPS signatures.
- Examine the resulting IPS configuration.
- Use a scanning tool to simulate an attack.
- Use the CCP Monitor to verify IPS functionality.

Background / Scenario

In this lab, you will configure the Cisco IOS Intrusion Prevention System (IPS), which is part of the Cisco IOS Firewall feature set. IPS examines certain attack patterns and alerts or mitigates when those patterns occur. IPS alone is not enough to make a router into a secure Internet firewall, but in addition to other security features, it can be a powerful defense.

You will configure IPS using the Cisco IOS CLI on one router and CCP on another router, and then test IPS functionality on both routers. You will load the IPS Signature package from a TFTP server and configure the public crypto key using the Cisco IOS CLI and CCP.

Note: The router commands and output in this lab are from a Cisco 1841 router with Cisco IOS Release 15.1(4)M8 (Advanced IP Services image). Other routers and Cisco IOS versions can be used. See the Router Interface Summary Table at the end of the lab to determine which interface identifiers to use based on the equipment in the lab. Depending on the router model and Cisco IOS version, the commands available and output produced might vary from what is shown in this lab.

Note: Ensure that the routers and switches have been erased and have no startup configurations.

Required Resources

- 3 Routers (Cisco 1841 with Cisco IOS Release 15.1(4)M8 Advanced IP Services image or comparable)
- 2 Switches (Cisco 2960 or comparable)
- 2 PCs (Windows Vista or Windows 7 with CCP 2.5, Tftpd32 server, Nmap/Zenmap, latest version of Java, Internet Explorer, and Flash Player)
- Serial and Ethernet cables as shown in the topology
- Console cables to configure Cisco networking devices
- IPS Signature package and public crypto key files on PC-A and PC-C (provided by instructor)

CCP Notes:

- If the PC on which CCP is installed is running Windows Vista or Windows 7, it may be necessary to right-click the **CCP** icon, and select **Run as administrator**.
- To run CCP, it may be necessary to temporarily disable antivirus programs and O/S firewalls. Ensure that all pop-up blockers are turned off in the browser.

Part 1: Configure Basic Router Settings

In Part 1, you will set up the network topology and configure basic settings, such as hostnames, interface IP addresses, static routing, device access, and passwords.

Note: Perform steps listed in Part 1 on all three routers; only R1 is shown below.

Step 1: Cable the network as shown in the topology.

Attach the devices, as shown in the topology diagram, and cable as necessary.

Step 2: Configure the basic settings for each router.

a. Configure the hostnames, as shown in the topology.

b. Configure the interface IP addresses, as shown in the IP Addressing table.

c. Configure a clock rate for serial router interfaces with a DCE serial cable attached.

```
R1(config)# interface S0/0/0
R1(config-if)# clock rate 64000
```

d. To prevent the router from attempting to translate incorrectly entered commands, disable DNS lookup.

```
R1(config)# no ip domain-lookup
```

Step 3: Configure static routing on the routers.

a. Configure a static default route from R1 to R2 and from R3 to R2.

b. Configure a static route from R2 to the R1 LAN and from R2 to the R3 LAN.

Step 4: Configure PC host IP settings.

Configure a static IP address, subnet mask, and default gateway for PC-A and PC-C, as shown in the IP Addressing table.

Step 5: Verify basic network connectivity.

a.   Ping from R1 to R3.

If the pings are unsuccessful, troubleshoot the basic device configurations before continuing.

b.   Ping from PC-A on the R1 LAN to PC-C on the R3 LAN.

If the pings are unsuccessful, troubleshoot the basic device configurations before continuing.

Note: If you can ping from PC-A to PC-C, you have demonstrated that the static routing protocol is configured and functioning correctly. If you cannot ping, but the device interfaces are up and IP addresses are correct, use the **show run** and **show ip route** commands to identify routing protocol-related problems.

Step 6: Configure and encrypt passwords.

Note: Passwords in this task are set to a minimum of 10 characters, but are relatively simple for the benefit of performing the lab. More complex passwords are recommended in a production network.

a.   Configure a minimum password length using the **security passwords** command to set a minimum password length of 10 characters.

```
R1(config)# security passwords min-length 10
```

b.   Configure a console password and enable login for router R1. For additional security, the **exec-timeout** command causes the line to log out after **5** minutes of inactivity. The **logging synchronous** command prevents console messages from interrupting command entry.

Note: To avoid repetitive logins during this lab, the **exec-timeout** command can be set to **0 0**, which prevents it from expiring; however, this is not considered to be a good security practice.

```
R1(config)# line console 0
R1(config-line)# password ciscoconpass
R1(config-line)# exec-timeout 5 0
R1(config-line)# login
R1(config-line)# logging synchronous
```

c.   Configure a password for the aux port for router R1.

```
R1(config)# line aux 0
R1(config-line)# password ciscoauxpass
R1(config-line)# exec-timeout 5 0
R1(config-line)# login
```

d.   Configure the password on the vty lines for router R1.

```
R1(config)# line vty 0 4
R1(config-line)# password ciscovtypass
R1(config-line)# exec-timeout 5 0
R1(config-line)# login
```

e.   Encrypt the console, aux, and vty clear text passwords.

```
R1(config)# service password-encryption
```

Issue the **show run** command. Can you read the console, aux, and vty passwords? Explain.

_____

Step 7: Save the basic configurations for all three routers.

Save the running configuration to the startup configuration from the privileged EXEC mode prompt.

```
R1# copy running-config startup-config
```

Part 2: Configuring IPS Using the Cisco IOS CLI

In Part 2 of this lab, you will configure IPS on R1 using the Cisco IOS CLI. You then review and test the resulting configuration.

Task 1: Verify Access to the R1 LAN from R2.

In this task, you will verify that without IPS configured, the external router R2 can ping the R1 S0/0/0 interface and PC-A on the R1 internal LAN.

Step 1: Ping from R2 to R1.

From R2, ping R1 interface S0/0/0 at IP address 10.1.1.1.

```
R2# ping 10.1.1.1
```

If the pings are unsuccessful, troubleshoot the basic device configurations before continuing.

Step 2: Ping from R2 to PC-A on the R1 LAN.

From R2, ping PC-A on the R1 LAN at IP address 192.168.1.3.

```
R2# ping 192.168.1.3
```

If the pings are unsuccessful, troubleshoot the basic device configurations before continuing.

Step 3: Display the R1 running configuration prior to configuring IPS.

Issue the **show run** command to review the current basic configuration on R1.

Are there any security commands related to IPS?

_____

_____

_____

Task 2: Prepare the Router and TFTP Server.

Step 1: Verify the availability of Cisco IOS IPS files.

To configure Cisco IOS IPS 5.x, the IOS IPS Signature package file and public crypto key file must be available on PC-A. Check with your instructor if these files are not on the PC. These files can be downloaded from www.cisco.com with a valid user account that has proper authorization.

a. Verify that the IOS-S*xxx*-CLI.pkg file is in a TFTP folder. This is the signature package. The *xxx* is the version number and varies depending on which file was downloaded.

b. Verify that the realm-cisco.pub.key.txt file is available and note its location on PC-A. This is the public crypto key used by IOS IPS.

Step 2: Verify or create the IPS directory in router flash on R1.

a. In this step, you will verify the existence of, or create a directory in, the router flash memory where the required signature files and configurations will be stored.

Note: Alternatively, you can use a USB flash drive connected to the router USB port to store the signature files and configurations. The USB flash drive must remain connected to the router USB port if it is used as the IOS IPS configuration directory location. IOS IPS also supports any Cisco IOS file system as its configuration location with proper write access.

b. From the R1 CLI, display the contents of flash memory using the **show flash** command and check for the **ipsdir** directory.

    ```
    R1# show flash
    ```

c. If the **ipsdir** directory is not listed, create it in privileged EXEC mode.

    ```
    R1# mkdir ipsdir
    Create directory filename [ipsdir]? <Enter>
    Created dir flash:ipsdir
    ```

d. If the directory already exists, the following message displays:

    ```
    %Error Creating dir flash:ipsdir (Can't create a file that exists)
    ```

    Use the **delete** command to erase the content of **ipsdir** directory.

    ```
    R1# delete flash:ipsdir/*
    Delete filename [/ipsdir/*]?
    Delete flash:/ipsdir/R1-sigdef-default.xml? [confirm]
    Delete flash:/ipsdir/R1-sigdef-delta.xml? [confirm]
    Delete flash:/ipsdir/R1-sigdef-typedef.xml? [confirm]
    Delete flash:/ipsdir/R1-sigdef-category.xml? [confirm]
    Delete flash:/ipsdir/R1-seap-delta.xml? [confirm]
    Delete flash:/ipsdir/R1-seap-typedef.xml? [confirm]
    ```

    Note: Use this command with caution. If there are no files in the **ipsdir** directory, the following message displays:

    ```
    R1# delete flash:ipsdir/*
    Delete filename [/ipsdir/*]?
    No such file
    ```

e. From the R1 CLI, verify that the directory is present using the **dir flash:** or **dir flash:ipsdir** command.

    ```
    R1# dir flash:
    Directory of flash:/

        5  -rw-    37081324  Dec 17 2008 21:57:10 +00:00  c1841-advipservicesk9-mz.124-
    24.T8dir .bin
        6  drw-           0  Jan 6 2009 11:19:14 +00:00   ipsdir
    ```

    or

    ```
    R1# dir flash:ipsdir


    Directory of flash:/ipsdir/


    No files in directory
    ```

    Note: The directory exists, but there are currently no files in it.

Task 3: Configuring the IPS Crypto Key.

The crypto key verifies the digital signature for the master signature file (sigdef-default.xml). The contents are signed by a Cisco private key to guarantee the authenticity and integrity at every release.

Step 1: Copy and paste the crypto key file into R1.

Select and copy the following crypto key file named **realm-cisco.pub.key.txt**.

```
crypto key pubkey-chain rsa
 named-key realm-cisco.pub signature
```

```
key-string
 30820122 300D0609 2A864886 F70D0101 01050003 82010F00 3082010A 02820101
 00C19E93 A8AF124A D6CC7A24 5097A975 206BE3A2 06FBA13F 6F12CB5B 4E441F16
 17E630D5 C02AC252 912BE27F 37FDD9C8 11FC7AF7 DCDD81D9 43CDABC3 6007D128
 B199ABCB D34ED0F9 085FADC1 359C189E F30AF10A C0EFB624 7E0764BF 3E53053E
 5B2146A9 D7A5EDE3 0298AF03 DED7A5B8 9479039D 20F30663 9AC64B93 C0112A35
 FE3F0C87 89BCB7BB 994AE74C FA9E481D F65875D6 85EAF974 6D9CC8E3 F0B08B85
 50437722 FFBE85B9 5E4189FF CC189CB9 69C46F9C A84DFBA5 7A0AF99E AD768C36
 006CF498 079F88F8 A3B3FB1F 9FB7B3CB 5539E1D1 9693CCBB 551F78D2 892356AE
 2F56D826 8918EF3C 80CA4F4D 87BFCA3B BFF668E9 689782A5 CF31CB6E B4B094D3
 F3020301 0001
quit
```

Step 2: Apply the contents of the text file to the router.

a. At the R1 privileged EXEC mode prompt, enter global configuration mode using the **config t** command.

b. Paste the copied crypto key content at the global configuration mode prompt.

```
R1(config)#
R1(config)# crypto key pubkey-chain rsa
R1(config-pubkey-chain)# named-key realm-cisco.pub signature
R1(config-pubkey-key)# key-string
Enter a public key as a hexidecimal number ....

R1(config-pubkey)#$2A864886 F70D0101 01050003 82010F00 3082010A 02820101
R1(config-pubkey)#$D6CC7A24 5097A975 206BE3A2 06FBA13F 6F12CB5B 4E441F16
R1(config-pubkey)#$912BE27F 37FDD9C8 11FC7AF7 DCDD81D9 43CDABC3 6007D128
R1(config-pubkey)#$085FADC1 359C189E F30AF10A C0EFB624 7E0764BF 3E53053E
R1(config-pubkey)#$0298AF03 DED7A5B8 9479039D 20F30663 9AC64B93 C0112A35
R1(config-pubkey)#$994AE74C FA9E481D F65875D6 85EAF974 6D9CC8E3 F0B08B85
R1(config-pubkey)#$5E4189FF CC189CB9 69C46F9C A84DFBA5 7A0AF99E AD768C36
R1(config-pubkey)#$A3B3FB1F 9FB7B3CB 5539E1D1 9693CCBB 551F78D2 892356AE
R1(config-pubkey)#$80CA4F4D 87BFCA3B BFF668E9 689782A5 CF31CB6E B4B094D3
R1(config-pubkey)#    F3020301 0001
R1(config-pubkey)#   quit
R1(config-pubkey-key)#
```

c. Exit global configuration mode and issue the **show run** command to confirm that the crypto key is configured.

Task 4: Configure IPS.

Step 1: Create an IPS rule.

a. On R1, create an IPS rule name using the **ip ips name name** command in global configuration mode. Name the IPS rule **iosips**. This will be used later on an interface to enable IPS.

```
R1(config)# ip ips name iosips
```

b. You can specify an optional extended or standard access control list (ACL) to filter the traffic that will be scanned by this rule name. All traffic permitted by the ACL is subject to inspection by the IPS. Traffic that is denied by the ACL is not inspected by the IPS.

c. To see the options available for specifying an ACL with the rule name, use the **ip ips name** command and the CLI help function (**?**).

```
R1(config)# ip ips name ips list ?
  <1-199>  Numbered access list
  WORD     Named access list
```

Step 2: Configure the IPS Signature storage location in router flash memory.

The IPS files will be stored in the **ipsdir** directory that was created in Task 2, Step 2. Configure the location using the **ip ips config location** command.

```
R1(config)# ip ips config location flash:ipsdir
```

Step 3: Enable IPS SDEE event notification.

The Cisco Security Device Event Exchange (SDEE) server is a Simple Object Access Protocol (SOAP) based, intrusion detection system (IDS) alert format and transport protocol specification. SDEE replaces Cisco RDEP.

To use SDEE, the HTTP server must be enabled with the **ip http server** command. If the HTTP server is not enabled, the router cannot respond to the SDEE clients, because it cannot see the requests. SDEE notification is disabled, by default, and must be explicitly enabled.

```
R1(config)# ip http server
```

Note: CCP Monitor uses HTTP and SDEE to capture IPS events.

To enable SDEE, use the following command:

```
R1(config)# ip ips notify sdee
```

Step 4: Enable IPS syslog support.

IOS IPS also supports the use of syslog to send event notifications. SDEE and syslog can be used independently or enabled at the same time to send IOS IPS event notification. Syslog notification is enabled by default.

a. If console logging is enabled, IPS syslog messages display. Enable syslog if it is not enabled.

```
R1(config)# ip ips notify log
```

b. Use the **show clock** command to verify the current time and date for the router. Use the **clock set** command in privileged EXEC mode to reset the clock if necessary. The following example shows how to set the clock:

```
R1# clock set 01:20:00 6 january 2009
```

c. Verify that the timestamp service for logging is enabled on the router using the **show run** command. Enable the timestamp service if it is not enabled.

```
R1(config)# service timestamps log datetime msec
```

d. To send log messages to the syslog server on PC-A, use the following command:

```
R1(config)# logging 192.168.1.3
```

e. To see the type and level of logging enabled on R1, use the **show logging** command.

```
R1# show logging
```

Note: Verify that you have connectivity between R1 and PC-A by pinging from PC-A to the R1 Fa0/1 interface IP address **192.168.1.1**. If it is not successful, troubleshoot as necessary before continuing.

The next step describes how to download one of the freeware syslog servers if one is unavailable on PC-A.

Step 5: (Optional) Download and start the syslog server.

If a syslog server is not currently available on PC-A, you can download the Tftpd32 from http://tftpd32.jounin.net/. If the syslog server is available on the PC, go to Step 6.

Start the syslog server software on PC-A to send log messages to it.

Step 6: Configure IOS IPS to use one of the pre-defined signature categories.

IOS IPS with Cisco 5.x format signatures operates with signature categories, just like Cisco IPS appliances do. All signatures are pre-grouped into categories, and the categories are hierarchical. This helps classify signatures for easy grouping and tuning.

Warning: The "all" signature category contains *all* signatures in a signature release. Because IOS IPS cannot compile and use all the signatures contained in a signature release at one time, do not unretire the "all" category. Otherwise, the router will run out of memory.

Note: When configuring IOS IPS, it is required to first retire all the signatures in the "all" category and then unretire selected signature categories.

In the following example, all signatures in the **all** category are retired, and then the **ios_ips basic** category is unretired:

```
R1(config)# ip ips signature-category
R1(config-ips-category)# category all
R1(config-ips-category-action)# retired true
R1(config-ips-category-action)# exit
R1(config-ips-category)# category ios_ips basic
R1(config-ips-category-action)# retired false
R1(config-ips-category-action)# exit
R1(config-ips-category)# exit
Do you want to accept these changes? [confirm] <Enter>


Jan  6 01:32:37.983: Applying Category configuration to signatures ...
```

Step 7: Apply the IPS rule to an interface.

a. Apply the IPS rule to an interface with the **ip ips** *name direction* command in interface configuration mode. Apply the rule you just created inbound on the S0/0/0 interface. After you enable IPS, some log messages will be sent to the console line indicating that the IPS engines are being initialized.

Note: The direction **in** means that IPS inspects only traffic going into the interface. Similarly, **out** means only traffic going out the interface. To enable IPS to inspect both in and out traffic, enter the IPS rule name for in and out separately on the same interface.

```
R1(config)# interface serial0/0/0
R1(config-if)# ip ips iosips in


Jan  6 03:03:30.495: %IPS-6-ENGINE_BUILDS_STARTED:  03:03:30 UTC Jan 6 2008
Jan  6 03:03:30.495: %IPS-6-ENGINE_BUILDING: atomic-ip - 3 signatures - 1 of 13
engines
Jan  6 03:03:30.511: %IPS-6-ENGINE_READY: atomic-ip - build time 16 ms - packets for
this engine will be scanned
Jan  6 03:03:30.511: %IPS-6-ALL_ENGINE_BUILDS_COMPLETE: elapsed time 16 ms
```

The message also displays on the syslog server if it is enabled. The Tftpd32 syslog server is shown here.

Note: The following message may display if the router does not have built-in IOS signature file:

```
*************************************************************************
The signature package is missing or was saved by a previous version
```

```
IPS Please load a new signature package
************************************************************************

Jan  6 01:22:17.383: %IPS-3-SIG_UPDATE_REQUIRED: IOS IPS requires a signature update
package to be loaded
```

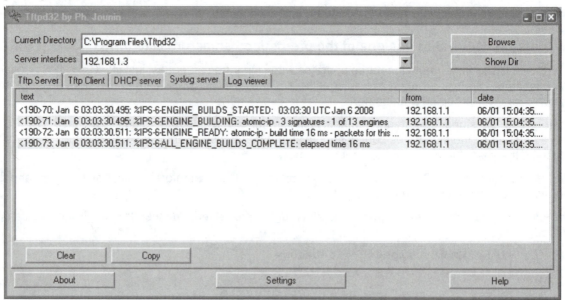

b. Although the R1 Fa0/1 interface is an internal interface, configure it with IPS to respond to internal attacks. Apply the IPS rule to the R1 Fa0/1 interface in the inbound direction.

```
R1(config)# interface fa0/1
R1(config-if)# ip ips iosips in
```

Step 8: Save the running configuration.

Enter privileged EXEC mode using the **enable** command and provide the enable password **cisco12345**.

```
R1# copy run start
```

Task 5: Load the IOS IPS Signature Package to the Router.

The most common way to load the signature package to the router is to use TFTP. Refer to Step 4 for alternative methods for loading the IOS IPS signature package. The alternative methods include the use of FTP and a USB flash drive.

Step 1: (Optional) Download the TFTP server.

The Tftpd32 freeware TFTP server is used in this task. Many other free TFTP servers are also available. If a TFTP server is currently unavailable on PC-A, you can download the latest version of Tftpd32 from http://tftpd32.jounin.net/. If it is already installed, go to Step 2.

Note: This lab uses the Tftpd32 TFTP server. This software also includes a syslog server, which runs simultaneously with the TFTP server.

Step 2: Start the TFTP server on PC-A and verify the IPS file directory.

a. Verify connectivity between R1 and PC-A, the TFTP server, using the **ping** command.

b. Verify that the PC has the IPS Signature package file in a directory on the TFTP server. This file is typically named IOS-S*xxx*-CLI.pkg, where *xxx* is the signature file version.

Note: If this file is not present, contact your instructor before continuing.

c. Start Tftpd32 or another TFTP server and set the default directory to the one with the IPS Signature package in it. The Tftpd32 screen is shown here with the C:\Program Files\Tftpd32\IPS directory contents displayed. Take note of the filename for use in the next step.

Note: It is recommended to use the latest signature file available in a production environment. However, if the amount of router flash memory is an issue in a lab environment, you may use an older version 5.x signature, which requires less memory. The S364 file is used with this lab for demonstration purposes, although newer versions are available. Consult CCO to determine the latest version.

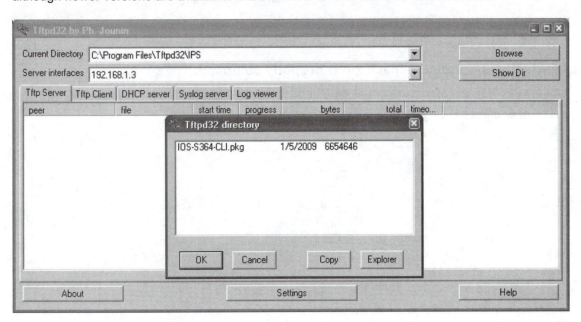

Step 3: Copy the signature package from the TFTP server to the router.

If you do not have a TFTP server available, and you are using a router with a USB port, go to Step 5 and use the procedure described there.

a. Use the **copy tftp** command to retrieve the signature file and load it into the Intrusion Detection Configuration. Use the **idconf** keyword at the end of the **copy** command.

Note: Immediately after the signature package is loaded to the router, signature compiling begins. You can see the messages on the router with logging level 6 or above enabled.

```
R1# copy tftp://192.168.1.3/IOS-S364-CLI.pkg idconf

Loading IOS-S364-CLI.pkg from 192.168.1.3 (via FastEthernet0/1):
!!!!!!!!!!!!!!!!!!!!!!!!!!!!!
[OK - 6654646 bytes]

Jan  6 03:18:36.799: %IPS-6-ENGINE_BUILDS_STARTED:  03:18:36 UTC Jan 6 2008
Jan  6 03:18:36.799: %IPS-6-ENGINE_BUILDING: multi-string - 8 signatures - 1 of 13
engines
Jan  6 03:18:36.811: %IPS-6-ENGINE_READY: multi-string - build time 12 ms - packets
for this engine will be scanned
Jan  6 03:18:36.831: %IPS-6-ENGINE_BUILDING: service-http - 629 signatures - 2 of 13
engines
Jan  6 03:18:46.755: %IPS-6-ENGINE_READY: service-http - build time 9924 ms - packets
for this engine will be scanned
<Output omitted>
```

b. Use the **dir flash** command to see the contents of the **ipsdir** directory created earlier. There should be six files, as shown here:

```
R1# dir flash:ipsdir
Directory of flash:/ipsdir/

16  -rw-    230621   Jan 6 2008 03:19:42 +00:00   R1-sigdef-default.xml
15  -rw-       255   Jan 6 2008 01:35:26 +00:00   R1-sigdef-delta.xml
14  -rw-      6632   Jan 6 2008 03:17:48 +00:00   R1-sigdef-typedef.xml
13  -rw-     28282   Jan 6 2008 03:17:52 +00:00   R1-sigdef-category.xml
10  -rw-       304   Jan 6 2008 01:35:28 +00:00   R1-seap-delta.xml
18  -rw-       491   Jan 6 2008 01:35:28 +00:00   R1-seap-typedef.xml
```

Step 4: Verify that the signature package is properly compiled.

a. Use the **show ip ips signature count** command to see the counts for the signature package compiled.

```
R1# show ip ips signature count

Cisco SDF release version S364.0
Trend SDF release version V0.0

Signature Micro-Engine: multi-string: Total Signatures 11
      multi-string enabled signatures: 9
      multi-string retired signatures: 11

Signature Micro-Engine: service-http: Total Signatures 662
      service-http enabled signatures: 163
      service-http retired signatures: 565
      service-http compiled signatures: 97
      service-http obsoleted signatures: 1

Signature Micro-Engine: string-tcp: Total Signatures 1148
      string-tcp enabled signatures: 622
      string-tcp retired signatures: 1031
      string-tcp compiled signatures: 117
      string-tcp obsoleted signatures: 21

<Output Omitted>

Total Signatures: 2435
   Total Enabled Signatures: 1063
   Total Retired Signatures: 2097
   Total Compiled Signatures: 338
   Total Obsoleted Signatures: 25
```

Note: If you see an error message during signature compilation, such as "%IPS-3-INVALID_ DIGITAL_SIGNATURE: Invalid Digital Signature found (key not found)," it means the public crypto key is invalid. Refer to Task 3, "Configure the IPS Crypto Key," to reconfigure the public crypto key.

b. Use the **show ip ips all** command to view the IPS configuration status summary. To which interfaces and in which direction is the iosips rule applied?

_____

_____

```
R1# show ip ips all

IPS Signature File Configuration Status
    Configured Config Locations: flash:ipsdir/
    Last signature default load time: 18:47:52 UTC Jan 6 2009
    Last signature delta load time: 20:11:35 UTC Jan 6 2009
    Last event action (SEAP) load time: -none-

    General SEAP Config:
    Global Deny Timeout: 3600 seconds
    Global Overrides Status: Enabled
    Global Filters Status: Enabled

IPS Auto Update is not currently configured

IPS Syslog and SDEE Notification Status
    Event notification through syslog is enabled
    Event notification through SDEE is enabled

IPS Signature Status
    Total Active Signatures: 339
    Total Inactive Signatures: 2096

IPS Packet Scanning and Interface Status
    IPS Rule Configuration
      IPS name iosips
    IPS fail closed is disabled
    IPS deny-action ips-interface is false
    Interface Configuration
      Interface Serial0/0/0
        Inbound IPS rule is iosips
        Outgoing IPS rule is not set
Interface FastEthernet0/1
        Inbound IPS rule is iosips
        Outgoing IPS rule is not set

IPS Category CLI Configuration:
    Category all:
        Retire: True
    Category ios_ips basic:
        Retire: False
```

Step 5: (Optional) Alternative methods of copying the signature package to the router.

If you used TFTP to copy the file and will not use one of these alternative methods, read through the procedures described here to become familiar with them. If you use one of these methods instead of TFTP, return to Step 4 to verify that the signature package loaded properly.

FTP method: Although the TFTP method is generally adequate, the signature file is rather large and FTP can provide another method of copying the file. You can use an FTP server to copy the signature file to the router with this command:

```
copy ftp://<ftp_user:password@Server_IP_address>/<signature_package> idconf
```

In the following example, the user **admin** must be defined on the FTP server with a password of **cisco**:

```
R1# copy ftp://admin:cisco@192.168.1.3/IOS-S364-CLI.pkg idconf
Loading IOS-S364-CLI.pkg !!!!!!!!!!!!!!!!!!!!!!!!!!!!!!!!!!!!
[OK - 7608873/4096 bytes]
```

USB method: If there is no access to a FTP or TFTP server, you can use a USB flash drive to load the signature package to the router.

a. Copy the signature package onto the USB drive.

b. Connect the USB drive to one of the USB ports on the router.

c. Use the **show file systems** command to see the name of the USB drive. In the following output, a 4 GB USB drive is connected to the USB port on the router as file system usbflash0:

```
R1# show file systems
File Systems:
```

	Size(b)	Free(b)	Type	Flags	Prefixes
	–	–	opaque	rw	archive:
	–	–	opaque	rw	system:
	–	–	opaque	rw	tmpsys:
	–	–	opaque	rw	null:
	–	–	network	rw	tftp:
	196600	185972	nvram	rw	nvram:
*	64012288	14811136	disk	rw	flash:#
	–	–	opaque	wo	syslog:
	–	–	opaque	rw	xmodem:
	–	–	opaque	rw	ymodem:
	–	–	network	rw	rcp:
	–	–	network	rw	pram:
	–	–	network	rw	http:
	–	–	network	rw	ftp:
	–	–	network	rw	scp:
	–	–	opaque	ro	tar:
	–	–	network	rw	https:
	–	–	opaque	ro	cns:
	4001378304	3807461376	usbflash	rw	usbflash0:

d. Verify the contents of the flash drive using the **dir** command.

```
R1# dir usbflash0:
Directory of usbflash0:/
90  -rw-  6654646  Jan 5 2009 14:49:34 +00:00  IOS-S364-CLI.pkg
91  -rw-      805  Jan 5 2009 14:49:34 +00:00  realm-cisco.pub.key.txt
```

e. Use the **copy** command with the **idconf** keyword to copy the signature package to the router.

```
R1# copy usbflash0:IOS-S364-CLI.pkg idconf
```

The USB copy process can take 60 seconds or more, and no progress indicator displays. When the copy process is complete, numerous engine building messages display. These must finish before the command prompt returns.

Task 6: Test the IPS Rule and Modify a Signature.

You can work with signatures in many ways. They can be retired and unretired, enabled and disabled, and their characteristics and actions can be changed. In this task, you first test the default behavior of IOS IPS by pinging it from the outside.

Step 1: Ping from R2 to the R1 serial 0/0/0 interface.

From the CLI on R2, ping R1 S0/0/0 at IP address **10.1.1.1**. The pings are successful because the ICMP Echo Request signature 2004:0 is retired.

Step 2: Ping from R2 to PC-A.

From the CLI on R2, ping PC-A at IP address **192.168.1.3**. These pings are also successful because of the retired signature. This is the default behavior of the IPS signatures.

```
R2# ping 192.168.1.3


Type escape sequence to abort.
Sending 5, 100-byte ICMP Echos to 192.168.1.3, timeout is 2 seconds:
!!!!!
Success rate is 100 percent (5/5), round-trip min/avg/max = 1/1/4 ms
```

Step 3: Modify the signature.

You can use the Cisco IOS CLI to change signature status and actions for one signature or a group of signatures based on signature categories.

The following example shows how to unretire the echo request signature, enable it, change the signature action to alert, and drop and reset for signature 2004 with a subsig ID of 0:

```
R1(config)# ip ips signature-definition
R1(config-sigdef)# signature 2004 0
R1(config-sigdef-sig)#status
R1(config-sigdef-sig-status)# retired false
R1(config-sigdef-sig-status)# enabled true
R1(config-sigdef-sig-status)# engine
R1(config-sigdef-sig-engine)# event-action produce-alert
R1(config-sigdef-sig-engine)# event-action deny-packet-inline
R1(config-sigdef-sig-engine)# event-action reset-tcp-connection
R1(config-sigdef-sig-engine)# exit
R1(config-sigdef-sig)# exit
R1(config-sigdef)# exit
Do you want to accept these changes? [confirm] <Enter>


*Jan  6 19:36:56.459: %IPS-6-ENGINE_BUILDS_STARTED: 19:36:56 UTC Jan 6 2009
*Jan  6 19:36:56.891: %IPS-6-ENGINE_BUILDING: atomic-ip - 306 signatures - 1
of 13 engines
*Jan  6 19:36:57.599: %IPS-6-ENGINE_READY: atomic-ip - build time 704 ms -
packets for this engine will be scanned
*Jan  6 19:36:57.979: %IPS-6-ALL_ENGINE_BUILDS_COMPLETE: elapsed time 1520 ms
```

Step 4: Ping from R2 to R1 serial 0/0/0 interface.

a. Start the syslog server.

b. From the CLI on R2, ping R1 S0/0/0 at IP address 10.1.1.1. Were the pings successful? Explain.

_____

_____

Step 5: Ping from R2 to PC-A.

a. From the CLI on R2, ping PC-A at IP address 192.168.1.3. Were the pings successful? Explain.

_____

_____

b. Notice the IPS messages from R1 on the syslog server screen below. How many messages were generated from the R2 pings to R1 and PC-A?

_____

_____

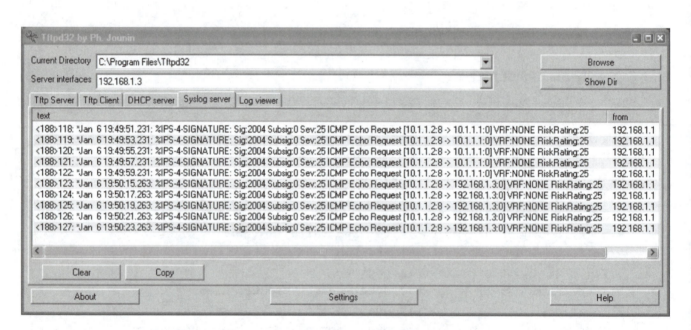

Note: The ICMP echo request IPS risk rating (severity level) is relatively low at 25. Risk rating can range from 0 to 100.

Task 7: Verify IPS with Zenmap.

Nmap/Zenmap is a network scanning tool that allows you to discover network hosts and resources, including services, ports, operating systems, and other fingerprinting information. Zenmap is the graphical interface for Nmap. Nmap **should not** be used to scan networks without prior permission. The act of network scanning can be considered as a form of network attack.

Nmap/Zenmap will test the IPS capabilities on R1. You will run the scanning program from PC-A and attempt to scan open ports on router R2 before and after applying IPS rule iosips on R1.

Step 1: Download and install Nmap/Zenmap.

a. If Nmap/Zenmap is not installed on PC-A, download **Nmap/Zenmap** at http://nmap.org/download.html.

b. Search for the appropriate binaries for your operating system.

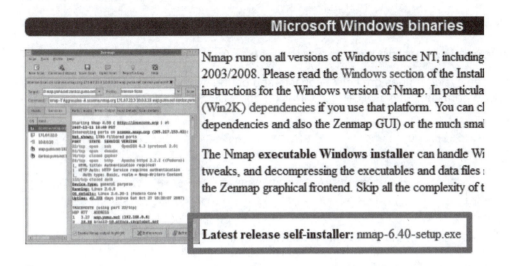

c. Install Nmap/Zenmap.

Step 2: Run Nmap/Zenmap and set scanning options.

a. Start **Zenmap** on PC-A.

b. Enter IP address **10.1.1.2** as the Target and verify that **Intense scan** is selected as the Profile. Click **Scan** to begin the scan.

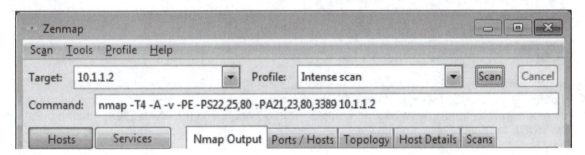

c. After the scan is complete, review the results displayed in the Nmap Output tab.

d. Click the **Ports/Hosts** tab. How many open ports did Nmap find on R2? What are the associated port numbers and services?

_____

_____

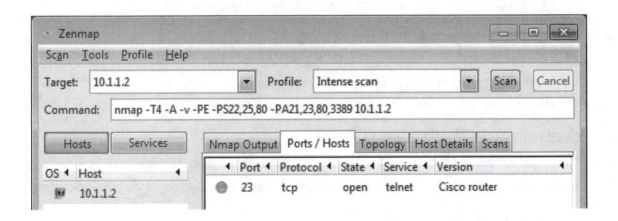

e.   Exit Zenmap.

Task 8: Observe the syslog messages on R1.

You should see syslog entries on the R1 console and on the syslog server if it is enabled. The descriptions should include phrases, such as TCP NULL Packet and TCP SYN/FIN Packet.

```
R1#
.Jan  6 01:51:13.050: %IPS-4-SIGNATURE: Sig:2004 Subsig:0 Sev:25 ICMP Echo Request
[192.168.1.3:8 -> 10.1.1.2:0] VRF:NONE RiskRating:25
.Jan  6 01:51:13.082: %IPS-4-SIGNATURE: Sig:3040 Subsig:0 Sev:100 TCP NULL Packet
[192.168.1.3:33455 -> 10.1.1.2:23] VRF:NONE RiskRating:100
.Jan  6 01:51:13.114: %IPS-4-SIGNATURE: Sig:3041 Subsig:0 Sev:100 TCP SYN/FIN Packet
[192.168.1.3:33456 -> 10.1.1.2:23] VRF:NONE RiskRating:100
```

a.   What is the IPS risk rating or severity level (Sev:) of the TCP NULL Packet, signature 3040?

_____

b.   What is the IPS risk rating or severity level (Sev:) of the TCP SYN/FIN packet, signature 3041?

_____

Part 3: Configuring an IPS using CCP

In Part 3 of this lab, you will configure IOS IPS on R3 using CCP.

Task 1: Configure Java Settings on PC-C.

The next-generation Java Plug-in must be enabled, and the Security setting must be set to **Medium** for the CCP configuration of IPS. To support the CCP configuration of IPS, PC-C should be running Java JRE version 6 or newer to set the Java heap to 256 MB. This is done using the **–Xmx256m** runtime parameter. The latest JRE for Windows can be downloaded from Oracle Corporation at http://www.oracle.com/.

Step 1: Enable the next-generation Java plug-in.

a.   Open the Control Panel, select **Java** to access the Java Control Panel.

b.   In the Java Control Panel, select the **Advanced** tab.

c.   Locate the **Java Plug-in** heading. Click the **Enable the next-generation Plug-in** check box, which requires browser restart.

d.   Click **Apply**.

e.   Click **Yes** to allow the changes, and then click **OK** to acknowledge the changes.

Step 2: Change the Java security settings.

a.   Select the **Security** tab.

b.   Change the Security Level to **Medium** by moving the slider.

c.   Click **Apply**.

Step 3: Change the Java Applet Runtime settings.

a.   Select the **Java** tab and click **View** to enter or change the Java Applet Runtime Settings.

b.   Double-click the empty box below the **Java Runtime Parameters** heading. In the box, type **–Xmx256m**.

c. Click **OK** twice to exit the Java Control Panel.

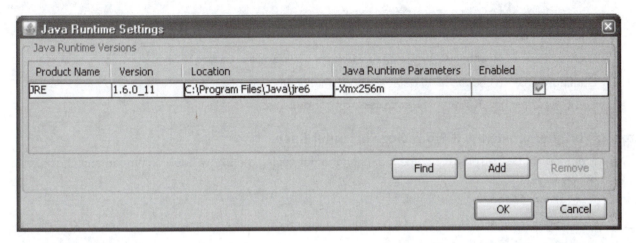

Step 4: Restart all web browsers, including CCP if opened, for the changes to take effect.

Task 2: Verify Access to the R3 LAN from R2.

In this task, you will verify that, without IPS configured, external router R2 can access the R3 S0/0/1 interface and PC-C on the R3 internal LAN.

Step 1: Ping from R2 to R3.

From R2, ping the R3 interface S0/0/1 at IP address **10.2.2.1**.

```
R2# ping 10.2.2.1
```

If the pings are not successful, troubleshoot the basic device configurations before continuing.

Step 2: Ping from R2 to PC-C on the R3 LAN.

From R2, ping PC-C on the R3 LAN at IP address **192.168.3.3**.

```
R2# ping 192.168.3.3
```

If the pings are unsuccessful, troubleshoot the basic device configurations before continuing.

Step 3: Display the R3 running configuration prior to starting CCP.

a. Issue the **show run** command to review the current basic configuration on R3.

b. Verify the R3 basic configuration as performed in Part 1 of this lab. Are there any security commands related to IPS?

_____

_____

_____

Task 3: Prepare the Router for CCP and IPS.

Step 1: Configure the enable secret password and secure HTTP router access prior to starting CCP.

a. From the CLI, configure the **enable secret** password for use with CCP on R3.

```
R3(config)# enable secret cisco12345
```

b. Enable the secure HTTP server on R3.

```
R3(config)# ip http secure-server
```

c. Add **admin** user to the local database.

```
R3(config)# username admin privilege 15 secret cisco12345
```

d. Configure CCP to use the local database to authenticate web sessions.

```
R3(config)# ip http authentication local
```

Step 2: Verify or create the IPS directory in router flash.

a. From the R3 CLI, display the content of flash memory using the **show flash** command and check for the **ipsdir** directory.

```
R3# show flash
```

If this directory is not listed, create it by entering the **mkdir ipsdir** command in privileged EXEC mode.

```
R3# mkdir ipsdir
Create directory filename [ipsdir]?
Created dir flash:ipsdir
```

b. If the directory already exists, the following message displays:

```
%Error Creating dir flash:ipsdir (Can't create a file that exists)
```

Use the **delete** command to erase the content of the **ipsdir** directory.

```
R1# delete flash:ipsdir/*
Delete filename [/ipsdir/*]?
Delete flash:/ipsdir/R1-sigdef-default.xml? [confirm]
Delete flash:/ipsdir/R1-sigdef-delta.xml? [confirm]
Delete flash:/ipsdir/R1-sigdef-typedef.xml? [confirm]
Delete flash:/ipsdir/R1-sigdef-category.xml? [confirm]
Delete flash:/ipsdir/R1-seap-delta.xml? [confirm]
Delete flash:/ipsdir/R1-seap-typedef.xml? [confirm]
```

Note: Use this command with caution. If there are no files in the **ipsdir** directory, the following message displays:

```
R1# delete flash:ipsdir/*
Delete filename [/ipsdir/*]?
No such file
```

c. From the R3 CLI, verify that the directory is present using the **dir flash:ipsdir** command.

```
R3# dir flash:ipsdir

Directory of flash:/ipsdir/

No files in directory
```

Note: The directory exists, but there are currently no files in it.

Task 4: Prepare the TFTP Server.

In this task, you will start the TFTP server on PC-C and verify the IPS file directory.

a. Download the **Tftpd32 server** from http://tftpd32.jounin.net/, if not installed on PC-C.

b. Verify connectivity between R3 and PC-C, the TFTP server, using the **ping** command.

c. Verify that the PC has the IPS Signature package file in a directory on the TFTP server. This file is typically named IOS-S*xxx*-CLI.pkg, where *xxx* is the signature file version.

    Note: If this file is not present, contact your instructor before continuing.

d. Start Tftpd32 or another TFTP server for IPS configuration in the next step.

e. Set the default directory to the one with the IPS Signature package. The Tftpd32 screen is shown here with the C:\Program Files\Tftpd32\IPS directory contents displayed. Take note of the filename for use in the next step.

    What is the name of the signature file?

    _____

    _____

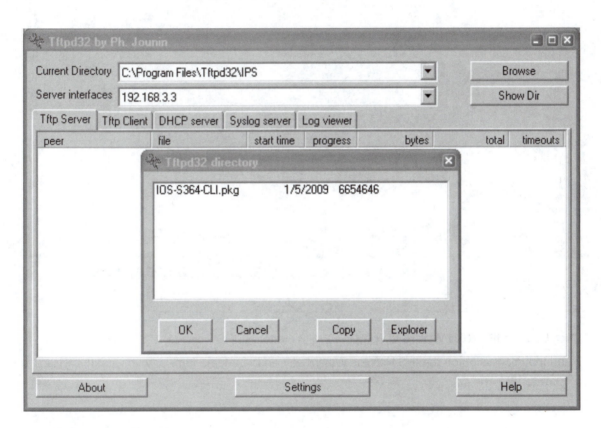

Task 5: Use CCP to Configure IPS.

Step 1: Access CCP and discover R3.

a. Start CCP on PC-C. In the Manage Devices window, add R3 IP address **192.168.3.1** in the first IP address field. In the Username field, enter **admin**, in the **Password** field, enter **cisco12345**, and select **Connect Securely**.

b. At the CCP Dashboard, click **Discover** to discover and connect to R3.

c. Click **Yes** to accept the Security Certificate Alert window displays.

d. If discovery fails, click **Discovery Details** to determine the problem.

    Note: If you are using Java version 1.6 or later, the Java console may display, by default, when CCP is run. If the Java console displays, you can close it. You can also start the Java plug-in application and select **Advanced** > **Java Console** > **Do not start console**. The Java console does not appear again unless you change the setting.

Step 2: Use the CCP IPS Wizard to configure Cisco IOS IPS.

a.   On the CCP menu bar, click **Configure**, and then select **Security** > **Intrusion Prevention** > **Create IPS**.

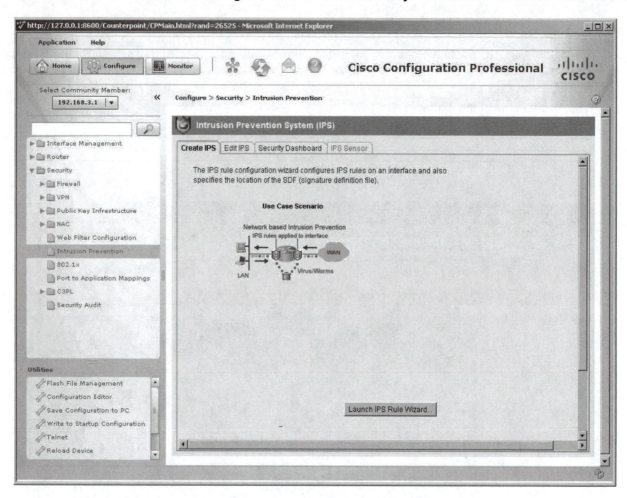

b.   Click **Launch IPS Rule Wizard** to open the Welcome to the IPS Policies Wizard window.

c.   Read the information on the IPS Policies Wizard screen to become familiar with what the wizard does, and click **Next**.

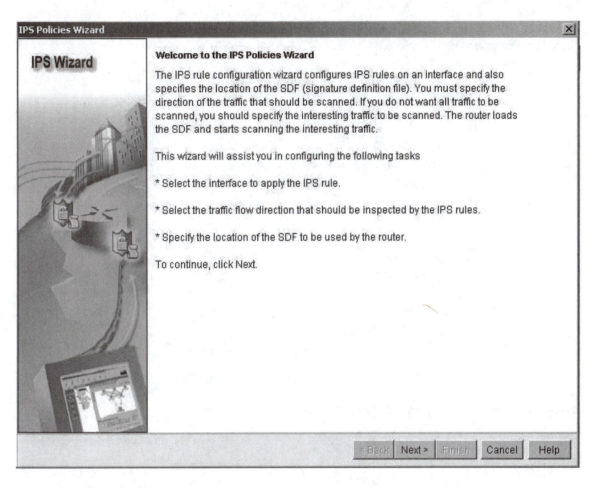

Note: SDEE dialog boxes might appear. Read the information and click **OK** for each dialog box.

d.   In the Select Interfaces window, click the **Inbound** check box for Fast Ethernet0/1 and Serial0/0/1, and click **Next**.

Note: Selecting inbound on both interfaces allows IPS to monitor attacks on the router from the internal and external network.

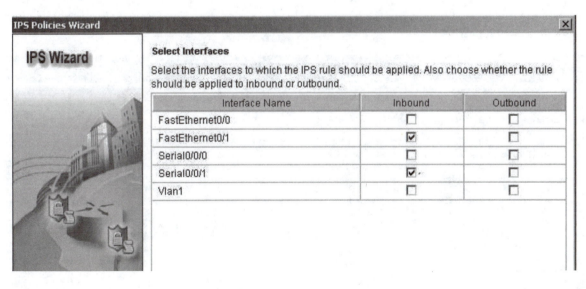

e.   In the Signature File and Public Key window, click the ellipsis (**...**) button next to Specify the Signature File You Want to Use with IOS IPS to open the Specify Signature File window. Confirm that the **Specify signature file using URL** option is selected.

f.   For Protocol, from the drop-down list, select **tftp**. Enter the IP address of the PC-C TFTP server and the filename. For example, 192.168.3.3/IOS-S364-CLI.pkg.

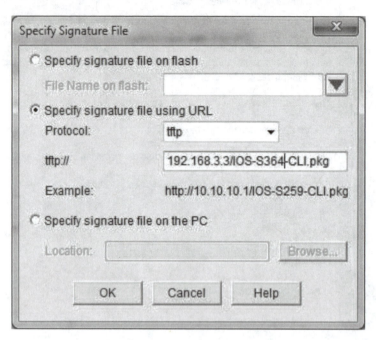

g.   What other options can be specified as a source for the Signature File?

_____

_____

h.   Click **OK** to return to the Signature File and Public Key window. In the Configure Public Key section in the Signature File and Public Key window, enter **realm-cisco.pub** in the Name field.

Each change to the signature configuration is saved in a delta file. This file must be digitally signed with a public key. You can obtain a key from Cisco.com and paste the information in the Name and Key fields. In this lab, you will copy and paste the key from a text file on PC-C.

i.   Open the realm-cisco-pub-key.txt file located on the PC-C desktop. The following is an example from the realm-cisco-pub-key.txt file.

```
realm-cisco_pub_key_v5x.txt - Notepad
File   Edit   Format   View   Help
crypto key pubkey-chain rsa
 named-key realm-cisco.pub signature
  key-string
   30820122 300D0609 2A864886 F70D0101 01050003 82010F00 3082010A 02820101
   00C19E93 A8AF124A D6CC7A24 5097A975 206BE3A2 06FBA13F 6F12CB5B 4E441F16
   17E630D5 C02AC252 912BE27F 37FDD9C8 11FC7AF7 DCDD81D9 43CDABC3 6007D128
   B199ABCB D34ED0F9 085FADC1 359C189E F30AF10A C0EFB624 7E0764BF 3E53053E
   5B2146A9 D7A5EDE3 0298AF03 DED7A5B8 9479039D 20F30663 9AC64B93 C0112A35
   FE3F0C87 89BCB7BB 994AE74C FA9E481D F65875D6 85EAF974 6D9CC8E3 F0B08B85
   50437722 FFBE85B9 5E4189FF CC189CB9 69C46F9C A84DFBA5 7A0AF99E AD768C36
   006CF498 079F88F8 A3B3FB1F 9FB7B3CB 5539E1D1 9693CCBB 551F78D2 892356AE
   2F56D826 8918EF3C 80CA4F4D 87BFCA3B BFF668E9 689782A5 CF31CB6E B4B094D3
   F3020301 0001
quit
exit
exit
```

j. Copy the text between the phrase **key-string** and the word **quit** from the realm-cisco_pub_key.txt file into the **Key** field in the Configure Public Key section. The Signature File and Public Key window should look similar to the following when the entries are complete.

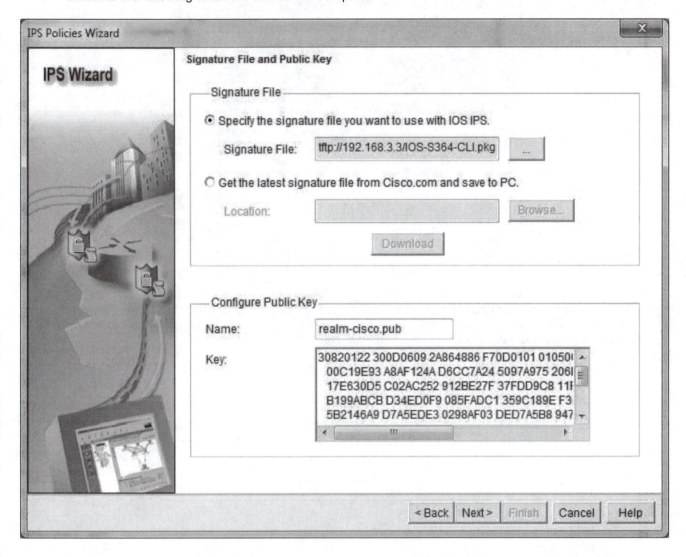

k. Click **Next** to display the Config Location and Category window, which specifies where to store the signature information. This file is used by the Cisco IOS IPS for detecting attacks from coming into the Fast Ethernet0/1 or Serial0/0/1 interfaces.

l. In the **Config Location and Category** window > **Config Location** section, click the ellipsis (**...**) button next to **Config Location** to add the location.

m. Verify that the **Specify the config location on this router** option is selected. Click the ellipsis (**...**) button. Click the plus sign (**+**) next to flash. Select the **ipsdir** folder, and then click **OK**.

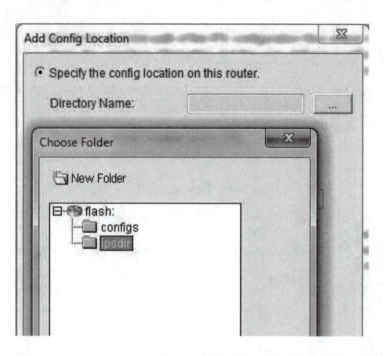

n.   Because router memory and resource constraints might prevent using all the available signatures, there
     are two categories of signatures: basic and advanced. In the **Config Location and Category** window >
     Choose Category field, select **basic**. The Config Location and Category window should look similar to
     the following screen excerpt when the entries are complete.

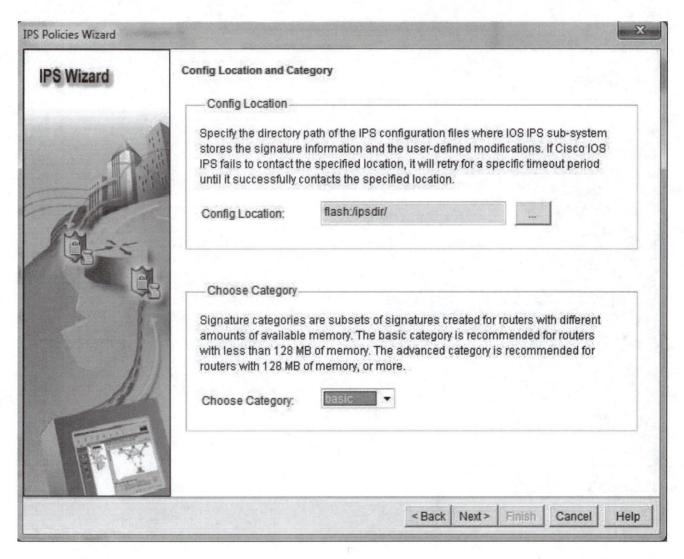

o. In the Cisco CCP IPS Policies Wizard window, click **Next**. The Summary window displays. Examine the
    IPS configuration information shown.

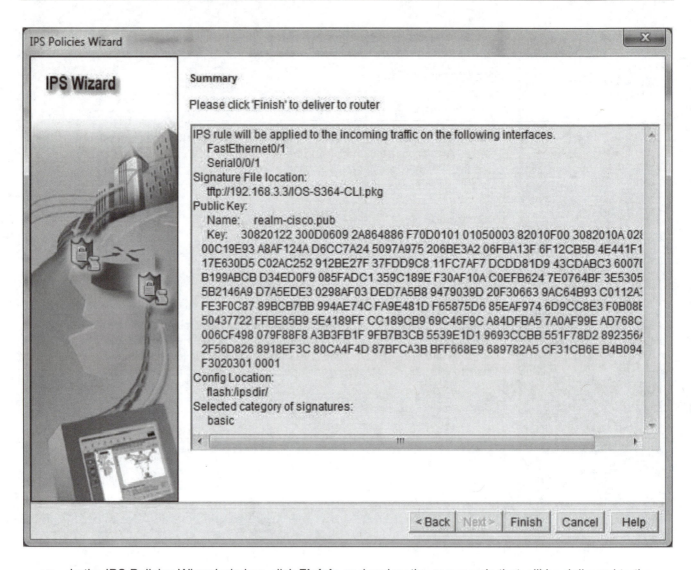

p. In the IPS Policies Wizard window, click **Finish**, and review the commands that will be delivered to the router.

q. Click **Deliver**. How many commands were delivered to the router?

_____

r. When the Commands Deliver Status window is ready, click **OK**. The IOS IPS Configuration Status window opens stating that it can take several minutes for the signatures to be configured.

s. When the signature configuration process is complete, you are returned to the IPS window with the Edit IPS tab selected. Your screen should look similar to the following:

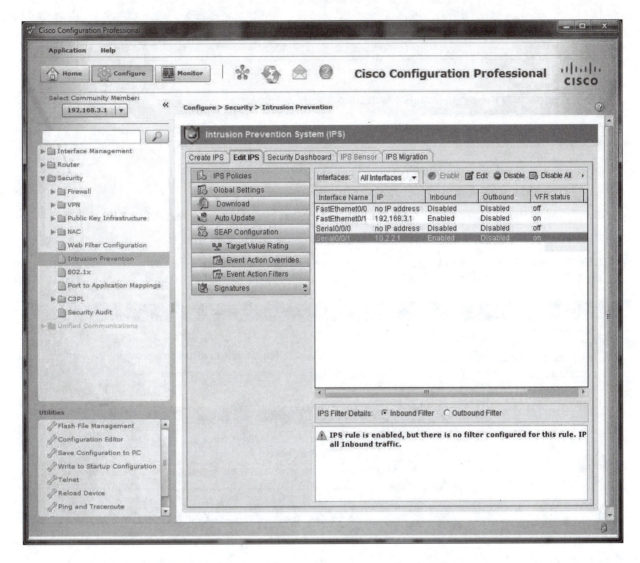

t.   Select interface **Serial0/0/1** from the list. What information is displayed at the bottom of the screen?

_____

_____

Task 6: Modify Signature Settings.

Step 1: Verify connectivity.

From PC-C, ping R3. The pings should be successful.

Step 2: Configure the IPS application to drop ping (echo request) traffic.

a.   On the CCP menu bar, click **Configure** and select **Security** > **Intrusion Prevention** > **Edit IPS** > **Signatures**. How many total signatures are there?

_____

Are all of them enabled? _____

b.   In the View By drop-down list, choose **Sig ID**.

c.   In the **Sig ID** field, enter **2004**, and then click **Go**. What is Sig ID 2004?

_____

d.   Do you know why the pings from PC-C in Step 1 were successful?

_____

e.   Select signature **2004**, click **Unretire**, and then click **Enable**.

f.   Right-click the signature and select **Actions**.

g.   Select **Deny Packet Inline** and leave the **Produce Alert** check box checked. Click **OK**.

h.   Click **Apply Changes**. It may take some time for the changes to take effect.

i.   CCP 2.5 will list all the signatures again. In the View By drop-down list, select **Sig ID**, in the **Sig ID** field, enter **2004**, and then click **Go**. Your screen should look similar to the following:

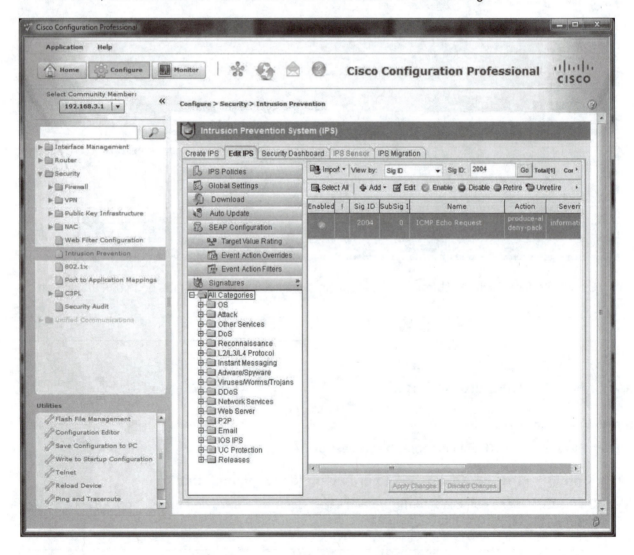

Return to PC-C and ping R3 again. Were the pings successful this time?

_____

_____

Task 7: Configure IPS Global Settings Using CCP.

In this task, you will enable the syslog and SDEE global settings using the Cisco CCP GUI.

a. On the CCP menu bar, click **Configure** and select **Security** > **Intrusion Prevention** > **Edit IPS** > **Global Settings**.

b. Verify that the syslog and SDEE options are enabled.

Note: Even if the syslog and SDEE options are already enabled, click **Edit** and explore the options available in the Edit Global Settings dialog box. Examine the options to learn whether Cisco IOS IPS has set the default to fail opened or to fail closed.

Task 8: Verify IPS Functionality with CCP Monitor and Ping.

In this task, you will demonstrate how the Cisco IOS IPS protects against an external attacker using ping.

a. From the R2 CLI, ping the R3 Fa0/1 interface at **192.168.3.1**. Were the pings successful? Explain.

_____

_____

b. On the CCP menu bar, click **Monitor** and select **Security** > **IPS Status**. The IPS Signature Statistics tab is selected by default. Wait for the screen to populate.

c. Scroll down to locate the signature ID 2004 ICMP echo request. You should see an entry similar to the one below indicating that IPS identified the ping attempt from R2. Notice that there are five hits and five drops for signature ID 2004, detected on Fa0/1 IP address 192.168.3.1.

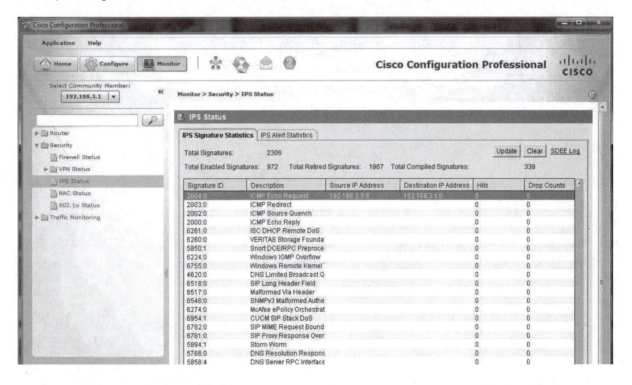

d. On the CCP menu bar, click **Configure** and select **Router** > **Logging**. In the Additional Tasks window, click **Edit** to ensure that syslog is running on R3. The window should be similar to the following:

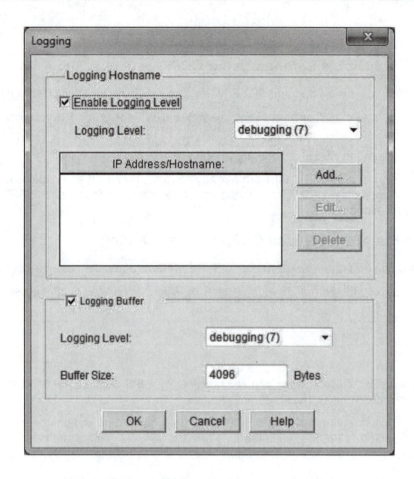

e. Click **OK**.

f. On the CCP menu bar, click **Monitor** and select **Router** > **Logging**.

g. A number of syslog messages display. Click **Clear** to clear the log.

h. From the R2 CLI, ping the R3 Fa0/1 interface at **192.168.3.1** again.

i. Click **Update**. You will see that the Cisco IOS IPS logged the ping attempts from R2.

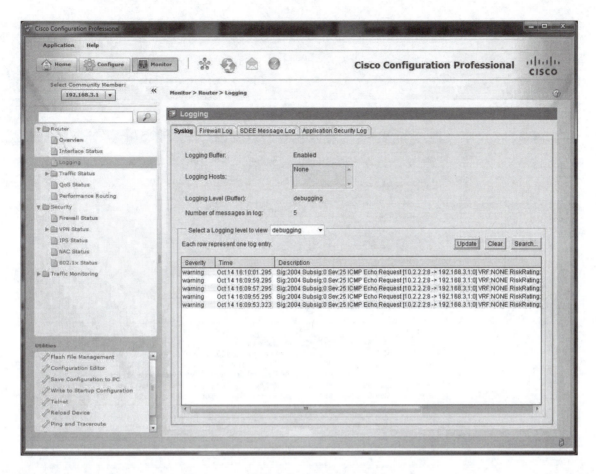

Task 9: Verify IPS Functionality with CCP Monitor and Zenmap.

In this task, you will demonstrate how the Cisco IOS IPS protects against an internal attacker that is using Nmap/Zenmap. Zenmap will test the IPS capabilities on R3. You will run the scanning program from PC-C and attempt to scan open ports on router R2. The IPS rule iosips, which is set on R3 Fa0/1 inbound, should intercept the scanning attempts and send messages to the R3 console and CCP syslog.

Step 1: Run Nmap/Zenmap and set scanning options.

a. Start Zenmap on PC-C.

b. Enter IP address **10.2.2.2** as the Target and verify the **Intense scan** is selected as the Profile, and then · click **Scan** to begin the scan.

c. After the scan is complete, review the results displayed in the Nmap Output tab.

Step 2: Check the results with CCP logging.

a. On the Cisco CCP menu bar, select **Monitor** > **Router** > **Logging**.

b. Click **Update**. You will see that the Cisco IOS IPS has been logging the port scans generated by Zenmap.

c. You should see syslog messages on R3 and entries in the CCP Monitor Log with descriptions that include one of these phrases: TCP SYN/FIN Packet or TCP NULL Packet.

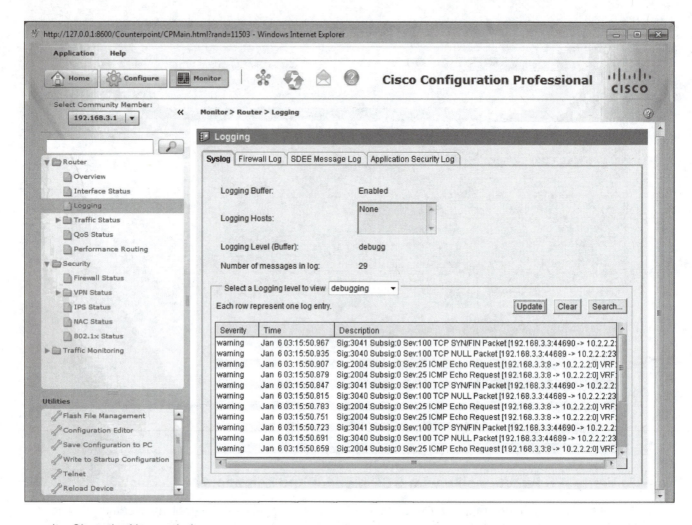

d.   Close the Nmap window.

Task 10: Compare the Results for Different IPS Configuration Methods.

a.   On R1, display the running configuration after IPS was configured with IOS CLI commands. Note the commands related to IPS.

b.   On R3, on the menu bar, click **Utilities** > **View** > **Show Running Config** to display the running configuration after IPS was configured with the CCP GUI. Note the commands related to IPS.

What differences are there between the CLI-based running configuration and the CCP-based running configuration?

_____

_____

_____

_____

_____

_____

Reflection

1. What are some advantages and disadvantages to using CLI or CCP to configure IPS?

    _____

    _____

    _____

    _____

    _____

    _____

    _____

2. With version 5.x signature files, if changes are made to a signature, are they visible in the router running configuration?

    _____

    _____

    _____

    _____

    _____

    _____

    _____

Router Interface Summary Table

Router Interface Summary				
Router Model	**Ethernet Interface #1**	**Ethernet Interface #2**	**Serial Interface #1**	**Serial Interface #2**
1800	Fast Ethernet 0/0 (Fa0/0)	Fast Ethernet 0/1 (Fa0/1)	Serial 0/0/0 (S0/0/0)	Serial 0/0/1 (S0/0/1)
1900	Gigabit Ethernet 0/0 (G0/0)	Gigabit Ethernet 0/1 (G0/1)	Serial 0/0/0 (S0/0/0)	Serial 0/0/1 (S0/0/1)
2801	Fast Ethernet 0/0 (Fa0/0)	Fast Ethernet 0/1 (Fa0/1)	Serial 0/1/0 (S0/1/0)	Serial 0/1/1 (S0/1/1)
2811	Fast Ethernet 0/0 (Fa0/0)	Fast Ethernet 0/1 (Fa0/1)	Serial 0/0/0 (S0/0/0)	Serial 0/0/1 (S0/0/1)
2900	Gigabit Ethernet 0/0 (G0/0)	Gigabit Ethernet 0/1 (G0/1)	Serial 0/0/0 (S0/0/0)	Serial 0/0/1 (S0/0/1)

Note: To find out how the router is configured, look at the interfaces to identify the type of router and how many interfaces the router has. There is no way to effectively list all the combinations of configurations for each router class. This table includes identifiers for the possible combinations of Ethernet and Serial interfaces in the device. The table does not include any other type of interface, even though a specific router may contain one. An example of this might be an ISDN BRI interface. The string in parenthesis is the legal abbreviation that can be used in Cisco IOS commands to represent the interface.

Chapter 6: Securing the Local Area Network

Lab 6.5.1.1 - Securing Layer 2 Switches

Topology

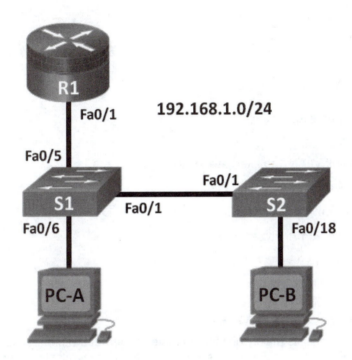

Note: ISR G2 devices use GigabitEthernet interfaces instead of FastEthernet interfaces.

IP Addressing Table

Device	Interface	IP Address	Subnet Mask	Default Gateway	Switch Port
R1	Fa0/1	192.168.1.1	255.255.255.0	N/A	S1 Fa0/5
S1	VLAN 1	192.168.1.2	255.255.255.0	N/A	N/A
S2	VLAN 1	192.168.1.3	255.255.255.0	N/A	N/A
PC-A	NIC	192.168.1.10	255.255.255.0	192.168.1.1	S1 Fa0/6
PC-B	NIC	192.168.1.11	255.255.255.0	192.168.1.1	S2 Fa0/18

Objectives

Part 1: Configure Basic Switch Settings

- Build the topology.
- Configure the hostname, IP address, and access passwords.

Part 2: Configure SSH Access to the Switches

- Configure SSH access on the switch.

- Configure an SSH client to access the switch.
- Verify the configuration.

Part 3: Configure Secure Trunks and Access Ports

- Configure trunk port mode.
- Change the native VLAN for trunk ports.
- Verify trunk configuration.
- Enable storm control for broadcasts.
- Configure access ports.
- Enable PortFast and BPDU guard.
- Verify BPDU guard.
- Enable root guard.
- Configure and verify port security.
- Disable unused ports.
- Move ports from default VLAN 1 to alternate VLAN.
- Configure the PVLAN Edge feature on a port.

Part 4: Configure SPAN and Monitor Traffic

- Configure the Switched Port Analyzer (SPAN).
- Monitor port activity using Wireshark.
- Analyze a sourced attack.

Background / Scenario

The Layer 2 infrastructure consists mainly of interconnected Ethernet switches. Most end-user devices, such as computers, printers, IP phones, and other hosts, connect to the network via Layer 2 access switches. As a result, switches can present a network security risk. Similar to routers, switches are subject to attack from malicious internal users. The switch Cisco IOS software provides many security features that are specific to switch functions and protocols.

In this lab, you will configure SSH access and Layer 2 security for S1 and S2. You will also configure various switch protection measures, including access port security, switch storm control, and Spanning Tree Protocol (STP) features, such as BPDU guard and root guard. Lastly, you use Cisco SPAN to monitor traffic to specific ports on the switch.

Note: The router commands and output in this lab are from a Cisco 1841 router using Cisco IOS software, release 15.1(4)M8 (Advanced IP Services image). The switch commands and output are from Cisco WS-C2960-24TT-L switches with Cisco IOS Release 15.0(2)SE4 (C2960-LANBASEK9-M image). Other routers, switches, and Cisco IOS versions can be used. See the Router Interface Summary Table at the end of the lab to determine which interface identifiers to use based on the equipment in the lab. Depending on the router, or switch model and Cisco IOS version, the commands available and output produced might vary from what is shown in this lab.

Note: Make sure that the routers and switches have been erased and have no startup configurations.

Required Resources

- 1 Router (Cisco 1841 with Cisco IOS Release 15.1(4)M8 Advanced IP Services image or comparable)
- 2 Switches (Cisco 2960 with cryptography IOS image for SSH support – Release 15.0(2)SE4 or comparable)
- 2 PCs (Windows Vista or Windows 7 with SSH Client, Wireshark, and Nmap/Zenmap)

- Ethernet cables as shown in the topology
- Console cables to configure Cisco networking devices

Part 1: Configure Basic Switch Settings

In Part 1, you will set up the network topology and configure basic settings, such as the hostnames, IP addresses, and device access passwords.

Step 1: Cable the network as shown in the topology.

Attach the devices, as shown in the topology diagram, and cable as necessary.

Step 2: Configure basic settings for the router and each switch.

Perform all tasks on R1, S1, and S2. The procedure for S1 is shown here as an example.

a. Configure hostnames, as shown in the topology.

b. Configure interface IP addresses, as shown in the IP Addressing Table. The following configuration displays the VLAN 1 management interface on S1:

```
S1(config)# interface vlan 1
S1(config-if)# ip address 192.168.1.2 255.255.255.0
S1(config-if)# no shutdown
```

c. To prevent the router or switch from attempting to translate incorrectly entered commands, disable DNS lookup. S1 is shown here as an example.

```
S1(config)# no ip domain-lookup
```

d. HTTP access to the switch is enabled by default. To prevent HTTP access, disable the HTTP server and HTTP secure server.

```
S1(config)# no ip http server
S1(config)# no ip http secure-server
```

Note: The switch must have a cryptography IOS image to support the **ip http secure-server** command. HTTP access to the router is disabled by default.

e. Configure the enable secret password.

```
S1(config)# enable secret cisco12345
```

f. Configure console password.

```
S1(config)# line console 0
S1(config-line)# password ciscoconpass
S1(config-line)# exec-timeout 5 0
S1(config-line)# login
S1(config-line)# logging synchronous
```

Step 3: Configure vty lines and password on R1.

```
R1(config)# line vty 0 4
R1(config-line)# password ciscovtypass
R1(config-line)# exec-timeout 5 0
R1(config-line)# login
```

Note: Do not configure the switch vty access at this time. The vty lines are configured on the switches in Part 2 for SSH access.

Step 4: Configure PC host IP settings.

Configure a static IP address, subnet mask, and default gateway for PC-A and PC-B, as shown in the IP Addressing Table.

Step 5: Verify basic network connectivity.

a. Ping from PC-A and PC-B to the R1 Fa0/1 interface at IP address **192.168.1.1**.

If the pings are unsuccessful, troubleshoot the basic device configurations before continuing.

b. Ping from PC-A to PC-B.

If the pings are unsuccessful, troubleshoot the basic device configurations before continuing.

Step 6: Save the basic configurations for the router and both switches.

Save the running configuration to the startup configuration from the privileged EXEC mode prompt.

```
S1# copy running-config startup-config
```

Part 2: Configure SSH Access to the Switches

In Part 2, you will configure S1 and S2 to support SSH connections and install SSH client software on the PCs.

Note: A switch IOS image that supports encryption is required to configure SSH. Otherwise, you cannot specify SSH as an input protocol for the vty lines and the **crypto** commands are unavailable.

Task 1: Configure the SSH Server on S1 and S2 Using the CLI.

In this task, use the CLI to configure the switch to be managed securely using SSH instead of Telnet. SSH is a network protocol that establishes a secure terminal emulation connection to a switch or other networking device. SSH encrypts all information that passes over the network link and provides authentication of the remote computer. SSH is rapidly replacing Telnet as the remote login tool of choice for network professionals. It is strongly recommended that SSH be used in place of Telnet on production networks.

Note: For a switch to support SSH, it must be configured with local authentication or AAA.

Step 1: Configure a domain name.

a. Enter global configuration mode and set the domain name.

```
S1# conf t
S1(config)# ip domain-name ccnasecurity.com
```

Step 2: Configure a privileged user for login from the SSH client.

a. Use the **username** command to create the user ID with the highest possible privilege level and a secret password.

```
S1(config)# username admin privilege 15 secret cisco12345
```

b. Exit to the initial switch login screen, and log in with this username. What was the switch prompt after you entered the password?

_____

_____

Step 3: Configure the incoming vty lines.

a. Configure vty access on lines 0 to 4. Specify a privilege level of 15 so that a user with the highest privilege level (**15**) will default to privileged EXEC mode when accessing the vty lines. Other users will default to user EXEC mode. Specify the use of local user accounts for mandatory login and validation, and accept only SSH connections.

```
S1(config)# line vty 0 4
S1(config-line)# privilege level 15
S1(config-line)# exec-timeout 5 0
S1(config-line)# login local
S1(config-line)# transport input ssh
S1(config-line)# exit
```

b. Disable login for switch vty lines 5 to 15 by allowing no transport input.

```
S1(config)# line vty 5 15
S1(config-line)# transport input none
```

Step 4: Generate the RSA encryption key pair for the router.

The switch uses the RSA key pair for authentication and encryption of transmitted SSH data.

Configure the RSA keys with **1024** for the number of modulus bits. The default is 512, and the range is from 360 to 2,048.

```
S1(config)# crypto key generate rsa general-keys modulus 1024
The name for the keys will be: S1.ccnasecurity.com

% The key modulus size is 1024 bits
% Generating 1024 bit RSA keys, keys will be non-exportable...[OK]

S1(config)#
00:15:36: %SSH-5-ENABLED: SSH 1.99 has been enabled
```

Step 5: Verify the SSH configuration.

a. Use the **show ip ssh** command to see the current settings.

```
S1# show ip ssh
```

b. Fill in the following information based on the output of the **show ip ssh** command:

SSH version enabled: _____

Authentication timeout: _____

Authentication retries: _____

Step 6: Configure SSH timeouts and authentication parameters.

The default SSH timeouts and authentication parameters can be altered to be more restrictive using the following commands.

```
S1(config)# ip ssh time-out 90
S1(config)# ip ssh authentication-retries 2
```

Step 7: Save the running configuration to the startup configuration.

```
S1# copy running-config startup-config
```

Task 2: Configure the SSH Client.

PuTTy and Tera Term are two terminal emulation programs that can support SSHv2 client connections. This lab uses PuTTY.

Step 1: (Optional) Download and install an SSH client on PC-A and PC-B.

If the SSH client is not already installed, download PuTTY from the following link:

http://www.chiark.greenend.org.uk/~sgtatham/putty/download.html

Note: The procedure described here is for PuTTY and pertains to PC-A.

Step 2: Verify SSH connectivity to S1 from PC-A.

a. Launch PuTTY by double-clicking the **putty.exe** icon (and clicking **Run** if prompted).

b. Input the S1 IP address **192.168.1.2** in the **Host Name (or IP address)** field.

c. Verify that the **SSH** radio button is selected. PuTTY defaults to SSH version 2.

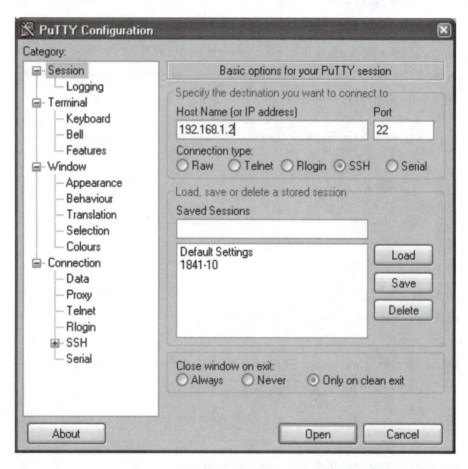

d. Click **Open**.

Note: Upon first connection, the user is prompted with a PuTTY Security Alert stating that the server's host key is not cached in the registry.

e. In the PuTTY Security Alert window, click **Yes** to cache the server's host key.

f. In the PuTTY window, enter the **admin** username and password **cisco12345**.

g. At the S1 privileged EXEC mode prompt, enter the **show users** command.

    S1# **show users**

    What users are connected to S1 at this time?

    _____

    _____

h. Close the PuTTy SSH session window with the **exit** or **quit** command.

    Try to open a Telnet session to S1 from PC-A. Were you able to open the Telnet session? Explain.

    _____

    _____

Step 3: Save the configuration.

Save the running configuration to the startup configuration from the privileged EXEC mode prompt.

    S1# **copy running-config startup-config**

Part 3: Configure Secure Trunks and Access Ports

In Part 3, you will configure trunk ports, change the native VLAN for trunk ports, verify trunk configuration, and enable storm control for broadcasts on the trunk ports.

Securing trunk ports can help stop VLAN hopping attacks. The best way to prevent a basic VLAN hopping attack is to explicitly disable trunking on all ports except the ones that specifically require trunking. On the required trunking ports, disable DTP (auto trunking) negotiations and manually enable trunking. If no trunking is required on an interface, configure the port as an access port. This disables trunking on the interface.

Note: Tasks should be performed on S1 or S2, as indicated.

Task 1: Secure Trunk Ports.

Step 1: Configure S1 as the root switch.

For the purpose of this lab, S2 is currently the root bridge. You will configure S1 as the root bridge by changing the bridge ID priority level.

a. From the console on S1, enter global configuration mode.

b. The default priority for S1 and S2 is 32769 (32768 + 1 with System ID Extension). Set S1 priority to **0** so that it becomes the root switch.

    S1(config)# **spanning-tree vlan 1 priority 0**
    S1(config)# **exit**

Note: You can also use the **spanning-tree vlan 1 root primary** command to make S1 the root switch for VLAN 1.

c. Issue the **show spanning-tree** command to verify that S1 is the root bridge and to see the ports in use and their status.

```
S1# show spanning-tree


VLAN0001
  Spanning tree enabled protocol ieee
  Root ID    Priority    1
             Address     001d.4635.0c80
             This bridge is the root
             Hello Time   2 sec  Max Age 20 sec  Forward Delay 15 sec

  Bridge ID  Priority    1        (priority 0 sys-id-ext 1)
             Address     001d.4635.0c80
             Hello Time   2 sec  Max Age 20 sec  Forward Delay 15 sec
             Aging Time 300


Interface         Role Sts Cost      Prio.Nbr Type
----------------- ---- --- --------- -------- --------------------------------
Fa0/1             Desg FWD 19        128.1    P2p
Fa0/5             Desg FWD 19        128.5    P2p
Fa0/6             Desg FWD 19        128.6    P2p
```

d. What is the S1 priority?

_____

What ports are in use and what is their status?

_____

_____

Step 2: Configure trunk ports on S1 and S2.

a. Configure port Fa0/1 on S1 as a trunk port.

```
S1(config)# interface FastEthernet 0/1
S1(config-if)# switchport mode trunk
```

Note: If performing this lab with a 3560 switch, the user must first enter the **switchport trunk encapsulation dot1q** command.

b. Configure port Fa0/1 on S2 as a trunk port.

```
S2(config)# interface FastEthernet 0/1
S2(config-if)# switchport mode trunk
```

c. Verify that S1 port Fa0/1 is in trunking mode with the **show interfaces trunk** command.

```
S1# show interfaces trunk


Port      Mode      Encapsulation  Status      Native vlan
Fa0/1     on        802.1q         trunking    1
```

```
Port            Vlans allowed on trunk
Fa0/1           1-4094


Port            Vlans allowed and active in management domain
Fa0/1           1


Port            Vlans in spanning tree forwarding state and not pruned
Fa0/1           1
```

Step 3: Change the native VLAN for the trunk ports on S1 and S2.

a. Changing the native VLAN for trunk ports to an unused VLAN helps prevent VLAN hopping attacks.

From the output of the **show interfaces trunk** command in the previous step, what is the current native VLAN for the S1 Fa0/1 trunk interface?

_____

b. Set the native VLAN on the S1 Fa0/1 trunk interface to an unused VLAN 99.

```
S1(config)# interface fa0/1
S1(config-if)# switchport trunk native vlan 99
S1(config-if)# end
```

c. The following message should display after a brief period of time:

```
02:16:28: %CDP-4-NATIVE_VLAN_MISMATCH: Native VLAN mismatch discovered on
FastEthernet0/1 (99), with S2 FastEthernet0/1 (1).
```

What does the message mean?

_____

_____

_____

_____

d. Set the native VLAN on the S2 Fa0/1 trunk interface to VLAN 99.

```
S2(config)# interface fa0/1
S2(config-if)# switchport trunk native vlan 99
S2(config-if)# end
```

Step 4: Prevent the use of DTP on S1 and S2.

Setting the trunk port to not negotiate also helps to mitigate VLAN hopping by turning off the generation of DTP frames.

```
S1(config)# interface fa0/1
S1(config-if)# switchport nonegotiate


S2(config)# interface fa0/1
S2(config-if)# switchport nonegotiate
```

Step 5: Verify the trunking configuration on port Fa0/1.

```
S1# show interfaces fa0/1 trunk
```

```
Port         Mode           Encapsulation  Status       Native vlan
Fa0/1        on             802.1q         trunking     99


Port         Vlans allowed on trunk
Fa0/1        1-4094


Port         Vlans allowed and active in management domain
Fa0/1        1


Port         Vlans in spanning tree forwarding state and not pruned
Fa0/1        1
```

S1# **show interfaces fa0/1 switchport**

```
Name: Fa0/1
Switchport: Enabled
Administrative Mode: trunk
Operational Mode: trunk
Administrative Trunking Encapsulation: dot1q
Operational Trunking Encapsulation: dot1q
Negotiation of Trunking: Off
Access Mode VLAN: 1 (default)
Trunking Native Mode VLAN: 99 (Inactive)
Administrative Native VLAN tagging: enabled
Voice VLAN: none
Administrative private-vlan host-association: none
Administrative private-vlan mapping: none
Administrative private-vlan trunk native VLAN: none
Administrative private-vlan trunk Native VLAN tagging: enabled
Administrative private-vlan trunk encapsulation: dot1q
Administrative private-vlan trunk normal VLANs: none
Administrative private-vlan trunk private VLANs: none
Operational private-vlan: none
Trunking VLANs Enabled: ALL
Pruning VLANs Enabled: 2-1001
Capture Mode Disabled
Capture VLANs Allowed: ALL

Protected: false
Unknown unicast blocked: disabled
Unknown multicast blocked: disabled
Appliance trust: none
```

Step 6: Enable storm control for broadcasts.

Enable storm control for broadcasts on the trunk port with a **50** percent rising suppression level using the **storm-control broadcast** command.

```
S1(config)# interface FastEthernet 0/1
S1(config-if)# storm-control broadcast level 50


S2(config)# interface FastEthernet 0/1
```

```
S2(config-if)# storm-control broadcast level 50
```

Step 7: Verify your configuration with the show run command.

Use the **show run** command to display the running configuration, beginning with the first line that has the text string "0/1" in it.

```
S1# show run | begin 0/1
interface FastEthernet0/1
 switchport trunk native vlan 99
 switchport mode trunk
 switchport nonegotiate
 storm-control broadcast level 50.00

<output omitted>
```

Task 2: Secure Access Ports.

By manipulating the STP root bridge parameters, network attackers hope to spoof their system, or a rogue switch that they add to the network, as the root bridge in the topology. If a port that is configured with PortFast receives a BPDU, STP can put the port into the blocking state by using a feature called BPDU guard.

Step 1: Disable trunking on S1 access ports.

a. On S1, configure Fa0/5, the port to which R1 is connected, as access mode only.

```
S1(config)# interface FastEthernet 0/5
S1(config-if)# switchport mode access
```

b. On S1, configure Fa0/6, the port to which PC-A is connected, as access mode only.

```
S1(config)# interface FastEthernet 0/6
S1(config-if)# switchport mode access
```

Step 2: Disable trunking on S2 access ports.

On S2, configure Fa0/18, the port to which PC-B is connected, as access mode only.

```
S2(config)# interface FastEthernet 0/18
S2(config-if)# switchport mode access
```

Task 3: Protect Against STP Attacks.

The topology has only two switches and no redundant paths, but STP is still active. In this step, you enable some switch security features that can help reduce the possibility of an attacker manipulating switches via STP-related methods.

Step 1: Enable PortFast on S1 and S2 access ports.

PortFast is configured on access ports that connect to a single workstation or server to enable them to become active more quickly.

a. Enable PortFast on the S1 Fa0/5 access port.

```
S1(config)# interface FastEthernet 0/5
S1(config-if)# spanning-tree portfast
```

The following Cisco IOS warning message displays:

```
%Warning: portfast should only be enabled on ports connected to a single host.
Connecting hubs, concentrators, switches, bridges, etc... to this interface when
portfast is enabled, can cause temporary bridging loops. Use with CAUTION

%Portfast has been configured on FastEthernet0/5 but will only
 have effect when the interface is in a non-trunking mode.
```

b. Enable PortFast on the S1 Fa0/6 access port.

```
S1(config)# interface FastEthernet 0/6
S1(config-if)# spanning-tree portfast
```

c. Enable PortFast on the S2 Fa0/18 access ports.

```
S2(config)# interface FastEthernet 0/18
S2(config-if)# spanning-tree portfast
```

Step 2: Enable BPDU guard on the S1 and S2 access ports.

BPDU guard is a feature that can help prevent rogue switches and spoofing on access ports.

a. Enable BPDU guard on the switch ports previously configured as access only.

```
S1(config)# interface FastEthernet 0/5
S1(config-if)# spanning-tree bpduguard enable

S1(config)# interface FastEthernet 0/6
S1(config-if)# spanning-tree bpduguard enable

S2(config)# interface FastEthernet 0/18
S2(config-if)# spanning-tree bpduguard enable
```

b. PortFast and BPDU guard can also be enabled globally with the **spanning-tree portfast default** and **spanning-tree portfast bpduguard** commands in global configuration mode.

Note: BPDU guard can be enabled on all access ports that have PortFast enabled. These ports should never receive a BPDU. BPDU guard is best deployed on user-facing ports to prevent rogue switch network extensions by an attacker. If a port enabled with BPDU guard receives a BPDU, it is disabled and must be manually re-enabled. An **err-disable timeout** can be configured on the port so that it can recover automatically after a specified time period.

c. Verify that BPDU guard is configured by using the **show spanning-tree interface fa0/5 detail** command on S1.

```
S1# show spanning-tree interface fa0/5 detail

Port 5 (FastEthernet0/5) of VLAN0001 is designated forwarding
   Port path cost 19, Port priority 128, Port Identifier 128.5.
   Designated root has priority 1, address 001d.4635.0c80
   Designated bridge has priority 1, address 001d.4635.0c80
   Designated port id is 128.5, designated path cost 0
   Timers: message age 0, forward delay 0, hold 0
   Number of transitions to forwarding state: 1
   The port is in the portfast mode
   Link type is point-to-point by default
   Bpdu guard is enabled
   BPDU: sent 3349, received 0
```

Step 3: (Optional) Enable root guard.

Root guard is another option in helping to prevent rogue switches and spoofing. Root guard can be enabled on all ports on a switch that are not root ports. It is normally enabled only on ports connecting to edge switches where a superior BPDU should never be received. Each switch should have only one root port, which is the best path to the root switch.

a. The following command configures root guard on S2 interface Gi0/1. Normally, this is done if another switch is attached to this port. Root guard is best deployed on ports that connect to switches that should not be the root bridge. In the lab topology, S1 Fa0/1 would be the most logical candidate for root guard. However, S2 Gi0/1 is shown here as an example, as Gigabit ports are more commonly used for inter-switch connections.

```
S2(config)# interface gigabitEthernet 0/1
S2(config-if)# spanning-tree guard root
```

b. Issue the **show run | begin Gig** command to verify that root guard is configured.

```
S2# show run | begin Gig
interface GigabitEthernet0/1
 spanning-tree guard root
```

Note: The S2 Gi0/1 port is not currently up, so it is not participating in STP. Otherwise, you could use the **show spanning-tree interface Gi0/1 detail** command.

Note: The expression in the command **show run | begin** is case-sensitive.

c. If a port that is enabled with BPDU guard receives a superior BPDU, it goes into a root-inconsistent state. Use the **show spanning-tree inconsistentports** command to determine if there are any ports currently receiving superior BPDUs that should not be.

```
S2# show spanning-tree inconsistentports

Name                    Interface              Inconsistency
-------------------- ---------------------- ------------------

Number of inconsistent ports (segments) in the system : 0
```

Note: Root guard allows a connected switch to participate in STP as long as the device does not try to become the root. If root guard blocks the port, subsequent recovery is automatic. If the superior BPDUs stop, the port returns to the forwarding state.

Task 4: Configure Port Security and Disable Unused Ports.

Switches can be subject to CAM table, also known as MAC address table, overflow, MAC spoofing attacks, and unauthorized connections to switch ports. In this task, you will configure port security to limit the number of MAC addresses that can be learned on a switch port and disable the port if that number is exceeded.

Step 1: Record the R1 Fa0/0 MAC address.

From the R1 CLI, use the **show interface** command and record the MAC address of the interface.

```
R1# show interfaces fa0/1

FastEthernet0/1 is up, line protocol is up
   Hardware is Gt96k FE, address is 001b.5325.256f (bia 001b.5325.256f)
   Internet address is 192.168.1.1/24
   MTU 1500 bytes, BW 100000 Kbit/sec, DLY 100 usec,
      reliability 255/255, txload 1/255, rxload 1/255
   Encapsulation ARPA, loopback not set
   Keepalive set (10 sec)
   Full-duplex, 100Mb/s, 100BaseTX/FX
```

What is the MAC address of the R1 Fa0/1 interface?

_____

_____

Step 2: Configure basic port security.

This procedure should be performed on all access ports that are in use. S1 port Fa0/5 is shown here as an example:

a. From the S1 CLI, enter interface configuration mode for the port that connects to the router (Fast Ethernet 0/5).

    ```
    S1(config)# interface FastEthernet 0/5
    ```

b. Shut down the switch port.

    ```
    S1(config-if)# shutdown
    ```

c. Enable port security on the port.

    ```
    S1(config-if)# switchport port-security
    ```

    Note: A switch port must be configured as an access port to enable port security.

    Note: Entering just the **switchport port-security** command sets the maximum MAC addresses to **1** and the violation action to **shutdown**. The **switchport port-security maximum** and **switchport port-security violation** commands can be used to change the default behavior.

d. Configure a static entry for the MAC address of R1 Fa0/1/ interface recorded in Step 1.

    ```
    S1(config-if)# switchport port-security mac-address xxxx.xxxx.xxxx
    ```

    (*xxxx.xxxx.xxxx* is the actual MAC address of the router Fast Ethernet 0/1 interface.)

    Note: Optionally, you can use the **switchport port-security mac-address sticky** command to add all the secure MAC addresses that are dynamically learned on a port (up to the maximum set) to the switch running configuration.

e. Enable the switch port.

    ```
    S1(config-if)# no shutdown
    ```

Step 3: Verify port security on S1 Fa0/5.

a. On S1, issue the **show port-security** command to verify that port security has been configured on S1 Fa0/5.

    ```
    S1# show port-security interface f0/5
    Port Security              : Enabled
    Port Status                : Secure-up
    Violation Mode             : Shutdown
    Aging Time                 : 0 mins
    Aging Type                 : Absolute
    SecureStatic Address Aging : Disabled
    Maximum MAC Addresses      : 1
    Total MAC Addresses        : 1
    Configured MAC Addresses   : 1
    Sticky MAC Addresses       : 0
    Last Source Address:Vlan   : 001b.5325.256f:1
    Security Violation Count   : 0
    ```

b. What is the status of the Fa0/5 port?

_____

_____

What is the Last Source Address and VLAN?

_____

_____

c. From the R1 CLI, ping PC-A to verify connectivity. This also ensures that the R1 Fa0/1 MAC address is learned by the switch.

    R1# **ping 192.168.1.10**

d. You will now violate security by changing the MAC address on the router interface. Enter interface configuration mode for the Fast Ethernet 0/1. Configure a MAC address for the interface on the interface, using **aaaa.bbbb.cccc** as the address.

    R1(config)# **interface FastEthernet 0/1**

    R1(config-if)# **mac-address aaaa.bbbb.cccc**

    R1(config-if)# **end**

    Note: You could also change the PC MAC address attached to S1 Fa0/6 and achieve similar results to those shown here.

e. From the R1 CLI, ping PC-A. Was the ping successful? Explain.

_____

_____

f. On S1 console, observe the messages when port Fa0/5 detects the violating MAC address.

    *Jan 14 01:34:39.750: %PM-4-ERR_DISABLE: psecure-violation error detected on Fa0/5, putting Fa0/5 in err-disable state

    *Jan 14 01:34:39.750: %PORT_SECURITY-2-PSECURE_VIOLATION: Security violation occurred, caused by MAC address aaaa.bbbb.cccc on port FastEthernet0/5.

    *Jan 14 01:34:40.756: %LINEPROTO-5-UPDOWN: Line protocol on Interface FastEthernet0/5, changed state to down

    *Jan 14 01:34:41.755: %LINK-3-UPDOWN: Interface FastEthernet0/5, changed state to down

g. On the switch, use the various **show port-security** command to verify that port security has been violated.

    S1# **show port-security**

    Secure Port MaxSecureAddr CurrentAddr SecurityViolation Security Action
                   (Count)   (Count)   (Count)

        Fa0/5   1   1   1   Shutdown

    Total Addresses in System (excluding one mac per port)   : 0
    Max Addresses limit in System (excluding one mac per port) : 8192

    S1# **show port-security interface fastethernet0/5**

    Port Security   : Enabled
    Port Status   : Secure-shutdown

```
Violation Mode            : Shutdown
Aging Time                : 0 mins
Aging Type                : Absolute
SecureStatic Address Aging : Disabled
Maximum MAC Addresses     : 1
Total MAC Addresses       : 1
Configured MAC Addresses  : 1
Sticky MAC Addresses      : 0
Last Source Address:Vlan  : aaaa.bbbb.cccc:1
Security Violation Count  : 1
```

```
S1# show port-security address
Secure Mac Address Table
-------------------------------------------------------------------------
Vlan    Mac Address      Type                      Ports    Remaining Age
                                                              (mins)
----    -----------      ----                      -----    -------------
  1     001b.5325.256f   SecureConfigured          Fa0/5        -
-------------------------------------------------------------------------
Total Addresses in System (excluding one mac per port)    : 0
Max Addresses limit in System (excluding one mac per port) : 8192
```

h. Remove the hard-coded MAC address from the router, and re-enable the Fast Ethernet 0/1 interface.

```
R1(config)# interface FastEthernet 0/1
R1(config-if)# no mac-address aaaa.bbbb.cccc
```

Note: This will restore the original FastEthernet interface MAC address.

From R1, try to ping the PC-A again at 192.168.1.10. Was the ping successful? Why or why not?

_____

_____

Step 4: Clear the S1 Fa0/5 error disabled status.

a. From the S1 console, clear the error and re-enable the port using the following commands. This will change the port status from Secure-shutdown to Secure-up.

```
S1(config)# interface FastEthernet 0/5
S1(config-if)# shutdown
S1(config-if)# no shutdown
```

Note: This assumes the device/interface with the violating MAC address has been removed and replaced with the one originally configured.

b. From R1, ping PC-A again. You should be successful this time.

```
R1# ping 192.168.1.10
```

Step 5: Remove basic port security on S1 Fa0/5.

From the S1 console, remove port security on Fa0/5. This procedure can also be used to re-enable the port, but **port security** commands must be reconfigured.

```
S1(config)# interface FastEthernet 0/5
S1(config-if)# no switchport port-security
S1(config-if)# no switchport port-security mac-address 001b.5325.256f
```

You can also use the following commands to reset the interface to its default settings:

```
S1(config)# default interface fastethernet 0/5
S1(config)# interface FastEthernet 0/5
```

Note: This **default interface** command also requires you to reconfigure the port as an access port to re-enable the security commands.

Step 6: (Optional) Configure port security for VoIP.

The following example shows a typical port security configuration for a voice port. Three MAC addresses are allowed, and should be learned dynamically. One MAC address is for the IP phone, one is for the switch, and the third IP address is for the PC connected to the IP phone. Violations of this policy result in the port being shut down. The aging timeout for the learned MAC addresses is set to two hours.

The following example displays S2 port Fa0/18:

```
S2(config)# interface fa0/18
S2(config-if)# switchport mode access
S2(config-if)# switchport port-security
S2(config-if)# switchport port-security maximum 3
S2(config-if)# switchport port-security violation shutdown
S2(config-if)# switchport port-security aging time 120
```

Step 7: Disable unused ports on S1 and S2.

As a further security measure, disable any ports not being used on the switch.

a. Ports Fa0/1, Fa0/5, and Fa0/6 are used on S1. The remaining Fast Ethernet ports and the two Gigabit Ethernet ports will be shut down.

```
S1(config)# interface range fa0/2 - 4
S1(config-if-range)# shutdown
S1(config-if-range)# interface range Fa0/7 - 24
S1(config-if-range)# shutdown
S1(config-if-range)# interface range gigabitethernet0/1 - 2
S1(config-if-range)# shutdown
```

b. Ports Fa0/1 and Fa0/18 are used on S2. The remaining Fast Ethernet ports and the Gigabit Ethernet ports will be shut down.

```
S2(config)# interface range fa0/2 - 17 , fa0/19 - 24 , g0/1 - 2
S2(config-if-range)# shutdown
```

Step 8: (Optional) Move active ports to a VLAN other than the default VLAN 1.

As a further security measure, you can move all active end user and router ports to a VLAN other than the default VLAN 1 on both switches.

a. Configure a new VLAN for users on each switch using the following commands:

```
S1(config)# vlan 20
S1(config-vlan)# name Users

S2(config)# vlan 20
S2(config-vlan)# name Users
```

b. Add the current active access (non-trunk) ports to the new VLAN.

```
S1(config)# interface range fa0/5 - 6
S1(config-if-range)# switchport access vlan 20
```

```
S2(config)# interface fa0/18
S2(config-if)# switchport access vlan 20
```

Note: This will prevent communication between end user hosts and the management VLAN IP address of the switch, which is currently VLAN 1. The switch can still be accessed and configured using the console connection.

To provide Telnet or SSH access to the switch, a specific port can be designated as the management port and added to VLAN 1 with a specific management workstation attached. A more elaborate solution is to create a new VLAN for switch management (or use the existing native trunk VLAN 99), and configure a separate subnet for the management and user VLANs. Enable trunking with subinterfaces on R1 to route between the management and user VLAN subnets.

Step 9: Configure a port with the PVLAN Edge feature.

Some applications require that no traffic be forwarded at Layer 2 between ports on the same switch so that one neighbor does not see the traffic generated by another neighbor. In such an environment, the use of the Private VLAN (PVLAN) Edge feature, also known as protected ports, ensures that there is no exchange of unicast, broadcast, or multicast traffic between these ports on the switch. The PVLAN Edge feature can only be implemented for ports on the same switch and is locally significant.

For example, to prevent traffic between host PC-A on S1 (port Fa0/6) and a host on another S1 port (e.g. port Fa0/7, which was previously shut down), you could use the **switchport protected** command to activate the PVLAN Edge feature on these two ports. To disable protected port, use the **no switchport protected** interface configuration command.

a.   Configure the PVLAN Edge feature in interface configuration mode using the following commands:

```
S1(config)# interface fastEthernet 0/6
S1(config-if)# switchport protected

S1(config-if)# interface fastEthernet 0/7
S1(config-if)# switchport protected
S1(config-if)# no shut
S1(config-if)# end
```

b.   Verify that the PVLAN Edge Feature (protected port) is enabled on Fa0/6.

```
S1# show interfaces fa0/6 switchport
Name: Fa0/6
Switchport: Enabled
Administrative Mode: dynamic auto
Operational Mode: static access
Administrative Trunking Encapsulation: dot1q
Negotiation of Trunking: On
Access Mode VLAN: 20 (Users)
Trunking Native Mode VLAN: 1 (default)
Administrative Native VLAN tagging: enabled
Voice VLAN: none
Administrative private-vlan host-association: none
Administrative private-vlan mapping: none
Administrative private-vlan trunk native VLAN: none
Administrative private-vlan trunk Native VLAN tagging: enabled
Administrative private-vlan trunk encapsulation: dot1q
Administrative private-vlan trunk normal VLANs: none
Administrative private-vlan trunk private VLANs: none
```

```
Operational private-vlan: none
Trunking VLANs Enabled: ALL
Pruning VLANs Enabled: 2-1001
Capture Mode Disabled
Capture VLANs Allowed: ALL

Protected: true
Unknown unicast blocked: disabled
Unknown multicast blocked: disabled
Appliance trust: none
```

c. Deactivate protected port on interfaces Fa0/6 and Fa0/7 using the following commands:

```
S1(config)# interface range fastEthernet 0/6 - 7
S1(config-if-range)# no switchport protected
```

Part 4: Configure SPAN and Monitor Traffic

Note: There are two tasks in this part of the lab, Task 1: Option 1 is to be performed using hands-on equipment. Task 2: Option 2 is modified to be compatible with the NETLAB+ system, but can also be performed using hands-on equipment.

Cisco IOS provides a feature that can be used to monitor traffic in general and network attacks in particular, called the Switched Port Analyzer (SPAN). Cisco IOS supports local SPAN and remote SPAN (RSPAN). With local SPAN, the source VLANs, source switch ports, and the destination switch ports are on the same physical switch.

In this part of the lab, you will configure a local SPAN to copy traffic from one port where a host is connected to another port where a monitoring station is connected. The monitoring station will run the Wireshark packet sniffer application to analyze traffic.

Note: SPAN allows you to select and copy traffic from one or more source switch ports or source VLANs onto one or more destination ports.

Task 1: Option 1 - Configure a SPAN Session Using Hands-On Equipment.

Note: Option 1 assumes you have physical access to the devices shown in the topology for this lab. NETLAB+ users accessing lab equipment remotely should proceed to Task 2: Option 2.

Step 1: Configure a SPAN session on S1 with a source and destination.

a. Set the SPAN source interface using the **monitor session** command in global configuration mode. The following configures a SPAN source port on FastEthernet 0/5 for ingress and egress traffic. Traffic copied on the source port can be ingress only, egress only or both. S1 port Fa0/5 is connected to R1, so ingress traffic from R1 and egress to R1 on switch port Fa0/5 will be monitored.

```
S1(config)# monitor session 1 source interface fa0/5 both
```

Note: You can specify monitor tx (transmit) or rx (receive) traffic. The **both** keyword includes **tx** and **rx**. The source can be a single interface, a range of interfaces, a single VLAN, or a range of VLANs.

b. Set the SPAN destination interface.

```
S1(config)# monitor session 1 destination interface fa0/6
```

All traffic from S1 Fa0/5, where R1 is connected, will be copied to the SPAN destination port Fa0/6, where PC-A with Wireshark is connected.

Note: The destination can be an interface or a range of interfaces.

Step 2: Verify the setup of the SPAN session on S1.

```
S1# show monitor session 1
```

```
Session 1
---------
Type                    : Local Session
Source Ports            :
    Both                : Fa0/5
Destination Ports       : Fa0/6
    Encapsulation       : Native
            Ingress     : Disabled
```

Step 3: (Optional) Download and install Wireshark on PC-A.

a. Wireshark is a network protocol analyzer, also called a packet sniffer. If Wireshark is not currently available on PC-A, you can download the latest version from http://www.wireshark.org/download.html. This lab uses Wireshark version 1.0.5. The initial Wireshark installation screen is shown here.

b. Click **I Agree** to the License agreement and accept the defaults by clicking **Next** when prompted.

Note: In the Install WinPcap screen, select the **install WinPcap** options, and select **Start WinPcap service** option to have other users besides those with administrative privileges run Wireshark.

Step 4: Monitor S1 port Fa0/5 ping activity using Wireshark on PC-A.

a. If Wireshark is available, start the application.

b. On the main menu, click **Capture** > **Interfaces**.

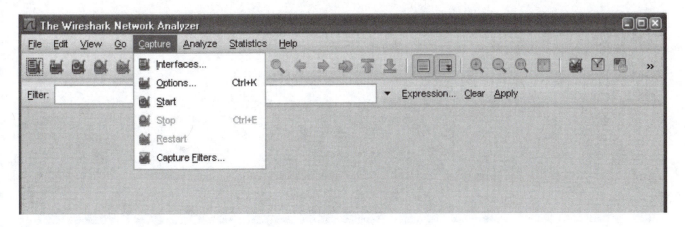

c. Click **Start** for the LAN interface adapter with IP address 192.168.1.10.

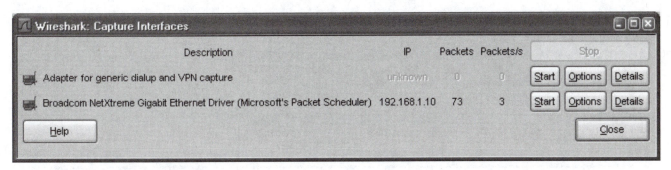

d. Generate some traffic from PC-B (192.168.1.11) to R1 interface Fa0/1 (**192.168.1.1**) using **ping**. This traffic will go from S2 port Fa0/18 to S2 port Fa0/1 across the trunk link to S1 port Fa0/1, and then exit interface Fa0/5 on S1 to reach R1.

```
PC-B:\> ping 192.168.1.1
```

e. Observe the results in Wireshark on PC-A. If you have not pinged 192.168.1.1 before, you will see the initial ARP request broadcast from PC-B (Intel NIC) to determine the MAC address of the R1 Fa0/1 interface with IP address 192.168.1.1 and the ARP reply from the R1 Cisco Ethernet interface. After the ARP request, the pings (echo request and replies) can be seen going from PC-B to R1 and from R1 to PC-B through the switch. The filter **!(ip.dst == 192.168.1.255)** was applied to the Wireshark results.

Note: Your screen should look similar to the one below. Some additional packets might be captured in addition to the pings, such as the R1 Fa0/1 LOOP reply.

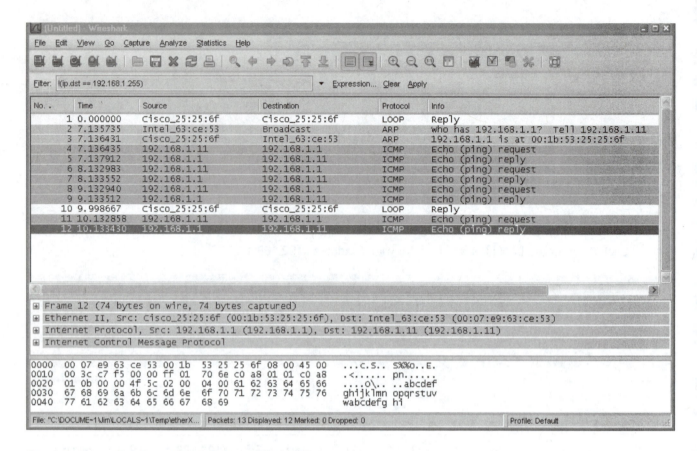

Step 5: Download and install Nmap/Zenmap.

Nmap/Zenmap is a network scanning tool which allows you to discover available hosts and resources. Zenmap is the graphical interface for Nmap. Nmap is used discovering what open ports exist on a network, including services, ports, operating systems, and other fingerprinting information. Nmap **should not** be used to scan networks without prior permission from the Network Administrator. The act of network scanning can be considered as a form of network attack.

a.   If Nmap/Zenmap is not installed on PC-B, download **Nmap/Zenmap** from the following link:

http://nmap.org/download.html

b.   Search for the appropriate binaries for your operating system.

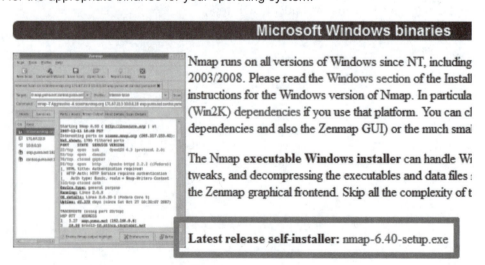

c.   Install **Nmap/Zenmap**.

Step 6: Monitor S1 port Fa0/5 Nmap activity using Wireshark on PC-A.

a. Start **Zenmap** on PC-B.

b. In the Target field, enter the IP address of R1 Fa0/1 (**192.168.1.1**).

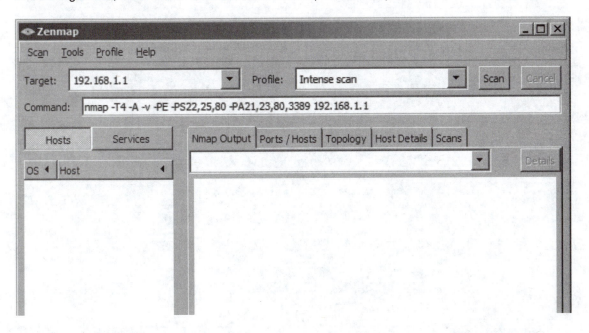

c. Clear the previous capture in Wireshark and start a new capture by clicking **Capture** > **Start**. When prompted, click **Continue without saving**.

d. In the Zenmap program, click **Scan** to start the simulated attack.

e. Observe the results on the Wireshark window on PC-A. Notice the number and types of ports tried by the simulated Zenmap attack from PC-B (192.168.1.11) to R1 Fa0/1 (192.168.1.1). The filter, **ip.host==192.168.1.1**, was applied to the Wireshark result. Your screen looks similar to the following:

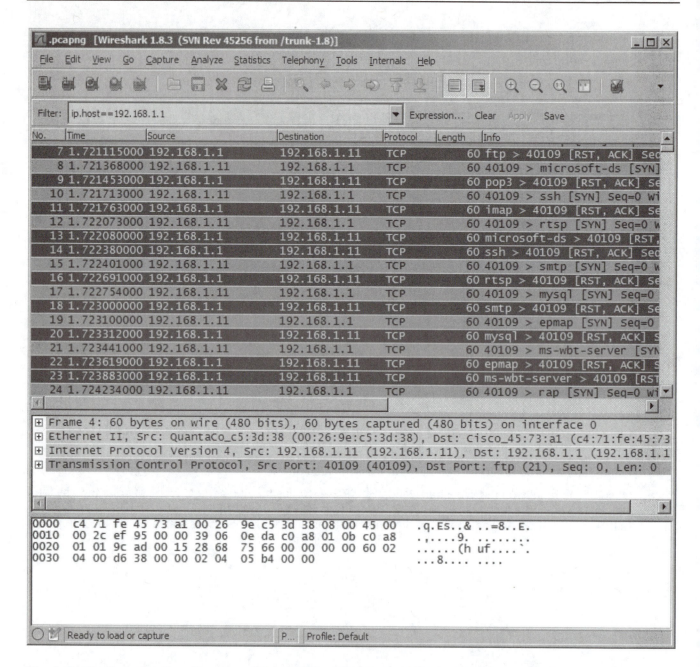

Task 2: Option 2 - Configure a SPAN Session Using NETLAB+ Remote Equipment.

Note: This portion of the lab has been rewritten to enhance compatibility with the NETLAB+ system.

On S1, you will configure a local SPAN to reflect the traffic exiting Port Fa0/5; in this case, the traffic from PC-A to R1's Fa0/1. This traffic should be received by S2 and forwarded to PC-B, where Wireshark captures the packets. Refer to the following diagram that illustrates the SPAN traffic flow.

Note: To perform this task, Wireshark should be installed on PC-B.

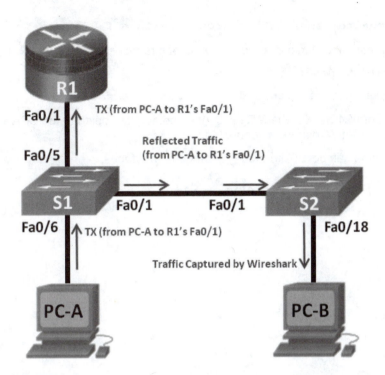

Note: S2 is acting as a regular switch, forwarding frames based on destination MAC addresses and switch ports. The traffic entering S2 through port Fa0/1 utilizes R1's MAC address as the destination for the Ethernet frame; therefore, to forward those packets to PC-B, the R1's MAC address must be the same as PC-B. To accomplish this, R1's Fa0/1 MAC address is modified using the IOS CLI to simulate PC-B's MAC address. This requirement is specific to the NETLAB+ environment.

Note: NETLAB+ VM NIC's must be configured for promiscuous mode for the capture part of this lab to work.

Step 1: Configure a SPAN session on S1 with a source and destination.

a. Return the switch ports to the default configuration.

```
S1(config)# default interface fastethernet 0/1
S1(config)# default interface fastethernet 0/5
S1(config)# default interface fastethernet 0/6

S2(config)# default interface fastethernet 0/1
S2(config)# default interface fastethernet 0/18
```

b. Display the MAC address for PC-B using the command prompt. Record the MAC address for PC-B in the space provided below.

```
PC> ipconfig /all
```

PC-B's MAC Address: _____

PC-B's MAC Address in this example is 000c-299a-e61a.

c. Configure the PC-B's MAC address on R1's Fa0/1.

```
R1(config)# interface fa0/1
R1(config-if)# mac-address 000c.299a.e61a
```

d. Set the SPAN Source Interface using the **monitor session** command in global configuration mode. The following example configures a SPAN source port on fastethernet0/5 for egress traffic. Traffic copied on the source port can be ingress only, egress only, or both. In this case, the egress traffic is the only one analyzed. On S1, port Fa0/5 is connected to R1 so traffic from the switch port Fa0/5 to R1 will be monitored.

```
S1(config)# monitor session 1 source interface fa0/5 tx
```

Note: The source can be a single interface, a range of interfaces, a single VLAN, or range of VLANs.

e.   Set the SPAN destination interface.

```
S1(config)# monitor session 1 destination interface fa0/1
```

All egress traffic from S1 Fa0/5, where R1 is connected, will be copied to the SPAN destination port Fa0/1, where PC-B with Wireshark is connected.

Note: The destination can be an interface or a range of interfaces.

Step 2: Verify the setup of the SPAN session on S1.

```
S1# show monitor session 1
Session 1
---------
Type                    : Local Session
Source Ports            :
    TX Only             : Fa0/5
Destination Ports       : Fa0/1
    Encapsulation       : Native
            Ingress     : Disabled
```

Step 3: (Optional) Download and install Wireshark on PC-B.

Wireshark is a network protocol analyzer, also called a packet sniffer. If Wireshark is not currently available on PC-B, you may download the latest version from http://www.wireshark.org/download.html and install it, as described in Part 4, Task 1, Step 3.

Step 4: Monitor S1 port Fa0/5 ping activity using Wireshark on PC-B.

a.   If Wireshark is available, start the application.

b.   On the main menu, click **Capture** > **Interfaces**.

c.   Click **Start** for the LAN interface adapter.

d.   Before pinging, delete the ARP table on PC-A to generate an ARP request.

```
C:\> arp -d *
```

Note: Administrative rights may be needed to run this command. Click **Start**, right-click **Command Prompt**, and select **Run as administrator**. Click **Yes** when the User Account Control dialog box displays.

Generate some traffic from PC-A (192.168.1.10) to R1 interface Fa0/1 (**192.168.1.1**) using ping. This traffic will go from S1 port Fa0/6 to S1 port Fa0/5. In addition, the traffic going from PC-A to R1 interface Fa0/1 is forwarded across the link between S1 and S2, and then S2 forwards this traffic to PC-B, where Wireshark is capturing the packets.

Note: The SPAN session is configured only on S1, and S2 operates as a normal switch.

```
C:\> ping 192.168.1.1
```

e.   Observe the results in Wireshark on PC-B. Notice the initial ARP request broadcast from PC-A to determine the MAC address of the R1 Fa0/1 interface with IP address 192.168.1.1 and the ARP reply from the R1 Cisco Ethernet interface. After the ARP request, the pings (echo requests) can be seen going from PC-A to R1 through the switch. Your screen should look similar to the one below.

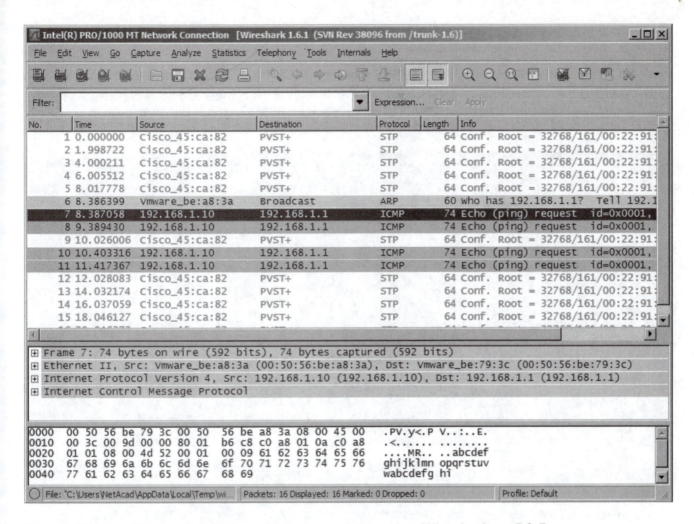

Step 5: Monitor S1 port Fa0/5 Nmap/Zenmap activity using Wireshark on PC-B.

a. Start the Zenmap on PC-A.

b. In the Target field, enter the IP address of R1 Fa0/1 (**192.168.1.1**).

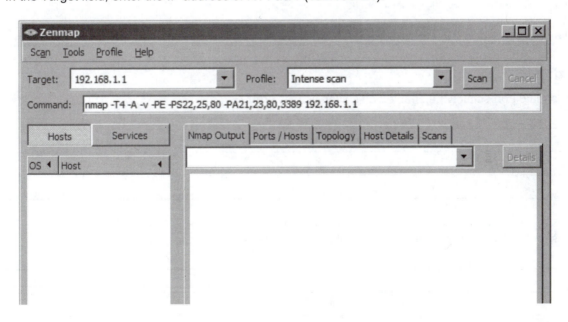

c. Clear the previous capture in Wireshark and start a new capture by clicking **Capture** > **Start**. When prompted, click **Continue without saving**.

d. In the Zenmap program, click **Scan** to start the simulated attack.

e. Observe the results on the Wireshark window on PC-B. Notice the number and types of ports tried by the simulated Zenmap attack from PC-A (192.168.1.10) to R1 Fa0/1 (192.168.1.1). A filter, such as **ip.host==192.168.1.1**, can be applied to the results. Your screen should look similar the following:

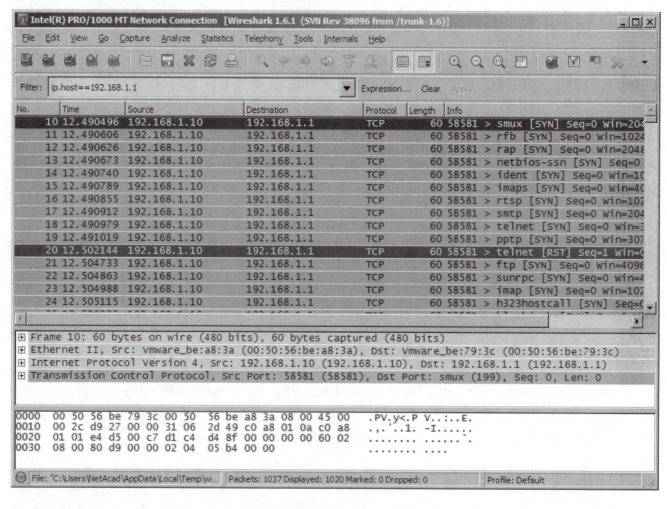

Reflection

1. Why should port security be enabled on switch access ports?

_____

_____

_____

_____

2. Why should port security be enabled on switch trunk ports?

_____

_____

_____

_____

3. Why should unused ports on a switch be disabled?

_____

_____

_____

_____

Router Interface Summary Table

Router Interface Summary				
Router Model	**Ethernet Interface #1**	**Ethernet Interface #2**	**Serial Interface #1**	**Serial Interface #2**
1800	Fast Ethernet 0/0 (Fa0/0)	Fast Ethernet 0/1 (Fa0/1)	Serial 0/0/0 (S0/0/0)	Serial 0/0/1 (S0/0/1)
1900	Gigabit Ethernet 0/0 (G0/0)	Gigabit Ethernet 0/1 (G0/1)	Serial 0/0/0 (S0/0/0)	Serial 0/0/1 (S0/0/1)
2801	Fast Ethernet 0/0 (Fa0/0)	Fast Ethernet 0/1 (Fa0/1)	Serial 0/1/0 (S0/1/0)	Serial 0/1/1 (S0/1/1)
2811	Fast Ethernet 0/0 (Fa0/0)	Fast Ethernet 0/1 (Fa0/1)	Serial 0/0/0 (S0/0/0)	Serial 0/0/1 (S0/0/1)
2900	Gigabit Ethernet 0/0 (G0/0)	Gigabit Ethernet 0/1 (G0/1)	Serial 0/0/0 (S0/0/0)	Serial 0/0/1 (S0/0/1)

Note: To find out how the router is configured, look at the interfaces to identify the type of router and how many interfaces the router has. There is no way to effectively list all the combinations of configurations for each router class. This table includes identifiers for the possible combinations of Ethernet and Serial interfaces in the device. The table does not include any other type of interface, even though a specific router may contain one. An example of this might be an ISDN BRI interface. The string in parenthesis is the legal abbreviation that can be used in Cisco IOS commands to represent the interface.

Chapter 7: Cryptographic Systems

Lab 7.5.1.1 - Exploring Encryption Methods

Objectives

Part 1: Decipher a Pre-encrypted Message Using the Vigenère Cipher

- Use an encrypted message, a cipher key, and the Vigenère cipher square to decipher the message.

Part 2: Create a Vigenère Cipher Encrypted Message and Decrypt It

- Work with a lab partner and agree on a secret password.
- Create a secret message using the Vigenère cipher and the key.
- Exchange messages and decipher them using the pre-shared key.
- Use an interactive Vigenère decoding tool to verify decryption.

Background

The Cisco IOS password encryption service uses a Cisco-proprietary algorithm that is based on the Vigenère cipher. Vigenère is an example of a common type of cipher mechanism called polyalphabetic substitution. Although not a strong encryption technique, Vigenère serves to illustrate a commonly used encryption and decryption process.

Note: Students can work in teams of two for this lab.

Required Resources

End user device with Internet access

Part 1: Decipher a Pre-encrypted Message Using the Vigenère Cipher

In Part 1, you analyze an encrypted message and decrypt it using a cipher key and the Vigenère cipher square.

Step 1: Review the encrypted message.

The following message has been encrypted using the Vigenère cipher:

VECIHXEJZXMA

Step 2: Review the cipher keyword.

The cipher keyword **TCPIP** was used to encrypt the message. The same keyword will be used to decrypt or decipher the message.

Step 3: Review the structure of the Vigenère square.

A standard Vigenère square or table is used with the keyword to decipher the message.

Step 4: Decrypt the message using the keyword and Vigenère square.

   a.   Use the table below to help you decrypt the message. Start by entering the letters of the encrypted
        message in the second row of cells, from left to right.

   b.   Enter the keyword TCPIP in the top row, repeating the letters until there is a keyword letter for each letter
        of the encrypted message, even if the keyword letters at the end do not represent the complete keyword.

   c.   Refer to the Vigenère square or table shown in Step 3 and find the horizontal row that starts with the first
        letter of the keyword (the letter T). Scan across that row and locate the first letter of the encrypted
        message in the row (the letter V). The letter at the top of the column where the encrypted message letter
        appears is the first letter of the decrypted message (the letter C).

   d.   Continue this process until you have decrypted the entire message and enter it in the following table.

Cipher Keyword												
Encrypted Message												
Decrypted Message												

Part 2: Create a Vigenère Cipher Encrypted Message and Decrypt It

In Part 2, work with a lab partner and agree on a secret password, referred to as the pre-shared key. Each lab partner creates a secret message using the Vigenère cipher and the key. Partners exchange messages and decipher them using their pre-shared key.

Note: If you do not have a partner, you can perform the steps by yourself.

Step 1: Determine the cipher keyword.

With your partner, establish a cipher keyword and enter it here.

_____

_____

Step 2: Create a plain text message and encrypt it (both partners).

a. Create a plain text (decrypted) message to be encrypted by your partner.

_____

_____

b. You can use the following table to help you encrypt the message. You can enter the unencrypted message and cipher keyword here, but do not let your partner see it.

c. In the Vigenère table, locate the row that starts with the first letter of the cipher keyword. Next locate the first letter to be encrypted at the top of the column in the table. The point (cell) at which the table row (key letter) and column (message letter) intersect is the first letter of the encrypted message. Continue this process until you have encrypted the entire message.

Note: This table is limited to messages of 12 characters. You can create longer messages if desired. Message encryption and decryption is not case-sensitive.

Cipher Keyword											
Encrypted Message											
Decrypted Message											

Step 3: Decrypt the message from your partner.

a. You can use the following table to help you decrypt your partner's encrypted message. Enter the encrypted message from your partner and the cipher keyword.

b. Use the same procedure described in Part 1, Step 4.

Note: This table is limited to messages of 12 characters. You can create longer messages if desired.

Cipher Keyword											
Encrypted Message											
Decrypted Message											

Step 4: Use an interactive decryption tool to confirm decryption.

a. An Internet search for "Vigenère decode" shows that various cipher encryption and decryption tools are available. Many of these are interactive.

b. One interactive tool is located at http://sharkysoft.com/vigenere/1.0/. At this site, enter the encrypted message from your partner in the top part of the screen and the cipher key in the middle. Click **Decode** to see the clear text version of the message. You can also use this tool to encrypt messages.

c. The following example shows using Sharky's Vigenère Cipher tool for decoding the encrypted message from Part 1.

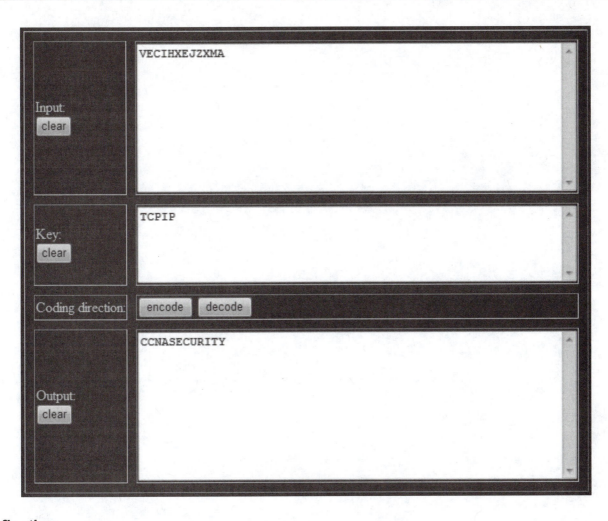

Reflection

1. Could the Vigenère cipher be used to decode messages in the field without a computer?

    _____

    _____

    _____

    _____

2. Search the Internet for Vigenère cipher cracking tools. Is the Vigenère cipher considered a strong encryption system that is difficult to crack?

    _____

    _____

    _____

    _____

Chapter 8: Implementing Virtual Private Networks

Lab 8.7.1.1 - Configuring a Site-to-Site VPN Using Cisco IOS and CCP

Topology

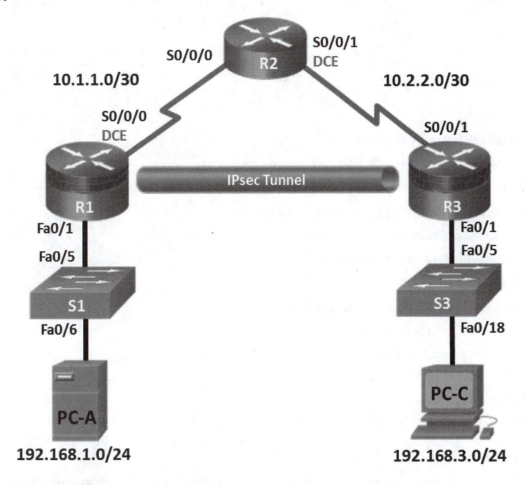

Note: ISR G2 devices use GigabitEthernet interfaces instead of FastEthernet interfaces.

IP Addressing Table

Device	Interface	IP Address	Subnet Mask	Default Gateway	Switch Port
R1	Fa0/1	192.168.1.1	255.255.255.0	N/A	S1 Fa0/5
	S0/0/0 (DCE)	10.1.1.1	255.255.255.252	N/A	N/A
R2	S0/0/0	10.1.1.2	255.255.255.252	N/A	N/A
	S0/0/1 (DCE)	10.2.2.2	255.255.255.252	N/A	N/A
R3	Fa0/1	192.168.3.1	255.255.255.0	N/A	S3 Fa0/5
	S0/0/1	10.2.2.1	255.255.255.252	N/A	N/A
PC-A	NIC	192.168.1.3	255.255.255.0	192.168.1.1	S1 Fa0/6
PC-C	NIC	192.168.3.3	255.255.255.0	192.168.3.1	S3 Fa0/18

Objectives

Part 1: Configure Basic Device Settings

- Configure hostnames, interface IP addresses, and access passwords.
- Configure the OSPF dynamic routing protocol.

Part 2: Configure a Site-to-Site VPN Using Cisco IOS

- Configure IPsec VPN settings on R1 and R3.
- Verify site-to-site IPsec VPN configuration.
- Test IPsec VPN operation.

Part 3: Configure a Site-to-Site VPN Using CCP

- Configure IPsec VPN settings on R1.
- Create a mirror configuration for R3.
- Apply the mirror configuration to R3.
- Verify the configuration.
- Test the VPN configuration using CCP.

Background / Scenario

VPNs can provide a secure method of transmitting data over a public network, such as the Internet. VPN connections can help reduce the costs associated with leased lines. Site-to-Site VPNs typically provide a secure (IPsec or other) tunnel between a branch office and a central office. Another common implementation that uses VPN technology is remote access to a corporate office from a telecommuter location, such as a small office or home office.

In this lab, you will build and configure a multi-router network, and then use Cisco IOS and CCP to configure a site-to-site IPsec VPN and then test it. The IPsec VPN tunnel is from router R1 to router R3 via R2. R2 acts as a pass-through and has no knowledge of the VPN. IPsec provides secure transmission of sensitive information over unprotected networks, such as the Internet. IPsec acts at the network layer, protecting and authenticating IP packets between participating IPsec devices (peers), such as Cisco routers.

The router commands and output in this lab are from a Cisco 1841 router using Cisco IOS software, release 15.1(4)M8 (Advanced IP Services image). Other routers and Cisco IOS versions can be used. See the Router Interface Summary Table at the end of the lab to determine which interface identifiers to use based on the equipment in the lab. Depending on the model of the router, the commands available and output produced may vary from what is shown in this lab.

Note: Make sure that the routers and the switches have been erased and have no startup configurations.

Required Resources

- 3 Routers (Cisco 1841 with Cisco IOS Release 15.1(4)M8 Advanced IP Services image or comparable)
- 2 Switches (Cisco 2960 or comparable)
- 2 PCs (Windows Vista or Windows 7 with CCP 2.5, latest Java version, Internet Explorer, and Flash Player)
- Serial and Ethernet cables as shown in the topology
- Console cables to configure Cisco networking devices

CCP Notes:

- If the PC on which CCP is installed is running Windows Vista or Windows 7, it may be necessary to right-click the **CCP** icon or menu item, and select **Run as administrator**.
- To run CCP, it may be necessary to temporarily disable antivirus programs and O/S firewalls. Make sure that all pop-up blockers are turned off in the browser.

Part 1: Configure Basic Device Settings

In Part 1, you will set up the network topology and configure basic settings, such as the interface IP addresses, dynamic routing, device access, and passwords.

Note: All tasks should be performed on R1, R2, and R3. The procedure for R1 is shown here as an example.

Step 1: Cable the network as shown in the topology.

Attach the devices as shown in the topology diagram, and cable as necessary.

Step 2: Configure basic settings for each router.

a. Configure hostnames, as shown in the topology.

b. Configure the interface IP addresses, as shown in the IP Addressing Table.

c. Configure a clock rate of **64000** for the serial router interfaces with a DCE serial cable attached.

Step 3: Disable DNS lookup.

To prevent the router from attempting to translate incorrectly entered commands, disable DNS lookup.

Step 4: Configure the OSPF routing protocol on R1, R2, and R3.

a. On R1, use the following commands:

```
R1(config)# router ospf 101
R1(config-router)# network 192.168.1.0 0.0.0.255 area 0
R1(config-router)# network 10.1.1.0 0.0.0.3 area 0
```

b. On R2, use the following commands:

```
R2(config)# router ospf 101
R2(config-router)# network 10.1.1.0 0.0.0.3 area 0
R2(config-router)# network 10.2.2.0 0.0.0.3 area 0
```

c. On R3, use the following commands:

```
R3(config)# router ospf 101
```

```
R3(config-router)# network 192.168.3.0 0.0.0.255 area 0
R3(config-router)# network 10.2.2.0 0.0.0.3 area 0
```

Step 5: Configure PC host IP settings.

a. Configure a static IP address, subnet mask, and default gateway for PC-A, as shown in the IP Addressing Table.

b. Configure a static IP address, subnet mask, and default gateway for PC-C, as shown in the IP Addressing Table.

Step 6: Verify basic network connectivity.

a. Ping from R1 to the R3 Fa0/1 interface at IP address **192.168.3.1**.

If the pings are unsuccessful, troubleshoot the basic device configurations before continuing.

b. Ping from PC-A on the R1 LAN to PC-C on the R3 LAN.

If the pings are unsuccessful, troubleshoot the basic device configurations before continuing.

Note: If you can ping from PC-A to PC-C, you have demonstrated that the OSPF routing protocol is configured and functioning correctly. If you cannot ping, but the device interfaces are up and IP addresses are correct, use the **show run** and **show ip route** commands to help identify routing protocol-related problems.

Step 7: Configure a minimum password length.

Note: Passwords in this lab are set to a minimum of 10 characters, but are relatively simple for the benefit of performing the lab. More complex passwords are recommended in a production network.

Use the **security passwords** command to set a minimum password length of **10** characters.

```
R1(config)# security passwords min-length 10
```

Step 8: Configure the basic console and vty lines.

a. Configure **ciscoconpass** as the console password and enable login for R1. For additional security, the **exec-timeout** command causes the line to log out after **5** minutes of inactivity. The **logging synchronous** command prevents console messages from interrupting command entry.

b. Configure **ciscovtypass** as the vty line password and enable login on R1. For additional security, the **exec-timeout** command causes the line to log out after **5** minutes of inactivity.

c. Repeat these configurations on both R2 and R3.

Step 9: Encrypt clear text passwords.

a. Use the **service password-encryption** command to encrypt the console, aux, and vty passwords.

```
R1(config)# service password-encryption
```

b. Issue the **show run** command. Can you read the console, aux, and vty passwords? Explain.

_____

_____

c. Repeat this configuration on both R2 and R3.

Step 10: Save the basic running configuration for all three routers.

Save the running configuration to the startup configuration from the privileged EXEC mode prompt on R1, R2, and R3.

```
R1# copy running-config startup-config
```

Step 11: Save the configuration on R1 and R3 for later restoration.

Save the R1 and R3 running configurations as text files so the configurations can be used later, in Part 3 of this lab, to restore the routers to configure the VPN with CCP.

Part 2: Configure a Site-to-Site VPN with Cisco IOS

In Part 2 of this lab, you will configure an IPsec VPN tunnel between R1 and R3 that passes through R2. You will configure R1 and R3 using the Cisco IOS CLI. You then review and test the resulting configuration.

Task 1: Configure IPsec VPN Settings on R1 and R3.

Step 1: Verify connectivity from the R1 LAN to the R3 LAN.

In this task, you will verify that with no tunnel in place, the PC-A on the R1 LAN can ping the PC-C on R3 LAN.

From PC-A, ping the PC-C IP address of **192.168.3.3**.

```
PC-A:\> ping 192.168.3.3
```

If the pings are unsuccessful, troubleshoot the basic device configurations before continuing.

Step 2: Enable IKE policies on R1 and R3.

IPsec is an open framework that allows the exchange of security protocols as new technologies, such as encryption algorithms, are developed.

There are two central configuration elements to the implementation of an IPsec VPN:

* Implement Internet Key Exchange (IKE) parameters

* Implement IPsec parameters

a. Verify that IKE is supported and enabled.

IKE Phase 1 defines the key exchange method used to pass and validate IKE policies between peers. In IKE Phase 2, the peers exchange and match IPsec policies for the authentication and encryption of data traffic.

IKE must be enabled for IPsec to function. IKE is enabled, by default, on IOS images with cryptographic feature sets. If it is disabled, you can enable it with the **crypto isakmp enable** command. Use this command to verify that the router IOS supports IKE and that it is enabled.

```
R1(config)# crypto isakmp enable
```

```
R3(config)# crypto isakmp enable
```

Note: If you cannot execute this command on the router, you must upgrade the IOS image that includes the Cisco cryptographic services.

b. Establish an Internet Security Association and Key Management Protocol (ISAKMP) policy and view the available options.

To allow IKE Phase 1 negotiation, you must create an ISAKMP policy and configure a peer association involving that ISAKMP policy. An ISAKMP policy defines the authentication and encryption algorithms and hash function used to send control traffic between the two VPN endpoints. When an ISAKMP security association has been accepted by the IKE peers, IKE Phase 1 has been completed. IKE Phase 2 parameters will be configured later.

Issue the **crypto isakmp policy number** global configuration mode command on R1 for policy 10.

```
R1(config)# crypto isakmp policy 10
```

c. View the various IKE parameters available using Cisco IOS help by typing a question mark (**?**).

```
R1(config-isakmp)# ?
ISAKMP commands:
   authentication  Set authentication method for protection suite
   default         Set a command to its defaults
   encryption      Set encryption algorithm for protection suite
   exit            Exit from ISAKMP protection suite configuration mode
   group           Set the Diffie-Hellman group
   hash            Set hash algorithm for protection suite
   lifetime        Set lifetime for ISAKMP security association
   no              Negate a command or set its defaults
```

Step 3: Configure ISAKMP policy parameters on R1 and R3.

Your choice of an encryption algorithm determines how confidential the control channel between the endpoints is. The hash algorithm controls data integrity, ensuring that the data received from a peer has not been tampered with in transit. The authentication type ensures that the packet was, indeed, sent and signed by the remote peer. The Diffie-Hellman group is used to create a secret key shared by the peers that has not been sent across the network.

a. Configure an ISAKMP policy with a priority of **10**. Use **pre-shared key** as the authentication type,.**aes 256** for the encryption algorithm, **sha** as the hash algorithm, and Diffie-Hellman group **5** key exchange. Give the policy a lifetime of **3600** seconds (one hour).

   Note: Older versions of Cisco IOS do not support AES 256 encryption and SHA as a hash algorithm. Substitute whatever encryption and hashing algorithm your router supports. Ensure that the same changes are made on the other VPN endpoint to be in sync.

```
R1(config)# crypto isakmp policy 10
R1(config-isakmp)# authentication pre-share
R1(config-isakmp)# encryption aes 256
R1(config-isakmp)# hash sha
R1(config-isakmp)# group 5
R1(config-isakmp)# lifetime 3600
R1(config-isakmp)# end
```

b. Configure the same policy on R3.

```
R3(config)# crypto isakmp policy 10
R3(config-isakmp)# authentication pre-share
R3(config-isakmp)# encryption aes 256
R3(config-isakmp)# hash sha
R3(config-isakmp)# group 5
R3(config-isakmp)# lifetime 3600
R3(config-isakmp)# end
```

c. Verify the IKE policy with the **show crypto isakmp policy** command.

```
R1# show crypto isakmp policy
Global IKE policy
Protection suite of priority 10
        encryption algorithm:   AES - Advanced Encryption Standard (256 bit keys).
        hash algorithm:         Secure Hash Standard
        authentication method:  Pre-Shared Key
        Diffie-Hellman group:   #5 (1536 bit)
        lifetime:               3600 seconds, no volume limit
```

Step 4: Configure pre-shared keys.

Because pre-shared keys are used as the authentication method in the IKE policy, a key must be configured on each router that points to the other VPN endpoint. These keys must match for authentication to be successful. The global configuration mode **crypto isakmp key key-string address address** command is used to enter a pre-shared key. Use the IP address of the remote peer, the remote interface that the peer would use to route traffic to the local router.

Which IP addresses should you use to configure the IKE peers, given the topology diagram and IP addressing table?

_____

_____

_____

a. Each IP address that is used to configure the IKE peers is also referred to as the IP address of the remote VPN endpoint. Configure the pre-shared key of **cisco123** on router R1. Production networks should use a complex key. This command points to the remote peer R3 S0/0/1 IP address.

```
R1(config)# crypto isakmp key cisco123 address 10.2.2.1
```

b. Configure the pre-shared key of **cisco123** on router R3. The command for R3 points to the R1 S0/0/0 IP address.

```
R3(config)# crypto isakmp key cisco123 address 10.1.1.1
```

Step 5: Configure the IPsec transform set and life times.

a. The IPsec transform set is another crypto configuration parameter that routers negotiate to form a security association. To create an IPsec transform set, use the **crypto ipsec transform-set tag** command. Use **?** to see which parameters are available.

```
R1(config)# crypto ipsec transform-set 50 ?
  ah-md5-hmac    AH-HMAC-MD5 transform
  ah-sha-hmac    AH-HMAC-SHA transform
  comp-lzs       IP Compression using the LZS compression algorithm
  esp-3des       ESP transform using 3DES(EDE) cipher (168 bits)
  esp-aes        ESP transform using AES cipher
  esp-des        ESP transform using DES cipher (56 bits)
  esp-md5-hmac   ESP transform using HMAC-MD5 auth
  esp-null       ESP transform w/o cipher
  esp-seal       ESP transform using SEAL cipher (160 bits)
  esp-sha-hmac   ESP transform using HMAC-SHA auth
```

b. On R1 and R3, create a transform set with tag **50** and use an Encapsulating Security Protocol (ESP) transform with an AES 256 cipher with ESP and the SHA hash function. The transform sets must match.

```
R1(config)# crypto ipsec transform-set 50 esp-aes 256 esp-sha-hmac
R1(cfg-crypto-trans)# exit


R3(config)# crypto ipsec transform-set 50 esp-aes 256 esp-sha-hmac
R3(cfg-crypto-trans)# exit
```

What is the function of the IPsec transform set?

_____

_____

_____

_____

c. You can also change the IPsec security association life times from the default of 3600 seconds. On R1 and R3, set the IPsec security association life time to 30 minutes, or **1800** seconds.

```
R1(config)# crypto ipsec security-association lifetime seconds 1800

R3(config)# crypto ipsec security-association lifetime seconds 1800
```

Step 6: Define interesting traffic.

To make use of the IPsec encryption with the VPN, it is necessary to define extended access lists to tell the router which traffic to encrypt. A packet that is permitted by an access list used for defining IPsec traffic is encrypted if the IPsec session is configured correctly. A packet that is denied by one of these access lists is not dropped, but sent unencrypted. Also, like any other access list, there is an implicit deny at the end, which, in this case, means the default action is to not encrypt traffic. If there is no IPsec security association correctly configured, no traffic is encrypted, and traffic is forwarded as unencrypted.

In this scenario, the traffic you want to encrypt is traffic going from R1's Ethernet LAN to R3's Ethernet LAN, or vice versa. These access lists are used outbound on the VPN endpoint interfaces and must mirror each other.

a. Configure the IPsec VPN interesting traffic ACL on R1.

```
R1(config)# access-list 101 permit ip 192.168.1.0 0.0.0.255 192.168.3.0 0.0.0.255
```

b. Configure the IPsec VPN interesting traffic ACL on R3.

```
R3(config)# access-list 101 permit ip 192.168.3.0 0.0.0.255 192.168.1.0 0.0.0.255
```

Does IPsec evaluate whether the access lists are mirrored as a requirement to negotiate its security association?

_____

_____

_____

Step 7: Create and apply a crypto map.

A crypto map associates traffic that matches an access list to a peer and various IKE and IPsec settings. After the crypto map is created, it can be applied to one or more interfaces. The interfaces that it is applied to should be the ones facing the IPsec peer.

To create a crypto map, use **crypto map name sequence-num type** command in global configuration mode to enter crypto map configuration mode for that sequence number. Multiple crypto map statements can belong to the same crypto map and are evaluated in ascending numerical order. Enter crypto map configuration mode on R1. Use a type of ipsec-isakmp, which means IKE is used to establish IPsec security associations.

a. Create the crypto map on R1, name it **CMAP**, and use **10** as the sequence number. A message displays after the command is issued.

```
R1(config)# crypto map CMAP 10 ipsec-isakmp
% NOTE: This new crypto map will remain disabled until a peer
and a valid access list have been configured.
```

b. Use the **match address access-list** command to specify which access list defines which traffic to encrypt.

```
R1(config-crypto-map)# match address 101
```

c. To view the list of possible **set** commands that you can do in a crypto map, use the help function.

```
R1(config-crypto-map)# set ?
  identity              Identity restriction.
  ip                    Interface Internet Protocol config commands
  isakmp-profile        Specify isakmp Profile
  nat                   Set NAT translation
  peer                  Allowed Encryption/Decryption peer.
  pfs                   Specify pfs settings
  reverse-route         Reverse Route Injection.
  security-association  Security association parameters
  transform-set         Specify list of transform sets in priority order
```

d. Setting a peer IP or hostname is required. Set it to R3's remote VPN endpoint interface using the following command.

```
R1(config-crypto-map)# set peer 10.2.2.1
```

e. Hard code the transform set to be used with this peer, using the **set transform-set tag** command. Set the perfect forwarding secrecy type using the **set pfs type** command, and also modify the default IPsec security association life time with the **set security-association lifetime seconds seconds** command.

```
R1(config-crypto-map)# set pfs group5
R1(config-crypto-map)# set transform-set 50
R1(config-crypto-map)# set security-association lifetime seconds 900
R1(config-crypto-map)# exit
```

f. Create a mirrored matching crypto map on R3.

```
R3(config)# crypto map CMAP 10 ipsec-isakmp
R3(config-crypto-map)# match address 101
R3(config-crypto-map)# set peer 10.1.1.1
R3(config-crypto-map)# set pfs group5
R3(config-crypto-map)# set transform-set 50
R3(config-crypto-map)# set security-association lifetime seconds 900
R3(config-crypto-map)# exit
```

g. The last step is applying the crypto map to interfaces.

Note: The security associations (SAs) are not established until the crypto map has been activated by interesting traffic. The router generates a notification that crypto is now on.

Apply the crypto maps to the appropriate interfaces on R1 and R3.

```
R1(config)# interface S0/0/0
R1(config-if)# crypto map CMAP
*Jan 28 04:09:09.150: %CRYPTO-6-ISAKMP_ON_OFF: ISAKMP is ON
R1(config)# end


R3(config)# interface S0/0/1
R3(config-if)# crypto map CMAP
*Jan 28 04:10:54.138: %CRYPTO-6-ISAKMP_ON_OFF: ISAKMP is ON
R3(config)# end
```

Task 2: Verify the Site-to-Site IPsec VPN Configuration.

Step 1: Verify the IPsec configuration on R1 and R3.

   a. Previously, you used the **show crypto isakmp policy** command to display the configured ISAKMP policies on the router. Similarly, the **show crypto ipsec transform-set** command displays the configured IPsec policies in the form of the transform sets.

```
R1# show crypto ipsec transform-set
Transform set 50: { esp-256-aes esp-sha-hmac  }
   will negotiate = { Tunnel,  },

Transform set #$!default_transform_set_1: { esp-aes esp-sha-hmac  }
  will negotiate = { Transport,  },

Transform set #$!default_transform_set_0: { esp-3des esp-sha-hmac  }
   will negotiate = { Transport,  },

R3# show crypto ipsec transform-set
Transform set 50: { esp-256-aes esp-sha-hmac  }
   will negotiate = { Tunnel,  },

Transform set #$!default_transform_set_1: { esp-aes esp-sha-hmac  }
   will negotiate = { Transport,  },

Transform set #$!default_transform_set_0: { esp-3des esp-sha-hmac  }
   will negotiate = { Transport,  },
```

   b. Use the **show crypto map** command to display the crypto maps that will be applied to the router.

```
R1# show crypto map
Crypto Map "CMAP" 10 ipsec-isakmp
        Peer = 10.2.2.1
        Extended IP access list 101
            access-list 101 permit ip 192.168.1.0 0.0.0.255 192.168.3.0 0.0.0.255
        Current peer: 10.2.2.1
        Security association lifetime: 4608000 kilobytes/900 seconds
        Responder-Only (Y/N): N
        PFS (Y/N): Y
        DH group:  group5
        Transform sets={
                50:  { esp-256-aes esp-sha-hmac  } ,
        }
        Interfaces using crypto map CMAP:
                Serial0/0/0

R3# show crypto map
Crypto Map "CMAP" 10 ipsec-isakmp
        Peer = 10.1.1.1
        Extended IP access list 101
            access-list 101 permit ip 192.168.3.0 0.0.0.255 192.168.1.0 0.0.0.255
        Current peer: 10.1.1.1
        Security association lifetime: 4608000 kilobytes/900 seconds
```

```
            Responder-Only (Y/N): N
            PFS (Y/N): Y
            DH group:  group5
            Transform sets={
                    50:  { esp-256-aes esp-sha-hmac  } ,
            }
            Interfaces using crypto map CMAP:
                    Serial0/0/1
```

Note: The output of these **show** commands does not change if interesting traffic goes across the connection. You test various types of traffic in the next task.

Task 3: Verify the IPsec VPN Operation.

Step 1: Display isakmp security associations.

The **show crypto isakmp sa** command reveals that no IKE SAs exist yet. When interesting traffic is sent, this command output changes.

```
R1# show crypto isakmp sa
IPv4 Crypto ISAKMP SA
dst             src             state           conn-id status


IPv6 Crypto ISAKMP SA
```

Step 2: Display IPsec security associations.

The **show crypto ipsec sa** command shows the unused SA between R1 and R3.

Note: The number of packets sent across and the lack of any security associations listed toward the bottom of the output. The output for R1 is shown here.

```
R1# show crypto ipsec sa

interface: Serial0/0/0
    Crypto map tag: CMAP, local addr 10.1.1.1

   protected vrf: (none)
   local  ident (addr/mask/prot/port): (192.168.1.0/255.255.255.0/0/0)
   remote ident (addr/mask/prot/port): (192.168.3.0/255.255.255.0/0/0)
   current_peer 10.2.2.1 port 500
     PERMIT, flags={origin_is_acl,}
    #pkts encaps: 0, #pkts encrypt: 0, #pkts digest: 0
    #pkts decaps: 0, #pkts decrypt: 0, #pkts verify: 0
    #pkts compressed: 0, #pkts decompressed: 0
    #pkts not compressed: 0, #pkts compr. failed: 0
    #pkts not decompressed: 0, #pkts decompress failed: 0
    #send errors 0, #recv errors 0

     local crypto endpt.: 10.1.1.1, remote crypto endpt.: 10.2.2.1
     path mtu 1500, ip mtu 1500, ip mtu idb Serial0/0/0
     current outbound spi: 0x0(0)
     PFS (Y/N): N, DH group: none

     inbound esp sas:
```

```
        inbound ah sas:

        inbound pcp sas:

        outbound esp sas:

        outbound ah sas:

        outbound pcp sas:
```

Why have no SAs been negotiated?

_____

_____

_____

Step 3: Generate some uninteresting test traffic and observe the results.

a. Ping from R1 to the R3 S0/0/1 interface IP address **10.2.2.1**. These pings should be successful.

b. Issue the **show crypto isakmp sa** command.

c. Ping from R1 to the R3 Fa01 interface IP address **192.168.3.1**. These pings should be successful.

d. Issue the **show crypto isakmp sa** command again. Was an SA created for these pings? Explain.

_____

_____

_____

e. Issue the **debug ip ospf hello** command. You should see OSPF hello packets passing between R1 and R3.

```
R1# debug ip ospf hello
OSPF hello events debugging is on
R1#
*Apr  7 18:04:46.467: OSPF: Send hello to 224.0.0.5 area 0 on FastEthernet0/1 from
192.168.1.1
*Apr  7 18:04:50.055: OSPF: Send hello to 224.0.0.5 area 0 on Serial0/0/0 from
10.1.1.1
*Apr  7 18:04:52.463: OSPF: Rcv hello from 10.2.2.2 area 0 from Serial0/0/0 10.1.1.2
*Apr  7 18:04:52.463: OSPF: End of hello processing
*Apr  7 18:04:55.675: OSPF: Send hello to 224.0.0.5 area 0 on FastEthernet0/1 from
192.168.1.1
*Apr  7 18:04:59.387: OSPF: Send hello to 224.0.0.5 area 0 on Serial0/0/0 from
10.1.1.1
*Apr  7 18:05:02.431: OSPF: Rcv hello from 10.2.2.2 area 0 from Serial0/0/0 10.1.1.2
*Apr  7 18:05:02.431: OSPF: End of hello processing
```

f. Turn off debugging with the **no debug ip ospf hello** or **undebug all** command.

g. Re-issue the **show crypto isakmp sa** command. Was an SA created between R1 and R3? Explain.

_____

_____

Step 4: Generate some interesting test traffic and observe the results.

a. Use an extended ping from R1 to the R3 Fa01 interface IP address **192.168.3.1**. Extended ping allows you to control the source address of the packets. Respond as shown in the following example. Press **Enter** to accept the defaults, except where a specific response is indicated.

```
R1# ping
Protocol [ip]:
Target IP address: 192.168.3.1
Repeat count [5]:
Datagram size [100]:
Timeout in seconds [2]:
Extended commands [n]: y
Source address or interface: 192.168.1.1
Type of service [0]:
Set DF bit in IP header? [no]:
Validate reply data? [no]:
Data pattern [0xABCD]:
Loose, Strict, Record, Timestamp, Verbose[none]:
Sweep range of sizes [n]:
Type escape sequence to abort.
Sending 5, 100-byte ICMP Echos to 192.168.3.1, timeout is 2 seconds:

Packet sent with a source address of 192.168.1.1
..!!!
Success rate is 100 percent (3/5), round-trip min/avg/max = 92/92/92 ms
```

b. Re-issue the **show crypto isakmp sa** command.

```
R1# show crypto isakmp sa
IPv4 Crypto ISAKMP SA
dst             src             state           conn-id status
10.2.2.1        10.1.1.1        QM_IDLE            1001 ACTIVE

IPv6 Crypto ISAKMP SA
```

Why was an SA created between R1 and R3 this time?

_____

_____

_____

What are the endpoints of the IPsec VPN tunnel?

_____

_____

_____

c. Ping from PC-A to PC-C. If the pings were successful, issue the **show crypto ipsec sa** command. How many packets have been transformed between R1 and R3?

_____

_____

_____

```
R1# show crypto ipsec sa

interface: Serial0/0/0
    Crypto map tag: CMAP, local addr 10.1.1.1

   protected vrf: (none)
   local  ident (addr/mask/prot/port): (192.168.1.0/255.255.255.0/0/0)
   remote ident (addr/mask/prot/port): (192.168.3.0/255.255.255.0/0/0)
   current_peer 10.2.2.1 port 500
     PERMIT, flags={origin_is_acl,}
    #pkts encaps: 7, #pkts encrypt: 7, #pkts digest: 7
    #pkts decaps: 7, #pkts decrypt: 7, #pkts verify: 7
    #pkts compressed: 0, #pkts decompressed: 0
    #pkts not compressed: 0, #pkts compr. failed: 0
    #pkts not decompressed: 0, #pkts decompress failed: 0
    #send errors 2, #recv errors 0

     local crypto endpt.: 10.1.1.1, remote crypto endpt.: 10.2.2.1
     path mtu 1500, ip mtu 1500, ip mtu idb Serial0/0/0
     current outbound spi: 0xC1DD058(203280472)

     inbound esp sas:
      spi: 0xDF57120F(3747025423)
        transform: esp-256-aes esp-sha-hmac ,
        in use settings ={Tunnel, }
        conn id: 2005, flow_id: FPGA:5, crypto map: CMAP
        sa timing: remaining key lifetime (k/sec): (4485195/877)
        IV size: 16 bytes
        replay detection support: Y
        Status: ACTIVE

     inbound ah sas:

     inbound pcp sas:

     outbound esp sas:
      spi: 0xC1DD058(203280472)
        transform: esp-256-aes esp-sha-hmac ,
        in use settings ={Tunnel, }
        conn id: 2006, flow_id: FPGA:6, crypto map: CMAP
        sa timing: remaining key lifetime (k/sec): (4485195/877)
```

```
        IV size: 16 bytes
        replay detection support: Y
        Status: ACTIVE

    outbound ah sas:

    outbound pcp sas:
```

d. The previous example used pings to generate interesting traffic. What other types of traffic would result in an SA forming and tunnel establishment?

_____

_____

_____

_____

_____

Part 3: Configure a Site-to-Site IPsec VPN with CCP

In Part 3, configure an IPsec VPN tunnel between R1 and R3 that passes through R2. Task 1 will restore the router to the basic settings using your saved configurations. In Task 2, configure R1 using Cisco CCP. In Task 3, mirror those settings to R3 using CCP utilities. Finally, review and test the resulting configuration.

Task 1: Restore Router R1 and R3 to the Basic Settings.

To avoid confusion as to what was entered in Part 2, start by restoring R1 and R3 to the basic configuration as described in Part 1 of this lab.

Step 1: Restore the basic configuration.

a. Connect to the R1 console using the **ciscoconpass** password.

b. Enter privileged EXEC mode.

c. Reload the router and enter **no** when prompted to save the configuration.

```
R1# reload
```

```
System configuration has been modified. Save? [yes/no]: no
Proceed with reload? [confirm]
```

d. Connect to the R1 console using the **ciscoconpass** password.

e. Enter privileged EXEC mode.

f. Repeat on R3.

Step 2: Verify connectivity.

Test connectivity by pinging from host PC-A to PC-C. If the pings are unsuccessful, troubleshoot the router and PC configurations before continuing.

Task 2: Configure IPsec VPN Settings on R1 Using CCP.

Step 1: Configure a username and password pair and enable HTTP router access.

a. From the CLI, configure a username **admin** and password **cisco12345** to use with CCP on R1 and R3.

```
R1(config)# username admin privilege 15 secret cisco12345

R3(config)# username admin privilege 15 secret cisco12345
```

b. Enable the secure HTTP server on R1 and R3.

```
R1(config)#ip http secure-server

R3(config)#ip http secure-server
```

c. Configure local database authentication of web sessions to support CCP connectivity.

```
R1(config)# ip http authentication local

R3(config)# ip http authentication local
```

Step 2: Access CCP and discover R1.

a. Run the CCP application on PC-A. In the Select/Manage Community window, in the Hostname/Address field, enter the R1 IP address **192.168.1.1**, in the Username field, enter **admin**, and in the Password field, **cisco12345**. Click the **Connect Securely** check box, and then click **OK**.

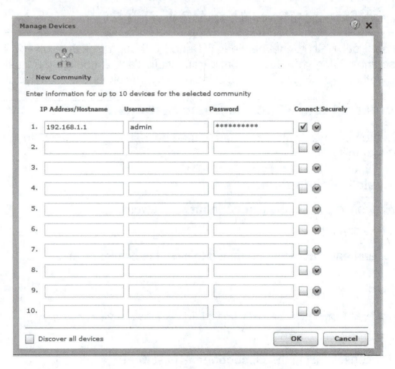

b. At the CCP Dashboard, click **Discover** to discover and connect to R1. If the discovery process fails, click **Discover Details** to determine the problem and resolve the issue.

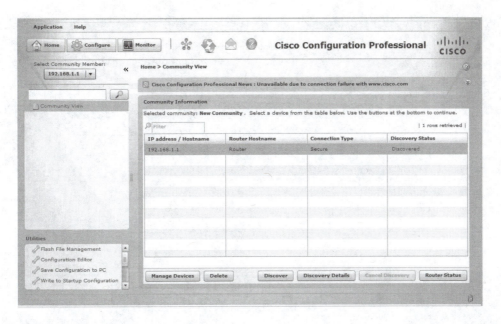

Step 3: Start the CCP VPN wizard to configure R1.

a. On the CCP menu bar, click **Configure**, and click **Security** > **VPN** > **Site-to-Site VPN**. Read through the description of this option.

What must you know to complete the configuration?

_____

_____

_____

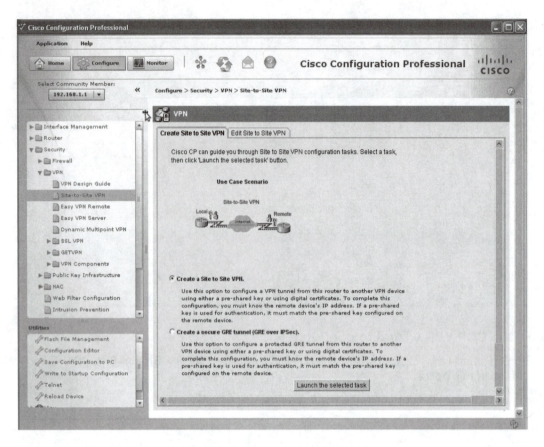

b. Click **Launch the selected task** to begin the CCP Site-to-Site VPN wizard.

c. On the initial Site-to-Site VPN Wizard window, the **Quick Setup** option is selected by default. Click **View Defaults** to see what settings this option uses. What type of encryption does the default transform set use?

_____

d. In the initial Site-to-Site VPN wizard window, choose the **Step by Step wizard**, and then click **Next**. Why would you use this option over the Quick setup option?

_____

_____

Step 4: Configure basic VPN connection information settings.

a. In the VPN Connection Information window, select the interface for the connection, which should be R1 **Serial0/0/0**.

b. In the Peer Identity section, select **Peer with static IP address**, and enter the IP address of remote peer R3 S0/0/1 (**10.2.2.1**).

c. In the Authentication section, click **Pre-shared Keys**, and enter the pre-shared VPN key **cisco12345**. Re-enter the key for confirmation. This key authenticates the initial exchange to establish the Security Association between devices. When finished, your screen should look similar to the following. When you have entered these settings correctly, click **Next**.

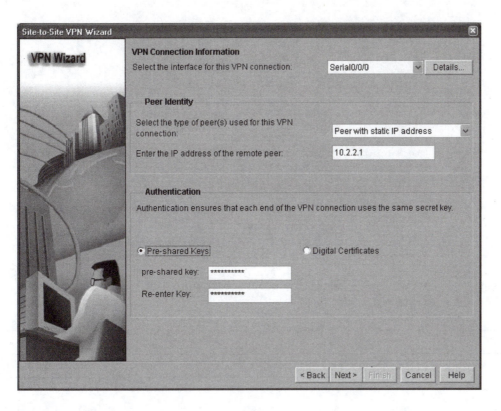

Step 5: Configure IKE policy parameters.

IKE policies are used while setting up the control channel between the two VPN endpoints for key exchange. This is also referred to as the IKE SA. In contrast, the IPsec policy is used during IKE Phase II to negotiate an IPsec SA to pass target data traffic.

a. In the IKE Proposals window, a default policy proposal is displayed. You can use this one or create a new one. What function does this IKE proposal serve?

_____

_____

_____

b. Click **Add** to create a new IKE policy.

c. Set up the security policy as shown in the Add IKE Policy dialog box. These settings are matched later on R3. When finished, click **OK** to add the policy, and click **Next**.

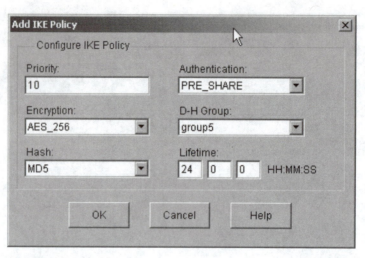

d. For assistance in answering the following questions, click **Help**. What is the function of the encryption algorithm in the IKE policy?

_____

_____

_____

What is the purpose of the hash function?

_____

_____

_____

What function does the authentication method serve?

_____

_____

_____

How is the Diffie-Hellman group in the IKE policy used?

_____

_____

_____

What event happens at the end of the IKE policy's lifetime?

_____

_____

_____

Step 6: Configure a transform set.

The transform set is the IPsec policy used to encrypt, hash, and authenticate packets that pass through the tunnel. The transform set is the IKE Phase 2 policy.

a. A CCP default transform set is displayed. Click **Add** to create a new transform set.

b. Set up the transform set, as shown in the Add Transform Set dialog box. These settings are matched later on R3. When finished, click **OK** to add the transform set, and click **Next**.

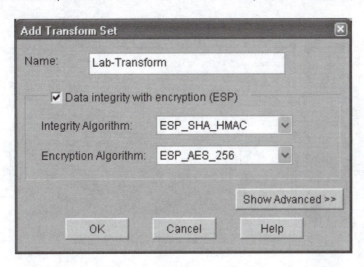

Step 7: Define interesting traffic.

You must define interesting traffic to be protected through the VPN tunnel. Interesting traffic is defined through an access list applied to the router. By entering the source and destination subnets that you would like to protect through the VPN tunnel, CCP generates the appropriate simple access list for you.

In the Traffic to protect window, enter the information as shown below. These are the opposite of the settings configured on R3 later in the lab. When finished, click **Next**.

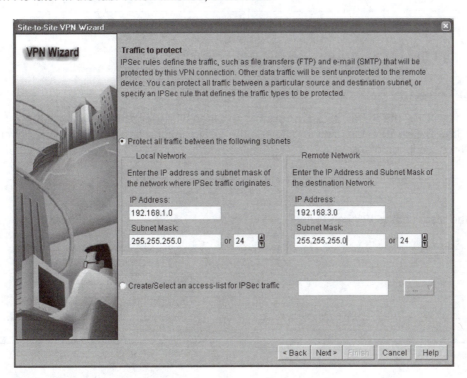

Step 8: Review the summary configuration and deliver commands to the router.

    a.   Review the Summary of the Configuration window. It should look similar to the one below. Do not click the **Test VPN connectivity after configuring** check box. This is done after configuring R3. Click **Finish** to continue.

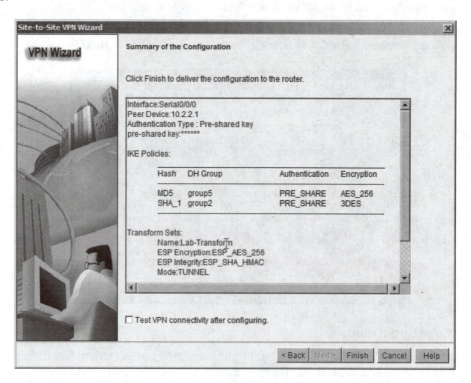

    b.   In the Deliver Configuration to router window, click **Deliver**. After the commands have been delivered, click **OK**. How many commands were delivered?

_____

Task 3: Create a Mirror Configuration for R3.

Step 1: Use CCP on R1 to generate a mirror configuration for R3.

    a.   On R1, on the CCP menu bar, click **Configure**, and then click **Security > VPN > Site-to-Site VPN**. Select the **Edit Site-to-Site VPN** tab. You should see the VPN configuration listed that you just created on R1. What is the description of the VPN?

_____

    b.   What is the status of the VPN and why?

_____

_____

_____

_____

_____

c. Select the VPN policy you just configured on R1 and click **Generate Mirror**. The Generate Mirror window displays the commands necessary to configure R3 as a VPN peer. Scroll through the window to see all the commands generated.

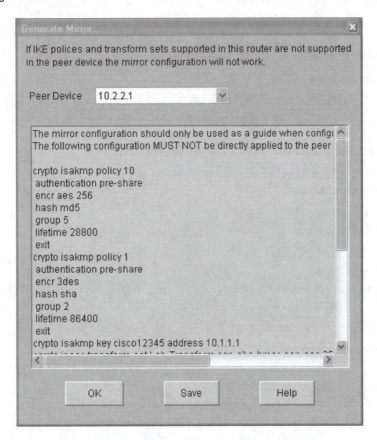

The text at the top of the window states that the configuration generated should only be used as a guide for setting up a site-to-site VPN. What commands are missing to allow this crypto policy to function on R3?

_____

_____

Hint: Look at the description entry following the **crypto map SDM_CMAP_1** command.

Step 2: Save the configuration commands for R3.

a. Click **Save** to create a text file for use in the next task.

b. Save the commands to the desktop or other location and name it **VPN-Mirror-Cfg-for-R3.txt**.

    Note: You can also copy the commands directly from the Generate Mirror window.

c. (Optional) Edit the file to remove the explanation text at the beginning and the description entry following the **crypto map SDM_CMAP_1** command.

Task 4: Apply the Mirror Configuration to R3 and Verify the Configuration.

Step 1: Access the R3 CLI and copy the mirror commands.

Note: You can also use CCP on R3 to create the appropriate VPN configuration, but copying and pasting the mirror commands generated from R1 is easier.

NETLAB+ Note: If you are using NETLAB+, Telnet into R3 (**10.2.2.1**) from PC-A to paste the commands generated for R3 using CCP. Use the **terminal monitor** command to view messages during Telnet session.

a.   On R3, enter privileged EXEC mode and then global configuration mode.

b.   Copy the commands from the text file into the R3 CLI.

Step 2: Apply the crypto map to the R3 S0/0/1 interface.

```
R3(config)# interface S0/0/1
R3(config-if)# crypto map SDM_CMAP_1
*Jan 30 13:00:38.184: %CRYPTO-6-ISAKMP_ON_OFF: ISAKMP is ON
```

Step 3: Verify the VPN configuration on R3 using Cisco IOS.

a.   Display the running configuration beginning with the first line that contains the string "0/0/1" to verify that the crypto map is applied to S0/0/1.

```
R3# show run | begin 0/0/1
interface Serial0/0/1
 ip address 10.2.2.1 255.255.255.252
 crypto map SDM_CMAP_1
```

b.   On R3, use the **show crypto isakmp policy** command to show the configured ISAKMP policies on the router.

Note: The default CCP policy is also present.

```
R3# show crypto isakmp policy
Global IKE policy
Protection suite of priority 1
        encryption algorithm:   Three key triple DES
        hash algorithm:         Secure Hash Standard
        authentication method:  Pre-Shared Key
        Diffie-Hellman group:   #2 (1024 bit)
        lifetime:               86400 seconds, no volume limit

Protection suite of priority 10
        encryption algorithm:   AES - Advanced Encryption Standard (256 bit keys).
        hash algorithm:         Message Digest 5
        authentication method:  Pre-Shared Key
        Diffie-Hellman group:   #5 (1536 bit)
        lifetime:               86400 seconds, no volume limit
```

c.   In the above output, how many ISAKMP policies are there?

_____

_____

_____

d.   Issue the **show crypto ipsec transform-set** command to display the configured IPsec policies in the form of the transform sets.

```
R3# show crypto ipsec transform-set
Transform set Lab-Transform: { esp-256-aes esp-sha-hmac  }
   will negotiate = { Tunnel,  },

Transform set #$!default_transform_set_1: { esp-aes esp-sha-hmac  }
```

```
    will negotiate = { Transport,  },

Transform set #$!default_transform_set_0: { esp-3des esp-sha-hmac  }
    will negotiate = { Transport,  },
```

e. Use the **show crypto map** command to display the crypto maps that will be applied to the router.

```
R3# show crypto map
Crypto Map "SDM_CMAP_1" 1 ipsec-isakmp
        Description: Apply the crypto map on the peer router's interface having IP
address 10.2.2.1 that connects to this router.
        Peer = 10.1.1.1
        Extended IP access list SDM_1
            access-list SDM_1 permit ip 192.168.3.0 0.0.0.255 192.168.1.0 0.0.0.255
        Current peer: 10.1.1.1
        Security association lifetime: 4608000 kilobytes/3600 seconds
        PFS (Y/N): N
        Transform sets={
                Lab-Transform:  { esp-256-aes esp-sha-hmac  } ,
        }
        Interfaces using crypto map SDM_CMAP_1:
                Serial0/0/1
```

In the above output, the ISAKMP policy being used by the crypto map is the CCP default policy with sequence number priority 1, indicated by the number 1 in the first output line: `Crypto Map` `"SDM_CMAP_1"` 1 ipsec-isakmp. Why is it not using the one you created in the CCP session—the one shown with priority 10 in Step 3b above?

_____

_____

_____

f. (Optional) In Part 3 Task 2 Step 5, ISAKMP policy 10 was configured on R1, in addition to the default ISAKMP policy 1. Both policies were included in the VPN policy that was generated in Part 3, Task 3. You can force the routers to use the more stringent policy that you created by changing the crypto map references in the R1 and R3 router configurations. In this example, the default ISAKMP policy 1 was removed from both routers.

```
R1(config)# interface S0/0/0
R1(config-if)# no crypto map SDM_CMAP_1
R1(config-if)# exit
*Jan 30 17:01:46.099: %CRYPTO-6-ISAKMP_ON_OFF: ISAKMP is OFF
R1(config)# no crypto map SDM_CMAP_1 1
R1(config)# crypto map SDM_CMAP_1 10 ipsec-isakmp
% NOTE: This new crypto map will remain disabled until a peer
        and a valid access list have been configured.
R1(config-crypto-map)# description Tunnel to 10.2.2.1
R1(config-crypto-map)# set peer 10.2.2.1
R1(config-crypto-map)# set transform-set Lab-Transform
R1(config-crypto-map)# match address 100
R1(config-crypto-map)# exit
R1(config)#interface S0/0/0
R1(config-if)# crypto map SDM_CMAP_1
```

```
R1(config-if)#
*Jan 30 17:03:16.603: %CRYPTO-6-ISAKMP_ON_OFF: ISAKMP is ON

R3(config)# interface S0/0/1
R3(config-if)# no crypto map SDM_CMAP_1
R3(config-if)# exit
R3(config)# no crypto map SDM_CMAP_1 1
R3(config)# crypto map SDM_CMAP_1 10 ipsec-isakmp
% NOTE: This new crypto map will remain disabled until a peer
         and a valid access list have been configured.
R3(config-crypto-map)# description Tunnel to 10.1.1.1
R3(config-crypto-map)# set peer 10.1.1.1
R3(config-crypto-map)# set transform-set Lab-Transform
R3(config-crypto-map)# match address SDM_1
R3(config-crypto-map)# exit
R3(config)# interface S0/0/1
R3(config-if)# crypto map SDM_CMAP_1
R3(config-if)#
*Jan 30 22:18:28.487: %CRYPTO-6-ISAKMP_ON_OFF: ISAKMP is ON
```

Task 5: Test the VPN Configuration Using CCP on R1.

a. On PC-A, use CCP to test the IPsec VPN tunnel between the two routers. Click **Security** > **VPN** > **Site-to-Site VPN**, and then select the **Edit Site-to-Site VPN** tab.

b. On the Edit Site-to-Site VPN tab, select the VPN and click **Test Tunnel**.

c. When the VPN Troubleshooting window displays, click **Start** to enable CCP to troubleshoot the tunnel.

d. When the CCP Warning window displays indicating that CCP will enable router debugs and generate some tunnel traffic, click **Yes** to continue.

e. In the next VPN Troubleshooting window, the IP address of the R1 Fa0/1 interface in the source network is displayed by default (192.168.1.1). Enter the IP address of the R3 Fa0/1 interface in the destination network field (**192.168.3.1**), and click **Continue** to begin the debugging process.

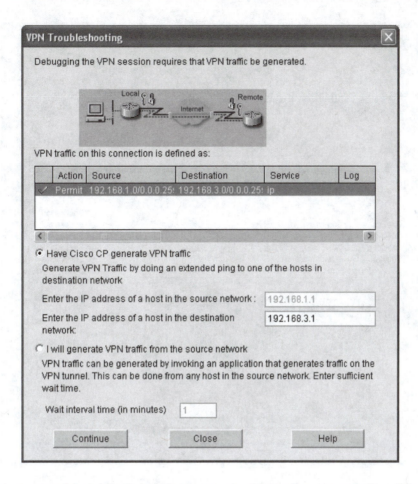

f.   If the debug is successful and the tunnel is up, you should see the screen below. If the testing fails, CCP
     displays failure reasons and recommended actions. Click **OK** to remove the window.

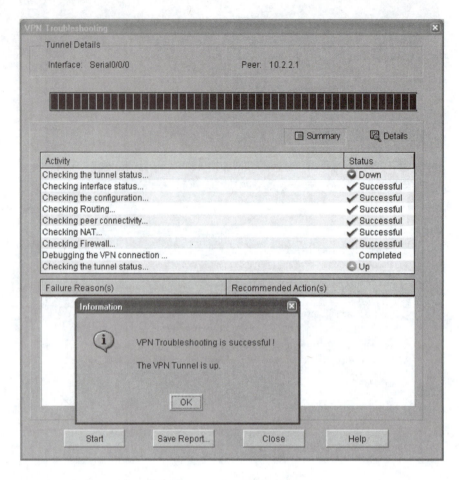

g. You can save the report if desired; otherwise, click **Close**.

Note: To reset the tunnel and test again, click **Clear Connection** in the Edit Site-to-Site VPN window. This can also be accomplished at the CLI using the **clear crypto session** command.

h. Issue the **show run interface s0/0/1** command to verify that the crypto map is applied to S0/0/1.

```
R3# show run interface s0/0/1
Building configuration...

Current configuration : 89 bytes
!
interface Serial0/0/1
 ip address 10.2.2.1 255.255.255.252
 crypto map SDM_CMAP_1
end
```

i. Issue the **show crypto isakmp sa** command on R3 to view the security association created.

```
R3# show crypto isakmp sa
IPv4 Crypto ISAKMP SA
dst             src             state           conn-id slot status
10.2.2.1        10.1.1.1        QM_IDLE            1001     0 ACTIVE

IPv6 Crypto ISAKMP SA
```

j. Issue the **show crypto ipsec sa** command. How many packets have been transformed between R1 and R3?

```
R3# show crypto ipsec sa

interface: Serial0/0/1
    Crypto map tag: SDM_CMAP_1, local addr 10.2.2.1

   protected vrf: (none)
   local  ident (addr/mask/prot/port): (192.168.3.0/255.255.255.0/0/0)
   remote ident (addr/mask/prot/port): (192.168.1.0/255.255.255.0/0/0)
   current_peer 10.1.1.1 port 500
     PERMIT, flags={origin_is_acl,}
    #pkts encaps: 116, #pkts encrypt: 116, #pkts digest: 116
    #pkts decaps: 116, #pkts decrypt: 116, #pkts verify: 116
    #pkts compressed: 0, #pkts decompressed: 0
    #pkts not compressed: 0, #pkts compr. failed: 0
    #pkts not decompressed: 0, #pkts decompress failed: 0
    #send errors 0, #recv errors 0

     local crypto endpt.: 10.2.2.1, remote crypto endpt.: 10.1.1.1
     path mtu 1500, ip mtu 1500, ip mtu idb Serial0/0/1
     current outbound spi: 0x207AAD8A(544910730)

     inbound esp sas:
      spi: 0xAF102CAE(2937072814)
        transform: esp-256-aes esp-sha-hmac ,
        in use settings ={Tunnel, }
        conn id: 2007, flow_id: FPGA:7, crypto map: SDM_CMAP_1
        sa timing: remaining key lifetime (k/sec): (4558294/3037)
        IV size: 16 bytes
        replay detection support: Y
        Status: ACTIVE

     inbound ah sas:

     inbound pcp sas:

     outbound esp sas:
      spi: 0x207AAD8A(544910730)
        transform: esp-256-aes esp-sha-hmac ,
        in use settings ={Tunnel, }
        conn id: 2008, flow_id: FPGA:8, crypto map: SDM_CMAP_1
        sa timing: remaining key lifetime (k/sec): (4558294/3037)
        IV size: 16 bytes
        replay detection support: Y
        Status: ACTIVE

     outbound ah sas:

     outbound pcp sas:
```

Reflection

1. Would traffic on the Fast Ethernet link between PC-A and the R1 Fa0/0 interface be encrypted by the site-to-site IPsec VPN tunnel? Explain.

_____

_____

_____

_____

_____

2. Compared to using the CCP VPN wizard GUI, what are some factors to consider when configuring site-to-site IPsec VPNs using the manual CLI?

_____

_____

_____

_____

_____

Router Interface Summary Table

Router Interface Summary				
Router Model	**Ethernet Interface #1**	**Ethernet Interface #2**	**Serial Interface #1**	**Serial Interface #2**
1800	Fast Ethernet 0/0 (Fa0/0)	Fast Ethernet 0/1 (Fa0/1)	Serial 0/0/0 (S0/0/0)	Serial 0/0/1 (S0/0/1)
1900	Gigabit Ethernet 0/0 (G0/0)	Gigabit Ethernet 0/1 (G0/1)	Serial 0/0/0 (S0/0/0)	Serial 0/0/1 (S0/0/1)
2801	Fast Ethernet 0/0 (Fa0/0)	Fast Ethernet 0/1 (Fa0/1)	Serial 0/1/0 (S0/1/0)	Serial 0/1/1 (S0/1/1)
2811	Fast Ethernet 0/0 (Fa0/0)	Fast Ethernet 0/1 (Fa0/1)	Serial 0/0/0 (S0/0/0)	Serial 0/0/1 (S0/0/1)
2900	Gigabit Ethernet 0/0 (G0/0)	Gigabit Ethernet 0/1 (G0/1)	Serial 0/0/0 (S0/0/0)	Serial 0/0/1 (S0/0/1)

Note: To find out how the router is configured, look at the interfaces to identify the type of router and how many interfaces the router has. There is no way to effectively list all the combinations of configurations for each router class. This table includes identifiers for the possible combinations of Ethernet and Serial interfaces in the device. The table does not include any other type of interface, even though a specific router may contain one. An example of this might be an ISDN BRI interface. The string in parenthesis is the legal abbreviation that can be used in Cisco IOS commands to represent the interface.

Lab 8.7.1.2 - Configuring a Remote Access VPN Server and Client

Topology

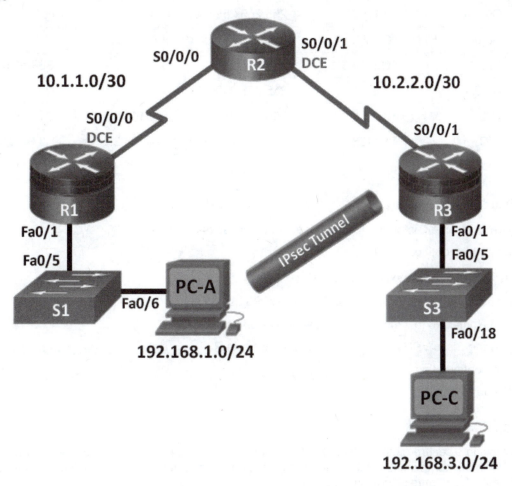

Note: ISR G2 devices use GigabitEthernet interfaces instead of FastEthernet interfaces.

IP Addressing Table

Device	Interface	IP Address	Subnet Mask	Default Gateway	Switch Port
R1	Fa0/1	192.168.1.1	255.255.255.0	N/A	S1 Fa0/5
	S0/0/0 (DCE)	10.1.1.1	255.255.255.252	N/A	N/A
R2	S0/0/0	10.1.1.2	255.255.255.252	N/A	N/A
	S0/0/1 (DCE)	10.2.2.2	255.255.255.252	N/A	N/A
R3	Fa0/1	192.168.3.1	255.255.255.0	N/A	S3 Fa0/5
	S0/0/1	10.2.2.1	255.255.255.252	N/A	N/A
PC-A	NIC	192.168.1.3	255.255.255.0	192.168.1.1	S1 Fa0/6
PC-C	NIC	192.168.3.3	255.255.255.0	192.168.3.1	S3 Fa0/18

Objectives

Part 1: Basic Router Configuration

- Configure hostnames, interface IP addresses, and access passwords.
- Configure static routing.

Part 2: Configuring a Remote Access VPN

- Configure a Zone-Based Policy Firewall (ZBF) on R3 using CCP.
- Configure Router R3 to support Cisco Easy VPN Server using CCP.
- Configure the Cisco VPN Client on PC-A and connect to R3.
- Verify the configuration.
- Test VPN functionality.

Background / Scenario

VPNs can provide a secure method of transmitting data over a public network, such as the Internet. A common VPN implementation is used for remote access to a corporate office from a telecommuter location such as a small office/home office (SOHO).

In this lab, you will build a multi-router network and configure the routers and hosts. You will configure a remote access IPsec VPN between a client computer and a simulated corporate network. You will use CCP to configure a Zoned-Based Policy Firewall (ZBF) to prevent connections from outside the corporate network. You will then use CCP to configure the Cisco Easy VPN Server on the corporate gateway router. Finally, you will configure the Cisco VPN Client on a host, and connect to the corporate network through a simulated ISP router.

The Cisco VPN Client allows organizations to establish end-to-end, encrypted (IPsec) VPN tunnels for secure connectivity for mobile employees or teleworkers. It supports Cisco Easy VPN, which allows the client to receive security policies upon a VPN tunnel connection from the central site VPN device (Cisco Easy VPN Server), minimizing configuration requirements at the remote location. The Cisco Easy VPN is a scalable solution for remote access deployments for which it is impractical to individually configure policies for multiple remote PCs.

Router R1 represents a remote site, and R3 represents the corporate headquarters. Host PC-A simulates an employee connecting from home or a small office over the Internet. Router R2 simulates an Internet ISP router and acts as a passthrough with no knowledge of the VPN connection running through it.

Note: The router commands and output in this lab are from a Cisco 1841 router with Cisco IOS Release 15.1(4)MT8 (Advanced IP Services image). Other routers and Cisco IOS versions can be used. See the

Router Interface Summary Table at the end of this lab to determine which interface identifiers to use based on the equipment in the lab. Depending on the router model and Cisco IOS version, the available commands and output produced might vary from what is shown in this lab.

Note: Ensure that the routers and switches have been erased and have no startup configurations.

Required Resources

- 3 Routers (Cisco 1841 with Cisco IOS Release 15.1(4)M8 Advanced IP Services image or comparable)
- 2 Switches (Cisco 2960 or comparable)
- 2 PCs (Windows Vista or Windows 7 with CCP 2.5, Cisco VPN Client, latest version of Java, Internet Explorer, and Flash Player)
- Serial and Ethernet cables as shown in the topology
- Console cables to configure Cisco networking devices

CCP Notes:

- If the PC on which CCP is installed is running Windows Vista or Windows 7, it may be necessary to right-click the **CCP** icon or menu item, and select **Run as administrator**.
- To run CCP, it may be necessary to temporarily disable antivirus programs and O/S firewalls. Ensure that all pop-up blockers are turned off in the browser.

Part 1: Basic Router Configuration

In Part 1, you will set up the network topology and configure basic settings, such as the interface IP addresses and static routing. Perform the steps on the routers as indicated.

Step 1: Cable the network as shown in the topology.

Attach the devices as shown in the topology diagram, and cable as necessary.

Step 2: Configure basic settings for all routers.

a. Configure hostnames as shown in the topology.

b. Configure the physical interface IP addresses as shown in the IP addressing table.

c. Configure a clock rate for the routers with a DCE serial cable attached to their serial interface.

```
R1(config)# interface S0/0/0
R1(config-if)# clock rate 64000
```

d. Disable DNS lookup to prevent the router from attempting to translate incorrectly entered commands as though they were hostnames.

```
R1(config)# no ip domain-lookup
```

Step 3: Configure static default routes on R1 and R3.

Configure a static default route from R1 to R2 and from R3 to R2.

```
R1(config)# ip route 0.0.0.0 0.0.0.0 10.1.1.2
```

```
R3(config)# ip route 0.0.0.0 0.0.0.0 10.2.2.2
```

Step 4: Configure static routes on R2.

a. Configure a static route from R2 to the R1 LAN.

```
R2(config)# ip route 192.168.1.0 255.255.255.0 10.1.1.1
```

b. Configure a static route from R2 to the R3 LAN.

```
R2(config)# ip route 192.168.3.0 255.255.255.0 10.2.2.1
```

Step 5: Configure PC host IP settings.

Configure a static IP address, subnet mask, and default gateway for PC-A and PC-C, as shown in the IP addressing table.

Step 6: Verify connectivity between PC-A and R3.

From PC-A, ping the R3 S0/0/1 interface at IP address **10.2.2.1**.

```
PC-A:\> ping 10.2.2.1
```

If the pings are unsuccessful, troubleshoot the basic device configurations before continuing.

Step 7: Configure a minimum password length.

Note: Passwords in this lab are set to a minimum of 10 characters, but are relatively simple for the benefit of performing the lab. More complex passwords are recommended in a production network.

Use the **security passwords** command to set a minimum password length of **10** characters.

```
R1(config)# security passwords min-length 10
```

Step 8: Configure the enable secret password and console and vty lines.

a. Configure the enable secret password **cisco12345** on R1.

```
R1(config)# enable secret cisco12345
```

b. Configure a console password and enable login for router R1. For additional security, the **exec-timeout** command causes the line to log out after five minutes of inactivity. The **logging synchronous** command prevents console messages from interrupting command entry.

Note: To avoid repetitive logins during this lab, the **exec-timeout** value can be set to 0 0, which prevents it from expiring; however, this is not considered a good security practice.

```
R1(config)# line console 0
R1(config-line)# password ciscoconpass
R1(config-line)# exec-timeout 5 0
R1(config-line)# login
R1(config-line)# logging synchronous
```

c. Configure the password on the vty lines for router R1.

```
R1(config)# line vty 0 4
R1(config-line)# password ciscovtypass
R1(config-line)# exec-timeout 5 0
R1(config-line)# login
```

d. Repeat these configurations on R2 and R3.

Step 9: Encrypt clear text passwords.

a. Use the **service password-encryption** command to encrypt the console, aux, and vty passwords.

```
R1(config)# service password-encryption
```

b. Issue the **show run** command. Can you read the console, aux, and vty passwords? Explain.

_____

_____

c. Repeat this configuration on R2 and R3.

Step 10: Configure a login warning banner on routers R1 and R3.

Configure a message-of-the-day (MOTD) warning banner to unauthorized users.

```
R1(config)# banner motd $Unauthorized access strictly prohibited and
prosecuted to the full extent of the law$
```

Step 11: Save the basic running configuration for all three routers.

Save the running configuration to the startup configuration from the privileged EXEC mode prompt.

```
R1# copy running-config startup-config
```

Part 2: Configuring a Remote Access VPN

In Part 2 of this lab, configure a firewall and a remote access IPsec VPN. You will use CCP to configure R3 as a VPN server. On PC-C, you will enable and configure the Cisco VPN client.

Task 1: Prepare R3 for CCP Access.

Step 1: Configure HTTP router access and an AAA user.

a. Enable the secure HTTP server on R3.

```
R3(config)# ip http secure-server
```

b. Create an **admin01** account on R3 with privilege level **15** and a password of **admin01pass** for use with AAA.

```
R3(config)# username admin01 privilege 15 password admin01pass
```

c. Configure R3 so that CCP uses the local database to authenticate web sessions.

```
R3(config)# ip http authentication local
```

Step 2: Access CCP and discover R3.

a. Run the CCP application on PC-C. In the Select/Manage Community window, in the Hostname/Address field, enter the R3 IP address **192.168.3.1**; in the Username field, enter **admin01**; and in the Password field, enter **admin01pass**. Click the **Connect Securely** check box, and click **OK**.

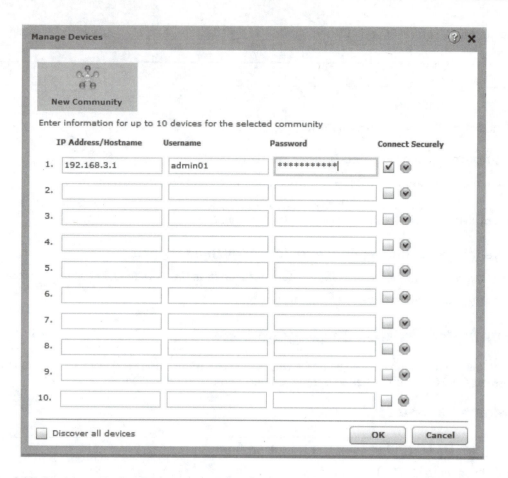

b. At the CCP Dashboard, click **Discover** to discover and connect to R3. If the discovery process fails, click **Discover Details** to determine the problem to resolve the issue.

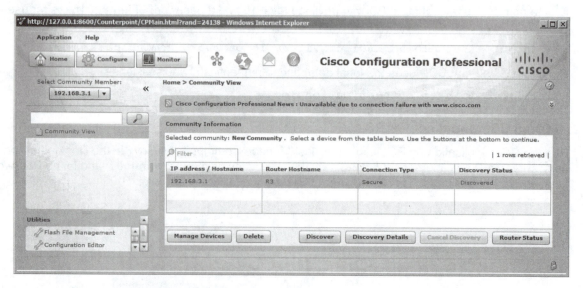

Task 2: Configure a ZBF Firewall on R3.

Step 1: Use the CCP firewall wizard to configure a Zone-Based Policy Firewall on R3.

a. On the CCP menu bar, click **Configure**. In the left pane, click **Security** > **Firewall** > **Firewall**.

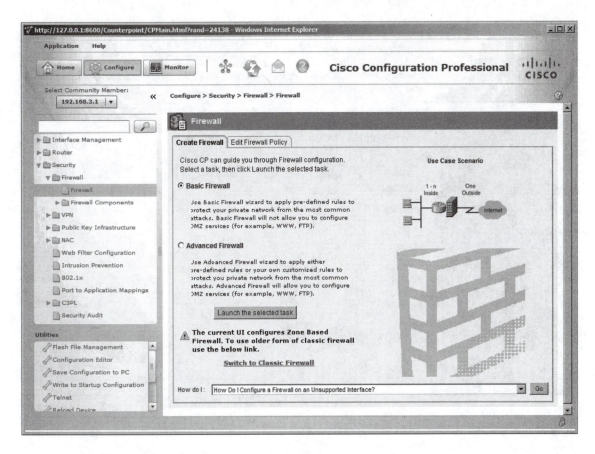

b. On the Create Firewall tab, select the **Basic Firewall** option, and click **Launch the selected task**. On the Basic Firewall Configuration wizard screen, click **Next**.

c. Click the **Inside (Trusted)** check box for **FastEthernet0/1** and the **Outside (Untrusted)** check box for **Serial0/0/1**. Click **Next**, then click **OK** when the CCP launch warning for Serial0/0/1 displays.

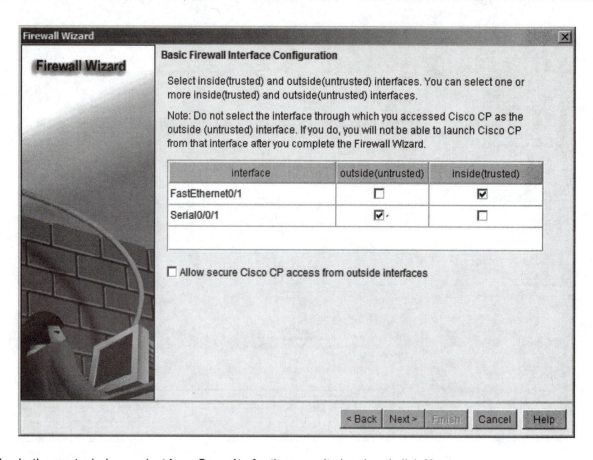

d.   In the next window, select **Low Security** for the security level and click **Next**.

e.   In the Summary window, click **Finish**.

f.   Click **Deliver** to send the commands to the router. In the Commands Delivery Status window, click **OK**. In the Information window, click **OK** to return to the Edit Firewall Policy tab.

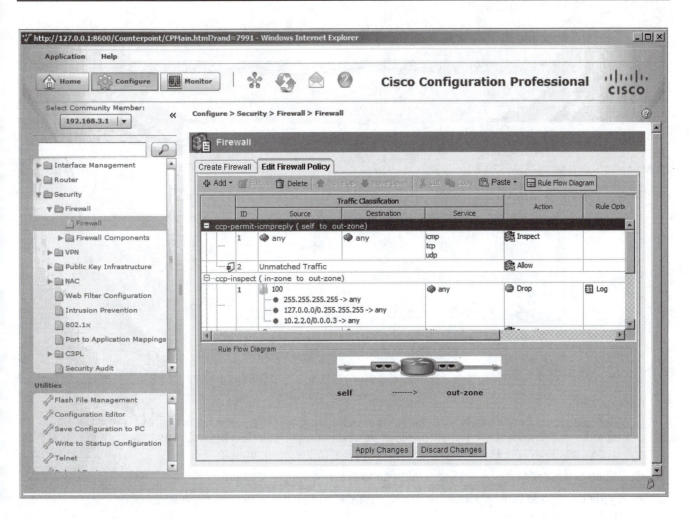

Step 2: Verify firewall functionality.

From PC-C, ping the R2 interface S0/0/1 at IP address **10.2.2.2**.

```
C:\> ping 10.2.2.2
```

Are the pings successful? Explain.

_____

_____

Step 3: From external router R2, ping PC-C at IP address 192.168.3.3.

```
R2# ping 192.168.3.3
```

Are the pings successful? Explain.

_____

_____

Task 3: Use the CCP VPN Wizard to Configure the Easy VPN Server.

Step 1: Launch the Easy VPN Server wizard and configure AAA services.

a. On the CCP menu bar, click **Configure**. In the left pane, click **Security** > **VPN** > **Easy VPN Server**.

b.   On the Create Easy VPN Server tab, click **Launch Easy VPN Server Wizard**.

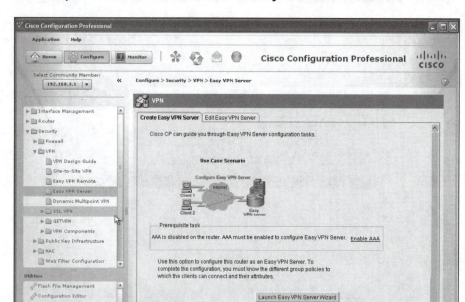

c.   The Easy VPN Server wizard checks the router configuration to see if AAA is enabled. If AAA is not enabled, the Enable AAA window displays. AAA must be enabled on the router before the Easy VPN Server configuration starts. Click **Yes** to continue with the configuration.

d.   When prompted to deliver the configuration to the router, click **Deliver**.

e.   In the Command Delivery Status window, click **OK**. When the "AAA has been successfully enabled on the router" message displays, click **OK**.

f.   Read through the descriptions of tasks displayed in the Easy VPN Server Wizard window.

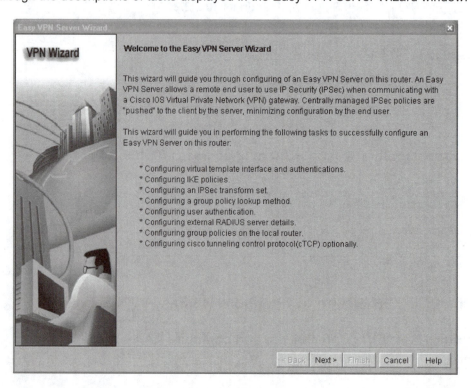

How does the client receive the IPsec policies?

_____

_____

How does the Easy VPN remote server configuration differ from the site-to-site?

_____

_____

_____

_____

g.   Click **Next** when you are finished answering the above questions.

Step 2: Configure the virtual tunnel interface and authentication.

a.   Select the interface on which the client connections terminate. Select the **Unnumbered to** option and, from the pull-down list, select the **Serial0/0/1** interface.

b.   Select the **Pre-shared Keys** option for the authentication type, and click **Next** to continue.

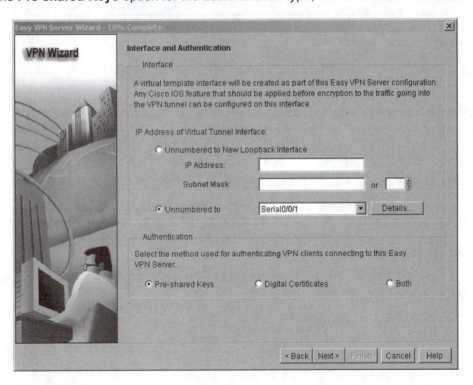

Step 3: Select an IKE proposal.

a.   In the IKE Proposals window, the default IKE proposal is used for R3.

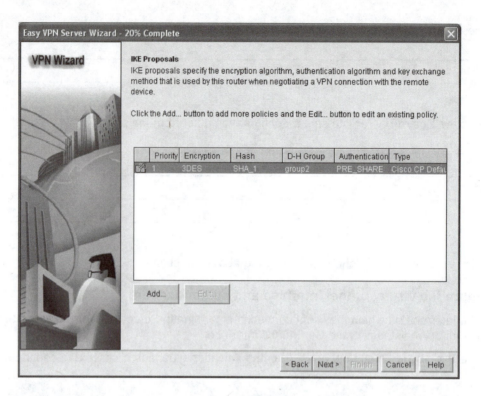

What is the encryption method used with the default IKE policy?

_____

What is the hash algorithm used to ensure that the keys have not been tampered with?

_____

b. Click **Next** to accept the default IKE policy.

Note: Configurations on both sides of the tunnel must match exactly. The Cisco VPN client automatically selects the proper configuration for itself. Therefore, an IKE configuration is unnecessary on the client PC.

Step 4: Select the transform set.

a. In the Transform Set window, the default CCP transform set is used. What ESP encryption method is used with the default transform set? _____

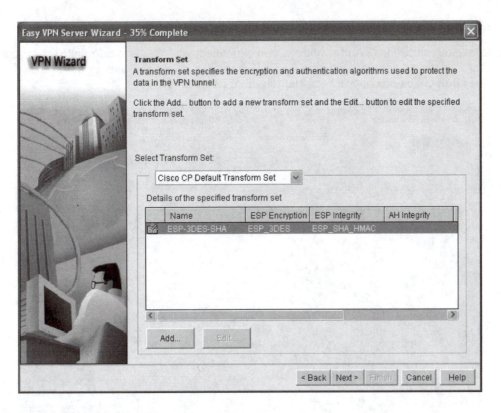

b. Click **Next** to accept the default transform set.

Step 5: Specify group authorization and group policy lookup.

a. In the Group Authorization and Group Policy Lookup window, select the **Local** option.

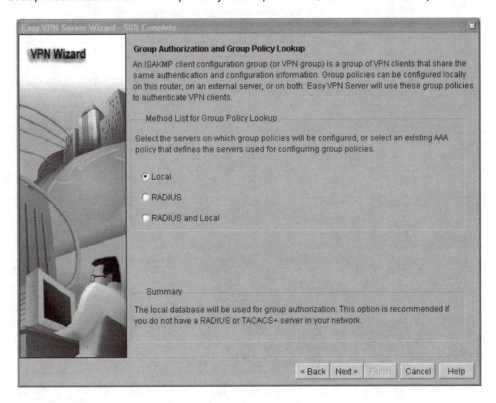

b. Click **Next** to create a new AAA method list for group policy lookup that uses the local router database.

Step 6: Configure user authentication (XAuth).

a. In the User Authentication (XAuth) window, you can select where user credentials will be configured. You can select an external server, such as a RADIUS server, a local database, or both. Click the **Enable User Authentication** check box and accept the default of **Local Only**.

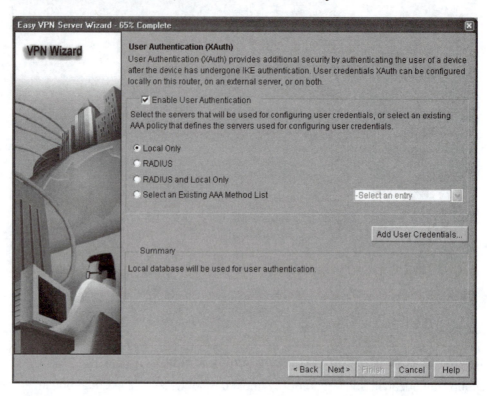

Where does the router look for valid user accounts and passwords to authenticate remote VPN users when they attempt to log in?

_____

_____

b. Click **Add User Credentials**. In the User Accounts window, you can view currently defined users or add new users.

What is the name of the user currently defined and what is the user privilege level?

_____

How was this user defined?

_____

c. In the User Accounts window, click **Add** to add another user. Enter the username **VPNuser1** with a password of **VPNuser1pass**. Select the **Encrypt password using the MD5 hash algorithm** check box for. Leave the privilege level at 1.

What is the range of privilege level that can be set for a user?

_____

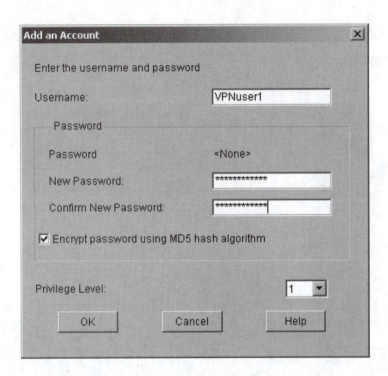

d. Click **OK** to accept the VPNuser1 entries, and then click **OK** to close the User Accounts window.

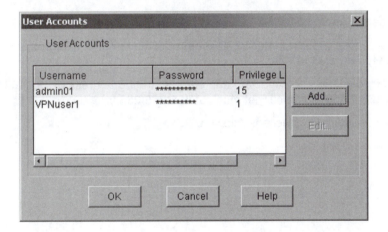

e. In the User Authentication (XAuth) window, click **Next** to continue.

Step 7: Specify group authorization and user group policies.

a. In the Group Authorization and User Group Policies window, you must create at least one group policy for the VPN server.

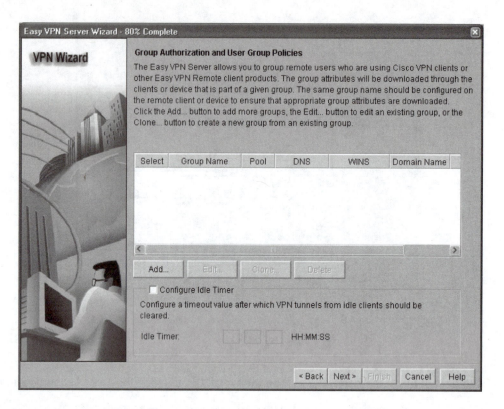

b. Click **Add** to create a group policy.

c. In the Add Group Policy window, enter **VPN-Access** as the name of this group. Enter a new pre-shared key of **cisco12345** and then re-enter it.

d. Leave the **Pool Information** box checked and enter a starting address of **192.168.3.100**, an ending address of **192.168.3.150**, and a subnet mask of **255.255.255.0**.

e. Enter **50** for the Maximum Connections Allowed.

f. Click **OK** to accept the entries.

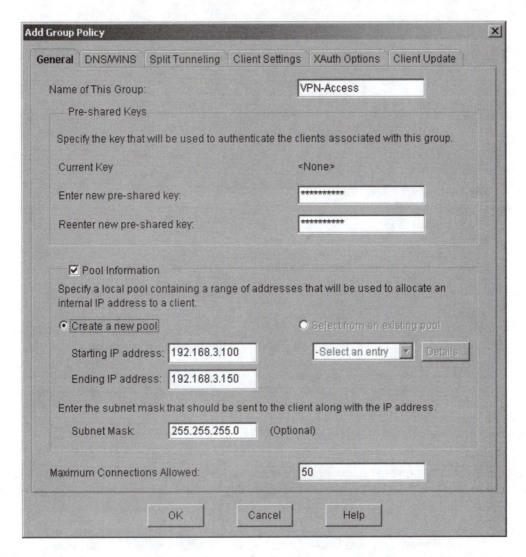

g. A CCP warning message displays indicating that the IP addresses in the pool and the IP address of the Fast Ethernet0/1 interface are in the same subnet. Click **Yes** to continue.

h. When you return to the Group Authorization window, click the **Configure Idle Timer** check box and enter one hour (**1**). This disconnects idle users if there is no activity for one hour and allows others to connect. Click **Next** to continue.

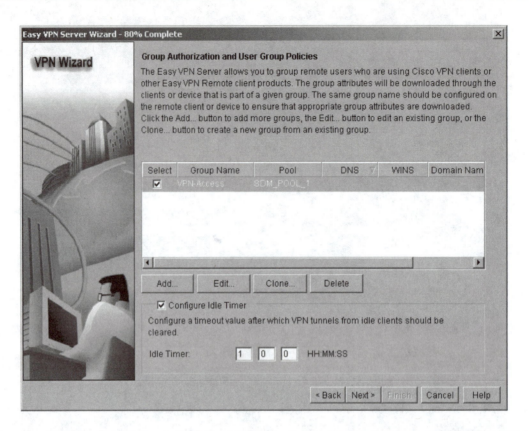

i.   When the Cisco Tunneling Control Protocol (cTCP) window displays, do not enable cTCP. Click **Next** to continue.

j.   When the Easy VPN Server Passthrough Configuration window displays, ensure that the **Action Modify** check box is checked. This option allows CCP to modify the firewall on S0/0/1 to allow IPsec VPN traffic to reach the internal LAN. Click **OK** to continue.

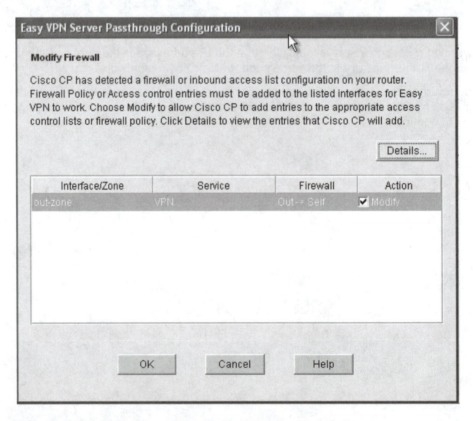

Step 8: Review the configuration summary and deliver the commands.

a. Scroll through the commands that CCP will send to the router. Do not click the **Test VPN connectivity after configuring** check box. Click **Finish**.

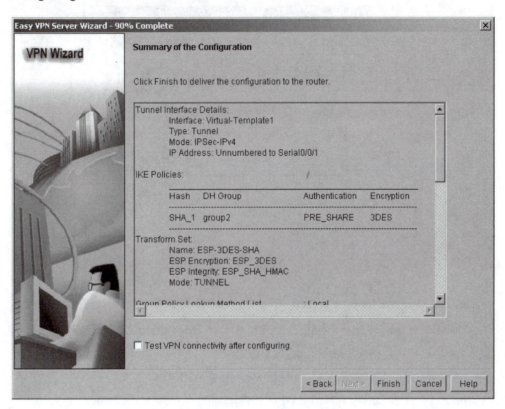

b. When prompted to deliver the configuration to the router, click **Deliver**.

In the Command Delivery Status window, click **OK**. How many commands are delivered?

Step 9: Test the VPN Server.

a. After completing Step 8b, you are returned to the main VPN window with the Edit Easy VPN Server tab selected. Click the **Test VPN Server** button in the lower-right corner of the screen.

b. In the VPN Troubleshooting window, click **Start**.

c. Your screen should look similar to the one below. Click **OK** to close the information window. Click **Close** to exit the VPN Troubleshooting window.

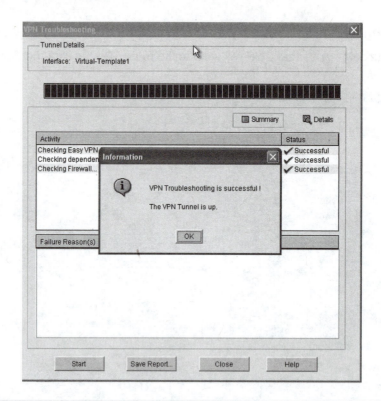

Note: If you receive a failure after testing the VPN server, close the VPN Troubleshooting window.

1. On the Edit Easy VPN Server tab, click **Edit**.

2. In the Edit Easy VPN Server Connection window, click **OK**.

3. In the Easy VPN Server Passthrough Configuration window, click **OK**.

4. Click the check box to the right of the FastEthernet0/1 interface, indicating that it is inside (Trusted).

5. On the Edit Easy VPN tab, click **Test VPN Server**.

6. Click **Start**, and the test should pass.

Task 4: Use the Cisco VPN Client to Test the Remote Access VPN.

Step 1: (Optional) Install the Cisco VPN client.

If the Cisco VPN Client software on host PC-A is not installed, install it now. If you do not have the Cisco VPN Client software, contact your instructor.

Step 2: Configure PC-A as a VPN client to access the R1 VPN server.

a. Start the Cisco VPN Client, select the **Connection Entries** tab, and click the **New** icon.

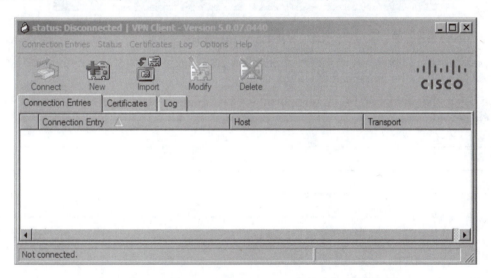

b. Enter the following information to define the new connection entry. Click **Save** when you are finished.

- Connection Entry: **VPN-R3**

- Description: **Connection to R3 internal network**

- Host: **10.2.2.1** (IP address of the R3 S0/0/1 interface)

- Group Authentication Name: **VPN-Access** (defines the address pool configured in Task 2)

- Password: **cisco12345** (pre-shared key configured in Task 2)

- Confirm Password: **cisco12345**

Note: The group authentication name and password are case-sensitive and must match the ones created on the VPN Server.

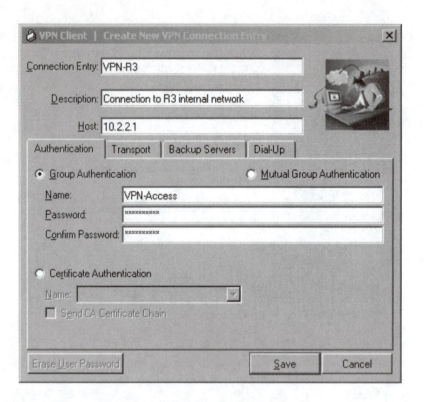

Step 3: Test access from PC-A without a VPN connection.

a. In the previous step, you created a VPN connection entry on the VPN client computer PC-A, but have not activated it, so the VPN tunnel is not yet up.

b. Open a command prompt on PC-A, and ping the PC-C IP address at **192.168.3.3** on the R3 LAN. Are the pings successful? Explain.

_____

_____

_____

_____

_____

Step 4: Establish a VPN connection and log in.

a. Select the newly created connection VPN-R3 and click the **Connect** icon. You can also double-click the connection entry.

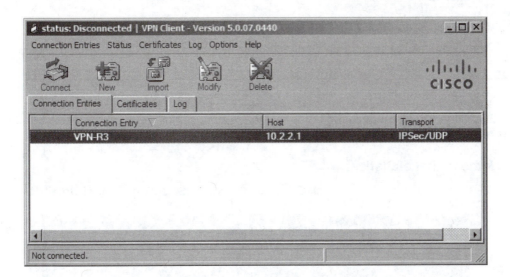

b. In the VPN Client User Authentication dialog box, enter the previously created username **VPNuser1**, and enter the password **VPNuser1pass**. Click **OK** to continue. The VPN Client window minimizes to a lock icon in the tools tray of the taskbar. When the lock is closed, the VPN tunnel is up. When it is open, the VPN connection is down.

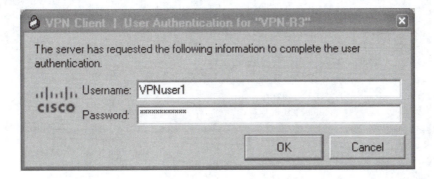

Task 5: Verify the VPN Tunnel between the Client, Server, and Internal Network.

Step 1: Open the VPN Client icon.

a. Double-click the VPN lock icon to expand the VPN Client window.

What does it say about the connection status at the top of the window?

_____

b. From the PC-A command line, issue the **ipconfig** command.

What is the IP address of the first Local Area Connection?

_____

What is the IP address of Local Area Connection 2?

_____

Step 2: Close the VPN connection and reopen it.

a. In the VPN Client window, click the **Disconnect** icon to close the VPN-R3 connection.

b. Click the **Connect** icon and log in again as VPNuser1.

What is the IP address of Local Area Connection 2 now?

_____

Note: Each time you disconnect and reconnect to the VPN server, you receive a new IP address until the limit is reached.

Step 3: Check the tunnel statistics.

a. On the VPN connection menu bar, click **Status > Statistics**. Select the **Tunnel Details** tab.

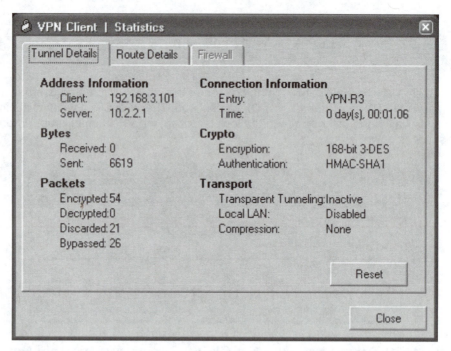

What is the current address obtained from the R3 VPN server? What is the range of addresses that can be assigned?

_____

_____

_____

What is the VPN server address?

_____

How many packets have been encrypted?

_____

What is the encryption method?

_____

What is the authentication method?

_____

b. Leave the VPN Client Statistics window open.

Step 4: Test access from the client PC-A using the VPN connection.

With the VPN connection from computer PC-A to router R3 activated, open a command prompt on PC-A, and ping the PC-C IP address at 192.168.3.3 on the R3 LAN. Were the pings successful? Explain.

_____

_____

_____

How many packets have now been encrypted?

_____

Step 5: Check the Cisco IOS message on R3 when the tunnel is created.

Open the console connection for R3 and locate the message displayed indicating that the virtual interface came up when the VPN Client connection was made.

What is the name of the interface on R3 that is activated for the VPN?

_____

_____

Step 6: Verify the VPN connection information for PC-A.

From the PC-A command prompt, issue the **ipconfig /all** command to see the network connections.

What is the configuration for the first Local Area Connection?

IP Address: _____

Subnet Mask: _____

Default Gateway: _____

Description: _____

What is the configuration for Local Area Connection 2?

IP Address: _____

Subnet Mask: _____

Default Gateway: _____

Description: _____

Step 7: Telnet from PC-A to R3.

a. From the PC-A command prompt, telnet to R3 at the Fa0/1 IP address **192.168.3.1**. Log in as **admin01** with a password of **admin01pass**. What is the router command prompt and why is this?

_____

_____

_____

b. Issue the **show run** command to view the various commands generated by CCP to configure the VPN server.

c. Issue the **show users** command to see connections to router R3. What connections are present?

_____

d. Close the Telnet connection using the **quit** or **exit** command.

Reflection

Why is VPN a good option for remote users?

_____

_____

_____

_____

_____

_____

Router Interface Summary Table

Router Interface Summary				
Router Model	**Ethernet Interface #1**	**Ethernet Interface #2**	**Serial Interface #1**	**Serial Interface #2**
1800	Fast Ethernet 0/0 (Fa0/0)	Fast Ethernet 0/1 (Fa0/1)	Serial 0/0/0 (S0/0/0)	Serial 0/0/1 (S0/0/1)
1900	Gigabit Ethernet 0/0 (G0/0)	Gigabit Ethernet 0/1 (G0/1)	Serial 0/0/0 (S0/0/0)	Serial 0/0/1 (S0/0/1)
2801	Fast Ethernet 0/0 (Fa0/0)	Fast Ethernet 0/1 (Fa0/1)	Serial 0/1/0 (S0/1/0)	Serial 0/1/1 (S0/1/1)
2811	Fast Ethernet 0/0 (Fa0/0)	Fast Ethernet 0/1 (Fa0/1)	Serial 0/0/0 (S0/0/0)	Serial 0/0/1 (S0/0/1)
2900	Gigabit Ethernet 0/0 (G0/0)	Gigabit Ethernet 0/1 (G0/1)	Serial 0/0/0 (S0/0/0)	Serial 0/0/1 (S0/0/1)

Note: To find out how the router is configured, look at the interfaces to identify the type of router and how many interfaces the router has. There is no way to effectively list all the combinations of configurations for each router class. This table includes identifiers for the possible combinations of Ethernet and Serial interfaces in the device. The table does not include any other type of interface, even though a specific router may contain one. An example of this might be an ISDN BRI interface. The string in parenthesis is the legal abbreviation that can be used in Cisco IOS commands to represent the interface.

Lab 8.7.1.3 - (Optional) Configuring a Remote Access VPN Server and Client

Topology

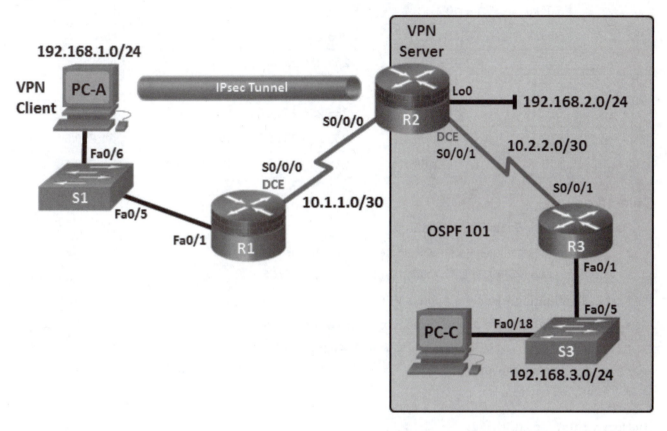

Note: ISR G2 devices use GigabitEthernet interfaces instead of FastEthernet interfaces.

IP Addressing Table

Device	Interface	IP Address	Subnet Mask	Default Gateway	Switch Port
R1	Fa0/1	192.168.1.1	255.255.255.0	N/A	S1 Fa0/5
	S0/0/0 (DCE)	10.1.1.1	255.255.255.252	N/A	N/A
R2	S0/0/0	10.1.1.2	255.255.255.252	N/A	N/A
	S0/0/1 (DCE)	10.2.2.2	255.255.255.252	N/A	N/A
	Lo0	192.168.2.1	255.255.255.0	N/A	N/A
R3	Fa0/1	192.168.3.1	255.255.255.0	N/A	S3 Fa0/5
	S0/0/1	10.2.2.1	255.255.255.252	N/A	N/A
PC-A	NIC	192.168.1.3	255.255.255.0	192.168.1.1	S1 Fa0/6
PC-C	NIC	192.168.3.3	255.255.255.0	192.168.3.1	S3 Fa0/18

Objectives

Part 1: Configure Basic Device Settings

*   Configure hostnames, interface IP addresses, and access passwords.
*   Configure the OSPF dynamic routing protocol on R2 and R3.

Part 2: Configuring a Remote Access VPN

*   Use CCP to configure a router to support an Easy VPN server.
*   Configure the Cisco VPN client on PC-A and connect to R2.
*   Verify the configuration.
*   Test VPN functionality.

Background / Scenario

VPNs can provide a secure method of transmitting data over a public network, such as the Internet. A common VPN implementation is used for remote access to a corporate office from a telecommuter location such as a small office or home office (SOHO).

In this lab, you build a multi-router network and configure the routers and hosts. You configure a remote access IPsec VPN between a client computer and a simulated corporate network. You use CCP to configure a Cisco Easy VPN server on the corporate edge gateway router and configure the Cisco VPN client on a host. Then you connect to the corporate network through a simulated ISP router.

The Cisco VPN client allows organizations to establish end-to-end, encrypted (IPsec) VPN tunnels for secure connectivity for mobile employees or teleworkers. It supports Cisco Easy VPN, which allows the client to receive security policies upon a VPN tunnel connection from the central site VPN device (Cisco Easy VPN Server), minimizing configuration requirements at the remote location. This is a scalable solution for remote access deployments where it is impractical to individually configure policies for multiple remote PCs.

Note: The router commands and output in this lab are from a Cisco 1841 router with Cisco IOS Release 15.1(4)M8 (Advanced IP Services image). Other routers and Cisco IOS versions can be used. See the Router Interface Summary Table at the end of the lab to determine which interface identifiers to use based on the equipment in the lab. Depending on the router model and Cisco IOS version, the commands available and output produced might vary from what is shown in this lab.

Note: Ensure that the routers and switches have been erased and have no startup configurations.

Required Resources

- 3 Routers (Cisco 1841 with Cisco IOS Release 15.1(4)M8 Advanced IP Services image or comparable)
- 2 Switches (Cisco 2960 or comparable)
- 2 PCs (Windows Vista or Windows 7 with CCP 2.5, Cisco VPN Client, latest version of Java, Internet Explorer, and Flash Player)
- Serial and Ethernet cables as shown in the topology
- Console cables to configure Cisco networking devices

CCP Notes:

- If the PC on which CCP is installed is running Windows Vista or Windows 7, it may be necessary to right-click the CCP icon or menu item, and select **Run as administrator**.
- To run CCP, it may be necessary to temporarily disable antivirus programs and O/S firewalls. Ensure that all pop-up blockers are turned off in the browser.

Part 1: Configure Basic Device Settings

In Part 1, you set up the network topology and configure basic settings, such as the interface IP addresses, dynamic routing, device access, and passwords.

Note: Perform all tasks on routers R1, R2, and R3. The procedure for R1 is shown here as an example.

Step 1: Cable the network as shown in the topology.

Attach the devices as shown in the topology diagram, and cable as necessary.

Step 2: Configure basic settings for each router.

a. Configure hostnames as shown in the topology.

b. Configure the physical interface IP addresses as shown in the IP addressing table.

c. Configure the logical loopback 0 interface on R2. This simulates the network from which the remote access clients receive addresses (192.168.2.0/24). Because loopback interfaces are up by default, it is not necessary to use the **no shutdown** command.

```
R2(config)# interface Loopback 0
R2(config-if)# ip address 192.168.2.1 255.255.255.0
```

d. Configure a clock rate for the serial router interfaces with a DCE serial cable attached.

```
R1(config)# interface S0/0/0
R1(config-if)# clock rate 64000
```

Step 3: Disable DNS lookup.

a. To prevent the router from attempting to translate incorrectly entered commands, disable DNS lookup.

```
R1(config)# no ip domain-lookup
```

Step 4: Configure the OSPF routing protocol on R2 and R3.

Note: R2 and R3 exchange routes in OSPF AS 101. R1 is acting as an ISP router and does not participate in the OSPF routing process.

a. On R2, use the following commands:

```
R2(config)# router ospf 101
R2(config-router)# network 10.2.2.0 0.0.0.3 area 0
```

```
R2(config-router)# network 192.168.2.0 0.0.0.255 area 0
```

b. On R3, use the following commands:

```
R3(config)# router ospf 101
R3(config-router)# network 192.168.3.0 0.0.0.255 area 0
R3(config-router)# network 10.2.2.0 0.0.0.3 area 0
```

Step 5: Configure a static default route on R2.

Router R1 represents a connection to the Internet. A default route is configured on R2 for all traffic whose destination network does not exist in the R2 routing table.

Note: Without the default route configured on R2, R2 cannot respond to the CCP HTTP connection from PC-A later in the lab. Because R1 is not part of the OSPF domain and is not advertising the PC-A LAN, R2 does not know about the 192.168.1.0/24 network.

a. Configure a static default route on R2 that points to the R1 S0/0/0 interface IP address.

```
R2(config)# ip route 0.0.0.0 0.0.0.0 10.1.1.1
```

b. Redistribute the static default into OSFP so that R3 also learns the route.

```
R2(config)# router ospf 101
R2(config-router)# default-information originate
```

Step 6: Configure PC host IP settings.

a. Configure a static IP address, subnet mask, and default gateway for PC-A, as shown in the IP addressing table.

b. Configure a static IP address, subnet mask, and default gateway for PC-C, as shown in the IP addressing table.

Step 7: Verify basic network connectivity.

a. Ping from PC-A to the R2 S0/0/0 interface at IP address **10.1.1.2**.

If the pings are unsuccessful, troubleshoot the basic device configurations before continuing.

Note: PC-A should be able to ping external R2 interface S0/0/0, but is unable to ping any of the internal OSPF network IP addresses on R2 and R3.

b. Ping from R2 to PC-C on the R3 LAN.

If the pings are unsuccessful, troubleshoot the basic device configurations before continuing.

Note: If you can ping from R2 to PC-C, you have demonstrated that the OSPF routing protocol is configured and functioning correctly. If you cannot ping, but the device interfaces are up and IP addresses are correct, use the **show run** and **show ip route** commands to help identify routing protocol-related problems.

Step 8: Configure a minimum password length.

Note: Passwords in this lab are set to a minimum of 10 characters, but are relatively simple for the benefit of performing the lab. More complex passwords are recommended in a production network.

Use the **security passwords** command to set a minimum password length of **10** characters.

```
R1(config)# security passwords min-length 10
```

Step 9: Configure the basic console and vty lines.

a. Configure a console password and enable login for router R1. For additional security, the **exec-timeout** command causes the line to log out after **5** minutes of inactivity. The **logging synchronous** command prevents console messages from interrupting command entry.

Note: To avoid repetitive logins during this lab, the **exec-timeout** can be set to 0 0, which prevents it from expiring; however, we do not recommend this.

```
R1(config)# line console 0
R1(config-line)# password ciscoconpass
R1(config-line)# exec-timeout 5 0
R1(config-line)# login
R1(config-line)# logging synchronous
```

b. Configure the password on the vty lines for router R1.

```
R1(config)# line vty 0 4
R1(config-line)# password ciscovtypass
R1(config-line)# exec-timeout 5 0
R1(config-line)# login
```

c. Repeat these configurations on both R2 and R3.

Step 10: Encrypt clear text passwords.

a. Use the **service password-encryption** command to encrypt the console, aux, and vty passwords.

```
R1(config)# service password-encryption
```

b. Issue the **show run** command. Can you read the console, aux, and vty passwords? Explain.

_____

_____

c. Repeat this configuration on both R2 and R3.

Step 11: Save the basic running configuration for all three routers.

Save the running configuration to the startup configuration from the privileged EXEC mode prompt.

```
R1# copy running-config startup-config
```

Part 2: Configuring a Remote Access VPN

In Part 2, you will configure a remote access IPsec VPN. You will use CCP to configure R2 as an Easy VPN server and configure the Cisco VPN client on PC-A. The PC-A host simulates an employee connecting from home over the Internet. Router R1 simulates an Internet ISP router.

Task 1: Prepare R2 for CCP Access and Easy VPN Server Setup.

Step 1: Configure user credentials for HTTPS router access prior to starting CCP.

a. Enable the secure HTTP server on R2.

```
R2(config)# ip http secure-server
```

b. Create an admin account on R2 with privilege level 15 for use with AAA and CCP.

```
R2(config)# username admin privilege 15 password cisco12345
```

c. Have CCP use the local database to authenticate web sessions.

```
R2(config)# ip http authentication local
```

Step 2: Access CCP and discover R2.

a. Run the CCP application on PC-A. In the Select/Manage Community window, in the IP Address/Hostname field, enter the R2 IP address **10.1.1.2**; in the Username field, enter **admin**; in the Password field, enter **cisco12345**. Click the **Connect Securely** check box, and then click **OK**.

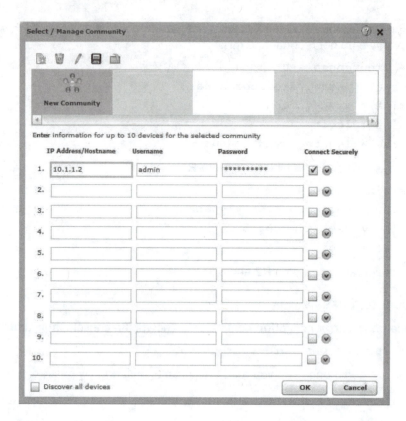

b. At the CCP Dashboard, click **Discover** to discover and connect to R1. If the discovery process fails, click **Discover Details** to determine the possible problem in order to resolve the issue.

c. Click **Yes** to accept the certificate when the Security Certificate Alert window displays.

Task 2: Use the CCP VPN Wizard to Configure the Easy VPN Server.

Step 1: Launch the Easy VPN server wizard and configure AAA services.

a. At the top of the CCP home screen, click **Configure**. In the left pane, click **Security** > **VPN** > **Easy VPN Server**.

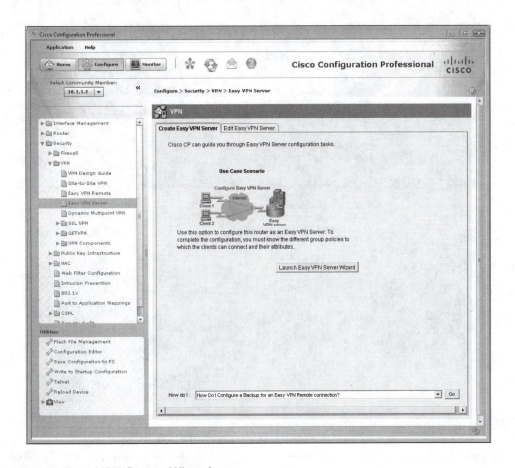

b. Click **Launch Easy VPN Server Wizard**.

The Easy VPN Server wizard checks the router configuration to see if AAA is enabled. If not, the Enable AAA window displays. AAA must be enabled on the router before the Easy VPN Server configuration starts.

c. Click **Yes** to continue with the configuration.

d. If prompted to deliver the configuration to the router, click **Deliver**.

e. In the Command Delivery Status window, click **OK**. When the "AAA has been successfully enabled on the router" message displays, click **OK**.

f. Now that AAA is enabled, you can start the Easy VPN Server wizard by clicking **Next** in the Welcome window. Read through the descriptions of the tasks that the wizard guides you through.

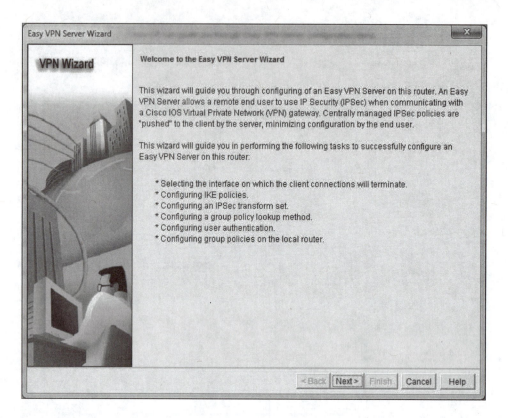

How does the client receive the IPsec policies?

_____

_____

How does the Easy VPN remote server configuration differ from the site-to-site?

_____

_____

g.   Click **Next** when you are finished answering the above questions.

Step 2: Configure the virtual tunnel interface and authentication

a.   From the pull-down list, select the **Serial0/0/0** interface as the interface for the Easy VPN Server. This is the interface on which the client connections terminate.

b.   Select the **Pre-shared Keys** option for the authentication type and click **Next** to continue.

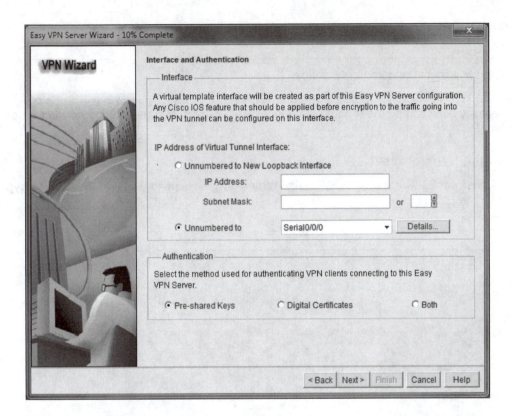

Step 3: Select the IKE proposal.

a.   In the Internet Key Exchange (IKE) Proposals window, the default IKE proposal is used for R2.

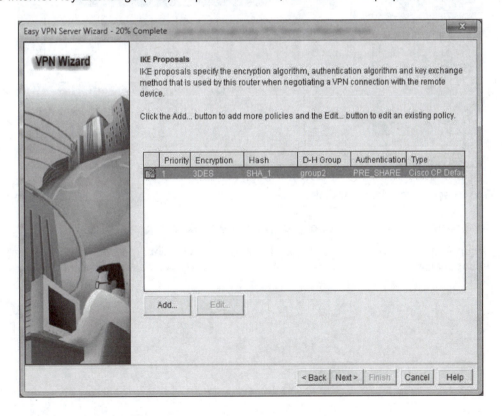

What is the encryption method used with the default IKE policy?

What is the hash algorithm used to ensure that the keys have not been tampered with?

_____

b.   Click **Next** to accept the default IKE policy.

Note: Configurations on both sides of the tunnel must match exactly. However, the Cisco VPN client automatically selects the proper configuration for itself. Therefore, no IKE configuration is necessary on the client PC.

Step 4: Select the transform set.

a.   In the Transform Set window, the CCP default transform set is used. What is the ESP encryption method used with the default transform set?

_____

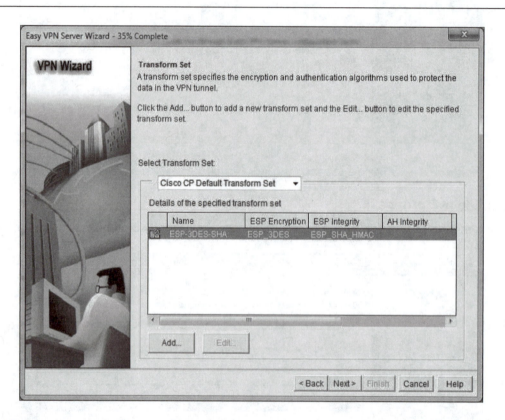

b.   Click **Next** to accept the default transform set.

Step 5: Specify group authorization and group policy lookup.

a.   In the Group Authorization and Group Policy Lookup window, select the **Local** option because a RADIUS server is not available.

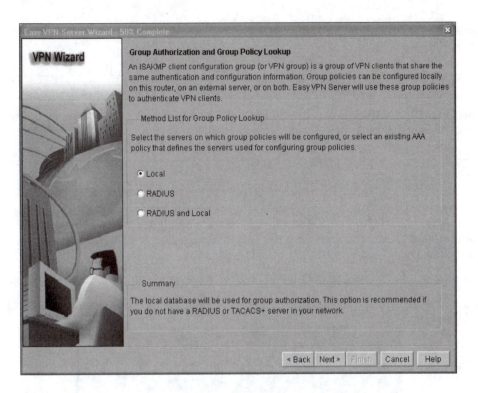

b. Click **Next** to create a new AAA method list for the group policy lookup that uses the local router database.

Step 6: Configure User Authentication (XAuth).

a. In the User Authentication (XAuth) window, you can specify where user information will be configured. Choices include an external server, such as a RADIUS server, a local database, or both. Check the **Enable User Authentication** check box and accept the default of **Local Only**.

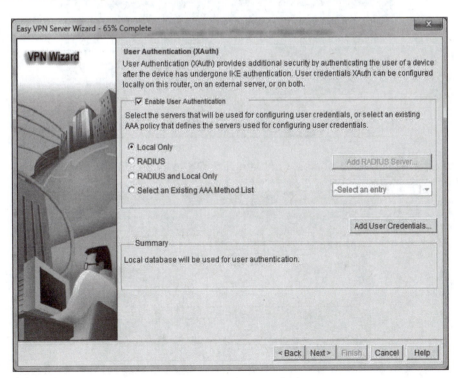

Where does the router look for valid user account and passwords to authenticate remote VPN users when they attempt to log in?

_____

_____

b.   Click **Add User Credentials**. In the User Accounts window, you can view currently defined users or add new users. What is the name of the user currently defined, and what is the user privilege level?

_____

How was this user defined?

_____

c.   In the User Accounts window, click **Add** to add another user. Enter the username **user01** with a password of **user01pass**, and check the Encrypt Password Using MD5 Hash Algorithm check box. Leave the privilege level at **1**.

What is the range of privilege levels that can be set for a user?

_____

d.   Click **OK** to accept the user01 entries, and then click **OK** to close the User Accounts window.

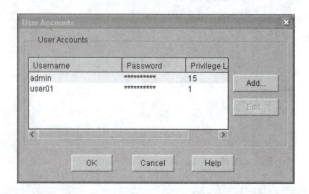

e.   In the User Authentication (XAuth) window, click **Next** to continue.

Step 7: Specify group authorization and user group policies.

a. In the Group Authorization and User Group Policies window, you must create at least one group policy for the VPN server.

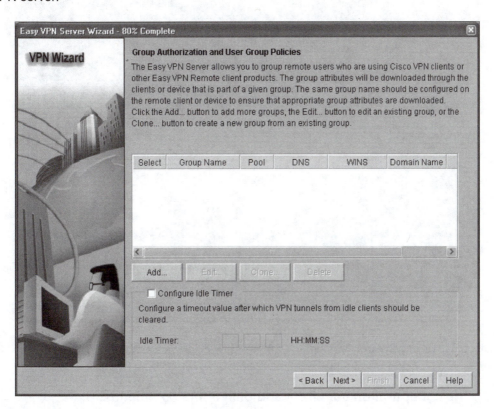

b. Click **Add** to create a group policy.

c. In the Add Group Policy window, enter **VPN-Access** as the name of this group. Enter a new pre-shared key of **cisco12345**, and then re-enter it.

d. Leave the **Pool Information** box checked. Enter a starting address of **192.168.2.101**, an ending address of **192.168.2.150**, and a subnet mask of **255.255.255.0**.

e. Enter **50** for the Maximum Connections Allowed.

f. Click **OK** to accept the entries.

g. If a CCP warning message displays, indicating that the IP addresses in the pool and the IP address of the Loopback0 interface are in the same subnet, click **Yes** to confirm.

Why use an IP network for the VPN clients pool that is associated with a loopback interface?

_____

_____

_____

How does R3 route traffic to the VPN clients?

_____

_____

_____

h. When you return to the Group Authorization window, click the **Configure Idle Timer** check box and enter one hour (**1**). This disconnects idle users if there is no activity for one hour and allows others to connect. Click **Next** to continue.

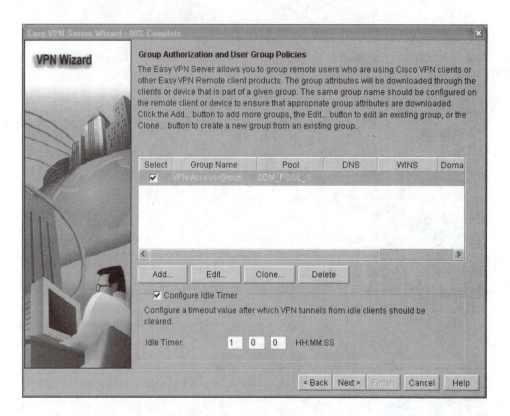

i.   If the Cisco Tunneling Control Protocol (cTCP) window displays, do not enable cTCP. Click **Next** to continue.

Step 8: Review the configuration summary and deliver the commands.

a.   Scroll through the commands that CCP will send to the router. Do not click the **Test VPN connectivity after configuring** check box. Click **Finish**.

b.   If prompted to deliver the configuration to the router, click **Deliver**.

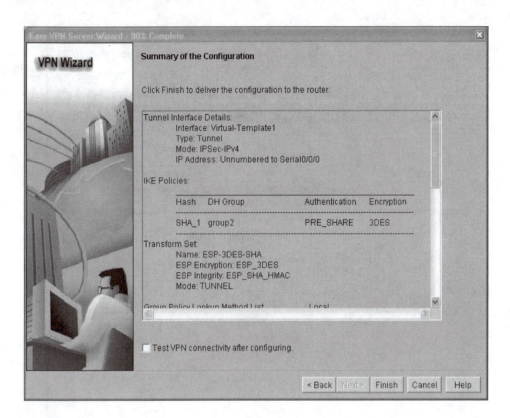

c.   In the Command Delivery Status window, click **OK**. How many commands were delivered?

Step 9: Test the VPN server.

a.   You are returned to the main VPN window with the **Edit Easy VPN Server** tab selected. Click **Test VPN Server** in the bottom-right corner of the screen.

b.   In the VPN Troubleshooting window, click **Start**.

c.   Your screen should look similar to the one below. Click **OK** to close the information window. Click **Close** to exit the VPN Troubleshooting window.

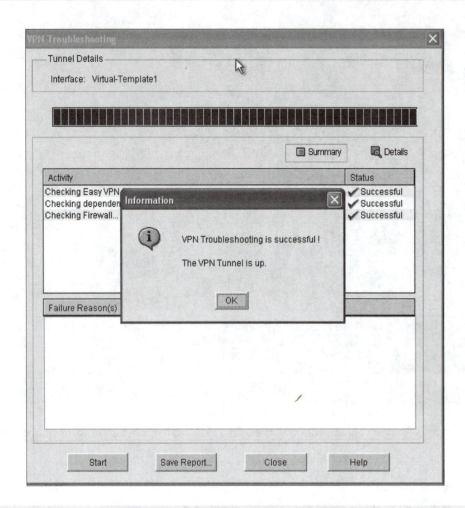

Note: If you receive a failure after testing the VPN server, close the VPN Troubleshooting window.

1) Click the **Edit** button on top-right of the Edit Easy VPN Server Tab.

2) Click **OK** in the Edit Easy VPN Server Connection window.

3) Click **OK** in the Easy VPN Server Passthrough Configuration window.

4) Click the box to the right of the FastEthernet0/1 interface indicating that it is inside (Trusted).

5) Rerun **Test VPN Server** by clicking on that button on the bottom-right of the Edit Easy VPN Server Tab.

6) Click **Start** button and test should pass this time.

Task 3: Use the Cisco VPN Client to Test the Remote Access VPN.

Step 1: (Optional) Install the Cisco VPN client.

If not already installed, install the Cisco VPN client software on host PC-A. If you do not have the Cisco VPN client software, contact your instructor.

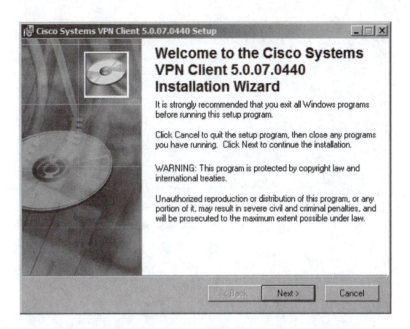

Step 2: Configure PC-A as a VPN client to access the R2 VPN server.

a. Start the Cisco VPN client and select the **Connection Entries** tab; click the **New** icon.

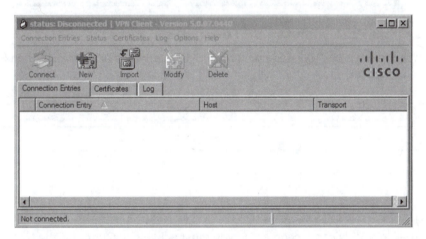

b. Enter the following information to define the new connection entry. Click **Save** when you are finished.

Connection Entry: **VPN-R2**

Description: **Connection to R2 internal network**

Host: **10.1.1.2** (IP address of the R2 S0/0/0 interface)

Group Authentication Name: **VPN-Access** (Defines the address pool configured in Task 2)

Password: **cisco12345** (Pre-shared key configured in Task 2)

Confirm Password: **cisco12345**

Note: The group authentication name and password are case-sensitive and must match the ones created on the VPN server.

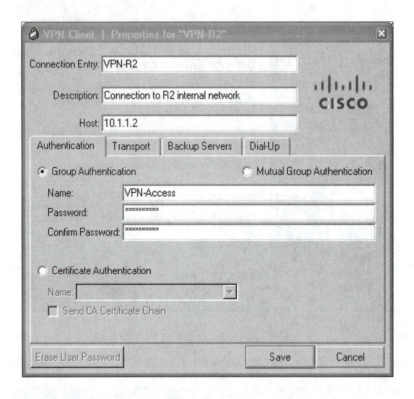

Step 3: Test access from PC-A without a VPN connection.

    a.   Open a command prompt on PC-A, and ping the PC-C IP address at **192.168.3.3** on the R3 LAN. Are the pings successful? Explain.

_____

_____

_____

_____

_____

_____

    Note: After creating a VPN connection entry, you must activate it. Currently, the VPN tunnel is not up.

Step 4: Establish a VPN connection and login.

    a.   Select the newly created connection VPN-R2 and click the **Connect** icon. You can also double-click the connection entry.

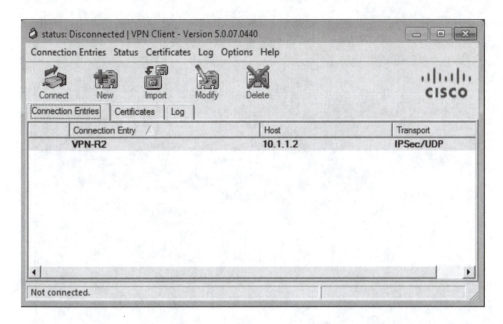

b.   Enter the username **user01** created previously on the VPN router, and enter the password **user01pass**.

c.   Click **OK** to continue. The VPN Client window minimizes to a lock icon in the tools system tray of the taskbar. When the lock is closed, the VPN tunnel is up. When it is open, the VPN connection is down.

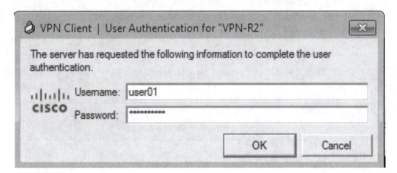

Task 4: Verify the VPN Tunnel Between the Client, Server, and Internal Network.

Step 1: Check the VPN Client status.

a.   Double-click the VPN lock icon to expand the VPN Client window.

b.   What does it say about the connection status at the top of the window?

_____

Step 2: Check the tunnel statistics.

a.   On the VPN connection menu bar, click **Status** > **Statistics** to display the Tunnel Details tab.

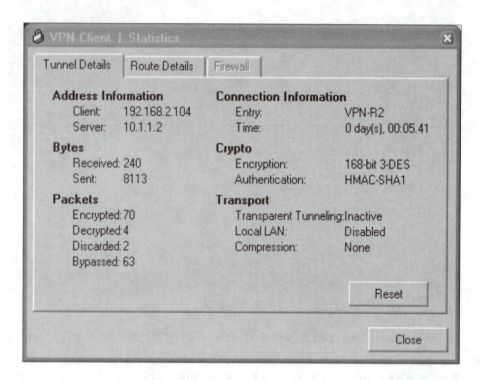

What is the Client IP address obtained from the VPN server?

_____

_____

Note: Each time you disconnect and reconnect to the VPN server, you receive a new IP address until the limit is reached.

b.   What is the VPN server address?

_____

How many packets have been encrypted?

_____

What is the encryption method being used?

_____

What is the authentication being used?

_____

Step 3: Check the Cisco IOS messages on R2 when the tunnel is created.

Open the console connection for R2 and locate the message displayed indicating that the virtual interface came up when the VPN Client connection was created.

```
R2#
*Feb  2 16:09:08.907: %LINEPROTO-5-UPDOWN: Line protocol on Interface Virtual-Access2,
changed state to up
R2#
```

Step 4: Verify the VPN connection.

a.   From the PC-A command prompt, issue the **ipconfig /all** command to see the network connections currently in use.

b. What is the configuration for the first local area connection?

IP Address: _____

Subnet Mask: _____

Default Gateway: _____

Description: _____

c. What is the configuration for Local Area Connection 2?

IP Address: _____

Subnet Mask: _____

Default Gateway: _____

Description: _____

Step 5: Test the access from the client with the VPN connection.

With the VPN connection from computer PC-A to router R2 activated, open a command prompt on PC-A, and ping the PC-C IP address at **192.168.3.3** on the R3 LAN. Are the pings successful? Explain.

_____

_____

_____

_____

_____

Step 6: Telnet to R2 from PC-A.

a. From the PC-A command prompt, telnet to R2 at the Lo0 IP address **192.168.2.1**. Log in as **admin** with the password **cisco12345**. What is the router command prompt and why?

_____

_____

_____

b. Issue the **show run** command to view the various commands generated by CCP to configure the VPN server.

c. Issue the **show users** command to see the connections to router R2. What connections are present?

_____

_____

d. Exit the Telnet session with the **quit** or **exit** command.

e. Telnet from PC-A to R2 again at the Lo0 IP address **192.168.2.1**. Log in as **user01** with the password **user01pass**. What is the router command prompt and why is this?

_____

_____

_____

f. Exit the Telnet session with the **quit** or **exit** command.

g. Right-click the **VPN Client** icon in the tools tray and select **Disconnect**, or click the **VPN-R2** connection and click the **Disconnect** icon.

Reflection

Why is VPN a good option for remote users?

_____

_____

_____

_____

_____

_____

Router Interface Summary Table

Router Interface Summary				
Router Model	**Ethernet Interface #1**	**Ethernet Interface #2**	**Serial Interface #1**	**Serial Interface #2**
1800	Fast Ethernet 0/0 (Fa0/0)	Fast Ethernet 0/1 (Fa0/1)	Serial 0/0/0 (S0/0/0)	Serial 0/0/1 (S0/0/1)
1900	Gigabit Ethernet 0/0 (G0/0)	Gigabit Ethernet 0/1 (G0/1)	Serial 0/0/0 (S0/0/0)	Serial 0/0/1 (S0/0/1)
2801	Fast Ethernet 0/0 (Fa0/0)	Fast Ethernet 0/1 (Fa0/1)	Serial 0/1/0 (S0/1/0)	Serial 0/1/1 (S0/1/1)
2811	Fast Ethernet 0/0 (Fa0/0)	Fast Ethernet 0/1 (Fa0/1)	Serial 0/0/0 (S0/0/0)	Serial 0/0/1 (S0/0/1)
2900	Gigabit Ethernet 0/0 (G0/0)	Gigabit Ethernet 0/1 (G0/1)	Serial 0/0/0 (S0/0/0)	Serial 0/0/1 (S0/0/1)
Note: To find out how the router is configured, look at the interfaces to identify the type of router and how many interfaces the router has. There is no way to effectively list all the combinations of configurations for each router class. This table includes identifiers for the possible combinations of Ethernet and Serial interfaces in the device. The table does not include any other type of interface, even though a specific router may contain one. An example of this might be an ISDN BRI interface. The string in parenthesis is the legal abbreviation that can be used in Cisco IOS commands to represent the interface.				

Chapter 9: Implementing the Cisco Adaptive Security Appliance (ASA)

Lab 9.4.1.1 - Configuring ASA Basic Settings and Firewall Using CLI

Topology

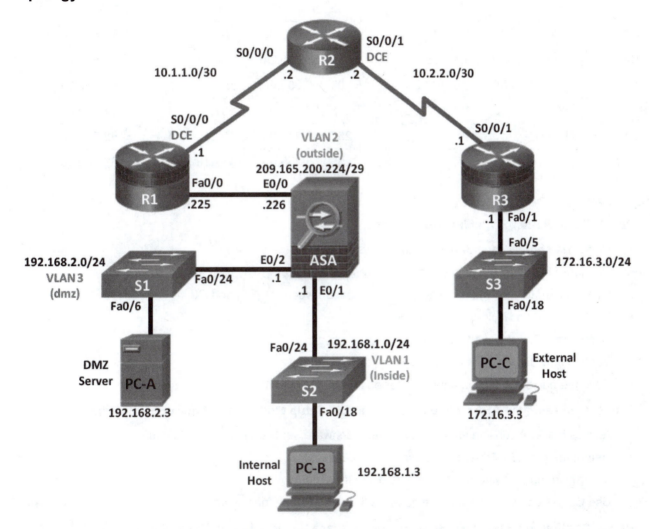

Note: ISR G2 devices use GigabitEthernet interfaces instead of FastEthernet interfaces.

IP Addressing Table

Device	Interface	IP Address	Subnet Mask	Default Gateway	Switch Port
R1	Fa0/0	209.165.200.225	255.255.255.248	N/A	ASA E0/0
R1	S0/0/0 (DCE)	10.1.1.1	255.255.255.252	N/A	N/A
R2	S0/0/0	10.1.1.2	255.255.255.252	N/A	N/A
R2	S0/0/1 (DCE)	10.2.2.2	255.255.255.252	N/A	N/A
R3	Fa0/1	172.16.3.1	255.255.255.0	N/A	S3 Fa0/5
R3	S0/0/1	10.2.2.1	255.255.255.252	N/A	N/A
ASA	VLAN 1 (E0/1)	192.168.1.1	255.255.255.0	NA	S2 Fa0/24
ASA	VLAN 2 (E0/0)	209.165.200.226	255.255.255.248	NA	R1 Fa0/0
ASA	VLAN 3 (E0/2)	192.168.2.1	255.255.255.0	NA	S1 Fa0/24
PC-A	NIC	192.168.2.3	255.255.255.0	192.168.2.1	S1 Fa0/6
PC-B	NIC	192.168.1.3	255.255.255.0	192.168.1.1	S2 Fa0/18
PC-C	NIC	172.16.3.3	255.255.255.0	172.16.3.1	S3 Fa0/18

Objectives

Part 1: Basic Router/Switch/PC Configuration

- Cable the network as shown in the topology.
- Configure hostnames and interface IP addresses for routers, switches, and PCs.
- Configure static routing, including default routes, between R1, R2, and R3.
- Enable HTTP and Telnet access for R1.
- Configure PC host IP settings.
- Verify connectivity between hosts, switches, and routers.
- Save the basic running configuration for each router and switch.

Part 2: Accessing the ASA Console and Using CLI Setup Mode to Configure Basic Settings

- Access the ASA console and view hardware, software, and configuration settings.
- Determine the ASA version, interfaces, and license.
- Determine the file system and contents of flash memory.
- Use CLI Setup mode to configure basic settings (hostname, passwords, clock, etc.).

Part 3: Configuring Basic ASA Settings and Interface Security Levels Using the CLI

- Configure the hostname and domain name.
- Configure the login and enable passwords.
- Set the date and time.
- Configure the inside and outside interfaces.
- Test connectivity to the ASA.
- Configure Telnet access to the ASA.
- Configure HTTPS access on the ASA for ASDM.

Part 4: Configuring Routing, Address Translation, and Inspection Policy Using the CLI

- Configure a static default route for the ASA.

- Configure port address translation (PAT) and network objects.

- Modify the MPF application inspection global service policy.

Part 5: Configuring DHCP, AAA, and SSH

- Configure the ASA as a DHCP server/client.

- Configure Local AAA user authentication.

- Configure SSH remote access to the AAA.

Part 6: Configuring DMZ, Static NAT, and ACLs

- Configure the DMZ interface VLAN3 on the ASA.

- Configure static NAT for the DMZ server using a network object.

- Configure an ACL to allow access to the DMZ for Internet users.

- Verify access to the DMZ server for external and internal users.

Background / Scenario

The Cisco Adaptive Security Appliance (ASA) is an advanced network security device that integrates a stateful firewall, VPN, and other capabilities. This lab employs an ASA 5505 to create a firewall and protect an internal corporate network from external intruders while allowing internal hosts access to the Internet. The ASA creates three security interfaces: Outside, Inside, and DMZ. It provides outside users limited access to the DMZ and no access to inside resources. Inside users can access the DMZ and outside resources.

This lab's focus is the configuration of the ASA as a basic firewall. Other devices will receive minimal configuration to support the ASA portion of this lab. This lab uses the ASA CLI, which is similar to the IOS CLI, to configure basic device and security settings.

In Part 1 of this lab, you will configure the topology and non-ASA devices. In Parts 2 through 4, you configure basic ASA settings and the firewall between the inside and outside networks. In Part 5, you configure the ASA for additional services such as DHCP, AAA, and SSH. In Part 6, you will configure a DMZ on the ASA and provide access to a server in the DMZ.

Your company has one location connected to an ISP. Router R1 represents a customer-premise equipment (CPE) device managed by the ISP. Router R2 represents an intermediate Internet router. Router R3 represents an ISP that connects an administrator from a network management company, who has been hired to manage your network remotely. The ASA is an edge security device that connects the internal corporate network and DMZ to the ISP while providing NAT and DHCP services to inside hosts. The ASA will be configured for management by an administrator on the internal network and by the remote administrator. Layer 3 VLAN interfaces provide access to the three areas created in the lab: Inside, Outside, and DMZ. The ISP has assigned the public IP address space of 209.165.200.224/29, which will be used for address translation on the ASA.

Note: The router commands and output in this lab are from a Cisco 1841 with Cisco IOS Release 15.1(4)M8 (Advanced IP Services image). Other routers and Cisco IOS versions can be used. See the Router Interface Summary Table at the end of this lab to determine which interface identifiers to use based on the equipment in the lab. Depending on the router model and Cisco IOS version, the available commands and output produced might vary from what is shown in this lab.

The ASA used with this lab is a Cisco model 5505 with an 8-port integrated switch, running OS version 8.4(2) and Adaptive Security Device Manager (ASDM) version 7.2(1), and comes with a Base license that allows a maximum of three VLANs.

Note: Ensure that the routers and switches have been erased and have no startup configurations.

Required Resources

- 3 Routers (Cisco 1841 with Cisco IOS Release 15.1(4)M8 Advanced IP Services image or comparable)
- 3 Switches (Cisco 2960 or comparable)
- 1 ASA 5505 (OS version 8.4(2) and ASDM version 7.2(1) and Base license or comparable)
- 3 PCs (Windows Vista or Windows 7 with CCP 2.5, Cisco VPN Client, latest version of Java, Internet Explorer, and Flash Player)
- Serial and Ethernet cables as shown in the topology
- Console cables to configure the routers via the console

CCP Notes:

- If the PC on which CCP is installed is running Windows Vista or Windows 7, it may be necessary to right-click the CCP icon or menu item, and select **Run as administrator**.
- To run CCP, it may be necessary to temporarily disable antivirus programs and O/S firewalls. Ensure that all pop-up blockers are turned off in the browser.

Part 1: Basic Router/Switch/PC Configuration

In Part 1 of this lab, you set up the network topology and configure basic settings on the routers, such as interface IP addresses and static routing.

Note: Do not configure any ASA settings at this time.

Step 1: Cable the network and clear previous device settings.

Attach the devices that are shown in the topology diagram and cable as necessary. Make sure that the routers and switches have been erased and have no startup configurations.

Step 2: Configure basic settings for routers and switches.

a. Configure hostnames as shown in the topology for each router.

b. Configure router interface IP addresses as shown in the IP Addressing Table.

c. Configure a clock rate for routers with a DCE serial cable attached to their serial interface. Router R1 is shown here as an example.

```
R1(config)# interface S0/0/0
R1(config-if)# clock rate 64000
```

d. Configure the host name for the switches. Other than the host name, the switches can be left in their default configuration state. Configuring the VLAN management IP address for the switches is optional.

Step 3: Configure static routing on the routers.

a. Configure a static default route from R1 to R2 and from R3 to R2.

```
R1(config)# ip route 0.0.0.0 0.0.0.0 Serial0/0/0

R3(config)# ip route 0.0.0.0 0.0.0.0 Serial0/0/1
```

b. Configure a static route from R2 to the R1 Fa0/0 subnet (connected to ASA interface E0/0) and a static route from R2 to the R3 LAN.

```
R2(config)# ip route 209.165.200.224 255.255.255.248 Serial0/0/0
R2(config)# ip route 172.16.3.0 255.255.255.0 Serial0/0/1
```

Step 4: Enable the HTTP server on R1 and set the enable and vty passwords.

a. Enable HTTP access to R1 using the **ip http server** command in global config mode. Also set the console and VTY passwords to **cisco**. This will provide web and Telnet targets for testing later in the lab.

```
R1(config)# ip http server
R1(config)# enable password class

R1(config)# line vty 0 4
R1(config-line)# password cisco
R1(config-line)# login

R1(config)# line con 0
R1(config-line)# password cisco
R1(config-line)# login
```

b. On routers R2 and R3, set the same enable, console and vty passwords as with R1.

Step 5: Configure PC host IP settings.

Configure a static IP address, subnet mask, and default gateway for PC-A, PC-B, and PC-C as shown in the IP Addressing Table.

Step 6: Verify connectivity.

Because the ASA is the focal point for the network zones and it has not yet been configured, there will be no connectivity between devices that are connected to it. However, PC-C should be able to ping the R1 interface. From PC-C, ping the R1 Fa0/0 IP address (**209.165.200.225**). If these pings are not successful, troubleshoot the basic device configurations before continuing.

Note: If you can ping from PC-C to R1 Fa0/0 and S0/0/0, you have demonstrated that static routing is configured and functioning correctly.

Step 7: Save the basic running configuration for each router and switch.

Part 2: Accessing the ASA Console and Using CLI Setup to Configure Basic Settings

In Part 2 of this lab, you will access the ASA via the console and use various **show** commands to determine hardware, software, and configuration settings. You will clear the current configuration and use the CLI interactive Setup utility to configure basic ASA settings.

Note: Do not configure any ASA settings at this time.

Step 1: Access the ASA console.

a. Accessing the ASA via the console port is the same as with a Cisco router or switch. Connect to the ASA console port with a rollover cable.

b. Use a terminal emulation program, such as TeraTerm or PuTTy to access the CLI. Then use the serial port settings of 9600 baud, 8 data bits, no parity, one stop bit, and no flow control.

c. Enter privileged mode with the **enable** command and password (if set). By default, the password is blank; press **Enter**. If the password has been changed to that specified in this lab, enter the word **class**. The default ASA hostname and prompt is **ciscoasa>**.

```
ciscoasa> enable
Password: class (or press Enter if none set)
```

Step 2: Determine the ASA version, interfaces, and license.

The ASA 5505 comes with an integrated 8-port Ethernet switch. Ports E0/0 to E0/5 are normal Fast Ethernet ports, and ports E0/6 and E0/7 are PoE ports for use with PoE devices, such as IP phones or network cameras.

Use the **show version** command to determine various aspects of this ASA device:

```
ciscoasa# show version

Cisco Adaptive Security Appliance Software Version 8.4(2)
Device Manager Version 6.4(5)

Compiled on Wed 15-Jun-11 18:17 by builders
System image file is "disk0:/asa842-k8.bin"
Config file at boot was "startup-config"

ciscoasa up 23 hours 0 mins

Hardware:   ASA5505, 512 MB RAM, CPU Geode 500 MHz
Internal ATA Compact Flash, 128MB
BIOS Flash M50FW016 @ 0xfff00000, 2048KB

Encryption hardware device : Cisco ASA-5505 on-board accelerator (revision 0x0)
                             Boot microcode         : CN1000-MC-BOOT-2.00
                             SSL/IKE microcode      : CNLite-MC-SSLm-PLUS-2.03
                             IPSec microcode        : CNlite-MC-IPSECm-MAIN-2.06
                             Number of accelerators: 1

 0: Int: Internal-Data0/0    : address is 0007.7dbf.5645, irq 11
 1: Ext: Ethernet0/0         : address is 0007.7dbf.563d, irq 255
 2: Ext: Ethernet0/1         : address is 0007.7dbf.563e, irq 255

<output omitted>
```

What software version is this ASA running?

_____

What is the name of the system image file and from where was it loaded?

_____

The ASA can be managed using a built-in GUI known as ASDM. What version of ASDM is this ASA running?

_____

How much RAM does this ASA have?

_____

How much flash memory does this ASA have?

_____

How many Ethernet ports does this ASA have?

_____

What type of license does this ASA have?

_____

How many VLANs can be created with this license?

_____

Step 3: Determine the file system and contents of flash memory.

a. Display the ASA file system using the **show file system** command to determine what prefixes are supported.

```
ciscoasa# show file system


File Systems:

     Size(b)        Free(b)       Type     Flags   Prefixes
* 128573440       55664640       disk      rw      disk0: flash:
           -             -       network   rw      tftp:
           -             -       opaque    rw      system:
           -             -       network   ro      http:
           -             -       network   ro      https:
           -             -       network   rw      ftp:
           -             -       network   rw      smb:
```

What is another name for flash:?_____

b. Display the contents of flash memory using one of these commands: **show flash**, **show disk0**, **dir flash:**, or **dir disk0:**.

```
ciscoasa# show flash:
--#--  --length--  -----date/time------  path
  168  25159680    Aug 29 2011 13:00:52  asa842-k8.bin
  122  0           Aug 29 2011 13:09:32  nat_ident_migrate
   13  2048        Aug 29 2011 13:02:14  coredumpinfo
   14  59          Aug 29 2011 13:02:14  coredumpinfo/coredump.cfg
  169  16280544    Aug 29 2011 13:02:58  asdm-645.bin
    3  2048        Aug 29 2011 13:04:42  log
    6  2048        Aug 29 2011 13:05:00  crypto_archive
  171  34816       Jan 01 1980 00:00:00  FSCK0000.REC
  173  36864       Jan 01 1980 00:00:00  FSCK0001.REC
  174  12998641    Aug 29 2011 13:09:22  csd_3.5.2008-k9.pkg
  175  2048        Aug 29 2011 13:09:24  sdesktop
  211  0           Aug 29 2011 13:09:24  sdesktop/data.xml
  176  6487517     Aug 29 2011 13:09:26  anyconnect-macosx-i386-2.5.2014-k9.pkg
  177  6689498     Aug 29 2011 13:09:30  anyconnect-linux-2.5.2014-k9.pkg
  178  4678691     Aug 29 2011 13:09:32  anyconnect-win-2.5.2014-k9.pkg
  <output omitted>
```

c. What is the name of the ASDM file in flash:? _____

Step 4: Determine the current running configuration.

The ASA 5505 is commonly used as an edge security device that connects a small business or teleworker to an ISP device, such as a DSL or cable modem, for access to the Internet. The default factory configuration for the ASA 5505 includes the following:

- An inside VLAN 1 interface is configured that includes the Ethernet 0/1 through 0/7 switch ports. The VLAN 1 IP address and mask are 192.168.1.1 and 255.255.255.0.

- An outside VLAN 2 interface is configured that includes the Ethernet 0/0 switch port. By default, VLAN 2 derives its IP address from the ISP using DHCP.

- The default route is also derived from the DHCP default gateway.

- All inside IP addresses are translated when accessing the outside, using interface PAT on the VLAN 2 interface.

- By default, inside users can access the outside with an access list, and outside users are prevented from accessing the inside.

- The DHCP server is enabled on the security appliance, so a PC connecting to the VLAN 1 interface receives an address between 192.168.1.5 and 192.168.1.36 (base license), though the actual range may vary.

- The HTTP server is enabled for ASDM and is accessible to users on the 192.168.1.0/24 network.

- No console or enable passwords are required and the default hostname is **ciscoasa**.

Note: In this lab, you will manually configure settings similar to those listed above, as well as some additional ones, using the ASA CLI.

a. Display the current running configuration using the **show running-config** command.

```
ciscoasa# show running-config
: Saved
:
ASA Version 8.4(2)
!
hostname ciscoasa
enable password 8Ry2YjIyt7RRXU24 encrypted
passwd 2KFQnbNIdI.2KYOU encrypted
names
!
interface Ethernet0/0
 switchport access vlan 2
!
interface Ethernet0/1
!
interface Ethernet0/2

<output omitted>
```

Note: To stop the output from a command using the CLI, press **Q**.

If you see VLANs 1 and 2 and other settings as described previously, the device is most likely configured with the default factory configuration. You may also see other security features, such as a global policy that inspects selected application traffic, which the ASA inserts by default, if the original startup configuration has been erased. The actual output varies depending on the ASA model, version, and configuration status.

b. You can restore the ASA to its factory default settings by using the **configure factory-default** command.

```
ciscoasa# conf t
ciscoasa(config)# configure factory-default

WARNING: The boot system configuration will be cleared.
The first image found in disk0:/ will be used to boot the
system on the next reload.
Verify there is a valid image on disk0:/ or the system will
not boot.

Begin to apply factory-default configuration:
Clear all configuration
WARNING: DHCPD bindings cleared on interface 'inside', address pool removed
Executing command: interface Ethernet 0/0
Executing command: switchport access vlan 2
Executing command: no shutdown
Executing command: exit
Executing command: interface Ethernet 0/1
Executing command: switchport access vlan 1
Executing command: no shutdown
Executing command: exit

<output omitted>
```

c. Review this output and pay particular attention to the VLAN interfaces, and NAT- and DHCP-related sections. These will be configured later in this lab using the CLI.

d. You may want to capture and print the factory-default configuration as a reference. Use the terminal emulation program to copy it from the ASA and paste it into a text document. You can then edit this file, if desired, so that it contains only valid commands. You should also remove password commands and enter the **no shut** command to bring up the desired interfaces.

Step 5: Clear the previous ASA configuration settings.

a. Use the **write erase** command to remove the **startup-config** file from flash memory.

```
ciscoasa# write erase
Erase configuration in flash memory? [confirm]
[OK]
ciscoasa#

ciscoasa# show start
No Configuration
```

Note: The IOS command **erase startup-config** is not supported on the ASA.

b. Use the **reload** command to restart the ASA. This causes the ASA to come up in CLI Setup mode. If prompted that the config has been modified, asking to save it, respond with **N**, and then press **Enter** to proceed with the reload.

```
ciscoasa# reload
Proceed with reload? [confirm]
ciscoasa#
***
*** --- START GRACEFUL SHUTDOWN ---
```

```
Shutting down isakmp
Shutting down File system
***
*** --- SHUTDOWN NOW ---
Process shutdown finished
Rebooting.....
CISCO SYSTEMS
Embedded BIOS Version 1.0(12)13 08/28/08 15:50:37.45
<output omitted>
```

Step 6: Use the Setup interactive CLI mode to configure basic settings.

When the ASA completes the reload process, it should detect that the **startup-config** file is missing and present a series of interactive prompts to configure basic ASA settings. If it does not come up in this mode, repeat Step 5. As an alternative, you can run the **setup** command at the global configuration mode prompt, but you must first create a VLAN interface (VLAN 1), name the VLAN **management** (using the **nameif** command), and assign the VLAN an IP address.

Note: The interactive prompt mode does not configure the ASA with factory defaults as described in Step 4. This mode can be used to configure minimal basic settings, such as hostname, clock, passwords, etc. You can also bypass this mode and go directly to the CLI to configure the ASA settings, as described in Part 3.

a.   Respond to the **Setup** interactive prompts as shown here, after the ASA reloads.

```
Pre-configure Firewall now through interactive prompts [yes]? <Enter>
Firewall Mode [Routed]: <Enter>
Enable password [<use current password>]: cisco
Allow password recovery [yes]? <Enter>
Clock (UTC):
  Year [2011]: <Enter>
  Month [Oct]: <Enter>
  Day [01]: <Enter>
  Time [12:24:42]: <Enter>
Management IP address: 192.168.1.1
Management network mask: 255.255.255.0
Host name: ASA-Init
Domain name: generic.com
IP address of host running Device Manager: <Enter>

The following configuration will be used:
Enable password: cisco
Allow password recovery: yes
Clock (UTC): 12:24:42 Sep 25 2011
Firewall Mode: Routed
Management IP address: 192.168.1.1
Management network mask: 255.255.255.0
Host name: ASA-Init
Domain name: generic.com


Use this configuration and write to flash? yes
INFO: Security level for "management" set to 0 by default.
```

```
WARNING: http server is not yet enabled to allow ASDM access.
Cryptochecksum: c8a535f0 e273d49e 5bddfd19 e12566b1


2070 bytes copied in 0.940 secs
Type help or '?' for a list of available commands.
ASA-Init>
```

Note: In the above configuration, the IP address of the host running ASDM was left blank. It is not necessary to install ASDM on a host. It can be run from the flash memory of the ASA device itself using the browser of the host. This process is described in Chapter 9 Lab B, "Configuring ASA Basic Settings and Firewall Using ASDM."

You may also see the warning above stating that the ASA HTTP server has not yet been enabled. This will be done in a subsequent step.

Note: The responses to the prompts are automatically stored in the **startup-config** and the **running config**. However, additional security-related commands, such as a global default inspection service policy, are inserted into the running-config by the ASA OS.

b.   Enter privileged EXEC mode with the **enable** command. Enter **cisco** for the password.

c.   Issue the **show run** command to see the additional security-related configuration commands that are inserted by the ASA.

d.   Issue the **copy run start** command to capture the additional security-related commands in the startup-config file.

e.   Issue the **reload** command to restart the ASA and load the startup configuration.

```
ASA-Init# reload
Proceed with reload? [confirm] <Enter>


<output omitted>
```

f.   Enter privileged EXEC mode with the **enable** command. Provide the password set in Step 6a (**cisco**). Issue the **show running-config** command. You should see the entries you provided in the interactive configuration process.

Part 3: Configuring ASA Settings and Interface Security Using the CLI

In Part 3, you will configure basic settings by using the ASA CLI, even though some of them were already configured using the Setup mode interactive prompts in Part 2. In this part, you will start with the settings configured in Part 2 and add to or modify them to create a more complete basic configuration.

Tip: You will find that many ASA CLI commands are similar to, if not the same, as those used with the Cisco IOS CLI. In addition, moving between configuration modes and submodes is essentially the same.

Note: You must complete Part 2 before beginning Part 3.

Step 1: Configure the hostname and domain name.

a.   Enter global configuration mode using the **config t** command. The first time you enter configuration mode after running Setup, you will be prompted to enable anonymous reporting. Respond with **no**.

```
ASA-Init# conf t
ASA-Init(config)#


****************************** NOTICE ******************************


Help to improve the ASA platform by enabling anonymous reporting,
which allows Cisco to securely receive minimal error and health
```

```
information from the device. To learn more about this feature,
please visit: http://www.cisco.com/go/smartcall

Would you like to enable anonymous error reporting to help improve
the product? [Y]es, [N]o, [A]sk later: n

In the future, if you would like to enable this feature,
issue the command "call-home reporting anonymous".

Please remember to save your configuration.
```

b. Configure the ASA hostname using the **hostname** command.

```
ASA-Init(config)# hostname CCNAS-ASA
```

c. Configure the domain name using the **domain-name** command.

```
CCNAS-ASA(config)# domain-name ccnasecurity.com
```

Step 2: Configure the login and enable mode passwords.

a. The login password is used for Telnet connections (and SSH prior to ASA version 8.4). By default, it is set to **cisco**. You can change the login password using the **passwd** or **password** command. For this lab, leave it set to the default of cisco.

b. Configure the privileged EXEC mode (enable) password using the **enable password** command.

```
CCNAS-ASA(config)# enable password class
```

Step 3: Set the date and time.

The date and time can be set manually using the **clock set** command. The syntax for the clock set command is **clock set** hh:mm:ss {month day | day month} year. The following example shows how to set the date and time using a 24-hour clock:

```
CCNAS-ASA(config)# clock set 14:25:00 april 15 2014
```

Step 4: Configure the inside and outside interfaces.

ASA 5505 interface notes:

The 5505 is different from the other 5500 series ASA models. With other ASAs, the physical port can be assigned a Layer 3 IP address directly, much like a Cisco router. With the ASA 5505, the eight integrated switch ports are Layer 2 ports. To assign Layer 3 parameters, you must create a switch virtual interface (SVI) or logical VLAN interface and then assign one or more of the physical Layer 2 ports to it. All eight switch ports are initially assigned to VLAN 1, unless the factory default config is present, in which case, port E0/0 is assigned to VLAN 2. In this step, you create internal and external VLAN interfaces, name them, assign IP addresses, and set the interface security level.

If you completed the initial configuration Setup utility, interface VLAN 1 is configured as the management VLAN with an IP address of 192.168.1.1. You will configure it as the inside interface for this lab. You will only configure the VLAN 1 (inside) and VLAN 2 (outside) interfaces at this time. The VLAN 3 (dmz) interface will be configured in Part 6 of the lab.

a. Configure a logical VLAN 1 interface for the inside network, 192.168.1.0/24, and set the security level to the highest setting of **100**.

```
CCNAS-ASA(config)# interface vlan 1
CCNAS-ASA(config-if)# nameif inside
CCNAS-ASA(config-if)# ip address 192.168.1.1 255.255.255.0
CCNAS-ASA(config-if)# security-level 100
```

b. Create a logical VLAN 2 interface for the outside network, 209.165.200.224/29, set the security level to the lowest setting of **0**, and bring up the VLAN 2 interface.

```
CCNAS-ASA(config-if)# interface vlan 2
CCNAS-ASA(config-if)# nameif outside
INFO: Security level for "outside" set to 0 by default.


CCNAS-ASA(config-if)# ip address 209.165.200.226 255.255.255.248
CCNAS-ASA(config-if)# no shutdown
```

Interface security-level notes:

You may receive a message that the security level for the inside interface was set automatically to 100 and the outside interface was set to 0. The ASA uses interface security levels from 0 to 100 to enforce the security policy. Security Level 100 (inside) is the most secure and level 0 (outside) is the least secure.

By default, the ASA applies a policy where traffic from a higher security level interface to one with a lower level is permitted and traffic from a lower security level interface to one with a higher security level is denied. The ASA default security policy permits outbound traffic, which is inspected, by default. Returning traffic is allowed due to stateful packet inspection. This default "routed mode" firewall behavior of the ASA allows packets to be routed from the inside network to the outside network, but not vice-versa. In Part 4 of this lab, you will configure NAT to increase the firewall protection.

c. Use the **show interface** command to ensure that ASA Layer 2 ports E0/0 (for VLAN 2) and E0/1 (for VLAN 1) are both up. An example is shown for E0/0. If either port is shown as down/down, check the physical connections. If either port is administratively down, bring it up with the **no shutdown** command.

```
CCNAS-ASA# show interface e0/0
Interface Ethernet0/0 "", is administratively down, line protocol is up
  Hardware is 88E6095, BW 100 Mbps, DLY 100 usec
        Auto-Duplex(Full-duplex), Auto-Speed(100 Mbps)
<output omitted>
```

d. Assign ASA Layer 2 port E0/1 to VLAN 1 and port E0/0 to VLAN 2, and use the **no shutdown** command to ensure they are up.

```
CCNAS-ASA(config)# interface e0/1
CCNAS-ASA(config-if)# switchport access vlan 1
CCNAS-ASA(config-if)# no shutdown
CCNAS-ASA(config-if)# interface e0/0
CCNAS-ASA(config-if)# switchport access vlan 2
CCNAS-ASA(config-if)# no shutdown
```

Note: Even though E0/1 is in VLAN 1 by default, the commands are provided above.

e. Display the status for all ASA interfaces using the **show interface ip brief** command.

Note: This command is different from the **show ip interface brief** IOS command. If any of the physical or logical interfaces previously configured are not up/up, troubleshoot as necessary before continuing.

Tip: Most ASA **show** commands, as well as **ping**, **copy**, and others, can be issued from within any configuration mode prompt without the **do** command required with IOS.

```
CCNAS-ASA(config)# show interface ip brief
```

Interface	IP-Address	OK? Method	Status	Protocol
Ethernet0/0	unassigned	YES unset	up	up
Ethernet0/1	unassigned	YES unset	up	up
Ethernet0/2	unassigned	YES unset	up	up
Ethernet0/3	unassigned	YES unset	down	down
Ethernet0/4	unassigned	YES unset	down	down

```
Ethernet0/5              unassigned       YES unset  down            down
Ethernet0/6              unassigned       YES unset  down            down
Ethernet0/7              unassigned       YES unset  down            down
Internal-Data0/0         unassigned       YES unset  up              up
Internal-Data0/1         unassigned       YES unset  up              up
Vlan1                    192.168.1.1      YES manual up              up
Vlan2                    209.165.200.226  YES manual up              up
Virtual0                 127.0.0.1        YES unset  up              up
```

f. Display the information for the Layer 3 VLAN interfaces using the **show ip address** command.

```
CCNAS-ASA(config)# show ip address
System IP Addresses:
Interface        Name      IP address        Subnet mask        Method
Vlan1            inside    192.168.1.1       255.255.255.0      manual
Vlan2            outside   209.165.200.226   255.255.255.248    manual

Current IP Addresses:
Interface        Name      IP address        Subnet mask        Method
Vlan1            inside    192.168.1.1       255.255.255.0      manual
Vlan2            outside   209.165.200.226   255.255.255.248    manual
```

g. Use the **show switch vlan** command to display the inside and outside VLANs configured on the ASA and to display the assigned ports.

```
CCNAS-ASA# show switch vlan
VLAN Name                              Status    Ports
---- ------------------------------    --------- -----------------------------
1    inside                            up        Et0/1, Et0/2, Et0/3, Et0/4
                                                 Et0/5, Et0/6, Et0/7
2    outside                           up        Et0/0
```

h. You may also use the **show running-config interface type/number** command to display the configuration for a particular interface from the running configuration.

```
CCNAS-ASA# show run interface vlan 1
!
interface Vlan1
 nameif inside
 security-level 100
 ip address 192.168.1.1 255.255.255.0
```

Step 5: Test connectivity to the ASA.

a. Ensure that PC-B has a static IP address of **192.168.1.3** along with subnet mask **255.255.255.0** and default gateway **192.168.1.1** (the IP address of ASA VLAN 1 inside interface).

b. You should be able to ping from PC-B to the ASA inside interface address and ping from the ASA to PC-B. If the pings fail, troubleshoot the configuration as necessary.

```
CCNAS-ASA# ping 192.168.1.3
Type escape sequence to abort.
Sending 5, 100-byte ICMP Echos to 192.168.1.3, timeout is 2 seconds:
!!!!!
Success rate is 100 percent (5/5), round-trip min/avg/max = 1/1/1 ms
```

c. From PC-B, ping the VLAN 2 (outside) interface at IP address **209.165.200.226**. You should not be able to ping this address.

d. From PC-B, Telnet to the ASA using address **192.168.1.1**. Were you able to make the connection? Explain.

_____

_____

_____

Step 6: Configure Telnet access to the ASA from the inside network.

a. You can configure the ASA to accept Telnet connections from a single host or a range of hosts on the inside network. Configure the ASA to allow Telnet connections from any host on the inside network 192.168.1.0/24, and set the Telnet timeout to **10** minutes (the default is 5 minutes).

```
CCNAS-ASA(config)# telnet 192.168.1.0 255.255.255.0 inside
CCNAS-ASA(config)# telnet timeout 10
```

b. From PC-B, Telnet to the ASA using address **192.168.1.1** to verify the Telnet access. Use the remote access login password **cisco** to access the ASA CLI prompt. Exit the Telnet session using the **quit** command.

Note: You cannot use Telnet to the lowest security interface (outside) from the outside, unless you use Telnet inside an IPsec tunnel. Telnet is not the preferred remote access tool due to its lack of encryption. In Part 5 of this lab, you will configure SSH access from the internal and external network.

Step 7: Configure ASDM access to the ASA.

a. You can configure the ASA to accept HTTPS connections using the **http** command. This allows access to the ASA GUI (ASDM). Configure the ASA to allow HTTPS connections from any host on the inside network 192.168.1.0/24.

```
CCNAS-ASA(config)# http server enable
CCNAS-ASA(config)# http 192.168.1.0 255.255.255.0 inside
```

b. Open a browser on PC-B and test the HTTPS access to the ASA by entering **https://192.168.1.1**. You will be prompted with a security certificate warning. Click **Continue** to this website. Click **Yes** for the other security warnings. You should see the Cisco ASDM Welcome screen that allows you to either Install ASDM Launcher and Run ASDM, Run ASDM, or Run Startup Wizard.

Note: If you are unable to launch ASDM, the IP address must be added to the allowed list of IP addresses in Java.

1) Access the Windows Control Panel and click **Java**.

2) In the Java Control Panel, select **Security** tab. Click **Edit Site List...**

3) In the Exception Site list, click **Add**. In the Location field, type **https://192.168.1.1** in the Location field.

4) Click **OK** to add the IP address.

5) Verify that the IP address has been added. Click **OK** to accept the changes.

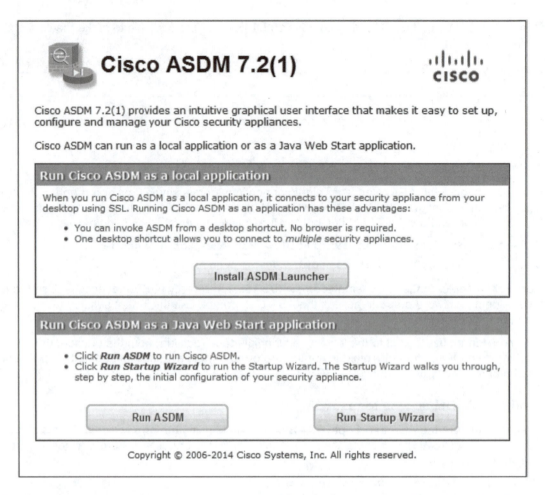

c. Close the browser. In the next lab, you will use ASDM extensively to configure the ASA. The objective here is not to use the ASDM configuration screens, but to verify HTTP/ASDM connectivity to the ASA. If you are unable to access ASDM, check your configurations or contact your instructor or do both.

Part 4: Configuring Routing, Address Translation, and Inspection Policy Using the CLI

In Part 4 of this lab, you will provide a default route for the ASA to reach external networks. You will configure address translation using network objects to enhance firewall security. You will then modify the default application inspection policy to allow specific traffic.

Note: You must complete Part 3 before going on to Part 4.

Step 1: Configure a static default route for the ASA.

In Part 3, you configured the ASA outside interface with a static IP address and subnet mask. However, the ASA does not have a gateway of last resort defined. To enable the ASA to reach external networks, you will configure a default static route on the ASA outside interface.

Note: If the ASA outside interface were configured as a DHCP client, it could obtain a default gateway IP address from the ISP. However, in this lab, the outside interface is configured with a static address.

a. Ping from the ASA to R1 Fa0/0 IP address **209.165.200.225**. Was the ping successful?

_____

_____

b. Ping from the ASA to R1 S0/0/0 IP address **10.1.1.1**. Was the ping successful?

_____

_____

c. Create a "quad zero" default route using the **route** command, associate it with the ASA outside interface, and point to the R1 Fa0/0 IP address **209.165.200.225** as the gateway of last resort. The default administrative distance is 1 by default.

```
CCNAS-ASA(config)# route outside 0.0.0.0 0.0.0.0 209.165.200.225
```

d. Issue the **show route** command to display the ASA routing table and the static default route just created.

```
CCNAS-ASA# show route
Codes: C - connected, S - static, I - IGRP, R - RIP, M - mobile, B - BGP
       D - EIGRP, EX - EIGRP external, O - OSPF, IA - OSPF inter area
       N1 - OSPF NSSA external type 1, N2 - OSPF NSSA external type 2
       E1 - OSPF external type 1, E2 - OSPF external type 2, E - EGP
       i - IS-IS, L1 - IS-IS level-1, L2 - IS-IS level-2, ia - IS-IS inter area
       * - candidate default, U - per-user static route, o - ODR
       P - periodic downloaded static route

Gateway of last resort is 209.165.200.225 to network 0.0.0.0

C    192.168.10.0 255.255.255.0 is directly connected, inside
C    209.165.200.224 255.255.255.248 is directly connected, outside
S*   0.0.0.0 0.0.0.0 [1/0] via 209.165.200.225, outside
```

e. Ping from the ASA to R1 S0/0/0 IP address **10.1.1.1**. Was the ping successful?

_____

_____

Step 2: Configure address translation using PAT and network objects.

Note: Beginning with ASA version 8.3, network objects are used to configure all forms of NAT. A network object is created and it is within this object that NAT is configured. In Step 2a, a network object **inside-net** is used to translate the inside network addresses 192.168.10.0/24 to the global address of the outside ASA interface. This type of object configuration is called Auto-NAT.

a. Create network object **inside-net** and assign attributes to it using the **subnet** and **nat** commands. In version 8.3 and newer, only the **nat** command is used and the **static** and **global** commands are no longer supported.

```
CCNAS-ASA(config)# object network inside-net
CCNAS-ASA(config-network-object)# subnet 192.168.1.0 255.255.255.0
CCNAS-ASA(config-network-object)# nat (inside,outside) dynamic interface
CCNAS-ASA(config-network-object)# end
```

b. The ASA splits the configuration into the object portion that defines the network to be translated and the actual **nat** command parameters. These appear in two different places in the running configuration. Display the NAT object configuration using the **show run object** and **show run nat** commands.

```
CCNAS-ASA# show run object
object network inside-net
 subnet 192.168.1.0 255.255.255.0
```

```
CCNAS-ASA# show run nat
!
object network inside-net
 nat (inside,outside) dynamic interface
```

c. From PC-B, attempt to ping the R1 Fa0/0 interface at IP address **209.165.200.225**. Were the pings successful? _____

d. Issue the **show nat** command on the ASA to see the translated and untranslated hits. Notice that, of the pings from PC-B, four were translated and four were not, because ICMP is not being inspected by the global inspection policy. The outgoing pings (echoes) were translated; the returning echo replies were blocked by the firewall policy. You will configure the default inspection policy to allow ICMP in the next step.

```
CCNAS-ASA# show nat

Auto NAT Policies (Section 2)
1 (inside) to (outside) source dynamic inside-net interface
    translate_hits = 4, untranslate_hits = 4
```

e. Ping from PC-B to R1 again and quickly issue the **show xlate** command to see the actual addresses being translated.

```
CCNAS-ASA# show xlate
1 in use, 28 most used
Flags: D - DNS, i - dynamic, r - portmap, s - static, I - identity, T - twice

ICMP PAT from inside:192.168.1.3/512 to outside:209.165.200.226/21469 flags ri idle
0:00:03 timeout 0:00:30
```

Note: The flags (r and i) indicate that the translation was based on a port map (r) and was done dynamically (i).

f. Open a browser on PC-B and enter the IP address of R1 Fa0/0 (**209.165.200.225**). You should be prompted by R1 for CCP GUI login. TCP-based HTTP traffic is permitted, by default, by the firewall inspection policy.

g. On the ASA, reissue the **show nat** and **show xlate** commands to see the hits and addresses being translated for the HTTP connection.

Step 3: Modify the default MPF application inspection global service policy.

For application layer inspection, as well as other advanced options, the Cisco Modular Policy Framework (MPF) is available on ASAs. Cisco MPF uses three configuration objects to define modular, object-oriented, hierarchical policies:

*   **Class maps:** Define a match criterion.

*   **Policy maps:** Associate actions to the match criteria.

*   **Service policies:** Attach the policy map to an interface, or globally to all interfaces of the appliance.

a. Display the default MPF policy map that performs the inspection on inside-to-outside traffic. Only traffic that was initiated from the inside is allowed back in to the outside interface. Notice that the ICMP protocol is missing.

```
CCNAS-ASA# show run
<output omitted>

class-map inspection_default
 match default-inspection-traffic
```

```
!
policy-map type inspect dns preset_dns_map
 parameters
  message-length maximum client auto
  message-length maximum 512

policy-map global_policy
 class inspection_default
  inspect dns preset_dns_map
  inspect ftp
  inspect h323 h225
  inspect h323 ras
  inspect ip-options
  inspect netbios
  inspect rsh
  inspect rtsp
  inspect skinny
  inspect esmtp
  inspect sqlnet
  inspect sunrpc
  inspect tftp
  inspect sip
  inspect xdmcp
!
service-policy global_policy global
```

b. Add the inspection of ICMP traffic to the policy map list using the following commands:

```
CCNAS-ASA(config)# policy-map global_policy
CCNAS-ASA(config-pmap)# class inspection_default
CCNAS-ASA(config-pmap-c)# inspect icmp
```

c. From PC-B, attempt to ping the R1 Fa0/0 interface at IP address **209.165.200.225**. The pings should be successful this time, because ICMP traffic is now being inspected and legitimate return traffic is being allowed.

Part 5: Configuring DHCP, AAA, and SSH

In Part 5, you will configure ASA features, such as DHCP and enhanced login security, using AAA and SSH.

Note: You must complete Part 4 before beginning Part 5.

Step 1: Configure the ASA as a DHCP server.

The ASA can be both a DHCP server and a DHCP client. In this step, you will configure the ASA as a DHCP server to dynamically assign IP addresses for DHCP clients on the inside network.

a. Configure a DHCP address pool and enable it on the ASA inside interface. This is the range of addresses to be assigned to inside DHCP clients. Attempt to set the range from **192.168.1.5** through **192.168.1.100**.

```
CCNAS-ASA(config)# dhcpd address 192.168.1.5-192.168.1.100 inside
Warning, DHCP pool range is limited to 32 addresses, set address range as:
192.168.1.5-192.168.1.36
```

Were you able to do this on this ASA?

Repeat the **dhcpd** command and specify the pool as 192.168.1.5-192.168.1.36.

```
CNAS-ASA(config)# dhcpd address 192.168.1.5-192.168.1.36 inside
```

b. (Optional) Specify the IP address of the DNS server to be given to clients.

```
CCNAS-ASA(config)# dhcpd dns 209.165.201.2
```

Note: Other parameters can be specified for clients, such as WINS server, lease length, and domain name.

c. Enable the DHCP daemon within the ASA to listen for DHCP client requests on the enabled interface (inside).

```
CCNAS-ASA(config)# dhcpd enable inside
```

d. Verify the DHCP daemon configuration by using the **show run dhcpd** command.

```
CCNAS-ASA(config)# show run dhcpd
dhcpd dns 209.165.201.2
!
dhcpd address 192.168.1.5-192.168.1.36 inside
dhcpd enable inside
```

e. Access the Network Connection IP Properties for PC-B and change it from a static IP address to a DHCP client so that it obtains an IP address automatically from the ASA DHCP server. The procedure to do this varies depending on the PC operating system. It may be necessary to issue the **ipconfig /renew** command on PC-B to force it to obtain a new IP address from the ASA.

Step 2: Configure AAA to use the local database for authentication.

a. Define a local user named **admin** by entering the **username** command. Specify a password of **cisco123**.

```
CCNAS-ASA(config)# username admin password cisco123
```

b. Configure AAA to use the local ASA database for Telnet and SSH user authentication.

```
CCNAS-ASA(config)# aaa authentication ssh console LOCAL
CCNAS-ASA(config)# aaa authentication telnet console LOCAL
```

Note: For added security, starting in ASA version 8.4(2), configure AAA authentication to support SSH connections. The Telnet/SSH default login is not supported. You can no longer connect to the ASA using SSH with the default username and the login password.

Step 3: Configure SSH remote access to the ASA.

You can configure the ASA to accept SSH connections from a single host or a range of hosts on the inside or outside network.

a. Generate an RSA key pair, which is required to support SSH connections. The modulus (in bits) can be 512, 768, 1024, or 2048. The larger the key modulus size you specify, the longer it takes to generate an RSA. Specify a modulus of **1024** using the **crypto key** command.

```
CCNAS-ASA(config)# crypto key generate rsa modulus 1024
INFO: The name for the keys will be: <Default-RSA-Key>
Keypair generation process begin. Please wait...
```

Note: You may receive a message that a RSA key pair is already defined. To replace the RSA key pair, enter **yes** at the prompt.

b. Save the RSA keys to persistent flash memory using either the **copy run start** or **write mem** command.

```
CCNAS-ASA# write mem
Building configuration...
Cryptochecksum: 3c845d0f b6b8839a f9e43be0 33feb4ef
3270 bytes copied in 0.890 secs
[OK]
```

c. Configure the ASA to allow SSH connections from any host on the inside network **192.168.1.0/24** and from the remote management host at the branch office (**172.16.3.3**) on the outside network. Set the SSH timeout to **10** minutes (the default is 5 minutes).

```
CCNAS-ASA(config)# ssh 192.168.1.0 255.255.255.0 inside
CCNAS-ASA(config)# ssh 172.16.3.3 255.255.255.255 outside
CCNAS-ASA(config)# ssh timeout 10
```

d. On PC-C, use an SSH client, such as PuTTY, to connect to the ASA outside interface at IP address **209.165.200.226**. The first time you connect, you may be prompted by the SSH client to accept the RSA host key of the ASA SSH server. Log in as user **admin** and provide the password **cisco123**. You can also connect to the ASA inside interface from a PC-B SSH client using IP address **192.168.1.1**.

Part 6: Configuring DMZ, Static NAT, and ACLs

Previously, you configured address translation using PAT for the inside network. In this part, you will create a DMZ on the ASA, configure static NAT to a DMZ server, and apply ACLs to control access to the server.

To accommodate the addition of a DMZ and a web server, you will use another address from the ISP range assigned, 209.165.200.224/29 (.224-.231). Router R1 Fa0/0 and the ASA outside interface are already using 209.165.200.225 and .226, respectively. You will use public address 209.165.200.227 and static NAT to provide address translation access to the server.

Step 1: Configure the DMZ interface VLAN 3 on the ASA.

a. Configure DMZ VLAN **3**, which is where the public access web server will reside. Assign it IP address **192.168.2.1/24**, name it **dmz**, and assign it a security level of **70**.

Note: If you are working with the ASA 5505 Base license, you will see the error message shown in the output below. The ASA 5505 Base license allows for the creation of up to three named VLAN interfaces. However, you must disable communication between the third interface and one of the other interfaces using the **no forward** command. This is not an issue if the ASA has a Security Plus license, which allows 20 named VLANs.

Because the server does not need to initiate communication with the inside users, disable forwarding to interface VLAN 1.

```
CCNAS-ASA(config)# interface vlan 3
CCNAS-ASA(config-if)# ip address 192.168.2.1 255.255.255.0
CCNAS-ASA(config-if)# nameif dmz
ERROR: This license does not allow configuring more than 2 interfaces with
nameif and without a "no forward" command on this interface or on 1 interface(s)
with nameif already configured.

CCNAS-ASA(config-if)# no forward interface vlan 1
CCNAS-ASA(config-if)# nameif dmz
INFO: Security level for "dmz" set to 0 by default.

CCNAS-ASA(config-if)# security-level 70
CCNAS-ASA(config-if)# no shut
```

b. Assign ASA physical interface E0/2 to DMZ VLAN 3 and enable the interface.

```
CCNAS-ASA(config-if)# interface Ethernet0/2
CCNAS-ASA(config-if)# switchport access vlan 3
CCNAS-ASA(config-if)# no shut
```

c. Display the status for all ASA interfaces using the **show interface ip brief** command.

```
CCNAS-ASA # show interface ip brief
Interface              IP-Address      OK? Method Status       Protocol
Ethernet0/0            unassigned      YES unset  up           up
Ethernet0/1            unassigned      YES unset  up           up
Ethernet0/2            unassigned      YES unset  up           up
Ethernet0/3            unassigned      YES unset  down         down
Ethernet0/4            unassigned      YES unset  down         down
Ethernet0/5            unassigned      YES unset  down         down
Ethernet0/6            unassigned      YES unset  down         down
Ethernet0/7            unassigned      YES unset  down         down
Internal-Data0/0       unassigned      YES unset  up           up
Internal-Data0/1       unassigned      YES unset  up           up
Vlan1                  192.168.1.1     YES manual up           up
Vlan2                  209.165.200.226 YES manual up           up
Vlan3                  192.168.2.1     YES manual up           up
Virtual0               127.0.0.1       YES unset  up           up
```

d. Display the information for the Layer 3 VLAN interfaces using the **show ip address** command.

```
CCNAS-ASA # show ip address
System IP Addresses:
Interface       Name        IP address       Subnet mask      Method
Vlan1           inside      192.168.1.1      255.255.255.0    manual
Vlan2           outside     209.165.200.226  255.255.255.248  manual
Vlan3           dmz         192.168.2.1      255.255.255.0    manual
<output omitted>
```

e. Display the VLANs and port assignments on the ASA using the **show switch vlan** command.

```
CCNAS-ASA(config)# show switch vlan
VLAN Name                               Status    Ports
---- ------------------------------     --------  ------------------------------
1    inside                             up        Et0/1, Et0/3, Et0/4, Et0/5
                                                  Et0/6, Et0/7
2    outside                            up        Et0/0
3    dmz                                up        Et0/2
```

Step 2: Configure static NAT to the DMZ server using a network object.

Configure a network object named **dmz-server** and assign it the static IP address of the DMZ server (**192.168.2.3**). While in object definition mode, use the **nat** command to specify that this object is used to translate a DMZ address to an outside address using static NAT, and specify a public translated address of **209.165.200.227**.

```
CCNAS-ASA(config)# object network dmz-server
CCNAS-ASA(config-network-object)# host 192.168.2.3
CCNAS-ASA(config-network-object)# nat (dmz,outside) static 209.165.200.227
```

Step 3: Configure an ACL to allow access to the DMZ server from the Internet.

Configure a named access list **OUTSIDE-DMZ** that permits any IP protocol from any external host to the internal IP address of the DMZ server. Apply the access list to the ASA outside interface in the **IN** direction.

```
CCNAS-ASA(config)# access-list OUTSIDE-DMZ permit ip any host 192.168.2.3
CCNAS-ASA(config)# access-group OUTSIDE-DMZ in interface outside
```

Note: Unlike IOS ACLs, the ASA ACL **permit** statement must permit access to the internal private DMZ address. External hosts access the server using its public static NAT address, and the ASA translates it to the internal host IP address and applies the ACL.

You can modify this ACL to allow only services that you want to be exposed to external hosts, such as web (HTTP) or file transfer (FTP).

Step 4: Test access to the DMZ server.

a. Create a loopback 0 interface on Internet router R2 representing an external host. Assign **Lo0** IP address **172.30.1.1** and a mask of **255.255.255.0**, Ping the DMZ server public address from R2 using the loopback interface as the source of the ping. The pings should be successful.

```
R2(config-if)# interface Lo0
R2(config-if)# ip address 172.30.1.1 255.255.255.0


R2# ping 209.165.200.227 source lo0

Type escape sequence to abort.
Sending 5, 100-byte ICMP Echos to 209.165.200.227, timeout is 2 seconds:
Packet sent with a source address of 172.30.1.1
!!!!!
Success rate is 100 percent (5/5), round-trip min/avg/max = 1/2/4 ms
```

b. Clear the NAT counters using the **clear nat counters** command.

```
CCNAS-ASA# clear nat counters
```

c. Ping from PC-C to the DMZ server at the public address **209.165.200.227**. The pings should be successful.

d. Issue the **show nat** and **show xlate** commands on the ASA to see the effect of the pings. Both the PAT (inside to outside) and static NAT (dmz to outside) policies are shown.

```
CCNAS-ASA# show nat

Auto NAT Policies (Section 2)
1 (dmz) to (outside) source static dmz-server 209.165.200.227
    translate_hits = 0, untranslate_hits = 4

2 (inside) to (outside) source dynamic inside-net interface
    translate_hits = 4, untranslate_hits = 0
```

Note: Pings from inside to outside are translated hits. Pings from outside host PC-C to the DMZ are considered untranslated hits.

```
CCNAS-ASA# show xlate
1 in use, 3 most used
Flags: D - DNS, i - dynamic, r - portmap, s - static, I - identity, T - twice
NAT from dmz:192.168.2.3 to outside:209.165.200.227
    flags s idle 0:22:58 timeout 0:00:00
```

Note the flag this time is "**s**" indicating a static translation.

e. Because the ASA inside interface (VLAN 1) is set to security level of 100 (the highest) and the DMZ interface (VLAN 3) is set to 70, you can also access the DMZ server from a host on the inside network. The ASA acts like a router between the two networks. Ping the DMZ server (PC-A) internal address (**192.168.2.3**) from inside network host PC-B (192.168.1.X). The pings should be successful due to the interface security level and the fact that ICMP is being inspected on the inside interface by the global inpseciton policy. The pings from PC-B to PC-A will not affect the NAT translation counts, because both PC-B and PC-A are behind the firewall and no translation takes place.

f. The DMZ server cannot ping PC-B on the inside network, because the DMZ interface VLAN 3 has a lower security level and the fact that, when the VLAN 3 interface was created, it was necessary to specify the **no forward** command. Try to ping from the DMZ server PC-A to PC-B at IP address **192.168.1.3**. The pings should not be successful.

g. Use the **show run** command to display the configuration for VLAN 3.

```
CCNAS-ASA# show run interface vlan 3
!
interface Vlan3
 no forward interface Vlan1
 nameif dmz
 security-level 70
 ip address 192.168.2.1 255.255.255.0
```

Note: An access list can be applied to the inside interface to control the type of access to be permitted or denied to the DMZ server from inside hosts.

Reflection

1. How does the configuration of the ASA firewall differ from that of an ISR?

_____

_____

_____

_____

_____

2. What does the ASA use to define address translation and what is the benefit?

_____

_____

_____

_____

_____

3. How does the ASA 5505 use logical and physical interfaces to manage security and how does this differ from other ASA models?

_____

_____

_____

_____

_____

Router Interface Summary Table

Router Interface Summary				
Router Model	Ethernet Interface #1	Ethernet Interface #2	Serial Interface #1	Serial Interface #2
1800	Fast Ethernet 0/0 (Fa0/0)	Fast Ethernet 0/1 (Fa0/1)	Serial 0/0/0 (S0/0/0)	Serial 0/0/1 (S0/0/1)
1900	Gigabit Ethernet 0/0 (G0/0)	Gigabit Ethernet 0/1 (G0/1)	Serial 0/0/0 (S0/0/0)	Serial 0/0/1 (S0/0/1)
2801	Fast Ethernet 0/0 (Fa0/0)	Fast Ethernet 0/1 (Fa0/1)	Serial 0/1/0 (S0/1/0)	Serial 0/1/1 (S0/1/1)
2811	Fast Ethernet 0/0 (Fa0/0)	Fast Ethernet 0/1 (Fa0/1)	Serial 0/0/0 (S0/0/0)	Serial 0/0/1 (S0/0/1)
2900	Gigabit Ethernet 0/0 (G0/0)	Gigabit Ethernet 0/1 (G0/1)	Serial 0/0/0 (S0/0/0)	Serial 0/0/1 (S0/0/1)
Note: To find out how the router is configured, look at the interfaces to identify the type of router and how many interfaces the router has. There is no way to effectively list all the combinations of configurations for each router class. This table includes identifiers for the possible combinations of Ethernet and Serial interfaces in the device. The table does not include any other type of interface, even though a specific router may contain one. An example of this might be an ISDN BRI interface. The string in parenthesis is the legal abbreviation that can be used in Cisco IOS commands to represent the interface.				

Lab 9.4.1.2 - Configuring ASA Basic Settings and Firewall Using ASDM

Topology

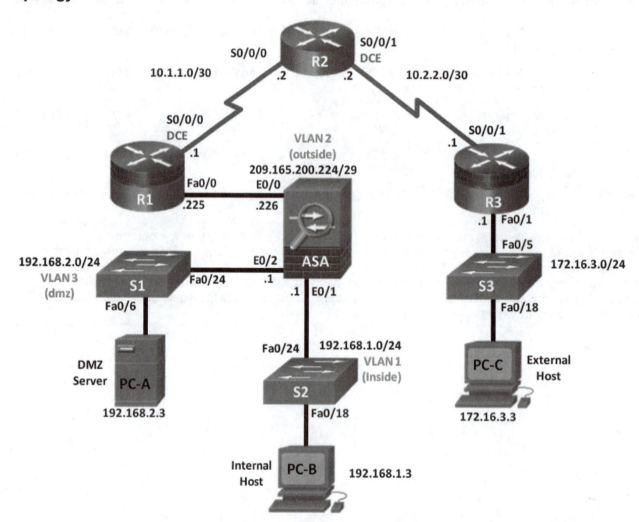

Note: ISR G2 devices use GigabitEthernet interfaces instead of FastEthernet interfaces.

IP Addressing Table

Device	Interface	IP Address	Subnet Mask	Default Gateway	Switch Port
R1	FA0/0	209.165.200.225	255.255.255.248	N/A	ASA E0/0
	S0/0/0 (DCE)	10.1.1.1	255.255.255.252	N/A	N/A
R2	S0/0/0	10.1.1.2	255.255.255.252	N/A	N/A
	S0/0/1 (DCE)	10.2.2.2	255.255.255.252	N/A	N/A
R3	FA0/1	172.16.3.1	255.255.255.0	N/A	S3 Fa0/5
	S0/0/1	10.2.2.1	255.255.255.252	N/A	N/A
ASA	VLAN 1 (E0/1)	192.168.1.1	255.255.255.0	NA	S2 Fa0/24
	VLAN 2 (E0/0)	209.165.200.226	255.255.255.248	NA	R1 Fa0/0
	VLAN 3 (E0/2)	192.168.2.1	255.255.255.0	NA	S1 Fa0/24
PC-A	NIC	192.168.2.3	255.255.255.0	192.168.2.1	S1 Fa0/6
PC-B	NIC	192.168.1.3	255.255.255.0	192.168.1.1	S2 Fa0/18
PC-C	NIC	172.16.3.3	255.255.255.0	172.16.3.1	S3 Fa0/18

Objectives

Part 1: Configure Basic Device Settings

- Cable the network and clear previous device settings.
- Configure basic settings for routers and switches.
- Configure static routing, including default routes, between R1, R2, and R3.
- Enable the HTTP server on R1 and set the enable and vty passwords.
- Configure PC host IP settings.
- Verify connectivity.

Part 2: Accessing the ASA Console and ASDM

- Access the ASA console and view hardware, software, and configuration settings.
- Clear previous ASA configuration settings.
- Bypass Setup mode and configure the ASDM VLAN interfaces.
- Configure ASDM and verify access to the ASA.
- Access ASDM and explore the GUI.

Part 3: Configuring ASA Settings and Firewall Using the ASDM Startup Wizard

- Access the Configuration menu and launch the Startup wizard.
- Configure the hostname, domain name, and enable the password.
- Configure the inside and outside VLAN interfaces.
- Configure DHCP, address translation, and administrative access.
- Review the summary and deliver the commands to the ASA.
- Test Telnet and SSH access to the ASA.

- Test access to an external website from PC-B.

- Test access to an external website using the ASDM Packet Tracer utility.

Part 4: Configuring ASA Settings from the ASDM Configuration Menu

- Set the ASA date and time.

- Configure a static default route for the ASA.

- Configure AAA user authentication using the local ASA database.

- Test connectivity using ASDM Ping and Traceroute.

- Modify the MPF application inspection policy.

Part 5: Configuring DMZ, Static NAT, and ACLs

- Configure the ASA DMZ VLAN 3 interface.

- Configure the DMZ server and static NAT.

- View the DMZ Access Rule (ACL) generated by ASDM.

- Test access to the DMZ server from the outside network.

Background / Scenario

The Cisco Adaptive Security Appliance (ASA) is an advanced network security device that integrates a stateful firewall, a VPN, and other capabilities. This lab employs an ASA 5505 to create a firewall and protect an internal corporate network from external intruders while allowing internal hosts access to the Internet. The ASA creates three security interfaces: Outside, Inside, and DMZ. It provides outside users limited access to the DMZ and no access to internal resources. Inside users can access the DMZ and outside resources.

This lab's focus is the configuration of the ASA as a basic firewall. Other devices will receive minimal configuration to support the ASA portion of the lab. This lab uses the ASA GUI interface ASDM, which is similar to Cisco Configuration Professional (CCP) used with Cisco ISRs, to configure basic device and security settings.

In Part 1 of this lab, you will configure the topology and non-ASA devices. In Part 2, you will prepare the ASA for Adaptive Security Device Manager (ASDM) access. In Part 3, you will use the ASDM **Startup wizard** to configure basic ASA settings and the firewall between the inside and outside networks. In Part 4, you will configure additional settings via the ASDM configuration menu. In Part 5, you will configure a DMZ on the ASA and provide access to a server in the DMZ.

Your company has one location connected to an ISP. Router R1 represents a customer-premise equipment (CPE) device managed by the ISP. Router R2 represents an intermediate Internet router. Router R3 connects an administrator from a network management company, who has been hired to manage your network remotely. The ASA is an edge security device that connects the internal corporate network and DMZ to the ISP while providing NAT and DHCP services to inside hosts. The ASA will be configured for management by an administrator on the internal network and the remote administrator. Layer 3 VLAN interfaces provide access to the three areas created in the lab: Inside, Outside, and DMZ. The ISP has assigned the public IP address space of 209.165.200.224/29, which will be used for address translation on the ASA.

Note: The router commands and output in this lab are from a Cisco 1841 router with Cisco IOS Release 15.1(4)M8 (Advanced IP Services image). Other routers and Cisco IOS versions can be used. See the Router Interface Summary Table at the end of this lab to determine which interface identifiers to use based on the equipment in the lab. Depending on the router model and Cisco IOS version, the commands available and output produced might vary from what is shown in this lab.

The ASA used with this lab is a Cisco model 5505 with an 8-port integrated switch, running OS version 8.4(2) and ASDM version 7.2(1) and comes with a Base license that allows a maximum of three VLANs.

Note: Ensure that the routers and switches have been erased and have no startup configurations.

Required Resources

- 3 Routers (Cisco 1841 with Cisco IOS Release 15.1(4)M8 Advanced IP Services image or comparable)
- 3 Switches (Cisco 2960 or comparable)
- 1 ASA 5505 (OS version 8.4(2) and ASDM version 7.2(1) and Base license or comparable)
- 3 PCs (Windows Vista or Windows 7 with CCP 2.5, latest version of Java, Internet Explorer, and Flash Player)
- Serial and Ethernet cables as shown in the topology
- Console cables to configure Cisco networking devices

CCP Notes:

- If the PC on which CCP is installed is running Windows Vista or Windows 7, it may be necessary to right-click the CCP icon or menu item, and choose **Run as administrator**.
- To run CCP, it may be necessary to temporarily disable antivirus programs and O/S firewalls. Make sure that all pop-up blockers are turned off in the browser.

Browser Note:

Use of a browser other than Internet Explorer 7 or newer on remote PC-C may produce results different from those shown in this lab. It may be necessary to create an exception when connecting to the ASA over the remote access VPN.

Part 1: Configure Basic Device Settings

In Part 1, you will set up the network topology and configure basic settings on the routers such as interface IP addresses and static routing.

Note: Do not configure any ASA settings at this time.

Step 1: Cable the network and clear previous device settings.

Attach the devices shown in the topology diagram and cable as necessary. Ensure that the routers and switches have been erased and have no startup configurations.

Step 2: Configure basic settings for routers and switches.

a. Configure hostnames as shown in the topology for each router.

b. Configure router interface IP addresses as shown in the IP Addressing table.

c. Configure a clock rate for routers with a DCE serial cable attached to the serial interface. R1 is shown here as an example:

```
R1(config)# interface S0/0/0
R1(config-if)# clock rate 64000
```

d. Configure the hostname for the switches. With the exception of the hostname, the switches can be left in their default configuration state. Configuring the VLAN management IP address for the switches is optional.

Step 3: Configure static routing on the routers.

a. Configure a static default route from R1 to R2 and from R3 to R2.

```
R1(config)# ip route 0.0.0.0 0.0.0.0 Serial0/0/0
```

```
R3(config)# ip route 0.0.0.0 0.0.0.0 Serial0/0/1
```

b.   Configure a static route from R2 to the R1 Fa0/0 subnet (connected to ASA interface E0/0) and a static route from R2 to the R3 LAN.

```
R2(config)# ip route 209.165.200.224 255.255.255.248 Serial0/0/0
R2(config)# ip route 172.16.3.0 255.255.255.0 Serial0/0/1
```

Step 4: Enable the HTTP server on R1 and set the enable and vty passwords.

Enable HTTP access to R1 using the **ip http server** command in global configuration mode. Configure an enable password of **class**. Also set the vty and console passwords to **cisco**. This provides web and Telnet targets for testing later in the lab.

```
R1(config)# ip http server
R1(config)# enable password class

R1(config)# line vty 0 4
R1(config-line)# password cisco
R1(config-line)# login

R1(config)# line con 0
R1(config-line)# password cisco
R1(config-line)# login
```

Step 5: Configure PC host IP settings.

Configure a static IP address, subnet mask, and default gateway for PC-A, PC-B, and PC-C as shown in the IP Addressing table.

Step 6: Verify connectivity.

Because the ASA is the focal point for the network zones and it has not yet been configured, there will be no connectivity between devices that are connected to it. However, PC-C should be able to ping the R1 interface Fa0/0. From PC-C, ping the R1 Fa0/0 IP address (**209.165.200.225**). If these pings are unsuccessful, troubleshoot the basic device configurations before continuing.

Note: If you can ping from PC-C to R1 Fa0/0 and S0/0/0, you have demonstrated that static routing is configured and functioning correctly.

Step 7: Save the basic running configuration for each router and switch.

Part 2: Accessing the ASA Console and ASDM

In Part 2, you will access the ASA via the console and use various **show** commands to determine hardware, software, and configuration settings. You will prepare the ASA for ASDM access and explore some of the ASDM screens and options.

Step 1: Access the ASA console.

a.   Accessing the ASA via the console port is the same as with a Cisco router or switch. Connect to the ASA console port with a rollover cable.

b.   Use a terminal emulation program to access the CLI. Use the serial port settings of 9600 baud, 8 data bits, no parity, one stop bit, and no flow control.

c.   If prompted to enter Interactive Firewall configuration (Setup mode), answer **no**.

d. Enter privileged mode with the **enable** command and password (if set). By default, the password is blank; press **Enter**. If the password has been changed to that specified in this lab, enter the password **class**. The default ASA hostname and prompt is **ciscoasa>**.

```
ciscoasa> enable
Password: class (or press Enter if no password is set)
```

Step 2: Clear previous ASA configuration settings.

a. Use the **write erase** command to remove the **startup-config** file from flash memory.

```
ciscoasa# write erase
Erase configuration in flash memory? [confirm]
[OK]
ciscoasa#

ciscoasa# show start
No Configuration
```

Note: The **erase startup-config** IOS command is not supported on the ASA.

b. Use the **reload** command to restart the ASA. This causes the ASA to come up in CLI Setup mode. If you see the `System config has been modified. Save? [Y]es/[N]o:` message, type **n** and then press **Enter**.

```
ciscoasa# reload
Proceed with reload? [confirm] <Enter>
ciscoasa#
***
*** --- START GRACEFUL SHUTDOWN ---
Shutting down isakmp
Shutting down File system
***
*** --- SHUTDOWN NOW ---
Process shutdown finished
Rebooting.....
CISCO SYSTEMS
Embedded BIOS Version 1.0(12)13 08/28/08 15:50:37.45
<output omitted>
```

Step 3: Bypass Setup mode and configure the ASDM VLAN interfaces.

When the ASA completes the reload process, it should detect that the **startup-config** file is missing and present a series of interactive prompts to configure basic ASA settings. If it does not come up in this mode, repeat Step 5.

a. When prompted to pre-configure the firewall through interactive prompts (Setup mode), respond with **no**.

```
Pre-configure Firewall now through interactive prompts [yes]? no
```

b. Enter privileged EXEC mode with the **enable** command. The password should be blank (no password) at this point.

c. Enter global configuration mode using the **config t** command. The first time you enter configuration mode after reloading, you will be prompted to enable anonymous reporting. Respond with **no**.

d. Configure the inside interface VLAN 1 to prepare for ASDM access. The Security Level should be automatically set to the highest level of **100**. The VLAN 1 logical interface will be used by PC-B to access ASDM on ASA physical interface E0/1.

```
ciscoasa(config)# interface vlan 1
ciscoasa(config-if)# nameif inside
INFO: Security level for "inside" set to 100 by default.
ciscoasa(config-if)# ip address 192.168.1.1 255.255.255.0
ciscoasa(config-if)# exit
```

PC-B is connected to switch S2 which is connected to ASA port E0/1. Why is it not necessary to add physical interface E0/1 to this VLAN?

_____

_____

ASA 5505 interface notes:

The 5505 is different from the other 5500 series ASA models. With other ASAs, the physical port can be assigned a Layer 3 IP address directly, much like a Cisco router. With the ASA 5505, the eight integrated switch ports are Layer 2 ports. To assign Layer 3 parameters, you must create a switch virtual interface (SVI) or logical VLAN interface and then assign one or more of the physical Layer 2 ports to it.

By default, all ASA physical interfaces are administratively down, unless the Setup utility has been run or the factory defaults have been reset. Because no physical interface in VLAN 1 has been enabled, the VLAN 1 status is down/down. Use the **show interface ip brief** command to verify this.

```
ciscoasa(config)# show interface ip brief
Interface        IP-Address   OK? Method Status                 Protocol
Ethernet0/0      unassigned   YES unset  administratively down  up
Ethernet0/1      unassigned   YES unset  administratively down  up
Ethernet0/2      unassigned   YES unset  administratively down  up
Ethernet0/3      unassigned   YES unset  administratively down  up
Ethernet0/4      unassigned   YES unset  administratively down  down
Ethernet0/5      unassigned   YES unset  administratively down  down
Ethernet0/6      unassigned   YES unset  administratively down  down
Ethernet0/7      unassigned   YES unset  administratively down  down
Internal-Data0/0 unassigned   YES unset  up                     up
Internal-Data0/1 unassigned   YES unset  up                     up
Vlan1            192.168.1.1  YES manual down                   down
Virtual0         127.0.0.1    YES unset  up                     up
```

e. Enable the E0/1 interface using the **no shutdown** command and verify the E0/1 and VLAN 1 interface status. The status and protocol for interface E0/1 and VLAN 1 should be up/up.

```
ciscoasa(config)# interface e0/1
ciscoasa(config-if)# no shut
ciscoasa(config-if)# exit
```

```
ciscoasa(config)# show interface ip brief
Interface        IP-Address   OK? Method Status                 Protocol
Ethernet0/0      unassigned   YES unset  administratively down  up
Ethernet0/1      unassigned   YES unset  up                     up
Ethernet0/2      unassigned   YES unset  administratively down  up
Ethernet0/3      unassigned   YES unset  administratively down  up
Ethernet0/4      unassigned   YES unset  administratively down  down
Ethernet0/5      unassigned   YES unset  administratively down  down
Ethernet0/6      unassigned   YES unset  administratively down  down
```

```
Ethernet0/7        unassigned    YES unset  administratively down down
Internal-Data0/0 unassigned    YES unset  up                   up
Internal-Data0/1 unassigned    YES unset  up                   up
Vlan1              192.168.1.1   YES manual up                   up
Virtual0           127.0.0.1     YES unset  up                   up
```

f. Also pre-configure outside interface VLAN 2, add physical interface E0/0 to VLAN 2, and bring up the E0/0 interface. You will assign the IP address using ASDM.

```
ciscoasa(config)# interface vlan 2
ciscoasa(config-if)# nameif outside
INFO: Security level for "outside" set to 0 by default.

ciscoasa(config-if)# interface e0/0
ciscoasa(config-if)# switchport access vlan 2
ciscoasa(config-if)# no shut
ciscoasa(config-if)# exit
```

g. Test connectivity to the ASA by pinging from PC-B to ASA interface VLAN 1 IP address **192.168.1.1**. The pings should be successful.

Step 4: Configure ASDM and verify access to the ASA.

a. Configure the ASA to accept HTTPS connections using the **http** command to allow access to ASDM from any host on the inside network 192.168.1.0/24.

```
ciscoasa(config)# http server enable
ciscoasa(config)# http 192.168.1.0 255.255.255.0 inside
```

b. Open a browser on PC-B and test the HTTPS access to the ASA by entering **https://192.168.1.1**.

Note: Be sure to specify the HTTPS protocol in the URL.

Step 5: Access ASDM and explore the GUI.

a. After entering the URL above, you should see a security warning about the website security certificate. Click **Continue to this website**. The ASDM Welcome page will display. From this screen, you can run ASDM as a local application on the PC (installs ASDM on the PC), run ASDM as a browser-based Java applet directly from the ASA, or run the Startup wizard.

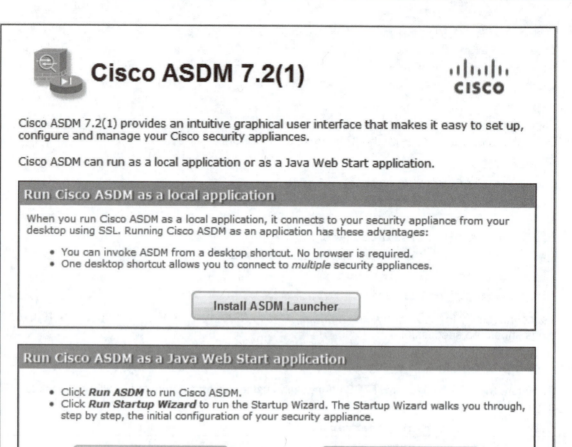

b. Click **Run ASDM**.

c. Click **Yes** for any other security warnings. You should see the **Cisco ASDM-IDM Launcher** dialog box where you can enter a username and password. Leave these fields blank as they have not yet been configured.

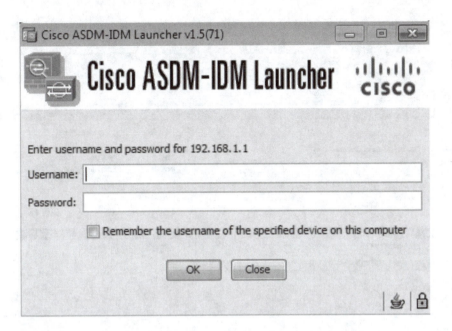

d.   Click **OK** to continue. ASDM will load the current configuration into the GUI.

e.   The initial GUI screen is displayed with various areas and options. The main menu at the top left of the screen contains three main sections; Home, Configuration, and Monitoring. The Home section is the default and has two dashboards: Device and Firewall. The Device dashboard is the default screen and shows device information such as Type (ASA 5505), ASA and ASDM version, amount of memory and firewall mode (routed). There are five areas on the Device Dashboard:

   o   Device Information

   o   Interface Status

   o   VPN Sessions

   o   System Resources Status

   o   Traffic Status

Note: If the Cisco Smart Call Home window appears, click **Do not enable Smart Call Home**, and then click **OK**.

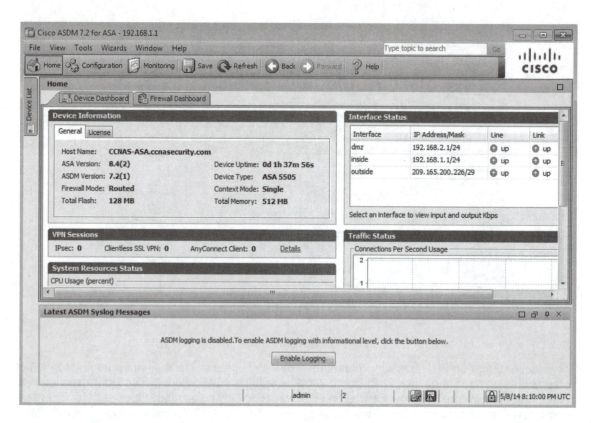

f.   Click the **Configuration** and **Monitoring** tabs to become familiar with their layout and to see what options are available.

Part 3: Configuring Basic ASA Settings and Firewall Using the ASDM Startup Wizard

Step 1: Access the Configuration menu and launch the Startup wizard.

a.   On the menu bar, click **Configuration**. There are five main configuration areas:

  o   Device Setup

  o   Firewall

  o   Remote Access VPN

  o   Site-to-Site VPN

  o   Device Management

b.   The Device Setup Startup wizard is the first option available and displays by default. Read through the on-screen text describing the Startup wizard, and then click **Launch Startup Wizard**.

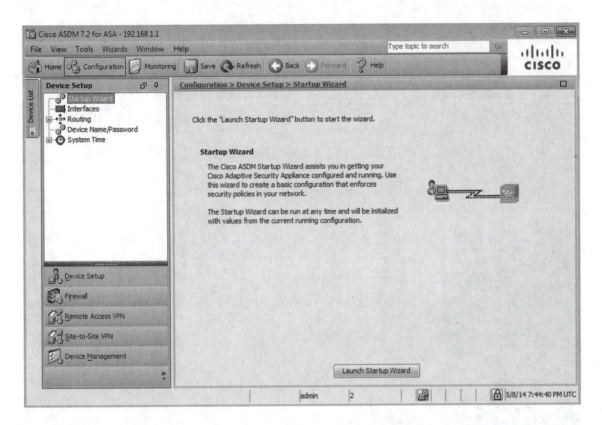

Step 2: Configure hostname, domain name, and enable the password.

a. On the first Startup Wizard screen, modify the existing configuration or reset the ASA to the factory defaults. With the **Modify Existing Configuration** option selected, click **Next** to continue.

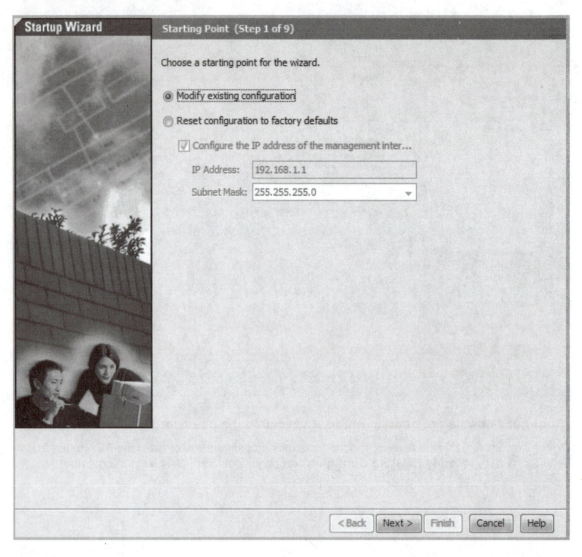

b. On the Startup Wizard Step 2 screen, configure the ASA hostname **CCNAS-ASA** and domain name **ccnasecurity.com**. Click the check box for changing the enable mode password, change it from blank (no password) to **class**, and enter it again to confirm. When the entries are completed, click **Next** to continue.

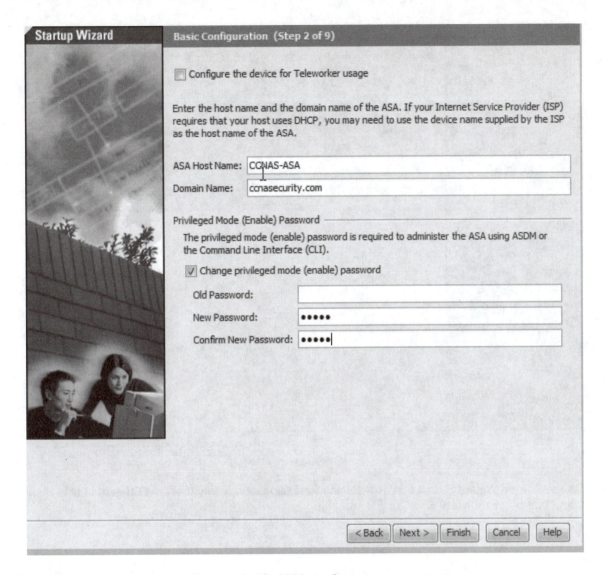

Step 3: Configure the inside and outside VLAN interfaces.

a. On the Startup Wizard Step 3 screen – Interface Selection, for the Outside and Inside VLANs, do not change the current settings because these were previously defined using the CLI. The inside VLAN is named **inside** and the security level is set to 100 (highest). The Outside VLAN interface is named **outside** and the security level set to 0 (lowest). Click **Next** to continue.

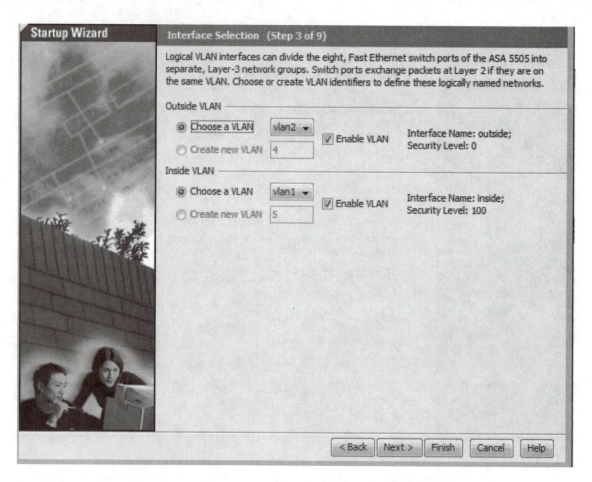

b. On the Startup Wizard Step 4 screen – Switch Port Allocation, verify that port **Ethernet1** is in Inside VLAN 1 and that port **Ethernet0** is in Outside VLAN 2.

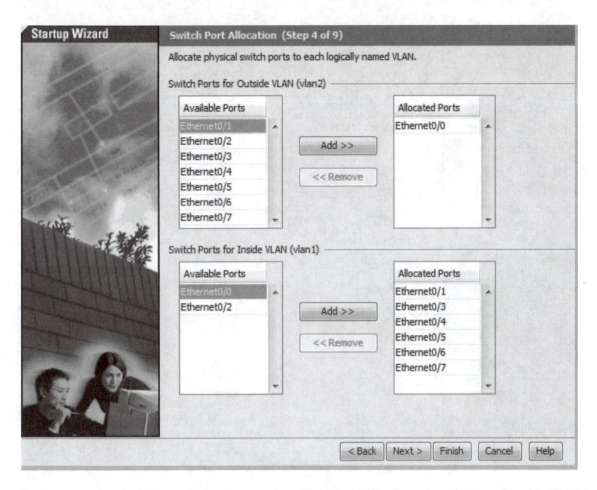

c. On the Startup Wizard Step 5 screen – Interface IP Address Configuration, enter an Outside IP Address of **209.165.200.226** and Mask **255.255.255.248**. You can use the pull-down menu to select the mask. Leave the inside interface IP address as **192.168.1.1** with a mask of **255.255.255.0**. Click **Next** to continue.

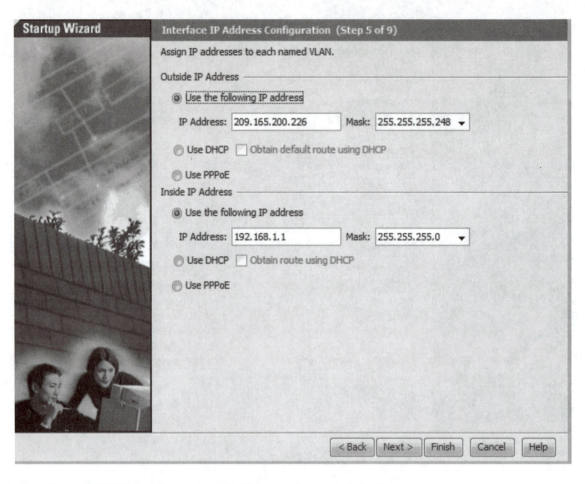

Step 4: Configure DHCP, address translation, and administrative access.

a. On the Startup Wizard Step 6 screen – DHCP Server, click the **Enable DHCP server on the inside interface** check box. Enter a Starting IP Address of **192.168.1.3** and Ending IP Address of **192.168.1.30**. Enter the DNS Server 1 address of **10.20.30.40** and Domain Name **ccnasecurity.com**. Do **NOT** check the box to enable Autoconfiguration from Interface. Click **Next** to continue.

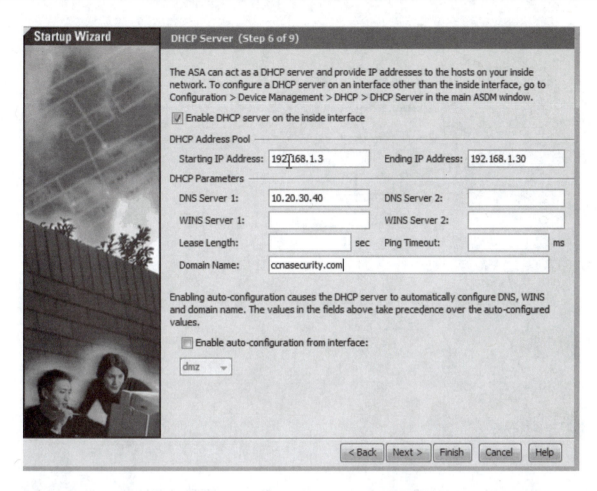

b. On the Startup Wizard Step 7 screen – Address Translation (NAT/PAT), click **Use Port Address Translation (PAT)**. The default is to use the IP address of the outside interface.

Note: You can also specify a particular IP address for PAT or a range of addresses with NAT. Click **Next** to continue.

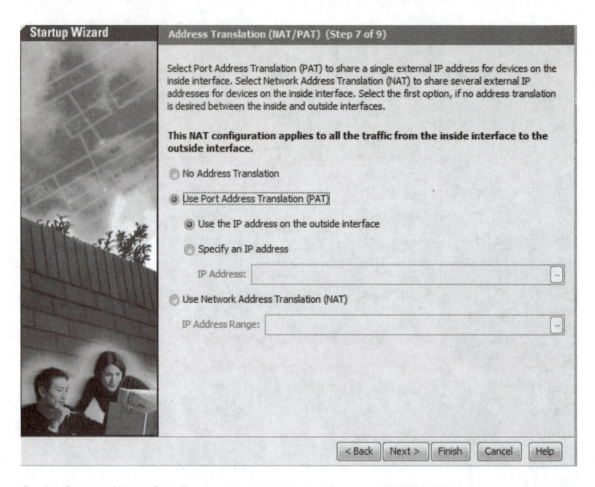

c. On the Startup Wizard Step 8 screen – Administrative Access, HTTPS/ASDM access is currently configured for hosts on inside network 192.168.1.0/24. Add **Telnet** access to the ASA for the **inside** network **192.168.1.0** with a subnet mask of **255.255.255.0**. Add **SSH** access to the ASA from host **172.16.3.3** on the **outside** network. Ensure that the **Enable HTTP server for HTTPS/ASDM access** check box is checked. Click **Next** to continue.

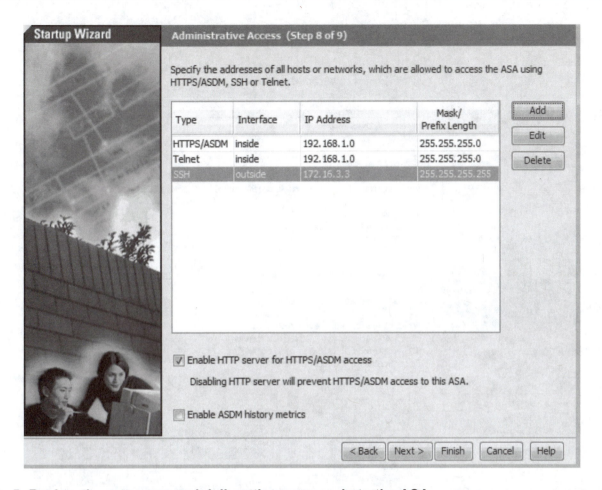

Step 5: Review the summary and deliver the commands to the ASA.

a. On the Startup Wizard Step 9 screen – Startup Wizard Summary, review the **Configuration Summary** and click **Finish**. ASDM will deliver the commands to the ASA device and then reload the modified configuration.

Note: If the GUI dialogue box stops responding during the reload process, close it, exit ASDM, and restart the browser and ASDM. If prompted to save the configuration to flash memory, respond with **Yes**. Even though ASDM may not appear to have reloaded the configuration, the commands were delivered. If there are errors encountered as ASDM delivers the commands, you will be notified with a list of commands that succeeded and those that failed.

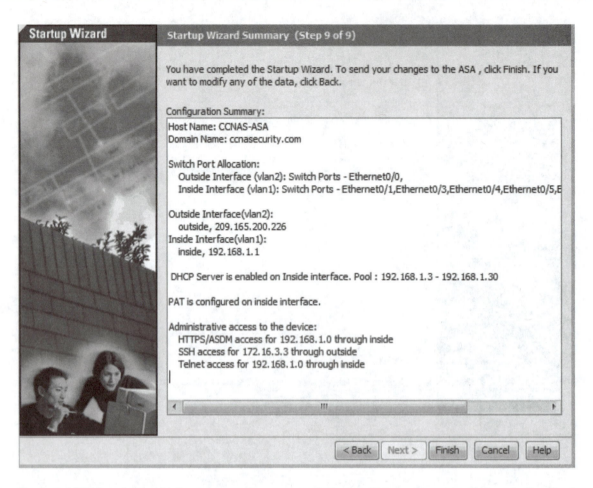

b. Restart ASDM and provide the new enable password **class** with no username. Return to the Device Dashboard and check the Interface Status window. You should see the inside and outside interfaces with IP address and status. The inside interface should show some number of Kb/s. The Traffic Status window may show the ASDM access as TCP traffic spike.

Step 6: Test Telnet and SSH access to the ASA.

a. From a command prompt or GUI Telnet client on PC-B, Telnet to the ASA inside interface at IP address **192.168.1.1**.

b. Log in to the ASA using the default login password **cisco**. Enter privileged EXEC mode by using the **enable** command and provide the password **class**. Exit the Telnet session by using the **quit** command.

c. In Step 4, SSH access was configured using the Startup wizard to allow access to the ASA from outside PC-C (172.16.3.3). From PC-C, open an SSH client, such as PuTTY, and attempt to connect to the ASA outside interface at **209.165.200.226**.

    Note: You will not be able to establish the connection, because SSH access (ASA version 8.4(2) and later) requires that you also configure AAA and provide an authenticated username. AAA will be configured in the Part 4 of this lab.

Step 7: Test access to an external website from PC-B.

a. Open a browser on PC-B and enter the IP address of the R1 Fa0/0 interface (**209.165.200.225**) to simulate access to an external website.

b. The R1 HTTP server was enabled in Part 1; you should be prompted with a user authentication login dialog box from the R1 GUI device manager. Leave the username blank and enter the password **class**. Exit the browser. You should see TCP activity in the ASDM Device Dashboard Traffic Status window.

Step 8: Test access to an external website using the ASDM Packet Tracer utility.

a. On the ASDM Home page, click **Tools** > **Packet Tracer**.

b. Select the **Inside** interface from the Interface drop-down list and click **TCP** from the Packet Type radio buttons. From the Source drop-down list, select **IP Address** and enter the address **192.168.1.3** (PC-B) with a source port of **1500**. From the Destination drop-down list, select **IP Address**, and enter **209.165.200.225** (R1 Fa0/0) with a Destination Port of **HTTP**. Click **Start** to begin the trace of the packet. The packet should be permitted.

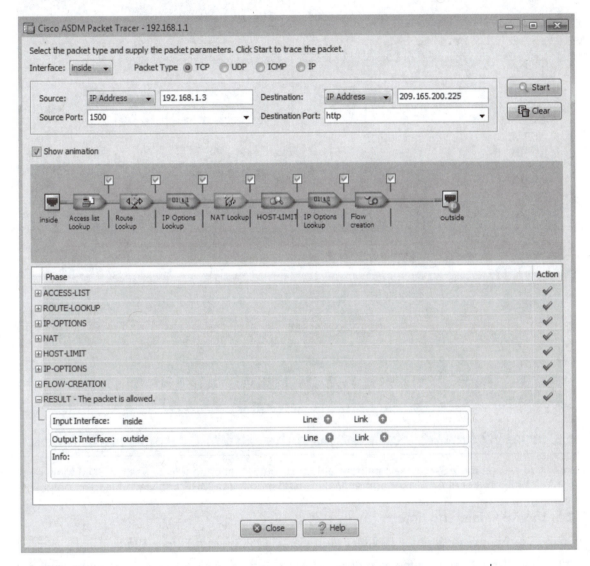

c. Click **Clear** to reset the entries. Try another trace and select **outside** from the **Interface** drop-down list and leave **TCP** as the packet type. From the **Sources** drop-down list, select **IP Address**, and enter **209.165.200.225** (R1 Fa0/0) and a Source Port of 1500. From the **Destination** drop-down list, select **IP Address** and enter the address **209.165.200.226** (ASA outside interface) with a Destination Port of telnet. Click **Start** to begin the trace of the packet. The packet should be dropped. Click **Close** to continue.

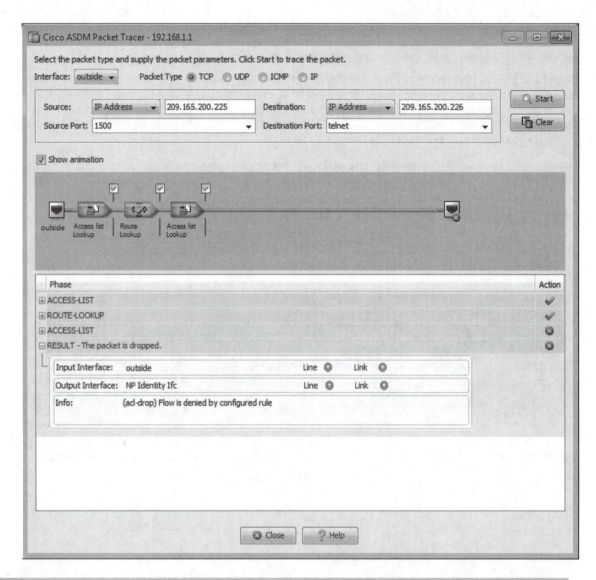

Part 4: Configuring ASA Settings from the ASDM Configuration Menu

In Part 4, you will set the ASA clock, configure a default route, test connectivity using ASDM tools ping and traceroute, configure Local AAA user authentication, and modify the MPF application inspection policy.

Step 1: Set the ASA date and time.

a.   On the **Configuration** screen > **Device Setup** menu, click **System Time** > **Clock**.

b.   Select your **Time Zone** from the drop-down list and enter the current date and time in the fields provided. (The clock is a 24-hour clock.) Click **Apply** to send the commands to the ASA.

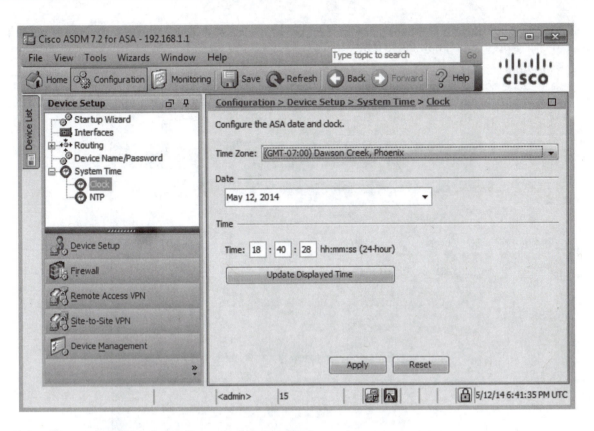

Step 2: Configure a static default route for the ASA.

a. On the **ASDM Tools** menu, select **Ping** and enter the IP address of router R1 S0/0/0 (**10.1.1.1**). The ASA does not have a default route to unknown external networks. The ping should fail because the ASA has no route to 10.1.1.1. Click **Close** to continue.

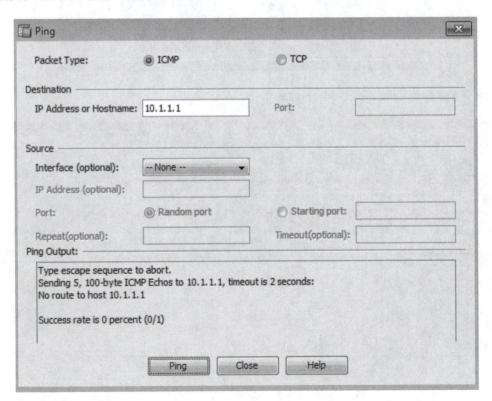

b. From the **Configuration** screen > **Device Setup** menu, click **Routing** > **Static Routes**. Click **IPv4 Only** and click **Add** to add a new static route.

c. On the Add Static Route dialog box, select the **outside** interface from the drop-down list. Click the ellipsis button to the right of **Network** and select **Any** from the list of network objects, and then click **OK**. The selection of **Any** translates to a "quad zero" route. For the Gateway IP, enter **209.165.200.225** (R1 Fa0/0).

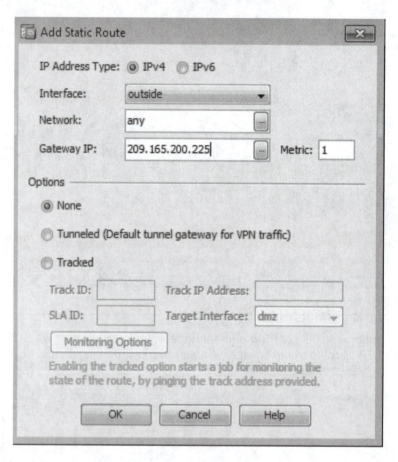

d. Click **OK** > **Apply** to send the commands to the ASA.

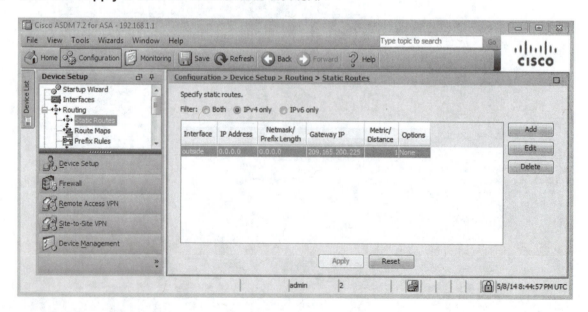

e. On the ASDM **Tools** menu, select **Ping** and enter the IP address of router R1 S0/0/0 (**10.1.1.1**). The ping should succeed this time. Click **Close** to continue.

f. On the ASDM **Tools** menu, select **Traceroute** and enter the IP address of external host PC-C (**172.16.3.3**). Click **Trace Route**. The traceroute should succeed and show the hops from the ASA through R1, R2, and R3 to host PC-C. Click **Close** to continue.

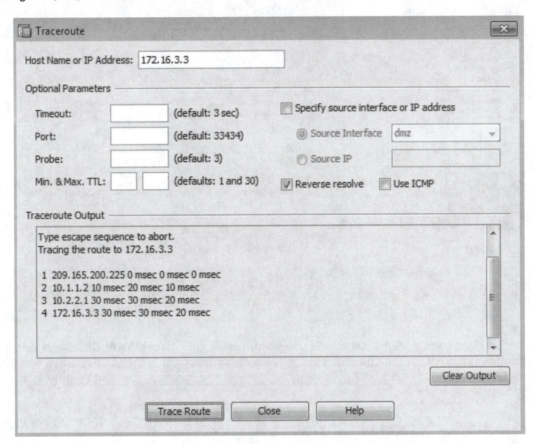

Step 3: Configure AAA user authentication using the local ASA database.

Enable AAA user authentication to access the ASA using SSH. You allowed SSH access to the ASA from the outside host PC-C when the **Startup wizard** was run. To allow the remote network administrator at PC-C to have SSH access to the ASA, you will create a user in the local database.

a. On the **Configuration** screen > **Device Management** area, click **Users/AAA**. Click **User Accounts** > **Add**. Create a new user named **admin** with a password of **cisco123** and enter the password again to confirm it. Allow this user **Full access** (ASDM, SSH, Telnet, and console) and set the privilege level to **15**. Click **OK** to add the user and click **Apply** to send the command to the ASA.

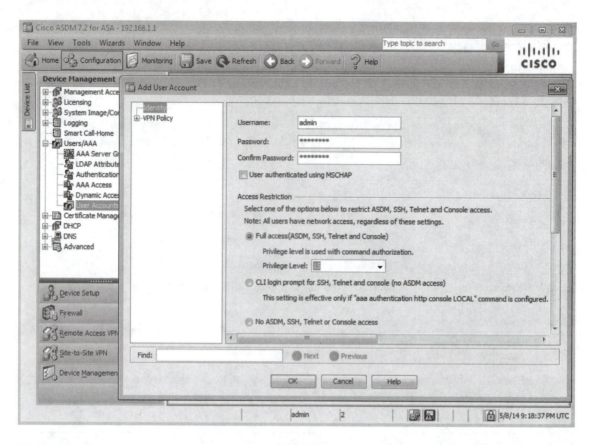

b. On the **Configuration** screen > **Device Management** area, click **Users/AAA**. Click **AAA Access**. On the **Authentication** tab, click the check box to require authentication for **HTTP/ASDM**, **SSH,** and **Telnet** connections and specify the **LOCAL** server group for each connection type. Click **Apply** to send the commands to the ASA.

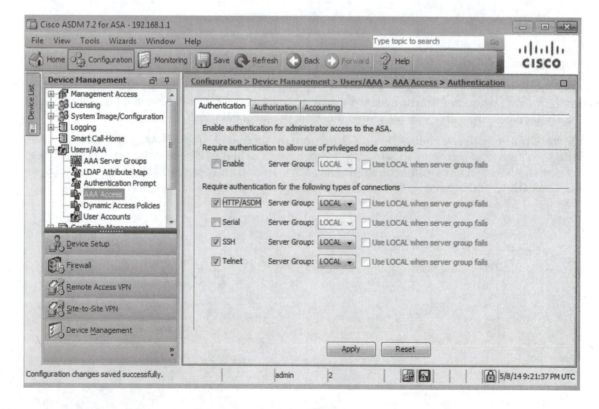

Note: The next action you attempt within ASDM will require you to log in as **admin** with password **cisco123**.

c.   From **PC-C**, open an SSH client, such as PuTTY, and attempt to access the ASA outside interface at **209.165.200.226**. You should be able to establish the connection. When prompted to log in, enter user name **admin** and password **cisco123**.

d.   After logging in to the ASA using SSH, enter the **enable** command and provide the password **class**. Issue the **show run** command to display the current configuration you have created using ASDM.

Note: The default timeout for Telnet and SSH is five minutes. You can increase this setting using the CLI as described in Lab 9A or go to ASDM **Device Management** > **Management Access** > **ASDM/HTTP/Telnet/SSH**.

Step 4: Modify the MPF application inspection policy.

For application layer inspection, and other advanced options, the Cisco Modular Policy Framework (MPF) is available on ASAs.

a.   The default global inspection policy does not inspect ICMP. To enable hosts on the internal network to ping external hosts and receive replies, ICMP traffic must be inspected. On the **Configuration** screen > **Firewall** area menu, click **Service Policy Rules**.

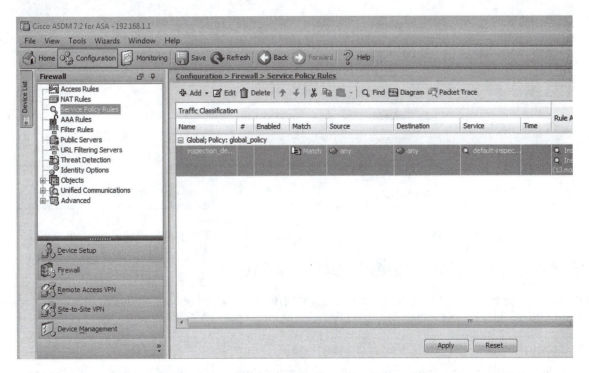

b.   Select the **inspection_default** policy and click **Edit** to modify the default inspection rules. On the Edit Service Policy Rule window, click the **Rule Actions** tab and select the **ICMP** check box. Do not change the other default protocols that are checked. Click **OK** > **Apply** to send the commands to the ASA. If prompted, log in as **admin** with password **cisco123**.

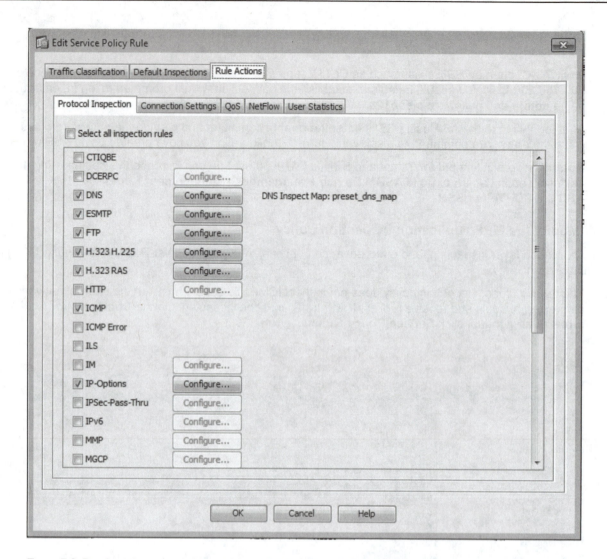

c.   From PC-B, **ping** the external interface of R1 S0/0/0 (**10.1.1.1**). The pings should be successful.

Part 5: Configuring DMZ, Static NAT, and ACLs

In Part 3, you configured address translation using PAT for the inside network. In this part, you will create a DMZ on the ASA, configure static NAT to a DMZ server, and apply an ACL to control access to the server.

Step 1: Configure the ASA DMZ VLAN 3 interface.

In this step, you will create a new interface VLAN 3 named **dmz**, assign physical interface E0/2 to the VLAN, set the security level to **70**, and limit communication from this interface to the inside (VLAN1) interface.

a.   On the **Configuration** screen > **Device Setup** menu, click **Interfaces**. The General tab is displayed by default and currently defined inside (VLAN 1, E0/1) and outside (VLAN 2, E0/0) interfaces are listed. Click **Add** to create a new interface.

b.   In the Add Interface dialog box, select port **Ethernet0/2** and click **Add**. You will be prompted to change the interface from the inside network. Click **OK** for the message to remove the port from the inside interface and add it to this new interface. In the Interface Name box, name the interface **dmz**, assign it a security level of **70**, and make sure the **Enable Interface** checkbox is checked.

c.   Ensure that the **Use Static IP** option is selected and enter an IP address of **192.168.2.1** with a subnet mask of **255.255.255.0**. Do NOT click OK at this time.

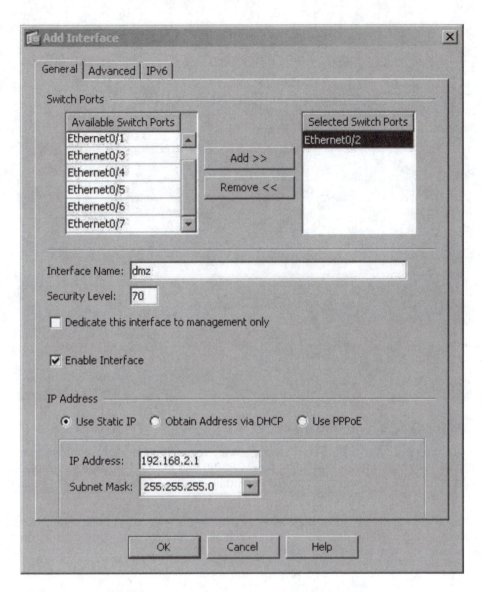

d. ASDM will configure this interface as VLAN ID 12 by default. Before clicking **OK** to add the interface, click the **Advanced** tab and specify this interface as VLAN ID **3**.

Note: If you are working with the ASA 5505 Base license, you are allowed to create up to three named interfaces. However, you must disable communication between the third interface and one of the other interfaces. Because the DMZ server does not need to initiate communication with the inside users, you can disable forwarding to interfaces VLAN 1.

e. On the Advanced tab, you also need to block traffic from this interface VLAN 3 (dmz) to the VLAN 1 (inside) interface. From the Block Traffic area, select **vlan1 (inside)** from the drop-down list. Click **OK** to return to the Interfaces window. You should see the new interface named **dmz**, in addition to the inside and outside interfaces. Click **Apply** to send the commands to the ASA.

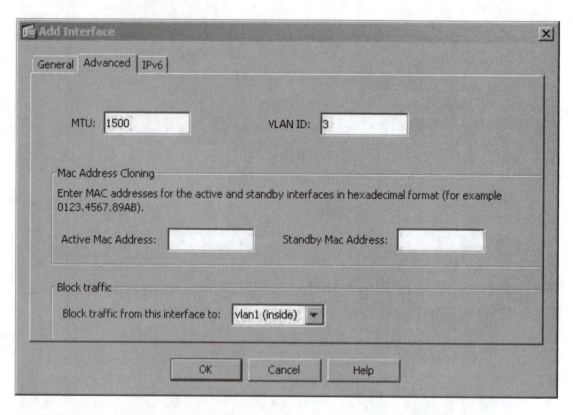

Step 2: Configure the DMZ server and static NAT.

To accommodate the addition of a DMZ and a web server, you will use another address from the ISP range assigned, 209.165.200.224/29 (.224-.231). Router R1 Fa0/0 and the ASA outside interface are already using 209.165.200.225 and .226, respectively. You will use public address **209.165.200.227** and static NAT to provide address translation access to the server.

a. On the **Firewall** menu, click the **Public Servers** option and click **Add** to define the DMZ server and services offered. In the Add Public Server dialog box, specify the Private Interface as **dmz**, the Public Interface as **outside**, and the Public IP address as **209.165.200.227**.

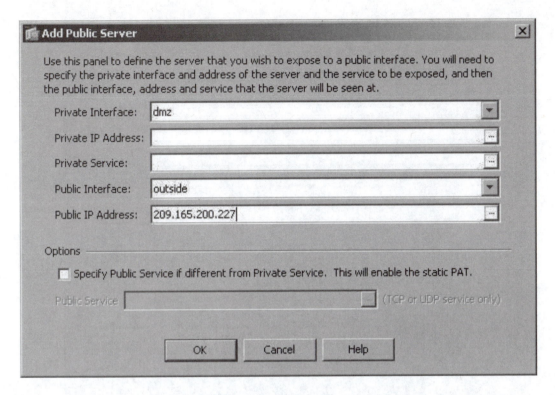

b. Click the ellipsis button to the right of Private IP Address. In the Browse Private IP Address window, click **Add** to define the server as a **Network Object**. Enter the name **DMZ-Server**, with a Type of **Host** and the Private IP Address of **192.168.2.3**.

c. While in the Add Network Object dialog box, click the double down arrow button for **NAT**. Click the checkbox for **Add Automatic Address Translation Rules** and enter the type as **Static**. Enter **209.165.200.227** as the Translated Address. When the screen looks like the following, click **OK** to add the server network object. From the Browse Private IP Address window, click **OK**. You will return to the Add Public Server dialog box.

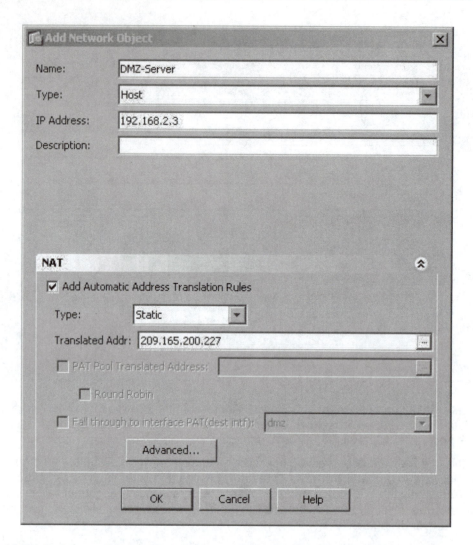

d.   In the Add Public Server dialog, click the ellipsis button to the right of Private Service. In the Browse Private Service window, double-click to select the following services: **tcp/http**, **tcp/ftp**, **icmp/echo**, and **icmp/echo-reply** (scroll down to see all services). Click **OK** to continue and return to the **Add Public Server** dialog.

Note: You can specify Public services if different from the Private services, using the option on this screen.

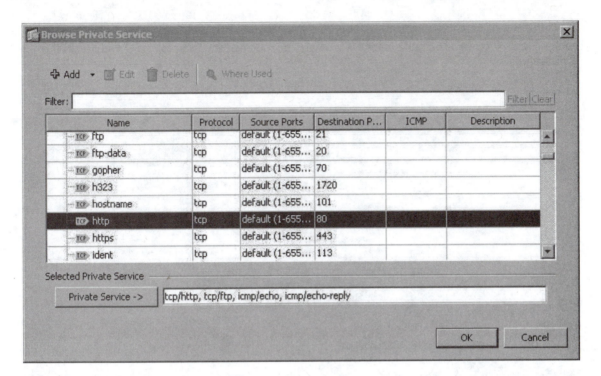

e. When you have completed all information in the Add Public Server dialog box, it should look like the one shown below. Click **OK** to add the server. Click **Apply** at the Public Servers screen to send the commands to the ASA.

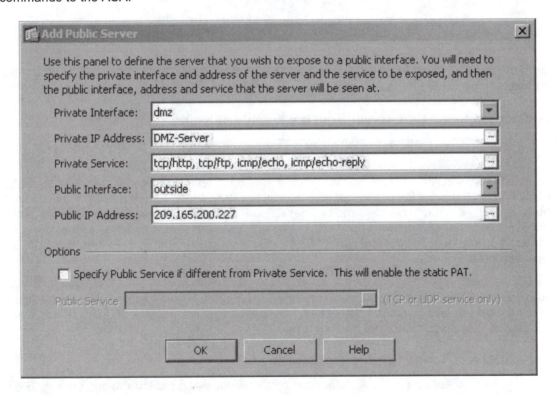

Step 3: View the DMZ Access Rule (ACL) generated by ASDM.

a. With the creation of the DMZ server object and selection of services, ASDM automatically generates an Access Rule (ACL) to permit the appropriate access to the server and applies it to the outside interface in the incoming direction.

b. View this Access Rule in ASDM by clicking **Configuration** > **Firewall** > **Access Rules**. It appears as an outside incoming rule. You can select the rule and use the horizontal scroll bar to see all of the components.

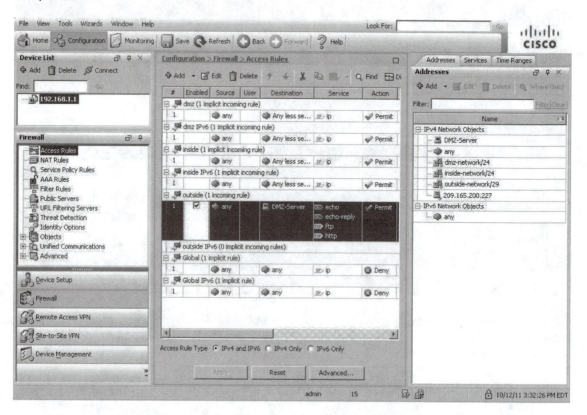

Note: You can also see the actual commands generated using the **Tools** > **Command Line Interface** and entering the **show run** command.

Step 4: Test access to the DMZ server from the outside network.

a. From PC-C, ping the IP address of the static NAT public server address (**209.165.200.227**). The pings should be successful.

b. Because the ASA inside interface (VLAN 1) is set to security level 100 (the highest) and the DMZ interface (VLAN 3) is set to 70, you can also access the DMZ server from a host on the inside network. The ASA acts like a router between the two networks. Ping the DMZ server (PC-A) internal address (**192.168.2.3**) from inside network host PC-B (192.168.1.X). The pings should be successful due to interface security level and the fact that ICMP is being inspected on the inside interface by the global inspection policy.

c. The DMZ server cannot ping PC-B on the inside network. This is because the DMZ interface VLAN 3 has a lower security level and the fact that, when the VLAN 3 interface was created, it was necessary to specify the **no forward** command. Try to ping from the DMZ server PC-A to PC-B at IP address 192.168.1.X. The pings should not be successful.

Step 5: Use ASDM Monitoring to graph packet activity.

There are a number of aspects of the ASA that can be monitored using the **Monitoring** screen. The main categories on this screen are **Interfaces**, **VPN**, **Routing**, **Properties**, and **Logging**. In this step, you will create a graph to monitor packet activity for the outside interface.

a. On the **Monitoring** screen > **Interfaces** menu, click **Interface Graphs** > **outside**. Select **Packet Counts** and click **Add** to add the graph. The exhibit below shows Packet Counts added.

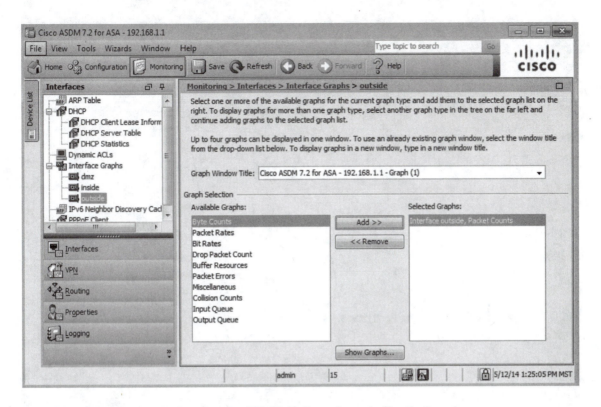

b. Click **Show Graphs** to display the graph. Initially there is no traffic displayed.

c. From a privileged mode command prompt on R2, simulate Internet traffic to the ASA by pinging the DMZ server public address with a repeat count of **1000**. You can increase the number of pings if desired.

    R2# **ping 209.165.200.227 repeat 1000**

    Type escape sequence to abort.
    Sending 1000, 100-byte ICMP Echos to 209.165.200.227, timeout is 2 seconds:
    !!!
    !!!
    <output omitted>
    !!!
    !!!!!!!!!!!!!!!!!!!!!
    Success rate is 100 percent (1000/1000), round-trip min/avg/max = 1/2/12 ms

d. You should see the results of the pings from R2 on the graph as an Input Packet Count. The scale of the graph is automatically adjusted depending on the volume of traffic. You can also view the data in tabular form by clicking the **Table** tab. Notice that the View selected at the bottom left of the Graph screen is Real-time, data every 10 seconds. Click the pull-down list to see the other available options.

e. Ping from PC-B to R1 Fa0/0 at **209.165.200.225** using the **–n** option (number of packets) to specify **100** packets.

    C:>\ **ping 209.165.200.225 –n 100**

    Note: The response from the PC is relatively slow and it may take a while to show up on the graph as Output Packet Count. The graph below shows an additional 2000 input packets and both input and output packet counts.

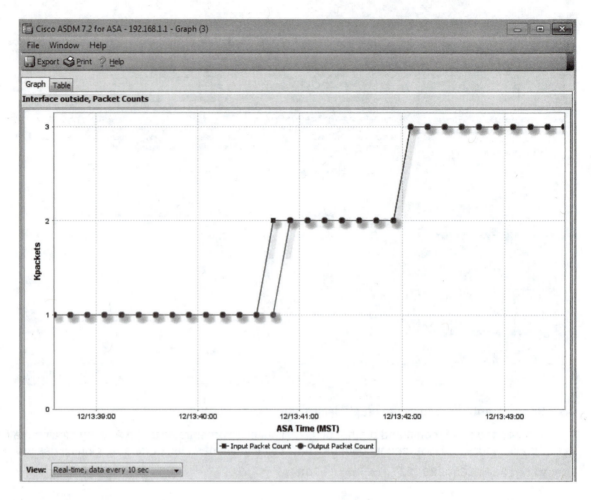

Reflection

1. What are some benefits to using ASDM over the CLI?

    _____

    _____

    _____

    _____

    _____

2. What are some benefits to using the CLI over ASDM?

    _____

    _____

    _____

    _____

    _____

Router Interface Summary Table

Router Interface Summary				
Router Model	**Ethernet Interface #1**	**Ethernet Interface #2**	**Serial Interface #1**	**Serial Interface #2**
1800	Fast Ethernet 0/0 (Fa0/0)	Fast Ethernet 0/1 (Fa0/1)	Serial 0/0/0 (S0/0/0)	Serial 0/0/1 (S0/0/1)
1900	Gigabit Ethernet 0/0 (G0/0)	Gigabit Ethernet 0/1 (G0/1)	Serial 0/0/0 (S0/0/0)	Serial 0/0/1 (S0/0/1)
2801	Fast Ethernet 0/0 (Fa0/0)	Fast Ethernet 0/1 (Fa0/1)	Serial 0/1/0 (S0/1/0)	Serial 0/1/1 (S0/1/1)
2811	Fast Ethernet 0/0 (Fa0/0)	Fast Ethernet 0/1 (Fa0/1)	Serial 0/0/0 (S0/0/0)	Serial 0/0/1 (S0/0/1)
2900	Gigabit Ethernet 0/0 (G0/0)	Gigabit Ethernet 0/1 (G0/1)	Serial 0/0/0 (S0/0/0)	Serial 0/0/1 (S0/0/1)

Note: To find out how the router is configured, look at the interfaces to identify the type of router and how many interfaces the router has. There is no way to effectively list all the combinations of configurations for each router class. This table includes identifiers for the possible combinations of Ethernet and Serial interfaces in the device. The table does not include any other type of interface, even though a specific router may contain one. An example of this might be an ISDN BRI interface. The string in parenthesis is the legal abbreviation that can be used in Cisco IOS commands to represent the interface.

Lab 9.4.1.3 - Configuring Clientless and AnyConnect Remote Access SSL VPNs Using ASDM

Topology

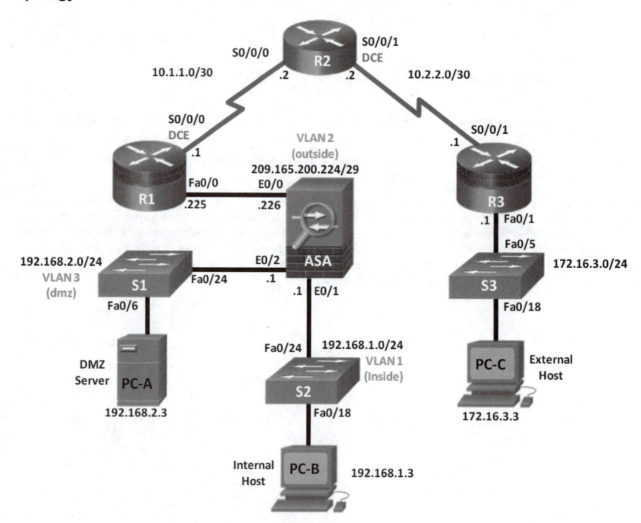

Note: ISR G2 devices use GigabitEthernet interfaces instead of FastEthernet interfaces.

IP Addressing Table

Device	Interface	IP Address	Subnet Mask	Default Gateway	Switch Port
R1	Fa0/0	209.165.200.225	255.255.255.248	N/A	ASA E0/0
	S0/0/0 (DCE)	10.1.1.1	255.255.255.252	N/A	N/A
R2	S0/0/0	10.1.1.2	255.255.255.252	N/A	N/A
	S0/0/1 (DCE)	10.2.2.2	255.255.255.252	N/A	N/A
R3	Fa0/1	172.16.3.1	255.255.255.0	N/A	S3 Fa0/5
	S0/0/1	10.2.2.1	255.255.255.252	N/A	N/A
ASA	VLAN 1 (E0/1)	192.168.1.1	255.255.255.0	NA	S2 Fa0/24
ASA	VLAN 2 (E0/0)	209.165.200.226	255.255.255.248	NA	R1 Fa0/0
ASA	VLAN 3 (E0/2)	192.168.2.1	255.255.255.0	NA	S1 Fa0/24
PC-A	NIC	192.168.2.3	255.255.255.0	192.168.2.1	S1 Fa0/6
PC-B	NIC	192.168.1.3	255.255.255.0	192.168.1.1	S2 Fa0/18
PC-C	NIC	172.16.3.3	255.255.255.0	172.16.3.1	S3 Fa0/18

Objectives

Part 1: Basic Router/Switch/PC Configuration

- Cable the network and clear previous device settings, as shown in the topology.
- Configure basic settings for routers and switches.
- Configure static routing, including default routes, between R1, R2, and R3.
- Enable the HTTP server on R1 and set the enable and vty passwords.
- Configure PC host IP settings.
- Verify connectivity.
- Save the basic running configuration for each router and switch.

Part 2: Access the ASA Console and ASDM

- Access the ASA console.
- Clear the previous ASA configuration settings.
- Bypass Setup mode.
- Configure the ASA by using the CLI script.
- Access ASDM.

Part 3: Configuring Clientless SSL VPN Remote Access Using ASDM

- Review the Remote Access VPN ASDM Assistant.
- Start the VPN wizard.
- Configure the SSL VPN user interface.
- Configure AAA user authentication.
- Configure the VPN group policy.

- Configure a bookmark list (clientless connections only).
- Review the configuration summary and deliver the commands to the ASA.
- Verify the ASDM SSL VPN connection profile.
- Verify VPN access from the remote host.
- Access the web portal page.
- View the clientless remote user session using the ASDM Monitor.

Part 4: Configuring AnyConnect Client SSL VPN Remote Access Using ASDM

- Clear the ASA configuration and access ASDM.
- Review the Remote Access VPN ASDM Assistant.
- Start the VPN wizard.
- Specify the VPN encryption protocol.
- Specify the client image to upload to AnyConnect users.
- Configure AAA local authentication.
- Configure the client address assignment.
- Configure the network name resolution.
- Exempt address translation for VPN traffic.
- Review the AnyConnect client deployment details.
- Review the Summary screen and apply the configuration to the ASA.
- Verify the AnyConnect client profile.
- Log in from the remote host.
- Perform platform detection (if required).
- Perform an automatic installation of the AnyConnect VPN Client (if required).
- Manually install the AnyConnect VPN Client (if required).
- Confirm VPN connectivity.

Background / Scenario

In addition to stateful firewall and other security features, the ASA can provide both site-to-site and remote access VPN functionality. The ASA provides two main deployment modes that are found in Cisco SSL remote access VPN solutions:

- **Clientless SSL VPN**—Clientless, browser-based VPN that lets users establish a secure, remote-access VPN tunnel to the ASA using a web browser and built-in SSL to protect VPN traffic. After authentication, users are presented with a portal page and can access specific, predefined internal resources from the portal.

- **Client-Based SSL VPN**—Provides full-tunnel SSL VPN connection, but requires a VPN client application to be installed on the remote host. After authentication, users can access any internal resource as if they were physically on the local network. The ASA supports both SSL and IPsec client-based VPNs.

In Part 1 of this lab, you will configure the topology and non-ASA devices. In Part 2, you will prepare the ASA for ASDM access. In Part 3, you will use the ASDM VPN wizard to configure a clientless SSL remote access VPN and verify access using a remote PC with a browser. In Part 4, you will configure an AnyConnect client-based SSL remote access VPN and verify connectivity.

Your company has two locations connected to an ISP. Router R1 represents a CPE device managed by the ISP. Router R2 represents an intermediate Internet router. Router R3 connects users at the remote branch office to the ISP. The ASA is an edge security device that connects the internal corporate network and DMZ to the ISP while providing NAT services to inside hosts.

Management has asked you to provide VPN access, using the ASA as a VPN concentrator, to teleworkers. They want you to test both the clientless access model, using SSL and a browser for client access, and the client-based model using SSL and the Cisco AnyConnect client.

Note: The router commands and output in this lab are from a Cisco 1841 router with Cisco IOS Release 15.1(4)M8 (Advanced IP Services image). Other routers and Cisco IOS versions can be used. See the Router Interface Summary Table at the end of the lab to determine which interface identifiers to use based on the equipment in the lab. Depending on the router model and Cisco IOS version, the commands available and output produced might vary from what is shown in this lab.

The ASA use with this lab is a Cisco model 5505 with an 8-port integrated switch, running OS version 8.4(2) and ASDM version 7.2(1) and comes with a Base license that allows a maximum of three VLANs.

Note: Ensure that the routers and switches have been erased and have no startup configurations.

Required Resources

- 3 Routers (Cisco 1841 with Cisco IOS Release 15.1(4)M8 Advanced IP Services image or comparable)
- 3 Switches (Cisco 2960 or comparable)
- 1 ASA 5505 (OS version 8.4(2) and ASDM version 7.2(1) and Base license or comparable)
- 3 PCs (Windows Vista or Windows 7 with CCP 2.5, latest version of Java, Internet Explorer, and Flash Player)
- Serial and Ethernet cables as shown in the topology
- Console cables to configure Cisco networking devices

CCP Notes:

- If the PC on which CCP is installed is running Windows Vista or Windows 7, it may be necessary to right-click the CCP icon or menu item, and select **Run as administrator**.
- To run CCP, it may be necessary to temporarily disable antivirus programs and O/S firewalls. Ensure that all pop-up blockers are turned off in the browser.

Browser Note:

Use of a browser other than Internet Explorer 7 or newer on remote PC-C may produce results different from those shown in this lab. It may be necessary to create an exception when connecting to the ASA over the remote access VPN.

Part 1: Basic Router/Switch/PC Configuration

In Part 1 of this lab, you will set up the network topology and configure basic settings on the routers, such as interface IP addresses and static routing.

Note: Do not configure any ASA settings at this time.

Step 1: Cable the network and clear previous device settings.

Attach the devices shown in the topology diagram and cable as necessary. Ensure that the routers and switches have been erased and have no startup configurations.

Step 2: Configure basic settings for routers and switches.

a. Configure hostnames as shown in the topology for each router.

b. Configure router interface IP addresses, as shown in the IP Addressing table.

c. Configure a clock rate for routers with a DCE serial cable attached to their serial interface. R1 is shown here as an example:

```
R1(config)# interface S0/0/0
R1(config-if)# clock rate 2000000
```

Note: It is recommended that the highest possible clock rate be used to shorten software download time in Part 4.

d. Configure the hostname for the switches. Other than hostname, the switches can be left in their default configuration state. Configuring the VLAN management IP address for the switches is optional.

Step 3: Configure static routing on the routers.

a. Configure a static default route from R1 to R2 and from R3 to R2.

```
R1(config)# ip route 0.0.0.0 0.0.0.0 Serial0/0/0


R3(config)# ip route 0.0.0.0 0.0.0.0 Serial0/0/1
```

b. Configure a static route from R2 to the R1 Fa0/0 subnet (connected to ASA interface E0/0) and a static route from R2 to the R3 LAN.

```
R2(config)# ip route 209.165.200.224 255.255.255.248 Serial0/0/0
R2(config)# ip route 172.16.3.0 255.255.255.0 Serial0/0/1
```

Step 4: Enable the HTTP server on R1 and set the enable and vty passwords.

a. Enable HTTP access to R1 using the **ip http server** command in global configuration mode. Also set the vty password to **cisco**.

b. Configure the same settings on R2 and R3. Router R1 is shown here as an example:

```
R1(config)# ip http server
R1(config)# enable password class


R1(config)# line vty 0 4
R1(config-line)# password cisco
R1(config-line)# login


R1(config)# line con 0
R1(config-line)# password cisco
R1(config-line)# login
```

Step 5: Configure PC host IP settings.

Configure a static IP address, subnet mask, and default gateway for PC-A, PC-B, and PC-C as shown in the IP Addressing Table.

Step 6: Verify connectivity.

Because the ASA is the focal point for the network zones and it has not yet been configured, there will be no connectivity between devices connected to it. However, PC-C should be able to ping the R1 interface Fa0/0. From PC-C, ping the R1 Fa0/0 IP address (**209.165.200.225**). If these pings are unsuccessful, troubleshoot the basic device configurations before continuing.

Note: If you can ping from PC-C to R1 Fa0/0, you have demonstrated that static routing is configured and functioning correctly.

Step 7: Save the basic running configuration for each router and switch.

Part 2: Accessing the ASA Console and ASDM

Step 1: Access the ASA console.

a. Accessing the ASA via the console port is the same as with a Cisco router or switch. Connect to the ASA console port with a rollover cable.

b. Use a terminal emulation program to access the CLI, and use the serial port settings of 9600 baud, 8 data bits, no parity, one stop bit, and no flow control.

c. If prompted to enter Interactive Firewall configuration (Setup mode), answer **no**.

d. Enter privileged EXEC mode with the **enable** command and password (if set). By default, the password is blank; press **Enter**. If the password has been changed to that specified in this lab, the password is **class**, and the hostname and prompt is **CCNAS-ASA>**, as shown in this example. The default ASA hostname and prompt is **ciscoasa>**.

```
CCNAS-ASA> enable
Password: class (or press Enter if none set)
```

Step 2: Clear the previous ASA configuration settings.

a. Use the **write erase** command to remove the **startup-config** file from flash memory.

```
CCNAS-ASA# write erase
Erase configuration in flash memory? [confirm]
[OK]
CCNAS-ASA#
```

Note: The **erase startup-config** IOS command is not supported on the ASA.

b. Use the **reload** command to restart the ASA. This causes the ASA to display in CLI Setup mode. If you see the `System config has been modified. Save? [Y]es/[N]o:` message, type **n**, and press **Enter**.

```
CCNAS-ASA# reload
Proceed with reload? [confirm] <Enter>
CCNAS-ASA#
***
*** --- START GRACEFUL SHUTDOWN ---
Shutting down isakmp
Shutting down File system
***
*** --- SHUTDOWN NOW ---
Process shutdown finished
Rebooting.....
CISCO SYSTEMS
Embedded BIOS Version 1.0(12)13 08/28/08 15:50:37.45
<output omitted>
```

Step 3: Bypass Setup mode.

When the ASA completes the reload process, it should detect that the startup configuration file is missing and go into Setup mode. If it does not come up in this mode, repeat Step 2.

a. When prompted to preconfigure the firewall through interactive prompts (Setup mode), respond with **no**.

```
Pre-configure Firewall now through interactive prompts [yes]? no
```

b. Enter privileged EXEC mode with the **enable** command. The password should be kept blank (no password).

Step 4: Configure the ASA by using the CLI script.

In this step, you will use a CLI script to configure basic settings, the firewall, and DMZ.

a. Other than the defaults that the ASA automatically inserts, use the **show run** command to confirm that there is no previous configuration in the ASA.

b. Enter global configuration mode. When prompted to enable anonymous call-home reporting, respond **no**.

```
ciscoasa> enable
Password: <Enter>

ciscoasa# conf t
ciscoasa(config)#
```

c. Copy and paste the Pre-VPN Configuration Script commands listed below at the ASA global configuration mode prompt to start configuring the SSL VPNs.

Observe the messages as the commands are applied to ensure that there are no warnings or errors. If prompted to replace the RSA key pair, respond **yes**.

Lab 9C Pre-VPN Configuration Script:

```
hostname CCNAS-ASA
!
domain-name ccnasecurity.com
!
enable password class
passwd cisco
!
interface Ethernet0/0
 switchport access vlan 2
 no shut
!
interface Ethernet0/1
 switchport access vlan 1
 no shut
!
interface Ethernet0/2
 switchport access vlan 3
 no shut
!
interface Vlan1
 nameif inside
 security-level 100
 ip address 192.168.1.1 255.255.255.0
!
interface Vlan2
 nameif outside
```

```
 security-level 0
 ip address 209.165.200.226 255.255.255.248
!
interface Vlan3
 no forward interface Vlan1
 nameif dmz
 security-level 70
 ip address 192.168.2.1 255.255.255.0
!
object network inside-net
 subnet 192.168.1.0 255.255.255.0
!
object network dmz-server
 host 192.168.2.3
!
access-list OUTSIDE-DMZ extended permit ip any host 192.168.2.3
!
object network inside-net
 nat (inside,outside) dynamic interface
!
object network dmz-server
 nat (dmz,outside) static 209.165.200.227
!
access-group OUTSIDE-DMZ in interface outside
!
route outside 0.0.0.0 0.0.0.0 209.165.200.225 1
!
username admin password cisco123
!
aaa authentication telnet console LOCAL
aaa authentication ssh console LOCAL
aaa authentication http console LOCAL
!
http server enable
http 192.168.1.0 255.255.255.0 inside
ssh 192.168.1.0 255.255.255.0 inside
telnet 192.168.1.0 255.255.255.0 inside
telnet timeout 10
ssh timeout 10
!
class-map inspection_default
 match default-inspection-traffic
policy-map type inspect dns preset_dns_map
 parameters
  message-length maximum client auto
  message-length maximum 512
```

```
policy-map global_policy
 class inspection_default
    inspect icmp
!
prompt hostname context
no call-home reporting anonymous
!
crypto key generate rsa modulus 1024
```

d. At the privileged EXEC mode prompt, issue the **write mem** (or **copy run start**) command to save the running configuration to the startup configuration and the RSA keys to non-volatile memory.

Step 5: Access ASDM.

a. Open a browser on PC-B and test the HTTPS access to the ASA by entering **https://192.168.1.1**.

    Note: Specify the HTTPS protocol in the URL.

b. After entering the https://192.168.1.1 URL, you should see a security warning about the website security certificate. Click **Continue to this website**. Click **Yes** for any other security warnings. At the ASDM welcome page, click **Run ASDM**. The ASDM-IDM Launcher will display. Log in as user **admin** with password **cisco123**. ASDM will load the current configuration into the GUI.

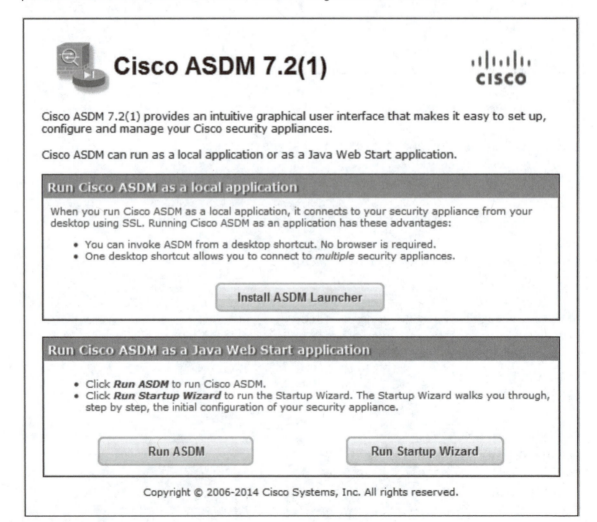

Part 3: Configuring Clientless SSL VPN Remote Access Using ASDM

Step 1: Review the Remote Access VPN ASDM Assistant.

a. On the ASDM menu bar, click **Configuration** > **Remote Access VPN** to display the Introduction screen, where you can access information on how to create any of the three types of remote access VPNs.

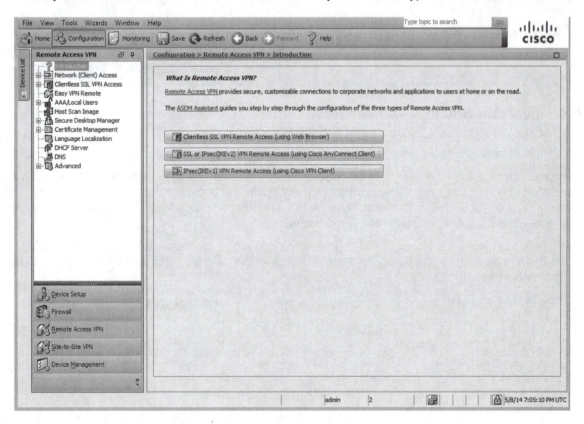

b. Click **Clientless SSL VPN Remote Access (using Web Browser)** to access the ASDM Assistant. Read through the information provided to get a better understanding of the process for creating this type of VPN.

Step 2: Start the VPN wizard.

a. On the ASDM main menu, click **Wizards** > **VPN Wizards** > **Clientless SSL VPN wizard**. The SSL VPN wizard Clientless SSL VPN Connection screen displays.

b. Review the on-screen text and topology diagram, and then click **Next** to continue.

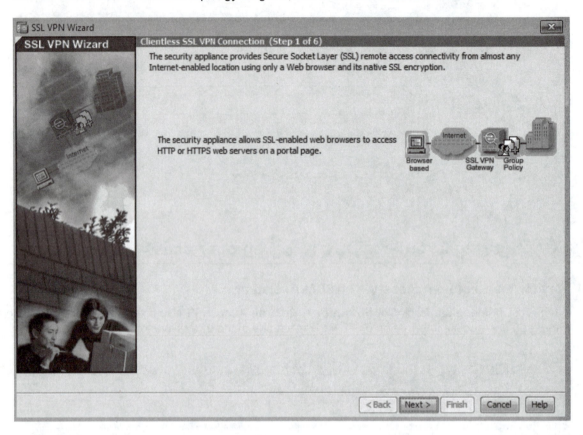

Step 3: Configure the SSL VPN user interface.

a. On the SSL VPN Interface screen, configure **ClientlessVPN-Con-Prof** as the Connection Profile Name, and specify **outside** as the interface to which outside users will connect.

Note: By default, the ASA uses a self-signed certificate to send to the client for authentication. Optionally, the ASA may be configured to use a third-party certificate that is purchased from a well-known certificate authority, such as VeriSign, to connect clients. In the event that a certificate is purchased, it may be selected in the Digital Certificate drop-down menu.

The SSL VPN Interface screen provides links in the Information section. These links identify the URLs that need to be used for the SSL VPN service access (login) and for Cisco ASDM access (to access the Cisco ASDM software).

b. Click **Next** to continue.

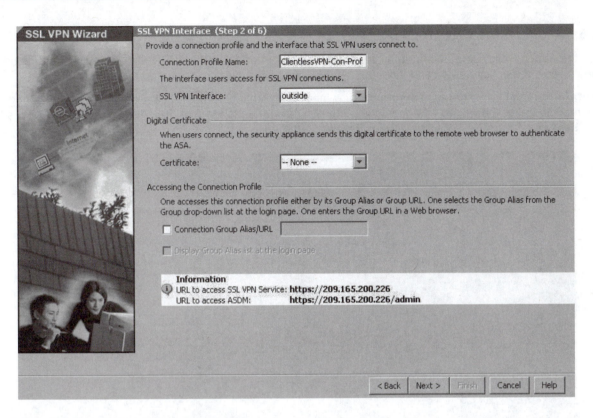

Step 4: Configure AAA user authentication.

On the User Authentication screen, click **Authenticate using the local user database** and enter the user name **VPN-User** with password **remote**. Click **Add** to create the new user and click **Next** to continue.

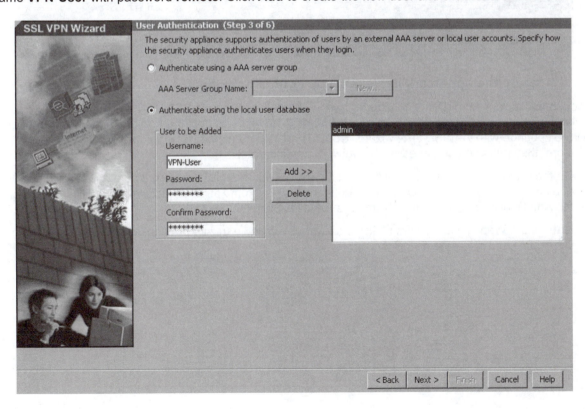

Step 5: Configure the VPN group policy.

On the Group Policy screen, create a new group policy named **ClientlessVPN-Grp-Pol**. (When configuring a new policy, the policy name cannot contain any spaces.) Click **Next** to continue.

Note: By default, the created user group policy inherits its settings from the DfltGrpPolicy. These settings may be modified after the wizard has been completed by navigating to the **Configuration** > **Remote Access VPN** > **Clientless SSL VPN Access** > **Group Policies** submenu.

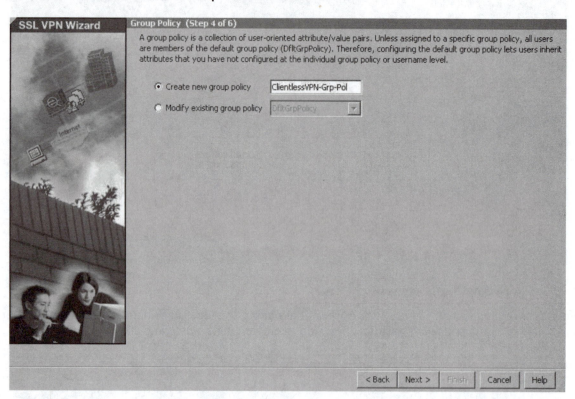

Step 6: Configure the bookmark list (clientless connections only).

A bookmark list is a set of URLs configured to be used in the clientless SSL VPN web portal. If there are bookmarks already listed, use the **Bookmark List** drop-down list, select the bookmark of choice, and click **Next** to continue with the SSL VPN wizard. **Note:** There are no configured bookmark lists by default and, therefore, they must be configured by the network administrator.

a. On the Clientless Connections Only – Bookmark List screen, click **Manage** to create an HTTP server bookmark in the bookmark list. In the Configure GUI Customization Objects window, click **Add** to open the Add Bookmark List window. Name the list **Web-Server**.

    Note: If the Web-Server bookmark list is shown as available from a previous configuration, you can delete it in ASDM and re-create it.

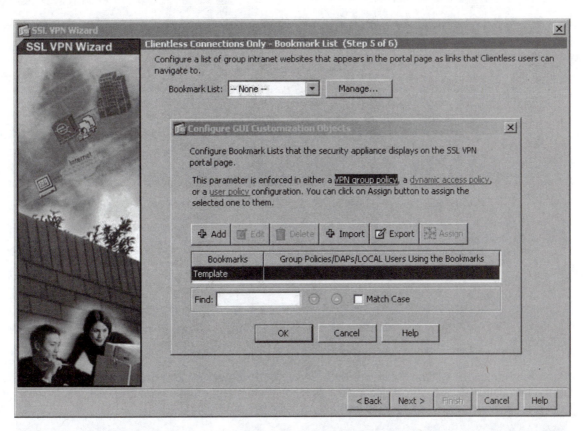

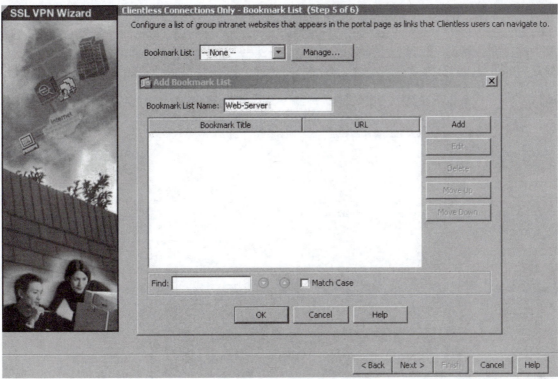

b. In the Add Bookmark List window, click **Add** to open the Add Bookmark window. Enter **Web Mail** as the Bookmark Title. Enter the server destination IP address or hostname as the URL to be used with the bookmark entry. In this example, the internal IP address of the DMZ server is specified. If this server has HTTP web services and web mail installed and functional, the outside users are able to access the server from the ASA portal when they connect.

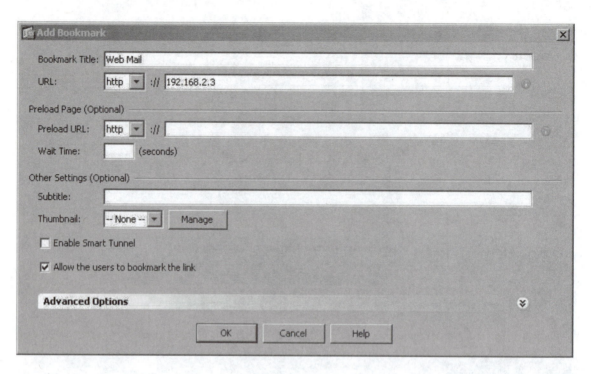

c. When the Bookmark Title and URL are entered, click **OK** in the Add Bookmark window to return to the Configure GUI Customization Objects window. Select the desired bookmark and click **OK** to return to the Bookmark List window. Click **Next** to continue.

Step 7: Review the configuration summary and deliver the commands to the ASA.

a. The Summary page is displayed next. Verify that the information configured in the SSL VPN wizard is correct. Click **Back** to make changes, or click **Cancel** and restart the VPN wizard.

b. Click **Finish** to complete the process and deliver the commands to the ASA.

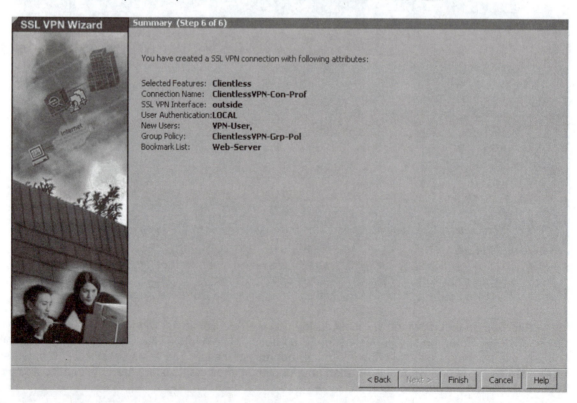

Step 8: Verify the ASDM SSL VPN connection profile.

In ASDM, click **Configuration** > **Remote Access VPN** > **Clientless SSL VPN Access** > **Connection Profiles**. In this window, the VPN configuration can be verified and edited.

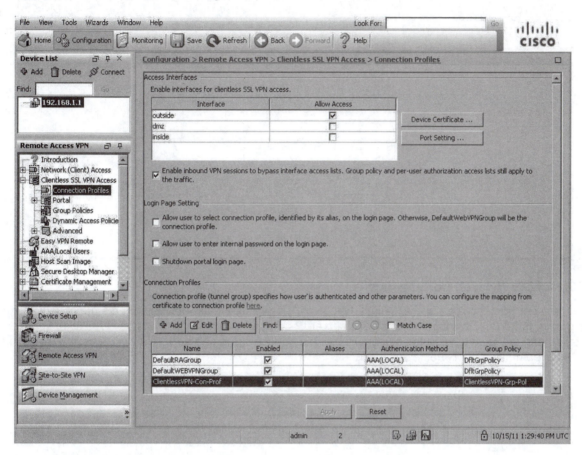

Step 9: Verify VPN access from the remote host.

a. Open the browser on PC-C and enter the login URL for the SSL VPN into the address field (**https://209.165.200.226**). Use secure HTTP (HTTPS) because SSL is required to connect to the ASA.

b. The Logon window should display. Enter the previously configured username **VPN-User** and password **remote**, and click **Logon** to continue.

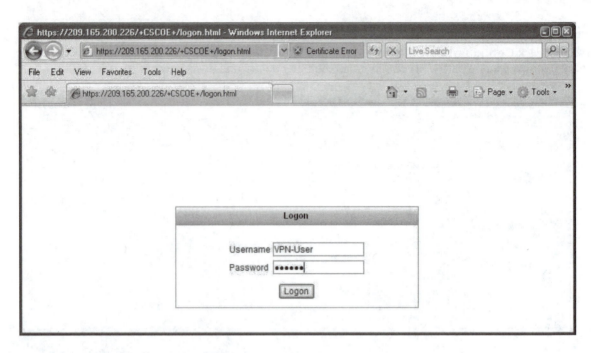

Step 10: Access the web portal window.

After the user authenticates, the ASA SSL web portal page lists the various bookmarks previously assigned to the profile. If the Bookmark points to a valid server IP address or hostname that has HTTP web services installed and functional, the outside user will be able to access the server from the ASA portal. **Note:** In this lab, the web mail server is not installed.

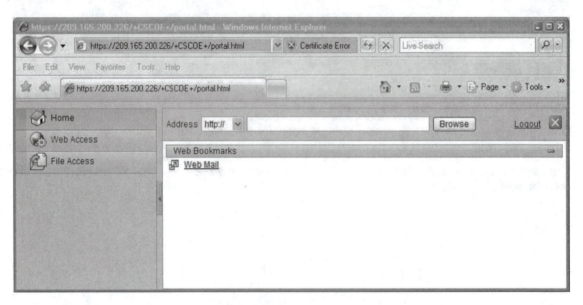

Step 11: View the clientless remote user session using the ASDM Monitor.

While the remote user at PC-C is still logged in and on the ASA portal page, you can view the session statistics using ASDM monitor.

On the menu bar, click **Monitoring** and then select **VPN** > **VPN Statistics** > **Sessions**. Click the **Filter By** pull-down list and select **Clientless SSL VPN**. You should see the VPN-User session logged in from PC-C (172.16.3.3).

Note: You may need to click **Refresh** to display the remote user session.

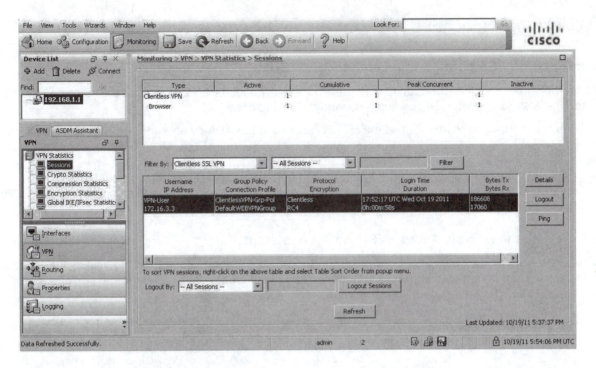

Step 12: Log out of the web portal page.

The user should log out of the web portal window using the **Logout** button when done (see Step 10). However, the web portal will also time out if there is no activity. In either case, a logout window will be displayed informing users that for additional security, they should clear the browser cache, delete the downloaded files, and close the browser window.

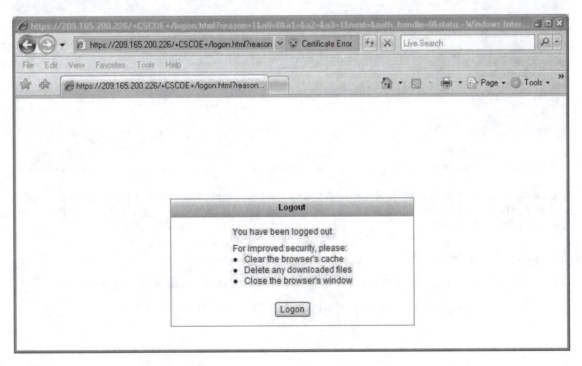

Part 4: Configuring AnyConnect SSL VPN Remote Access Using ASDM

Step 1: Clear the ASA configuration and access ASDM.

Before beginning Part 4 of this lab, use the procedure described in Part 2 to remove the current VPN settings, return the ASA to its base configuration, and verify ASDM access.

a. Open a browser on PC-B and test the HTTPS access to the ASA by entering **https://192.168.1.1**.

   Note: Specify the HTTPS protocol in the URL.

b. After entering the https://192.168.1.1 URL, you should see a security warning about the security certificate of the website. Click **Continue to this website**. The ASDM welcome page will display. Click **Run ASDM** and log in as **admin** with password **cisco123**.

Step 2: Review the Remote Access VPN ASDM Assistant.

a. On the ASDM menu bar, click **Configuration** and select **Remote Access VPN** to display the Introduction screen. From here, you can access information on how to create each of the three types of remote access VPNs that are supported by the ASA.

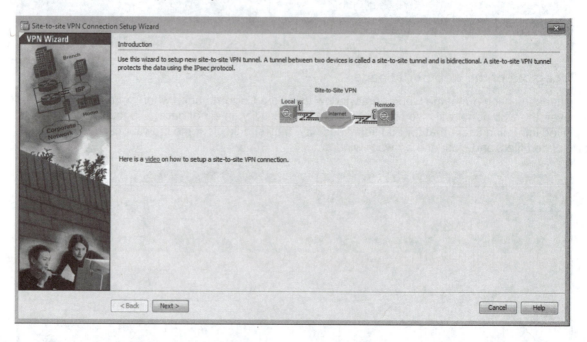

b. Click **SSL or IPsec(IKEv2) VPN Remote Access (using Cisco AnyConnect Client)** to access the ASDM Assistant. Read through the information provided to get a better understanding of the process for creating this type of VPN.

Step 3: Start the VPN wizard.

a. On the ASDM main menu, click **Wizards > VPN Wizards > AnyConnect VPN Wizard**.

b. Review the on-screen text and topology diagram, and then click **Next** to continue.

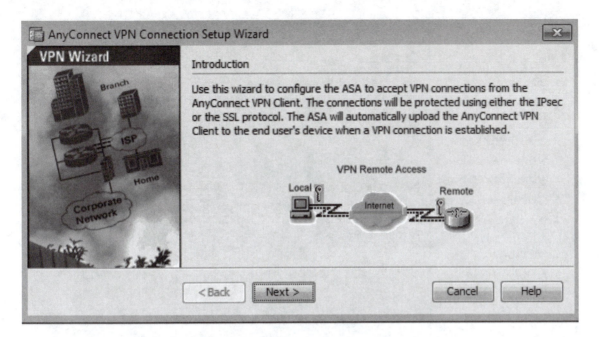

Step 4: Configure the SSL VPN interface connection profile.

On the Connection Profile Identification screen, enter **AnyC-SSL-VPN-Con-Prof** as the Connection Profile Name and specify the **outside** interface as the VPN Access Interface. Click **Next** to continue.

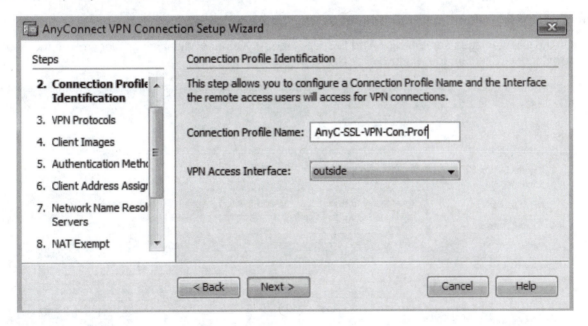

Step 5: Specify the VPN encryption protocol.

On the VPN Protocols screen, uncheck the **IPsec** check box and leave the **SSL** check box checked. Do not specify a device certificate. Click **Next** to continue.

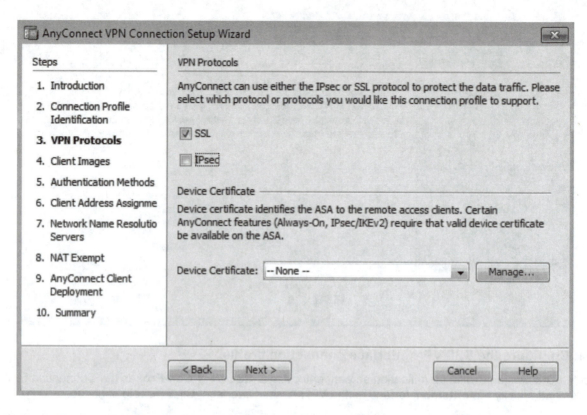

Step 6: Specify the client image to upload to AnyConnect users.

  a.   On the Client Images screen, click **Add** to specify the AnyConnect client image filename. In the Add
       AnyConnect Client Image window, click **Browse Flash**.

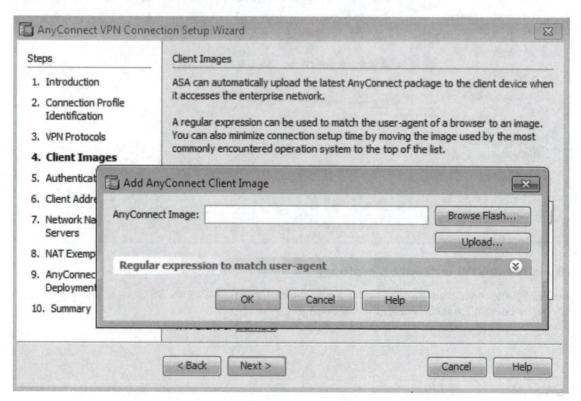

b. In the Browse Flash window, select the AnyConnect package file for Windows (**anyconnect-win-3.1.05160-k9.pkg**, in the example). Click **OK** to return to the AnyConnect Client Images window, and then click **OK** again. On the Client Images screen, click **Next** to continue.

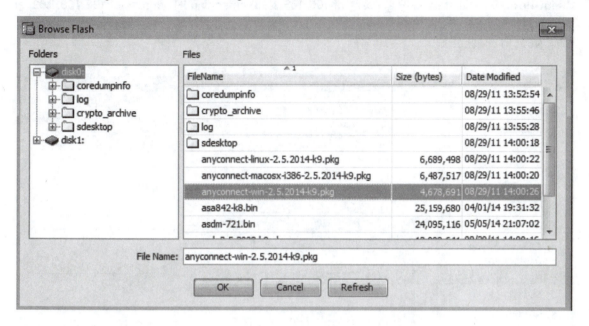

Step 7: Configure AAA local authentication.

a. On the Authentication Methods screen, ensure that the AAA Server Group is specified as **LOCAL**.

b. Enter a new user named **VPN-User** with a password of **remote**. Click **Add** to create the new user. Click **Next** to continue.

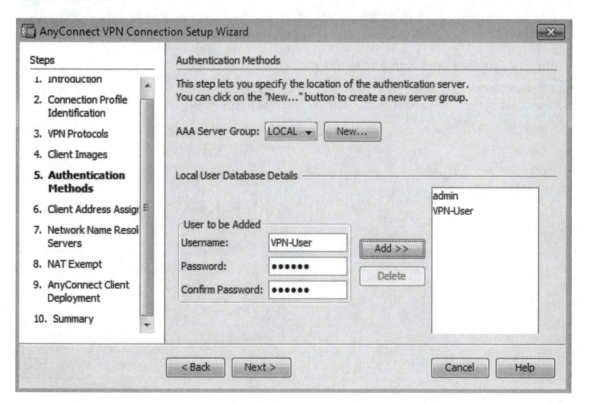

Step 8: Configure the client address assignment.

a. On the Client Address Assignment screen, click **New** to create an IPv4 address pool named **AnyC-VPN-Client-Pool**. Enter a starting IP address of **192.168.1.33**, an ending IP address of **192.168.1.62**, and subnet mask of **255.255.255.224**. Click **OK**.

b. Click **Next** to continue.

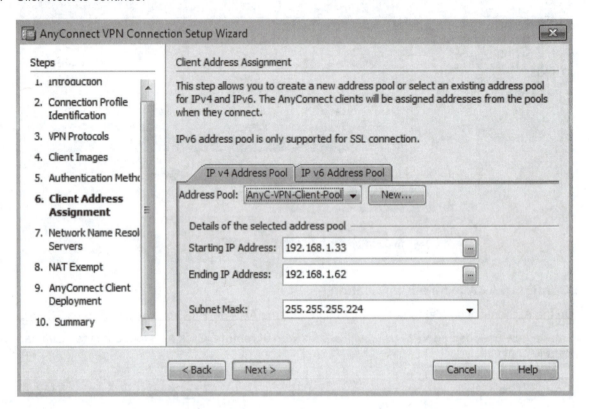

Step 9: Configure the network name resolution.

On the Network Name Resolution Servers screen, enter the IP address of a DNS server (**10.20.30.40**). Leave the current domain name as **ccnasecurity.com**. Click **Next** to continue.

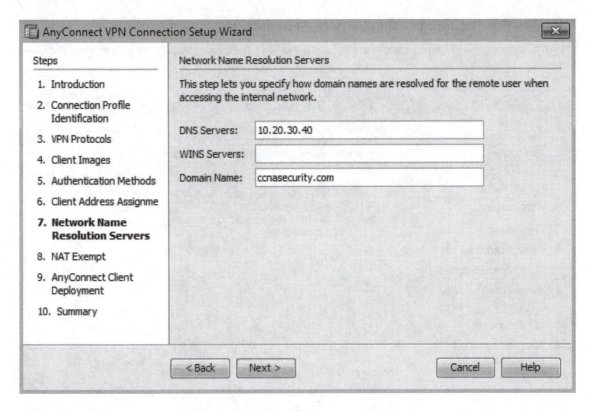

Step 10: Exempt address translation for VPN traffic.

a. On the NAT Exempt screen, click the **Exempt VPN traffic from network address translation** check box.

b. Leave the default entries for the Inside Interface (**inside**) and the Local Network (**any**) as they are. Click **Next** to continue.

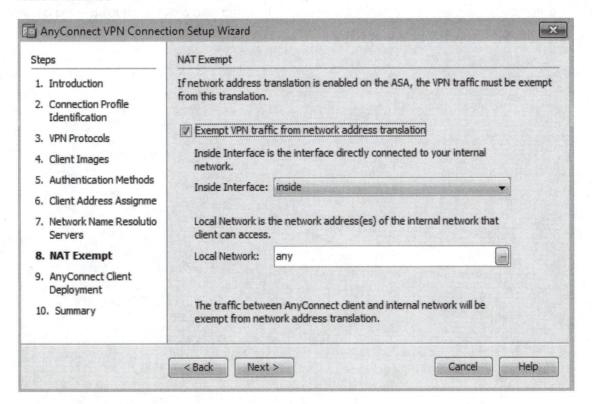

Step 11: Review the AnyConnect client deployment details.

On the AnyConnect Client Deployment screen, read the text describing the options, and then click **Next** to continue.

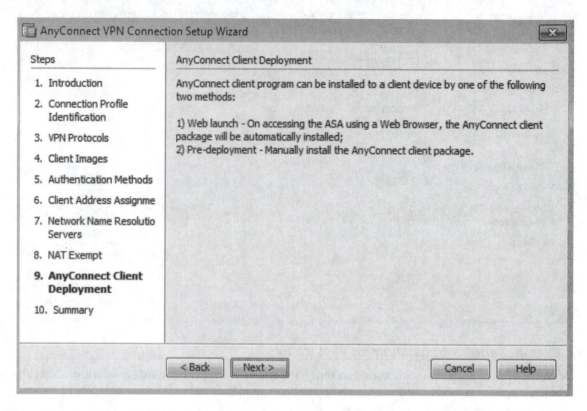

Step 12: Review the Summary screen and apply the configuration to the ASA.

On the Summary screen, review the configuration description, and then click **Finish** to send the commands to the ASA.

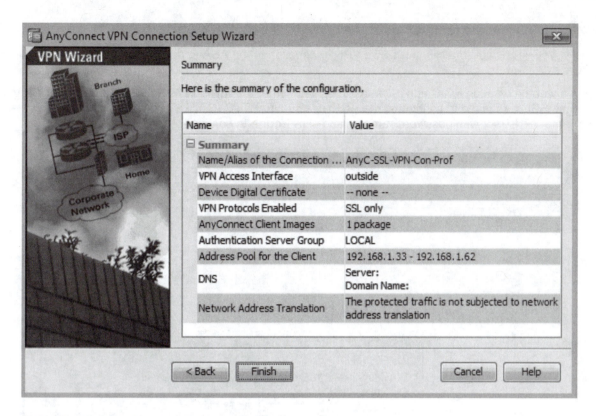

Step 13: Verify the AnyConnect client profile.

After the configuration is delivered to the ASA, the AnyConnect Connection Profiles screen displays.

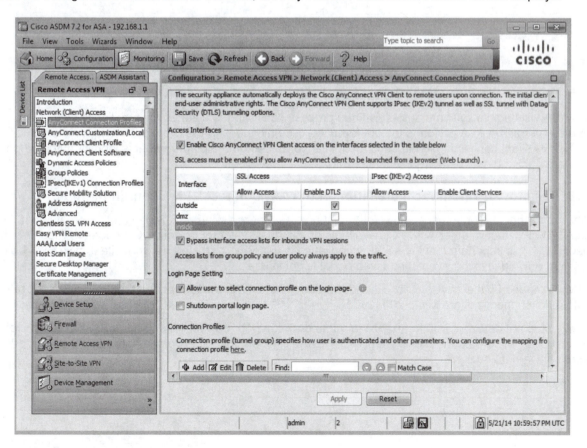

Step 14: Log in from the remote host.

Initially, you will establish a clientless SSL VPN connection to the ASA to download the AnyConnect client software.

Open a web browser on PC-C and in the address field, enter the **https://209.165.200.226** for the SSL VPN. Because SSL is required to connect to the ASA, use secure HTTP (HTTPS). Enter the previously created username **VPN-User** with password **remote**, and click **Logon** to continue.

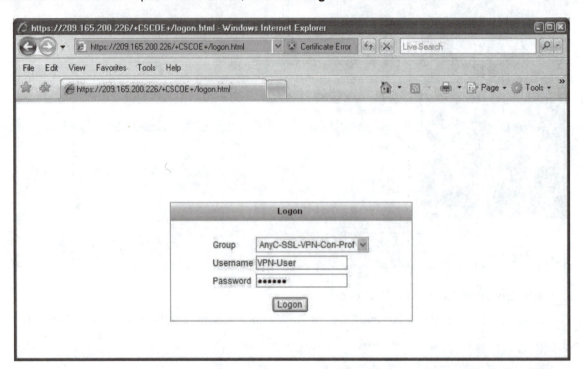

Note: The ASA may request confirmation that this is a trusted site. If requested, then click **Yes** to proceed.

Step 15: Perform platform detection (if required).

The ASA will begin a software auto-download process consisting of a series of compliance checks for the target system. The ASA performs the platform detection by querying the client system in an attempt to identify the type of client connecting to the security appliance. Based on the platform that is identified, the proper software package may be auto-downloaded.

Step 16: Perform an automatic installation of the AnyConnect VPN Client (if required).

If the AnyConnect client must be downloaded, then a security warning will display on the remote host. Then the ASA will detect whether ActiveX is available on the host system. For ActiveX to operate properly with the Cisco ASA, it is important that the security appliance is added as a trusted network site. ActiveX will be used for client download in the event that a web portal is not in use.

Note: To speed up the AnyConnect client download process, it is recommended that the DCE clock rates on both serial connections are set to **2000000**.

If ActiveX is not detected, you may be required to download AnyConnect client manually. If you receive the Manual Installation window, skip to Step 17 for instructions on how to download and install the AnyConnect client software manually.

a. To continue, click **Install**. If requested, click **Yes**. The VPN Client Installer begins and another security alert window may appear. If required, click **Yes** to continue and accept the security certificate.

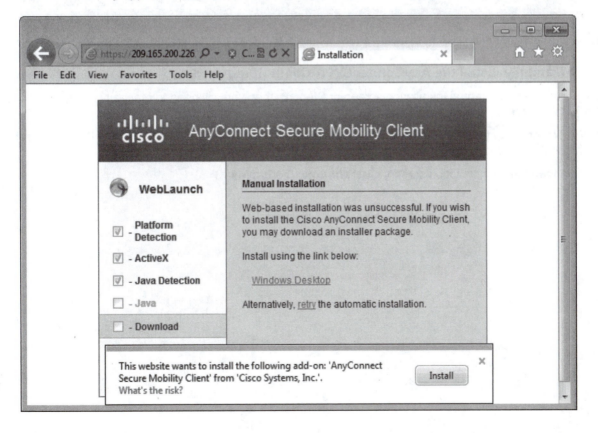

b. When the client completes the auto-download of the Cisco AnyConnect SSL VPN Client, the web session automatically launches the Cisco AnyConnect SSL VPN Client and attempts to log in the user to the network using the same credentials that are supplied when logging into the web portal.

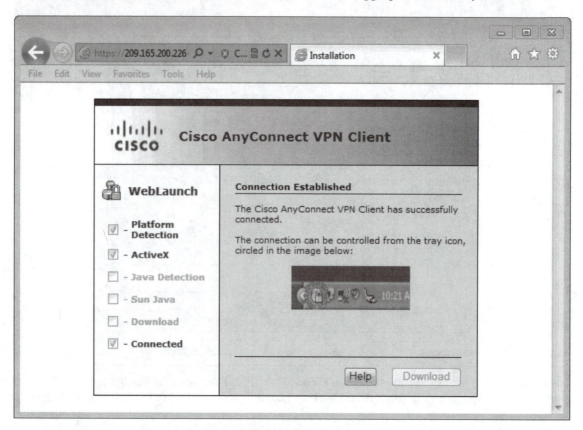

c. If the AnyConnection client software successfully downloaded and installed, you can skip to Step 18.

Step 17: Manually install the AnyConnect VPN Client (if required).

If you received the Manual Installation screen at Step 16, then you will need to manually install the AnyConnect client.

Note: To speed up the AnyConnect client download process, it is recommended that the DCE clock rates on both serial connections are set to **2000000**.

a. On the Manual Installation screen, click **Windows 7/Vista/64/XP**.

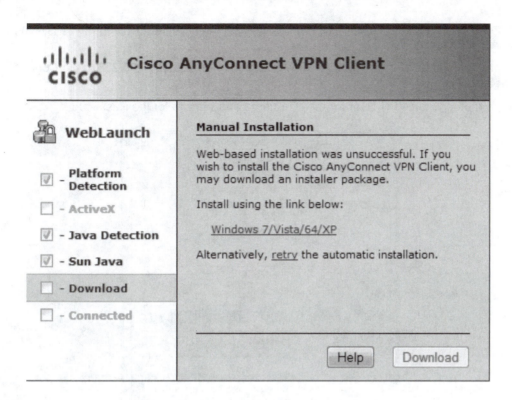

b. Click **Run** to install the AnyConnect VPN client.

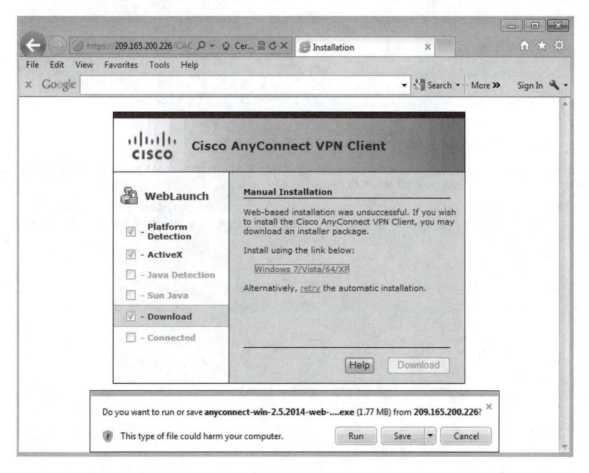

c. Respond to the installation prompts and security warning messages to finish the installation process.

d. When the AnyConnect VPN client has been installed, manually start the program by clicking **Start >
    Cisco AnyConnect VPN Client**.

e. When prompted to enter the secure gateway address, enter **209.165.200.226** in the Connect to: field, and
    click **Select**.

f. When prompted, enter **VPN-User** for the Username and **remote** for the Password.

Step 18: Confirm VPN connectivity.

When the full tunnel SSL VPN connection is established, an icon will appear in the system tray that signifies
that the client has successfully connected to the SSL VPN network.

a. Display connection statistics and information by double-clicking the **AnyConnect** icon in the system tray.
    This client interface may also be used to log out the user. **Note:** The inside IP address that is assigned to
    the client from the VPN pool (192.168.1.33-.62).

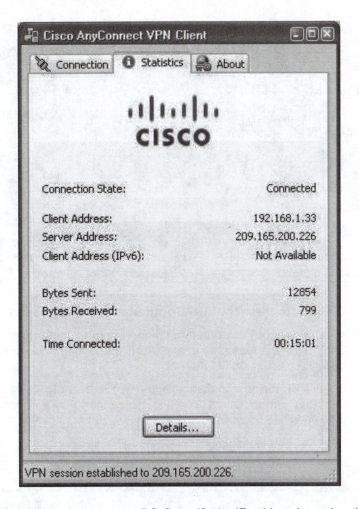

b.   From a command prompt on remote host PC-C, verify the IP addressing using the **ipconfig** command. There should be two IP addresses listed. One is for the PC-C remote host local IP address (172.16.3.3) and the other is the IP address assigned for the SSL VPN tunnel (192.168.1.33).

```
Command Prompt                                                   _ □ X
Windows IP Configuration

Ethernet adapter Local Area Connection:

        Connection-specific DNS Suffix  . :
        IP Address. . . . . . . . . . . . : 172.16.3.3
        Subnet Mask . . . . . . . . . . . : 255.255.255.0
        Default Gateway . . . . . . . . . :

Ethernet adapter Cisco AnyConnect VPN Client Connection:

        Connection-specific DNS Suffix  . : ccnasecurity.com
        IP Address. . . . . . . . . . . . : 192.168.1.33
        Subnet Mask . . . . . . . . . . . : 255.255.255.224
        Default Gateway . . . . . . . . . : 192.168.1.34

C:\>
```

c.   From remote host PC-C, ping inside host PC-B (**192.168.1.3**) to verify connectivity.

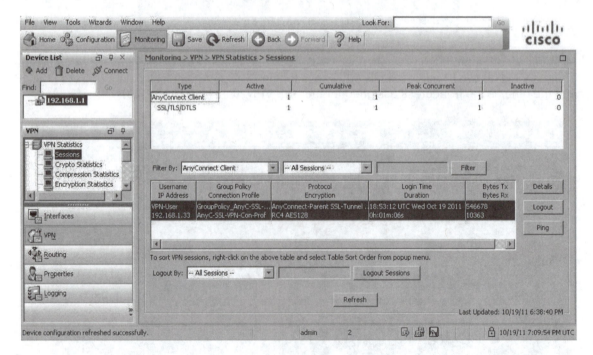

Step 19: Use the ASDM Monitor to view the AnyConnect remote user session.

Note: Future SSL VPN sessions can be launched through the web portal or through the installed Cisco AnyConnect SSL VPN client. While the remote user at PC-C is still logged in using the AnyConnect client, you can view the session statistics using ASDM monitor.

On the ASDM menu bar, click **Monitoring** and then select **VPN** > **VPN Statistics** > **Sessions**. Click the **Filter By** pull-down list and select **AnyConnect Client**. You should see the **VPN-User** session logged in from PC-C, which has been assigned an inside network IP address of 192.168.1.33 by the ASA.

Note: You may need to click **Refresh** to display the remote user session.

Reflection

1. What are some benefits of clientless vs. client-based VPNs?

_____

_____

_____

_____

_____

_____

2. What are some benefits of client-based vs. clientless VPNs?

_____

_____

_____

_____

_____

_____

3. What are some differences when using SSL as compared to IPsec for remote access tunnel encryption?

_____

_____

_____

_____

_____

_____

Router Interface Summary Table

Router Interface Summary				
Router Model	**Ethernet Interface #1**	**Ethernet Interface #2**	**Serial Interface #1**	**Serial Interface #2**
1800	Fast Ethernet 0/0 (Fa0/0)	Fast Ethernet 0/1 (Fa0/1)	Serial 0/0/0 (S0/0/0)	Serial 0/0/1 (S0/0/1)
1900	Gigabit Ethernet 0/0 (G0/0)	Gigabit Ethernet 0/1 (G0/1)	Serial 0/0/0 (S0/0/0)	Serial 0/0/1 (S0/0/1)
2801	Fast Ethernet 0/0 (Fa0/0)	Fast Ethernet 0/1 (Fa0/1)	Serial 0/1/0 (S0/1/0)	Serial 0/1/1 (S0/1/1)
2811	Fast Ethernet 0/0 (Fa0/0)	Fast Ethernet 0/1 (Fa0/1)	Serial 0/0/0 (S0/0/0)	Serial 0/0/1 (S0/0/1)
2900	Gigabit Ethernet 0/0 (G0/0)	Gigabit Ethernet 0/1 (G0/1)	Serial 0/0/0 (S0/0/0)	Serial 0/0/1 (S0/0/1)

Note: To find out how the router is configured, look at the interfaces to identify the type of router and how many interfaces the router has. There is no way to effectively list all the combinations of configurations for each router class. This table includes identifiers for the possible combinations of Ethernet and Serial interfaces in the device. The table does not include any other type of interface, even though a specific router may contain one. An example of this might be an ISDN BRI interface. The string in parenthesis is the legal abbreviation that can be used in Cisco IOS commands to represent the interface.

Lab 9.4.1.4 - Configuring a Site-to-Site IPsec VPN Using CCP and ASDM

Topology

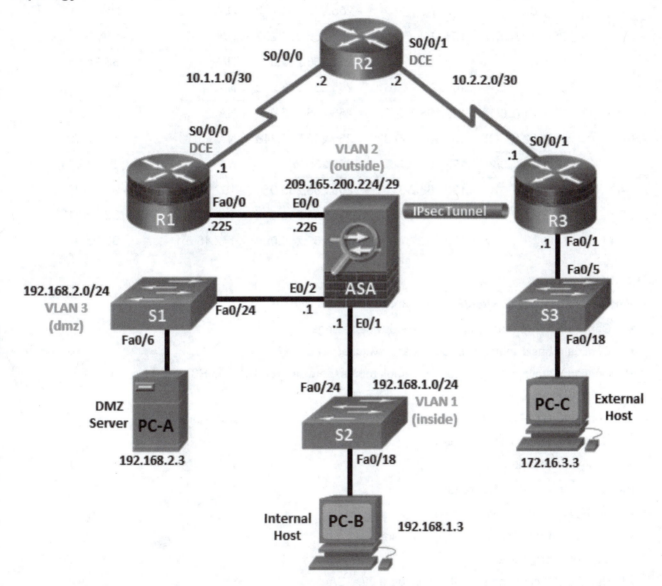

Note: ISR G2 devices use GigabitEthernet interfaces instead of FastEthernet interfaces.

IP Addressing Table

Device	Interface	IP Address	Subnet Mask	Default Gateway	Switch Port
R1	Fa0/0	209.165.200.225	255.255.255.248	N/A	ASA E0/0
	S0/0/0 (DCE)	10.1.1.1	255.255.255.252	N/A	N/A
R2	S0/0/0	10.1.1.2	255.255.255.252	N/A	N/A
	S0/0/1 (DCE)	10.2.2.2	255.255.255.252	N/A	N/A
R3	Fa0/1	172.16.3.1	255.255.255.0	N/A	S3 Fa0/5
	S0/0/1	10.2.2.1	255.255.255.252	N/A	N/A
ASA	VLAN 1 (E0/1)	192.168.1.1	255.255.255.0	NA	S2 Fa0/24
	VLAN 2 (E0/0)	209.165.200.226	255.255.255.248	NA	R1 Fa0/0
	VLAN 3 (E0/2)	192.168.2.1	255.255.255.0	NA	S1 Fa0/24
PC-A	NIC	192.168.2.3	255.255.255.0	192.168.2.1	S1 Fa0/6
PC-B	NIC	192.168.1.3	255.255.255.0	192.168.1.1	S2 Fa0/18
PC-C	NIC	172.16.3.3	255.255.255.0	172.16.3.1	S3 Fa0/18

Objectives

Part 1: Basic Router/Switch/PC Configuration

- Cable the network and clear previous device settings.
- Configure basic settings for routers and switches.
- Configure static routing, including default routes, between R1, R2, and R3.
- Configure the enable and vty passwords on R3.
- Configure HTTP access, a username, and local authentication prior to starting CCP.
- Configure PC host IP settings.
- Verify connectivity.

Part 2: Basic ASA Configuration

- Access the ASA console.
- Clear the previous ASA configuration settings.
- Bypass Setup mode.
- Use the CLI command script to configure the ASA.
- Verify HTTP ASDM access.

Part 3: Configuring the ISR as a Site-to-Site IPsec VPN Endpoint Using CCP

- Run the CCP application on PC-C and discover R3.
- Start the CCP VPN wizard to configure R3.
- Configure basic VPN connection information settings.
- Specify IKE policy parameters.
- Configure a transform set.

- Specify traffic to protect.

- Review the summary of the configuration.

- Review the site-to-site VPN tunnel configuration.

Part 4: Configuring the ASA as a Site-to-Site IPsec VPN Endpoint Using ASDM

- Access ASDM.

- Review the ASDM Home screen.

- Start the VPN wizard.

- Configure peer device identification.

- Specify the traffic to protect.

- Configure authentication.

- Configure miscellaneous settings.

- Review the configuration summary and deliver the commands to the ASA.

- Verify the ASDM VPN connection profile.

- Test the VPN configuration from R3 using CCP.

- Use ASDM monitoring to verify the tunnel.

Background / Scenario

In addition to acting as a remote access VPN concentrator, the ASA can provide Site-to-Site IPsec VPN tunneling. The tunnel can be configured between two ASAs or between an ASA and another IPsec VPN-capable device, such as an ISR, as is the case with this lab.

Your company has two locations connected to an ISP. Router R1 represents a CPE device managed by the ISP. Router R2 represents an intermediate Internet router. Router R3 connects users at the remote branch office to the ISP. The ASA is an edge security device that connects the internal corporate network and DMZ to the ISP while providing NAT services to inside hosts.

Management has asked you to provide a dedicated Site-to-Site IPsec VPN tunnel between the ISR router at the remote branch office and the ASA device at the corporate site. This tunnel will protect traffic between the branch office LAN and the corporate LAN, as it passes through the Internet. The Site-to-Site VPN does not require a VPN client on the remote or corporate site host computers. Traffic from either LAN to other Internet destinations is routed by the ISP and is not protected by the VPN tunnel. The VPN tunnel will pass through R1 and R2; both are not aware of its existence.

In Part 1 of this lab, you will configure the topology and non-ASA devices. In Part 2, you will prepare the ASA for ASDM access. In Part 3, you will use the CCP VPN Wizard to configure the R3 ISR as a Site-to-Site IPsec VPN endpoint. In Part 4, you will configure the ASA as a Site-to-Site IPsec VPN endpoint using the ASDM VPN wizard.

Note: The router commands and output in this lab are from a Cisco 1841 router with Cisco IOS Release 15.1(4)M8 (Advanced IP Services image). Other routers and Cisco IOS versions can be used. See the Router Interface Summary Table at the end of this lab to determine which interface identifiers to use based on the equipment in the lab. Depending on the router model and Cisco IOS version, the commands available, and output produced might vary from what is shown in this lab.

The ASA that is used with this lab is a Cisco model 5505 with an 8-port integrated switch, running OS version 8.4(2) and ASDM version 7.2(1) and comes with a Base license that allows a maximum of three VLANs.

Note: Ensure that the routers and switches have been erased and have no startup configurations.

Required Resources

- 3 Routers (Cisco 1841 with Cisco IOS Release 5.1(4)M8 Advanced IP Services image or comparable)
- 3 Switches (Cisco 2960 or comparable)
- 1 ASA 5505 (OS version 8.4(2) and ASDM version 7.2(1) and Base license or comparable)
- 3 PCs (Windows Vista or Windows 7 with CCP 2.5, latest version of Java, Internet Explorer, and Flash Player)
- Serial and Ethernet cables as shown in the topology
- Console cables to configure Cisco networking devices

CCP Notes:

- If the PC on which CCP is installed is running Windows Vista or Windows 7, it may be necessary to right-click the CCP icon or menu item, and select **Run as administrator**.
- To run CCP, it may be necessary to temporarily disable antivirus programs and O/S firewalls. Make sure that all pop-up blockers are turned off in the browser.

Part 1: Basic Router/Switch/PC Configuration

In Part 1 of this lab, you will set up the network topology and configure basic settings on the routers, such as interface IP addresses and static routing.

Note: Do not configure any ASA settings at this time.

Step 1: Cable the network and clear previous device settings.

Attach the devices shown in the topology diagram and cable as necessary. Ensure that the routers and switches have been erased and have no startup configurations.

Step 2: Configure basic settings for routers and switches.

a. Configure hostnames, as shown in the topology for each router.

b. Configure router interface IP addresses, as shown in the IP Addressing table.

c. Configure a clock rate for routers with a DCE serial cable attached to their serial interface. Router R1 is shown here as an example:

```
R1(config)# interface S0/0/0
R1(config-if)# clock rate 64000
```

d. Configure the hostname for the switches. Other than the hostname, the switches can be left in their default configuration state. Configuring the VLAN management IP address for the switches is optional.

Step 3: Configure static routing on the routers.

a. Configure a static default route from R1 to R2 and from R3 to R2.

```
R1(config)# ip route 0.0.0.0 0.0.0.0 Serial0/0/0

R3(config)# ip route 0.0.0.0 0.0.0.0 Serial0/0/1
```

b. Configure a static route from R2 to the R1 Fa0/0 subnet (connected to ASA interface E0/0) and a static route from R2 to the R3 LAN.

```
R2(config)# ip route 209.165.200.224 255.255.255.248 Serial0/0/0
R2(config)# ip route 172.16.3.0 255.255.255.0 Serial0/0/1
```

Step 4: Configure the enable and vty passwords on R3.

On R3, set the enable password to class and the console and vty passwords to **cisco**. Configure these settings on R1 and R2. R3 is shown here as an example:

```
R3(config)# enable secret class

R3(config)# line vty 0 4
R3(config-line)# password cisco
R3(config-line)# login

R3(config)# line con 0
R3(config-line)# password cisco
R3(config-line)# login
```

Step 5: Configure HTTP access, a username, and local authentication prior to starting CCP.

a. From the CLI, configure a username and password for use with CCP on R3.

```
R3(config)# ip http server
R3(config)# ip http secure-server
R3(config)# username admin privilege 15 secret cisco123
```

b. Use the local database to authenticate web sessions with CCP.

```
R3(config)# ip http authentication local
```

Step 6: Configure PC host IP settings.

Configure a static IP address, subnet mask, and default gateway for PC-A, PC-B, and PC-C, as shown in the IP Addressing table.

Step 7: Verify connectivity.

From PC-C, ping the R1 Fa0/0 IP address (**209.165.200.225**). If these pings are not successful, troubleshoot the basic device configurations before continuing.

Note: If you can ping from PC-C to R1 Fa0/0, you have demonstrated that static routing is configured and functioning correctly.

Step 8: Save the basic running configuration for each router and switch.

Part 2: Basic ASA Configuration

Step 1: Access the ASA console.

a. Accessing the ASA via the console port is the same as with a Cisco router or switch. Connect to the ASA Console port with a rollover cable.

b. Use a terminal emulation program, such as TeraTerm or PuTTy, to access the CLI, and use the serial port settings of 9600 baud, 8 data bits, no parity, one stop bit, and no flow control.

c. If prompted to enter Interactive Firewall configuration (Setup mode), answer **no**.

d. Enter privileged EXEC mode with the **enable** command and password (if set). By default, the password is blank; press **Enter**. If the password has been changed to that specified in this lab, the password will be **class**. In addition, the hostname and prompt will be **CCNAS-ASA>**, as shown here. The default ASA hostname and prompt is `ciscoasa>`.

```
CCNAS-ASA> enable
Password: class (or press Enter if none set)
```

Step 2: Clear the previous ASA configuration settings.

a. Use the **write erase** command to remove the **startup-config** file from flash memory.

```
CCNAS-ASA# write erase
Erase configuration in flash memory? [confirm]
[OK]
CCNAS-ASA#
```

Note: The **erase startup-config** IOS command is not supported on the ASA.

b. Use the **reload** command to restart the ASA. This will cause the ASA to come up in CLI Setup mode. If you see the System config has been modified. Save? [Y]es/[N]o: message, respond with **N**.

```
CCNAS-ASA# reload
Proceed with reload? [confirm] <Enter>
CCNAS-ASA#
***
*** --- START GRACEFUL SHUTDOWN ---
Shutting down isakmp
Shutting down File system
***
*** --- SHUTDOWN NOW ---
Process shutdown finished
Rebooting.....
CISCO SYSTEMS
Embedded BIOS Version 1.0(12)13 08/28/08 15:50:37.45
<output omitted>
```

Step 3: Bypass Setup mode.

When the ASA completes the reload process, it should detect that the startup configuration file is missing and go into Setup mode. If it does not come up in this mode, repeat Step 2.

a. When prompted to preconfigure the firewall through interactive prompts (Setup mode), respond with **no**.

```
Pre-configure Firewall now through interactive prompts [yes]? no
```

b. Enter privileged EXEC mode with the **enable** command. The password should be kept blank (no password).

Step 4: Use the CLI script to configure the ASA.

In this step, you will use a CLI script to configure basic settings, the firewall, and DMZ.

a. Ensure that there is no previous configuration in the ASA, other than the defaults that the ASA automatically inserts, using the **show run** command.

b. Enter global configuration mode. When prompted to enable anonymous call-home reporting, respond **no**.

```
ciscoasa> enable
Password: <Enter>

ciscoasa# conf t
ciscoasa(config)#
```

c. The first time you enter configuration mode after running reload, you will be asked to enable anonymous reporting. Respond with **no**.

d. Copy and paste the **Pre-VPN Configuration Script** commands listed below at the global configuration mode prompt to bring it to the point where you can start configuring the SSL VPNs.

e. Observe the messages as the commands are applied to ensure that there are no warnings or errors. If prompted to replace the RSA key pair, respond **yes**.

f. Issue the **write mem** (or **copy run start**) command to save the running configuration to the startup configuration and the RSA keys to non-volatile memory.

Lab 10D Pre-VPN ASA Configuration Script:

```
hostname CCNAS-ASA
!
domain-name ccnasecurity.com
!
enable password class
passwd cisco
!
interface Ethernet0/0
 switchport access vlan 2
 no shut
!
interface Ethernet0/1
 switchport access vlan 1
 no shut
!
interface Ethernet0/2
 switchport access vlan 3
 no shut
!
interface Vlan1
 nameif inside
 security-level 100
 ip address 192.168.1.1 255.255.255.0
!
interface Vlan2
 nameif outside
 security-level 0
 ip address 209.165.200.226 255.255.255.248
!
interface Vlan3
 no forward interface Vlan1
 nameif dmz
 security-level 70
 ip address 192.168.2.1 255.255.255.0
!
object network inside-net
```

```
  subnet 192.168.1.0 255.255.255.0
 !
object network dmz-server
 host 192.168.2.3
 !
access-list OUTSIDE-DMZ extended permit ip any host 192.168.2.3
 !
object network inside-net
 nat (inside,outside) dynamic interface
 !
object network dmz-server
 nat (dmz,outside) static 209.165.200.227
 !
access-group OUTSIDE-DMZ in interface outside
 !
route outside 0.0.0.0 0.0.0.0 209.165.200.225 1
 !
username admin password cisco123
 !
aaa authentication telnet console LOCAL
aaa authentication ssh console LOCAL
aaa authentication http console LOCAL
 !
http server enable
http 192.168.1.0 255.255.255.0 inside
ssh 192.168.1.0 255.255.255.0 inside
telnet 192.168.1.0 255.255.255.0 inside
telnet timeout 10
ssh timeout 10
 !
class-map inspection_default
 match default-inspection-traffic
policy-map type inspect dns preset_dns_map
 parameters
  message-length maximum client auto
  message-length maximum 512
policy-map global_policy
 class inspection_default
   inspect icmp
 !
prompt hostname context
no call-home reporting anonymous
 !
crypto key generate rsa modulus 1024
```

Step 5: Verify HTTPS ASDM access.

Note: This step is intended to verify HTTPS connectivity from PC-B to the ASA. ASDM settings will be configured in Part 4 of this lab.

a. Open a browser on PC-B and test the HTTPS access to the ASA by entering **https://192.168.1.1**.

b. After entering https://192.168.1.1, you should see a security warning about the website's security certificate. Click **Continue to this website**. The ASDM welcome page will display. From this screen, you can install ASDM on the PC, run ASDM as browser-based Java applet directly from the ASA, or run the Startup wizard. Click **Run ASDM**.

Note: The process may vary depending on the browser used. This example is for Internet Explorer.

Part 3: Configuring the ISR as a Site-to-Site IPsec VPN Endpoint Using CCP

In Part 3 of this lab, you will configure R3 as an IPsec VPN endpoint for the tunnel between R3 and the ASA. Routers R1 and R2 are unaware of the tunnel.

Step 1: Run the CCP application on PC-C and discover R3.

a. Run the CCP application on PC-C. In the **Select/Manage Community** window, enter the R3 Fa0/0 IP address **172.16.3.1**, username **admin**, and password **cisco123**. Click the **Connect Securely** check box to use secure-server for your connection. Click **OK**.

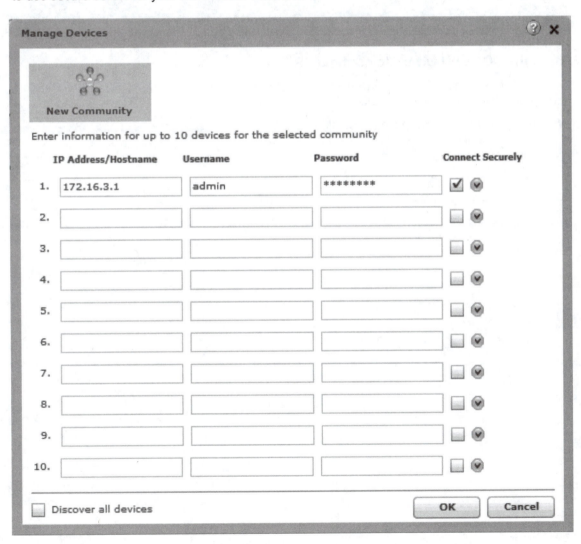

b.   In the **Community Information** panel, click **Discover** to discover and connect to R3. If the PC-C CCP application can make an HTTP connection to R3, the **Discovery Status** changes to **Discovered**. If the discovery process fails, click **Discover Details** to determine the problem so that you can resolve the issue.

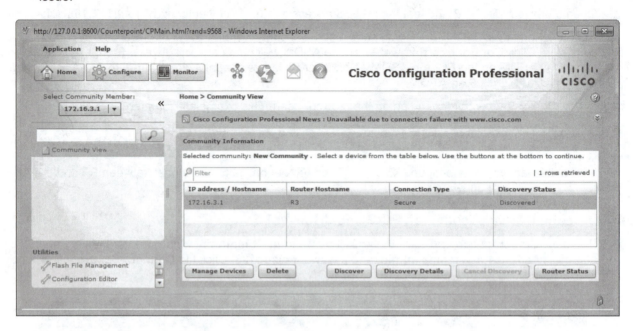

Step 2: Start the CCP VPN wizard to configure R3.

a.   On the CCP menu bar, click **Configure** , and select **Security** > **VPN** > **Site-to-Site VPN**. Read the on-screen text describing the Site-to-Site VPN.

What must you know to complete the configuration?

_____

_____

_____

_____

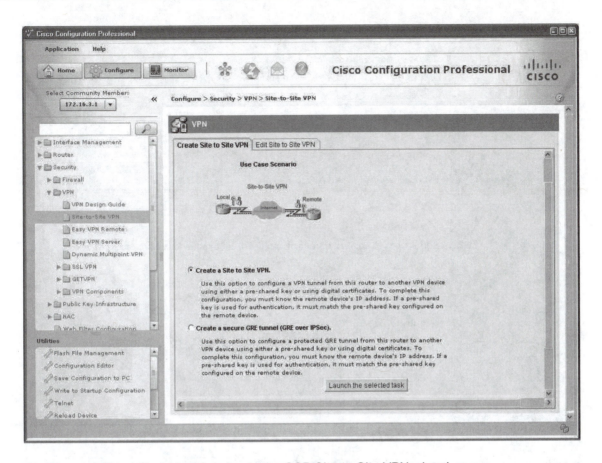

b. Click **Launch the selected task** to begin the CCP Site-to-Site VPN wizard.

c. From the initial Site-to-Site VPN wizard screen, select the **Step by Step wizard**, and then click **Next**.

Step 3: Configure basic VPN connection information settings.

a. On the VPN Connection Information screen, select the interface for the connection, which should be **Serial0/0/1**.

b. In the Peer Identity section, select **Peer with static IP address** and enter the IP address of the remote peer, ASA VLAN 2 interface E0/0 (**209.165.200.226**).

c. In the Authentication section, click **Pre-shared Keys**, and enter the pre-shared VPN key **cisco12345**. Re-enter the key for confirmation. This key authenticates the initial exchange to establish the Security Association between devices. When finished, your screen should look similar to the following. When you have entered these settings correctly, click **Next**.

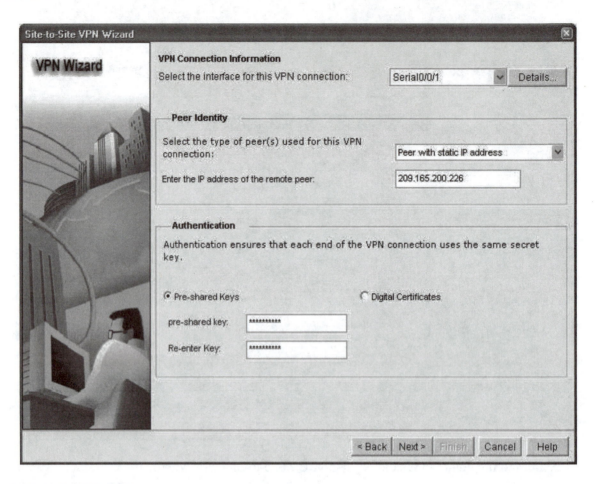

Step 4: Specify IKE policy parameters.

IKE policies are used while setting up the control channel between the two VPN endpoints for key exchange. This is also referred to as the IKE secure association (SA). In contrast, the IPsec policy is used during IKE Phase II to negotiate an IPsec security association to pass target data traffic.

a. On the IKE Proposals screen, a default policy proposal is displayed with a priority of 1. You can use this one or create a new one, if necessary. In this lab, you will configure the R3 end of the VPN tunnel using the default IKE proposal. Click **Next** to continue.

Settings for the CCP default IKE Phase 1 policy for this ISR are:

o   **Priority** = 1

o   **Encryption** = 3DES

o   **Hash** = SHA_1

o   **D-H Group** = group2

o   **Authentication** = PRE_SHARE

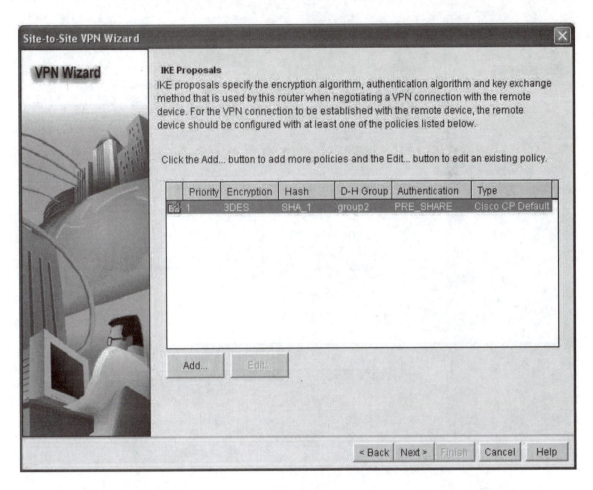

Step 5: Configure a transform set.

The transform set is the IPsec policy used to encrypt, hash, and authenticate packets that pass through the tunnel. The transform set is the IKE Phase 2 policy.

On the Transform Set screen, a default transform set is displayed. You can use this one or create a new one, if necessary. In this lab, you will configure the R3 end of the VPN tunnel using the default transform set. Click **Next** to continue.

Settings for the CCP default IKE Phase 2 policy transform set for this ISR are:

- o **Name** = ESP-3DES-SHA
- o **ESP Encryption** = ESP_3DES
- o **ESP Integrity** = ESP_SHA_HMAC
- o **Mode** = Tunnel

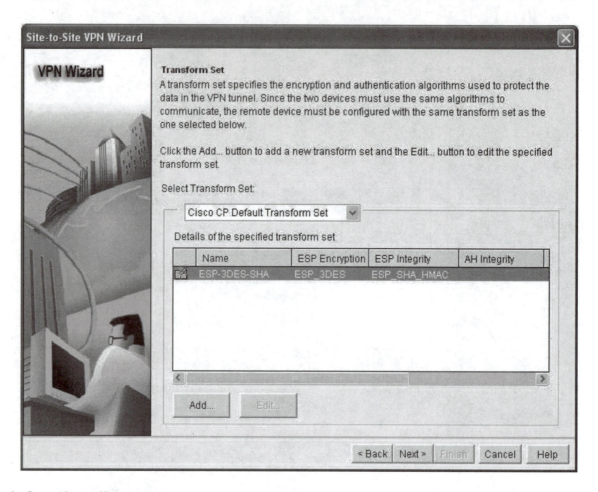

Step 6: Specify traffic to protect.

You must define "interesting" traffic to be protected through the VPN tunnel. Interesting traffic is defined through an access list that is applied to the router. By entering the source and destination subnets that you would like to protect through the VPN tunnel, CCP generates the appropriate simple access list for you.

On the Traffic to protect screen, enter the information shown below. These are the opposite of the settings configured on the ASA later in the lab. When finished, click **Next**.

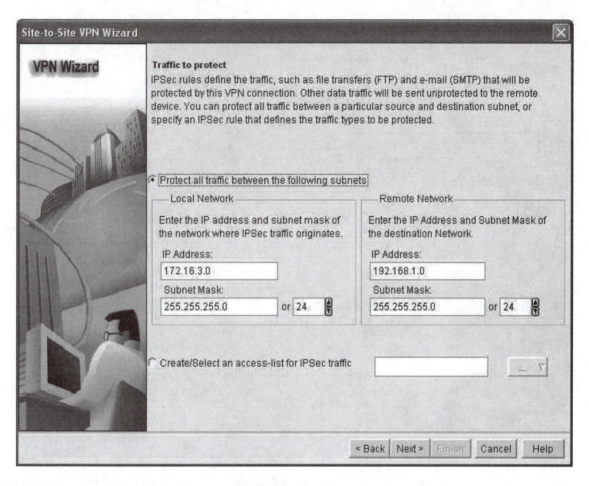

Step 7: Review the summary of the configuration.

a. Review the Summary of the Configuration screen. It should look similar to the one below. You can scroll down to see the IPsec rule (ACL) that CCP creates for R3, which permits all traffic from network 172.16.3.0/24 to network 192.168.1.0/24.

b. Do NOT click the **Test VPN connectivity after configuring** check box. This will be done after you configure the ASA side of the VPN tunnel. Click **Finish** to go to the Deliver Configuration to Device screen.

    Note: Pay particular attention to the IKE Policies and Transform Set. You will configure the ASA to match these settings in the next part of this lab.

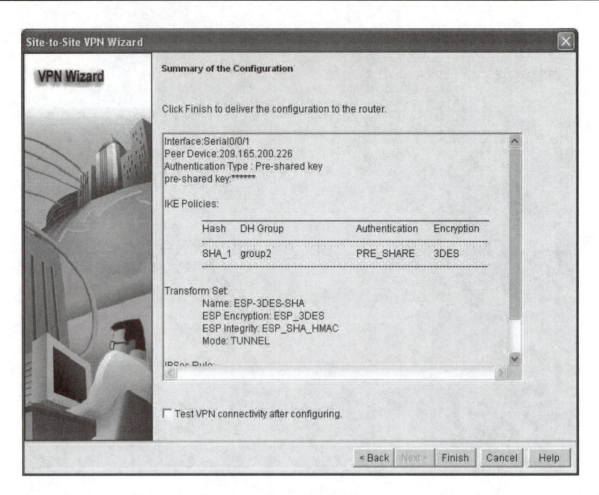

c. On the Deliver Configuration to Device screen, select **Save running config to device's startup config** and click **Deliver**. After the commands have been delivered, click **OK**.

d. You can also save these configuration commands for later editing or documentation purposes by clicking **Save to file**.

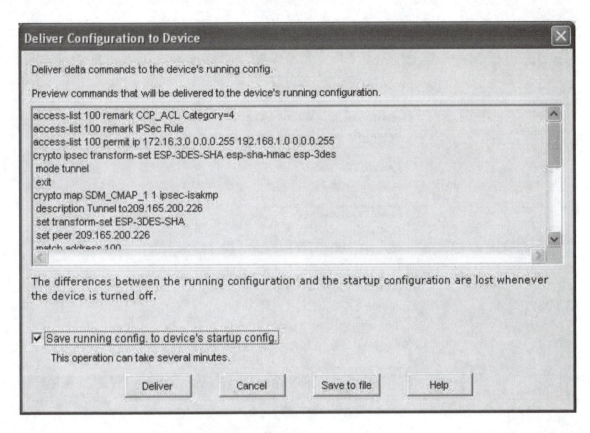

```
Deliver Configuration to Device                                    X

Deliver delta commands to the device's running config.

Preview commands that will be delivered to the device's running configuration.

access-list 100 remark CCP_ACL Category=4
access-list 100 remark IPSec Rule
access-list 100 permit ip 172.16.3.0 0.0.0.255 192.168.1.0 0.0.0.255
crypto ipsec transform-set ESP-3DES-SHA esp-sha-hmac esp-3des
 mode tunnel
 exit
crypto map SDM_CMAP_1 1 ipsec-isakmp
 description Tunnel to209.165.200.226
 set transform-set ESP-3DES-SHA
 set peer 209.165.200.226
 match address 100

The differences between the running configuration and the startup configuration are lost whenever
the device is turned off.

☑ Save running config. to device's startup config.
    This operation can take several minutes.

        Deliver        Cancel        Save to file        Help
```

Note: If you receive an error message that CCP was unable to copy the running-config to the startup configuration, you can verify that the commands were delivered by using the **show startup-config** CLI command on R3. If the startup configuration has not been updated, use the **copy run start** command on R3.

e. You can view the running configuration and startup configuration from within CCP. To view the running config, click **Home**, and under the Utilities section, click **View > Running Configuration**.

f. To view the startup configuration, click **Home** > **Utilities** > **View** > **IOS Show Commands**. Click the pull-down list next to the command window, select the **show startup-config** command, and then click **Show**.

Note: There are several predefined **show** commands listed in the pull-down list, but you can also enter any valid IOS command, such as **show ip interface brief**, and then click **Show**.

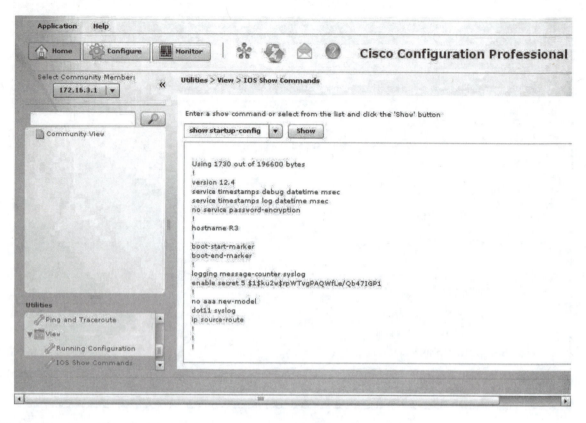

Step 8: Review the Site-to-Site VPN tunnel configuration.

a.   The Edit Site-to-Site VPN screen displays after the commands are delivered. Use the scroll buttons to examine the configuration. The tunnel status is down at this point, because the ASA end of the tunnel is not yet configured.

Note: Leave CCP running and connected to R3 on PC-C. Click **Test Tunnel** to verify VPN functionality after configuring the ASA end of the tunnel.

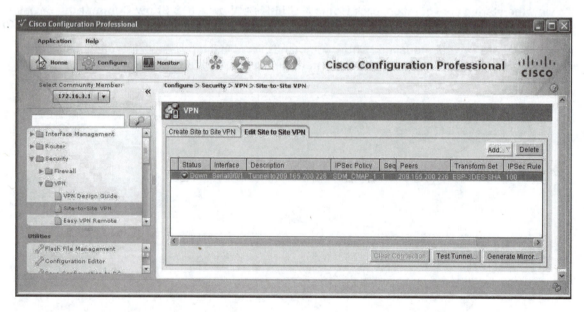

Part 4: Configuring the ASA as a Site-to-Site IPsec VPN Endpoint Using ASDM

In Part 4 of this lab, you will configure the ASA as an IPsec VPN tunnel endpoint. The tunnel between the ASA and R3 passes through R1 and R2.

Step 1: Access ASDM.

a. Open a browser on PC-B and test the HTTPS access to the ASA by entering **https://192.168.1.1**.

b. After entering https://192.168.1.1, you should see a security warning about the website security certificate. Click **Continue to this website**. Click **Yes** for any other security warnings. At the ASDM welcome page, click **Run ASDM**. The ASDM-IDM Launcher displays. Log in as user **admin** with password **cisco123**. ASDM then loads the current configuration into the GUI.

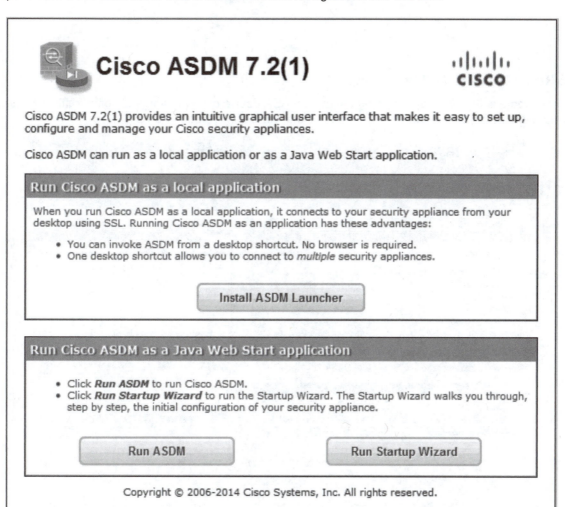

Cisco ASDM 7.2(1)

CISCO

Cisco ASDM 7.2(1) provides an intuitive graphical user interface that makes it easy to set up, configure and manage your Cisco security appliances.

Cisco ASDM can run as a local application or as a Java Web Start application.

Run Cisco ASDM as a local application

When you run Cisco ASDM as a local application, it connects to your security appliance from your desktop using SSL. Running Cisco ASDM as an application has these advantages:

- You can invoke ASDM from a desktop shortcut. No browser is required.
- One desktop shortcut allows you to connect to *multiple* security appliances.

Install ASDM Launcher

Run Cisco ASDM as a Java Web Start application

- Click *Run ASDM* to run Cisco ASDM.
- Click *Run Startup Wizard* to run the Startup Wizard. The Startup Wizard walks you through, step by step, the initial configuration of your security appliance.

Run ASDM   **Run Startup Wizard**

Copyright © 2006-2014 Cisco Systems, Inc. All rights reserved.

Step 2: Review the ASDM Home screen.

a. The Home screen displays showing the current ASA device configuration and some traffic flow statistics. Note the inside, outside, and DMZ interfaces that were configured in Part 2.

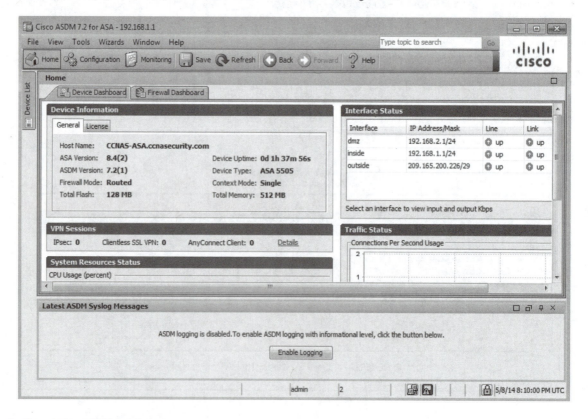

Step 3: Start the VPN wizard.

a. On the ASDM main menu, click **Wizards** > **VPN Wizards** > **Site-to-Site VPN Wizard**. The Site-to-Site VPN Connection Setup Wizard Introduction screen displays.

b. Review the on-screen text and topology diagram, and then click **Next** to continue.

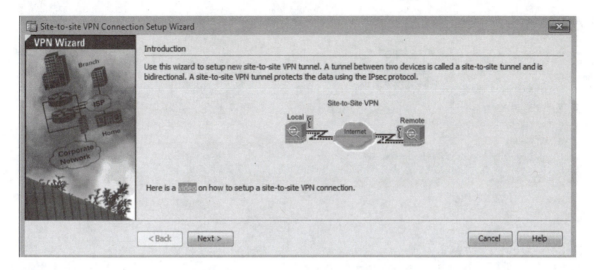

Step 4: Configure peer device identification.

On the Peer Device Identification screen, enter the IP address of the R3 Serial0/0/1 interface (**10.2.2.1**) as the Peer IP Address. Leave the default VPN Access Interface set to **outside**. The VPN tunnel will be between R3 S0/0/1 and the ASA outside interface (VLAN 2 E0/0). Click **Next** to continue.

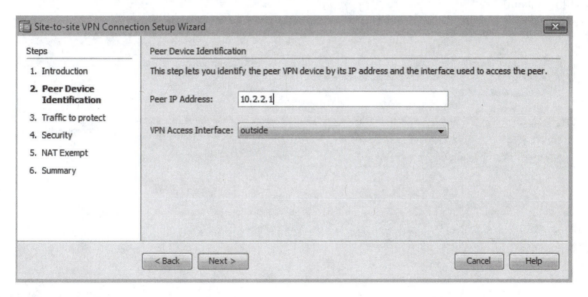

Step 5: Specify the traffic to protect.

On the Traffic to protect screen, click **IPv4** and enter the inside network **192.168.1.0/24** as the **Local Network** and the R3 LAN **172.16.3.0/24** as the Remote Network. Click **Next** to continue. A message may display that the certificate information is being retrieved.

Note: If the ASA does not respond, you may need to close the window and continue to the next step. If prompted to authenticate, log in again as **admin** with the password **cisco123**.

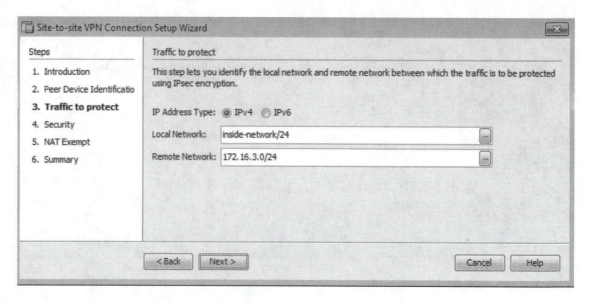

Step 6: Configure authentication.

On the Security screen, enter a pre-shared key of **cisco12345**. You will not be using a device certificate. Click **Next** to continue.

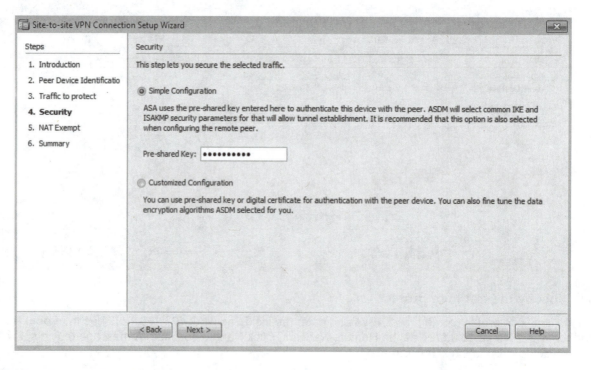

Step 7: Configure miscellaneous settings.

On the NAT Exempt screen, click the **Exempt ASA side host/network from address translation** check box for the **inside** interface. Click **Next** to continue.

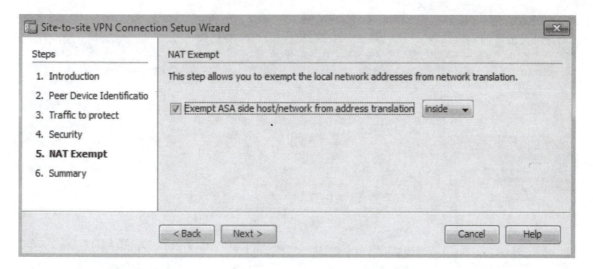

Step 8: Review the configuration summary and deliver the commands to the ASA.

a. The Summary page is displayed next. Verify that the information configured in the Site-to-Site VPN
    wizard is correct. You can click **Back** to make changes, or click **Cancel**, and restart the VPN wizard
    (recommended).

b. Click **Finish** to complete the process and deliver the commands to the ASA. If prompted to authenticate,
    log in again as **admin** with password **cisco123**.

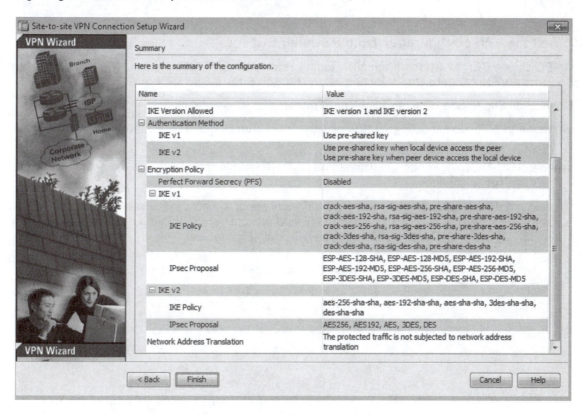

Step 9: Verify the ASDM VPN connection profile.

The ASDM **Configurations** > **Site-to-Site VPN** > **Connection Profiles** screen displays the settings you just
configured. From this window, the VPN configuration can be verified and edited.

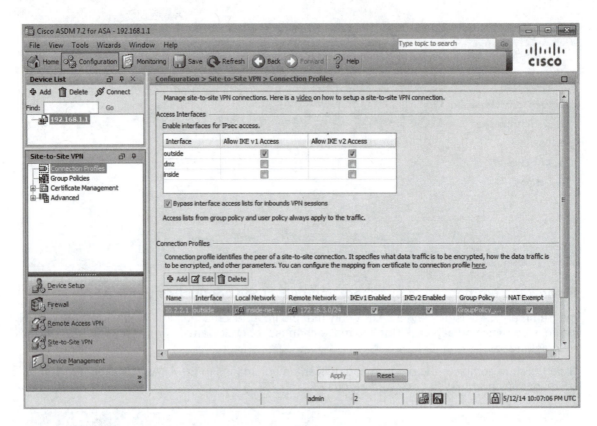

Step 10: Test the VPN configuration from R3 using CCP.

a. On PC-C, use CCP to test the IPsec VPN tunnel between the R3 ISR and the ASA. Click **Configure** > **Security** > **VPN** > **Site-to-Site VPN** and select the **Edit Site-to-Site VPN** tab.

b. On the Edit Site-to-Site VPN tab, click **Test Tunnel**.

c. When the VPN Troubleshooting window displays, click **Start** to have CCP start troubleshooting the tunnel.

d. When the CCP warning window indicates that CCP will enable router debugs and generate some tunnel traffic, click **Yes** to continue.

e. On the next VPN Troubleshooting screen, the IP address of the host in the source network is displayed by default (R3 FA0/1 = 172.16.3.1). Enter the IP address of host PC-B in the destination network field (**192.168.1.3**) and click **Continue** to begin the debugging process.

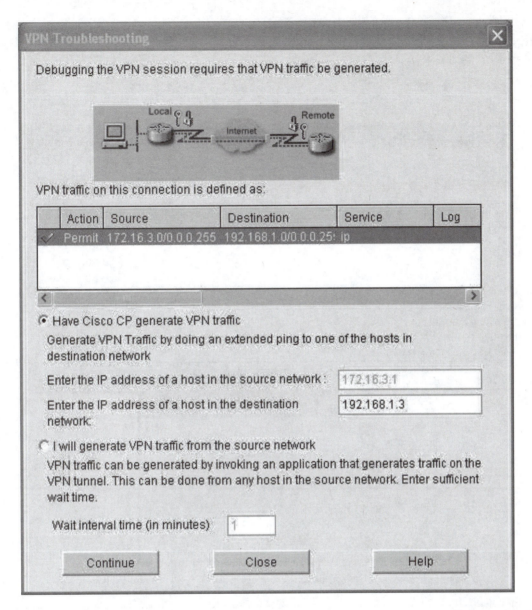

f.   If the debug is successful and the tunnel is up, you should see the screen below. If the testing fails, CCP
     displays failure reasons and recommended actions. Click **OK** to remove the window.

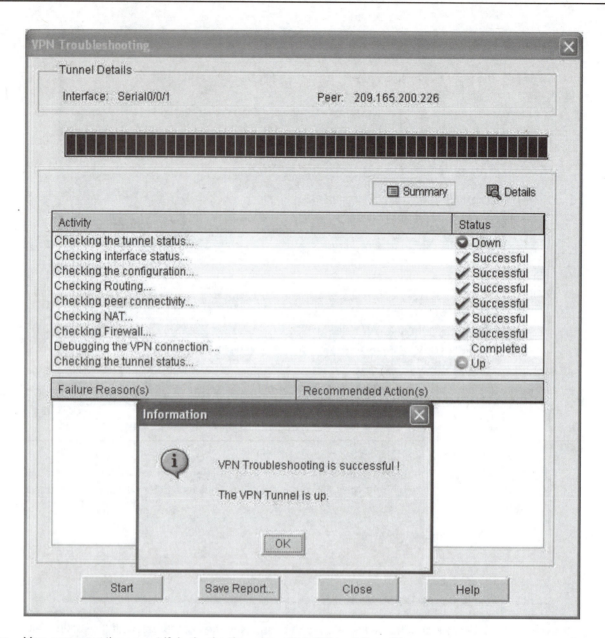

g. You can save the report if desired; otherwise, click **OK** and then **Close**.

h. On R3, click **Configure** > **Security** > **VPN** > **Site-to-Site VPN** and select the **Edit Site-to-Site VPN** tab. The tunnel Status should now be **up**.

    Note: To reset the tunnel and test again, click **Clear Connection** on the **Edit Site-to-Site VPN** window.

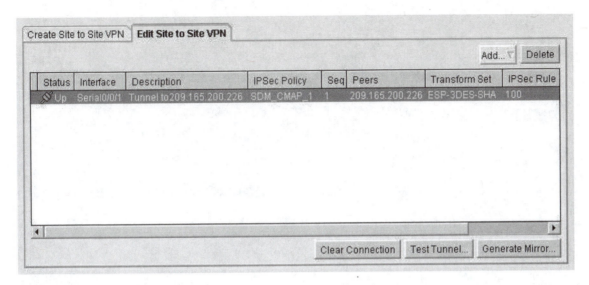

i.   You can further verify tunnel functionality by pinging from branch office PC-C to PC-B on the internal network. The pings should be successful.

Note: Without the tunnel in place and bypassing NAT, it would be impossible for PC-C on the external network to ping PC-B on the private internal network.

Step 11: Use ASDM monitoring to verify the tunnel.

a.   On the ASDM menu bar, click **Monitoring** > **VPN** from the panels at the lower left of the screen. Click **VPN Statistics** > **Sessions**. You should see the Site-to-Site IPsec VPN tunnel listed and active.

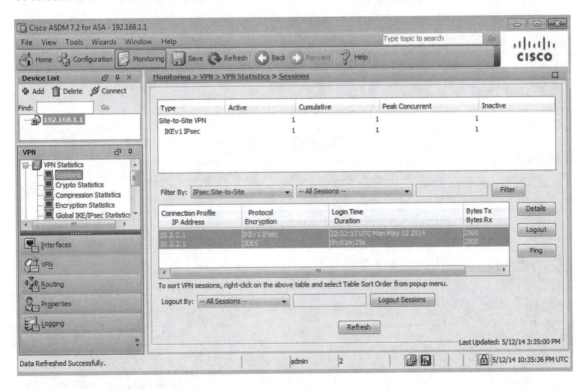

b.   Click **Encryption Statistics**. You should see one or more sessions using the 3DES encryption algorithm.

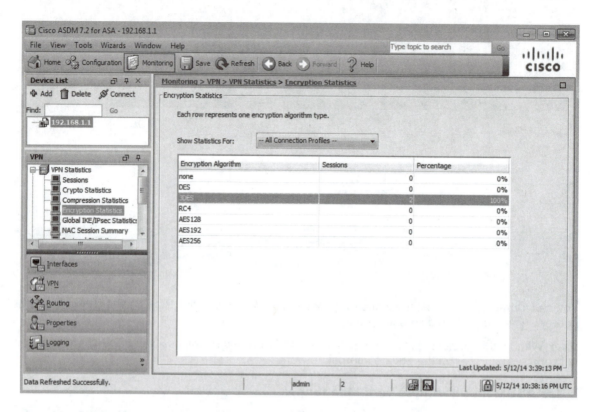

c.   Click **Crypto Statistics**. You should see values for the number of packets encrypted and decrypted, security association (SA) requests, etc.

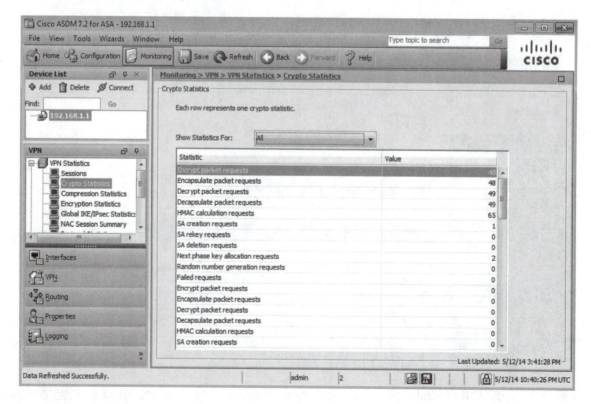

Reflection

1. What are some situations where a site-to-site IPsec VPN would be preferable as compared to a remote access SSL VPN?

_____

_____

_____

_____

_____

_____

_____

2. What are some situations where a remote access VPN would be preferable as compared to site-to-site VPN?

_____

_____

_____

_____

_____

_____

_____

Router Interface Summary Table

Router Interface Summary				
Router Model	**Ethernet Interface #1**	**Ethernet Interface #2**	**Serial Interface #1**	**Serial Interface #2**
1800	Fast Ethernet 0/0 (Fa0/0)	Fast Ethernet 0/1 (Fa0/1)	Serial 0/0/0 (S0/0/0)	Serial 0/0/1 (S0/0/1)
1900	Gigabit Ethernet 0/0 (G0/0)	Gigabit Ethernet 0/1 (G0/1)	Serial 0/0/0 (S0/0/0)	Serial 0/0/1 (S0/0/1)
2801	Fast Ethernet 0/0 (Fa0/0)	Fast Ethernet 0/1 (Fa0/1)	Serial 0/1/0 (S0/1/0)	Serial 0/1/1 (S0/1/1)
2811	Fast Ethernet 0/0 (Fa0/0)	Fast Ethernet 0/1 (Fa0/1)	Serial 0/0/0 (S0/0/0)	Serial 0/0/1 (S0/0/1)
2900	Gigabit Ethernet 0/0 (G0/0)	Gigabit Ethernet 0/1 (G0/1)	Serial 0/0/0 (S0/0/0)	Serial 0/0/1 (S0/0/1)

Note: To find out how the router is configured, look at the interfaces to identify the type of router and how many interfaces the router has. There is no way to effectively list all the combinations of configurations for each router class. This table includes identifiers for the possible combinations of Ethernet and Serial interfaces in the device. The table does not include any other type of interface, even though a specific router may contain one. An example of this might be an ISDN BRI interface. The string in parenthesis is the legal abbreviation that can be used in Cisco IOS commands to represent the interface.

Chapter 10: Managing a Secure Network

Lab 10.8.1.1 - CCNA Security Comprehensive Lab

Topology

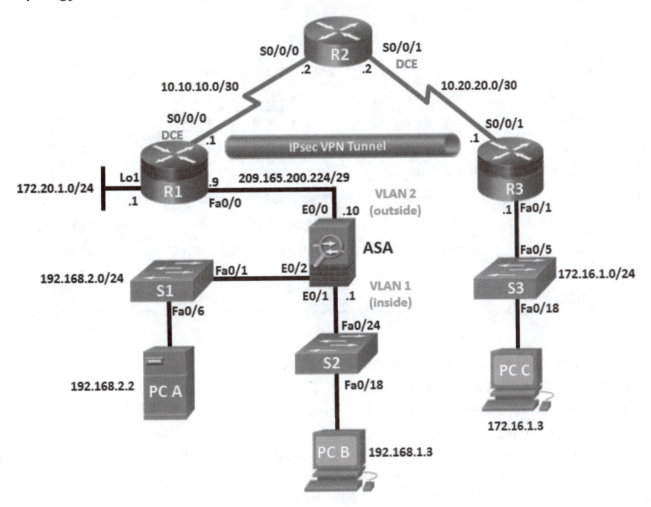

IP Addressing Table

Device	Interface	IP Address	Subnet Mask	Default Gateway	Switch Port
R1	Fa0/0	209.165.200.9	255.255.255.248	N/A	ASA E0/0
	S0/0/0 (DCE)	10.10.10.1	255.255.255.252	N/A	N/A
	Loopback 1	172.20.1.1	255.255.255.0	N/A	N/A
R2	S0/0/0	10.10.10.2	255.255.255.252	N/A	N/A
	S0/0/1 (DCE)	10.20.20.2	255.255.255.252	N/A	N/A
R3	Fa0/1	172.16.1.1	255.255.255.0	N/A	S3 Fa0/5
	S0/0/1	10.20.20.1	255.255.255.252	N/A	N/A
S1	VLAN 1	192.168.2.11	255.255.255.0	192.168.2.1	N/A
S2	VLAN 1	192.168.1.11	255.255.255.0	192.168.1.1	N/A
S3	VLAN 1	172.16.1.11	255.255.255.0	172.30.3.1	N/A
ASA	VLAN 1 (E0/1)	192.168.1.1	255.255.255.0	N/A	S2 Fa0/24
	VLAN 2 (E0/0)	209.165.200.10	255.255.255.248	N/A	R1 Fa0/0
	VLAN 2 (E0/2)	192.168.2.1	255.255.255.0	N/A	S1 Fa0/24
PC-A	NIC	192.168.2.3	255.255.255.0	192.168.2.1	S1 Fa0/6
PC-B	NIC	192.168.1.3	255.255.255.0	192.168.1.1	S2 Fa0/18
PC-C	NIC	172.16.1.3	255.255.255.0	172.16.1.1	S3 Fa0/18

Objectives

Part 1: Create a Basic Technical Security Policy

Part 2: Configure Basic Device Settings

Part 3: Configure Secure Router Administrative Access

- Configure encrypted passwords and a login banner.
- Configure the EXEC timeout value on console and vty lines.
- Configure login failure rates and vty login enhancements.
- Configure Secure Shell (SSH) access and disable Telnet.
- Configure local authentication, authorization, and accounting (AAA) user authentication.
- Secure the router against login attacks, and secure the IOS image, and configuration file.
- Configure a router NTP server and router NTP clients.
- Configure router syslog reporting and a syslog server on a local host.

Part 4: Configure a Site-to-Site VPN Between ISRs

- Configure an IPsec site-to-site VPN between R1 and R3 using the Cisco Configuration Professional (CCP).

Part 5: Configure a Zone-Based Policy Firewall and Intrusion Prevention System

- Configure a Zone-Based Policy Firewall (ZBF) on an ISR using CCP.
- Configure an intrusion prevention system (IPS) on an ISR using CCP.

Part 6: Secure Network Switches

- Configure passwords and a login banner.
- Configure management VLAN access.
- Secure access ports.
- Protect against Spanning Tree Protocol (STP) attacks.
- Configure port security and disable unused ports.

Part 7: Configure ASA Basic Settings and Firewall

- Configure basic settings, passwords, date, and time.
- Configure the inside and outside VLAN interfaces.
- Configure port address translation (PAT) for the inside network.
- Configure a Dynamic Host Configuration Protocol (DHCP) server for the inside network.
- Configure administrative access via Telnet and SSH.
- Configure a static default route for the Adaptive Security Appliance (ASA).
- Configure Local AAA user authentication.
- Configure a DMZ with a static NAT and ACL.
- Verify address translation and firewall functionality.

Part 8: Configure a DMZ, Static NAT, and ACLs

Part 9: Configure ASA Clientless SSL VPN Remote Access

- Configure a remote access SSL VPN using the Cisco Adaptive Security Device Manager (ASDM).
- Verify SSL VPN access to the portal.

Background / Scenario

This comprehensive lab is divided into nine parts. The parts should be completed sequentially. In Part 1, you will create a basic technical security policy. In Part 2, you configure the basic device settings. In Part 3, you will secure a network router using the command-line interface (CLI) to configure various IOS features, including AAA and SSH. In Part 4, you will configure a site-to-site VPN between R1 and R3 through the ISP router (R2). In Part 5, you will configure a ZBF and IPS on an ISR. In Part 6, you will configure a network switch using the CLI. In Parts 7 to 9, you will configure the ASA firewall functionality and clientless SSL VPN remote access.

Note: The router commands and output in this lab are from a Cisco 1841 router using Cisco IOS software, release 15.1(4)M8 (Advanced IP Services image). The switch commands and output are from Cisco WS-C2960-24TT-L switches with Cisco IOS Release 15.0(2)SE4 (C2960-LANBASEK9-M image). Other routers, switches, and Cisco IOS versions can be used. See the Router Interface Summary Table at the end of the lab to determine which interface identifiers to use based on the equipment in the lab. Depending on the router, or switch model and Cisco IOS version, the commands available and output produced might vary from what is shown in this lab.

The ASA used with this lab is a Cisco model 5505 with an 8-port integrated switch, running OS version 8.4(2) and the Adaptive Security Device Manager (ASDM) version 7.2(1) and comes with a Base license that allows a maximum of three VLANs.

Note: Ensure that the routers and switches have been erased and have no startup configurations.

Required Resources

- 3 Routers (Cisco 1841 with Cisco IOS Release 15.1(4)M8 Advanced IP Services image or comparable)
- 3 Switches (Cisco 2960 with cryptography IOS image for SSH support – Release 15.0(2)SE4 or comparable)

- 1 ASA 5505 (OS version 8.4(2) and ASDM version 7.2(1) and Base license or comparable)
- 3 PCs (Windows Vista or Windows 7 with CCP 2.5, Cisco VPN Client, latest version of Java, Internet Explorer, and Flash Player)
- Serial and Ethernet cables as shown in the topology
- Console cables to configure Cisco networking devices

CCP Notes:

- If the PC on which CCP is installed is running Windows Vista or Windows 7, it may be necessary to right-click on the CCP icon or menu item, and choose Run as administrator.
- In order to run CCP, it may be necessary to temporarily disable antivirus programs and O/S firewalls. Make sure that all pop-up blockers are turned off in the browser.

Part 1: Create a Basic Technical Security Policy (Chapters 1 and 10)

In Part 1, you will create a Network Device Security Guidelines document that can serve as part of a comprehensive network security policy. This document addresses specific router and switch security measures and describes the security requirements to be implemented on the infrastructure equipment.

Task 1: Identify Potential Sections of a Basic Network Security Policy.

A network security policy should include several key sections that can address potential issues for users, network access, device access, and other areas. List some key sections you think could be part of good basic security policy.

_____

_____

_____

_____

Task 2: Create a "Network Equipment Security Guidelines" Document As a Supplement to a Basic Security Policy.

Step 1: Review the objectives from previous CCNA Security labs.

a. Open each of the previous labs completed from Chapters 1 to 9, and review the objectives listed for each one.

b. Copy the objectives to a separate document for use as a starting point. Focus mainly on those objectives that involve security practices and device configuration.

Step 2: Create a "Network Device Security Guidelines" document for router and switch security.

Create a high-level list of tasks to include for network access and device security. This document should reinforce and supplement the information presented in a basic Security Policy. It is based on the content of previous CCNA Security labs and on the networking devices present in the course lab topology.

Note: The "Network Device Security Guidelines" document should be no more than two pages, and is the basis for the equipment configuration in the remaining parts of the lab.

Step 3: Submit the Network Device Security Guidelines to your instructor.

Provide the "Network Device Security Guidelines" documents to your instructor for review before starting Part 2 of this lab. You can send them as e-mail attachments or put them on removable storage media, such as a flash drive.

Part 2: Configure Basic Device Settings (Chapters 2 and 6)

Step 1: Cable the network as shown in the topology.

Attach the devices as shown in the topology diagram, and cable as necessary.

Step 2: Configure basic settings for all routers.

a. Configure hostnames as shown in the topology.

b. Configure the interface IP addresses as shown in the IP addressing table.

c. Configure a serial interface DCE clock rate of **128000** for the routers, if using routers other than those specified with this lab.

d. Disable DNS lookup on each router.

Step 3: Configure static default routes on routers R1 and R3.

a. Configure a static default route from R1 to R2 and from R3 to R2.

b. Configure static routes from R2 to the R1 simulated LAN (Loopback 1), the R1 Fa0/0-to-ASA subnet, and the R3 LAN.

Step 4: Configure basic settings for each switch.

a. Configure hostnames, as shown in the topology.

b. Configure the VLAN 1 management address on each switch, as shown in the IP Addressing table.

c. Configure the IP default gateway for each of the three switches.

d. Disable DNS lookup on each switch.

Step 5: Configure PC host IP settings.

Configure a static IP address, subnet mask, and default gateway for each PC, as shown in the IP Addressing table.

Step 6: Verify connectivity between PC-C and R1 Lo1 and Fa0/0.

Step 7: Save the basic running configuration for each router and switch.

Part 3: Configure Secure Router Administrative Access (Chapters 2 and 3)

You use the CLI to configure passwords and device access restrictions.

Task 1: Configure Access Passwords on All the Routers.

Step 1: Configure the enable secret password.

Use **ciscoenapa55** as the **enable secret** password..

Step 2: Configure the console line.

Configure a console password of **ciscoconpa55** and enable login. Set the **exec-timeout** value to log out after 15 minutes of inactivity. Prevent console messages from interrupting command entry.

Step 3: Configure the vty lines.

Configure the password for vty lines to be **ciscovtypa55** and enable login. Set the **exec-timeout** value to log out a session after **15** minutes of inactivity.

Task 2: Configure Settings for R1 and R3.

Step 1: Configure a minimum password length of 10 characters.

Step 2: Encrypt plaintext passwords.

Step 3: Configure a login warning banner.

Configure a warning to unauthorized users with a message-of-the-day (MOTD) banner that says: **Unauthorized access strictly prohibited and prosecuted to the full extent of the law!**.

Step 4: Configure the router to log login activity.

a. Configure the router to generate system logging messages for both successful and failed login attempts. Configure the router to log every successful login and log failed login attempts after every second failed login.

b. Issue the **show login** command. What additional information is displayed?

_____

_____

Step 5: Enable HTTP access.

a. Enable the HTTP server on R1 to simulate an Internet target for later testing.

b. Enable secure HTTP server on R3 for a secure CCP access.

Step 6: Configure the local user database.

Create a local user account of **Admin01** with a secret password of **Admin01pa55** and a privilege level of **15**, and configure the local database to authenticate and access the HTTP sessions.

Task 3: Configure Local Authentication with AAA on R1 and R3.

Step 1: Configure the local user database.

Create a local user account of **Admin01** with a secret password of **Admin01pa55** and a privilege level of **15**.

Step 2: Enable AAA services.

Step 3: Implement AAA services using the local database.

Create the default login authentication method list using case-sensitive local authentication as the first option, and the enable password as the backup option to use if an error occurs in relation to local authentication.

Task 4: Configure the SSH Server on R1 and R3.

Step 1: Configure the domain name.

Configure a domain name of **ccnasecurity.com**.

Step 2: Change the vty lines to accept SSH connections only.

Specify that the router vty lines will accept only SSH connections and only using the local database.

Step 3: Generate the RSA encryption key pair.

Configure the RSA keys with **1024** as the number of modulus bits.

Step 4: Configure the SSH version.

Specify that the router accept only **SSH version 2** connections.

Step 5: Configure SSH timeouts and authentication parameters.

The default SSH timeouts and authentication parameters can be altered to be more restrictive. Configure SSH timeout to **90** seconds and the number of authentication attempts to **2**.

Step 6: Verify SSH connectivity to R1 from PC-C.

Launch the SSH client on PC-C, enter the R1 S0/0/0 IP address (**10.10.10.1**) and log in as **Admin01** with the password **Admin01pa55**. If prompted by the SSH client with a security alert regarding the server's host key, click **Yes**.

Task 5: Secure Against Login Attacks and Secure the IOS and Configuration File on R1 and R3.

Step 1: Configure enhanced login security.

If a user fails to log in twice within a **30**-second time span, then disable logins for **1** minute. Log all failed login attempts.

Step 2: Secure the Cisco IOS image and archive a copy of the running configuration.

a. The **secure boot-image** command enables Cisco IOS image resilience, which hides the file from the **dir** and **show** commands. The file cannot be viewed, copied, modified, or removed using EXEC mode commands. (It can be viewed in ROMMON mode.)

b. The **secure boot-config** command takes a snapshot of the router running configuration and securely archives it in persistent storage (flash).

Step 3: Verify that your image and configuration are secured.

a. You can use only the **show secure bootset** command to display the archived filename. Display the status of configuration resilience and the primary bootset filename.

What is the name of the archived running config file and on what is the name based?

_____

_____

b. Save the running configuration to the startup configuration from the privileged EXEC mode prompt.

Task 6: Configure a Synchronized Time Source Using NTP.

R2 will be the master NTP clock source for R1 and R3.

Step 1: Set up the NTP master using Cisco IOS commands.

R2 is the master NTP server in this lab. All other routers and switches learn the time from it, either directly or indirectly. For this reason, you must ensure that R2 has the correct Coordinated Universal Time (UTC) set.

a. Use the **show clock** command to display the current time set on the router.

b. Use the **clock set** *time* command to set the time on the router.

c. Configure R2 as the NTP master using the **ntp master** *stratum-number* command in global configuration mode. The stratum number indicates the distance from the original source. For this lab, use a stratum number of 3 on R2. When a device learns the time from an NTP source, its stratum number becomes one greater than the stratum number of its source.

Step 2: Configure R1 and R3 as NTP clients using the CLI.

a. R1 and R3 will become NTP clients of R2. To configure R1, use the **ntp server** *hostname* global configuration mode command. The hostname can also be an IP address. The **ntp update-calendar** command periodically updates the calendar with the NTP time.

b. Verify that R1 has made an association with R2 with the **show ntp associations** command. You can also use the more verbose version of the command by adding the *detail* argument. It might take some time for the NTP association to form.

c. Verify the time on R1 and R3 after they have made NTP associations with R2.

Task 7: Configure Syslog Support on R3 and PC-C.

Step 1: Install the syslog server on PC-C.

a. The Tftpd32 software from jounin.net is free to download and install, and it includes a TFTP server, TFTP client, and a syslog server and viewer. If not already installed, download Tftpd32 at http://tftpd32.jounin.net and install it on PC-C.

b. Run the **Tftpd32.exe** file, click **Settings**, and ensure that the **syslog server** check box is checked. In the **SYSLOG** tab, you can configure a file for saving syslog messages. Close the settings and in the main Tftpd32 interface window, note the server interface IP address, and select the **Syslog server** tab to bring it to the foreground.

Step 2: Configure R3 to log messages to the syslog server using the CLI.

a. Verify that you have connectivity between R3 and PC-C by pinging the R1 Fa0/1 interface IP address **172.16.1.3**. If it is unsuccessful, troubleshoot as necessary before continuing.

b. NTP was configured in Task 2 to synchronize the time on the network. Displaying the correct time and date in syslog messages is vital when using syslog to monitor a network. If the correct time and date of a message is not known, it can be difficult to determine what network event caused the message.

   Verify that the timestamp service for logging is enabled on the router using the **show run** command. Use the **service timestamps log datetime msec** command if the timestamp service is not enabled.

c. Configure the syslog service on the router to send syslog messages to the syslog server.

Step 3: Configure the logging severity level on R3.

Logging traps can be set to support the logging function. A trap is a threshold that when reached, triggers a log message. The level of logging messages can be adjusted to allow the administrator to determine what kinds of messages are sent to the syslog server. Routers support different levels of logging. The eight levels range from 0 (emergencies), indicating that the system is unstable, to 7 (debugging), which sends messages that include router information.

Note: The default level for syslog is 6, informational logging. The default for console and monitor logging is 7, debugging.

a. Use the **logging trap** command to set the severity level for R3 to level 4, **warnings**.

b. Use the **show logging** command to see the type and level of logging enabled.

Part 4: Configure a Zone-Based Policy Firewall and Intrusion Prevention System (Chapters 4 and 5)

In Part 4, you will configure a ZBF and IPS on R3 using CCP.

Task 1: Configure a ZBF on R3 Using CCP.

Step 1: Access CCP and discover R3.

a. Start CCP on PC-C. In the Manage Devices window, add R3 IP address (**172.16.1.1**) in the first IP address field. In the Username field, enter **Admin01**, and in the Password field, **Admin01pa55**. Ensure that the **Connect Securely** check box is selected.

b. At the CCP Dashboard, click **Discover** to discover and connect to R3.

Step 2: Use the CCP Firewall wizard to configure ZBF.

a. On the CCP menu bar, click **Configure** > **Security** > **Firewall** > **Firewall**.

b. Select **Basic Firewall** and click **Launch the selected task**.

c. Specify **Fa0/1** interface as the **Inside (trusted)** interface and **S0/0/1** as the **Outside (untrusted)** interface.

d. Click **OK** when the warning displays, informing you that you cannot launch CCP from the S0/0/1 interface after the Firewall wizard completes.

e. Select **Low Security**, and complete the Firewall wizard.

f. Deliver the configuration to the router.

Step 3: Verify firewall functionality.

a. From PC-C, ping external router R2 interface S0/0/1 at IP address **10.20.20.2**. The pings should be successful.

b. From external router R2, ping PC-C at IP address **172.16.1.3**. The pings should NOT be successful.

c. From PC-C on the R3 internal LAN, Telnet to R2 at IP address **10.20.20.2** and use password **ciscovtypa55**.

d. With the Telnet session open from PC-C to R2, issue the **show policy-map type inspect zone-pair sessions** command on R3 from the privileged EXEC mode prompt. Continue pressing **Enter** until you see an Established Sessions section toward the end.

Task 2: Configure IPS on R3 Using CCP.

Step 1: Prepare router R3 and the TFTP server.

To configure Cisco IOS IPS 5.x, the IOS IPS signature package file and public crypto key files must be available on the PC with the TFTP server installed. R3 uses PC-C as the TFTP server. Check with your instructor if these files are not on the PC.

a. Verify that the **IOS-Sxxx-CLI.pkg** signature package file is in the default TFTP folder. The *xxx* is the version number and varies depending on which file was downloaded from Cisco.com.

b. Verify that the **realm-cisco.pub.key.txt** file is available and note its location on PC-C. This is the public crypto key used by Cisco IOS IPS.

c. Verify or create the IPS directory (**ipsdir**) in router flash on R3. From the R3 CLI, display the content of flash memory and check to see if the **ipsdir** directory exists.

    Note: For router R3, the IPS signature (.xml) files in the **flash:/ipsdir/** directory should have been deleted and the directory removed prior to starting the SBA. The files must be deleted from the directory to remove it.

d. If the **ipsdir** directory is not listed, create it in privileged EXEC mode, using the **mkdir** command.

    Note: If the ipsdir directory is listed and there are files in it, contact your instructor. This directory must be empty before configuring IPS. If there are no files in it, you may proceed to configure IPS.

Step 2: Verify the IOS IPS signature package location and TFTP server setup.

a. Verify connectivity between R3 and PC-C, the TFTP server, using the **ping** command.

b. Start Tftpd32 (or other TFTP server) and set the default directory to the one with the IPS signature package in it. Note the filename for use in the next step.

Step 3: Access CCP and discover R3 (if required).

a. Start CCP on PC-C. In the Manage Devices window, add R3 IP address (**172.16.1.1**) in the first IP address field.

b. In the Username field, enter **Admin01**, and in the Password field, **Admin01pa55**. Ensure that the **Connect Securely** check box is selected. Enter the same username and password for subsequent login dialog boxes, if prompted. Click **OK** > **Discover** (on the next screen).

Step 4: Use the CCP IPS wizard to configure IPS.

NETLAB+ Users: It may be necessary to copy the text from the public key file before starting the IPS configuration process with CCP. If you are not using **NETLAB+** to perform the SBA, go to Step 4a.

a. On the CCP menu bar, click **Configure** > **Security** > **Intrusion Prevention** > **Create IPS**.

b. Click **Launch IPS Rule Wizard** to open the Welcome to the IPS Policies Wizard window.

c. Apply the IPS rule in the **inbound** direction for **Serial0/0/1**.

d. In the Signature File and Public Key window, specify the signature file with a URL and use TFTP to retrieve the file from PC-C. Enter the IP address of the PC-C TFTP server and the filename.

e. In the Signature File and Public Key window, enter the name of the public key file, **realm-cisco.pub**.

f. On PC-C, open the public key file and copy the text that is between the phrase "key-string" and the word "quit". In the Configure Public Key section, paste the text into the **Key** field.

g. In the Config Location and Category window, specify the **flash:/ipsdir/** directory name as the location to store the signature information.

h. In the **Config Location and Category** window > Choose **Category** field, select **basic**.

i. Click **Next** to display the Summary window, and click **Finish**.

j. On the Deliver Configuration to Device screen, click **Deliver** to deliver the commands to the router.

   Note: Allow the signature configuration process to complete. This can take several minutes.

Part 5: Configure a Site-to-Site IPsec VPN Between ISRs (Chapter 8)

In Part 5, you will use CCP to configure an IPsec VPN tunnel between R1 and R3 that passes through R2.

Task 1: Configure the Site-to-Site VPN Between R1 and R3.

Step 1: Use the CCP VPN wizard to configure R3.

a. On the CCP menu bar, click **Configure** > **Security** > **VPN** > **Site-to-Site VPN**.

b. Select the **Create a Site to Site VPN** option to configure the R3 side of the site-to-site VPN. Click **Launch the selected task**.

c. Verify that **Quick setup** option is selected, and click **Next**.

Step 2: Configure basic VPN connection information settings.

a. On the VPN Connection Information screen, select R3 **S0/0/1** as the interface for the connection.

b. In the **Peer Identity** section, specify R1 interface S0/0/0 (**10.10.10.1**) as the remote peer static IP address.

c. In the **Authentication** section, specify the pre-shared VPN key **cisco12345**.

d. In the **Traffic to encrypt** section, specify the R1 source interface **FastEthernet0/1** and the destination IP address of the R1 Loopback 1 network (**172.20.1.0/24**). Click **Next**.

e. Click **Finish** on the Summary of the Configuration screen.

Step 3: Generate a mirror configuration from R3 and apply it to R1.

a. When returned to the CCP **VPN Edit Site-to-Site VPN** screen on R3, click **Generate mirror** to create the IOS commands for application to router R1.

b. Click **Save** and save the generated configuration CLI commands to a text file on the desktop or flash drive on PC-C.

c. Edit the file as necessary to remove notes and non-essential components.

d. From PC-C, SSH to R1 using SSH client. Log in to R1 using **Admin01** and **Admin01pa55** for the password. The enable password on R1 is **ciscoenapa55**.

e. Copy the mirrored commands from the text file that you saved on PC-C to the R1 command prompt in global configuration mode.

f. Apply the **crypto map** named in the configuration to the R1 **S0/0/0** interface.

Task 2: Test the Site-to-Site IPsec VPN Using CCP.

Step 1: On R3 (PC-C), use CCP to test the IPsec VPN tunnel between the two routers.

a. On the CCP menu bar, click **Configure** > **Security** > **VPN** > **Site-to-Site VPN** and select the **Edit Site-to-Site VPN** tab.

b. In the Edit Site-to-Site VPN tab, select the VPN you just configured, and click **Test Tunnel**.

c. When the VPN Troubleshooting window displays, click **Start** to have CCP troubleshoot the tunnel.

d. When the CCP Warning window displays, indicating that CCP will enable router debugs and generate some tunnel traffic, click **Yes** to continue.

e. In the next VPN Troubleshooting window, the IP address of the R3 Fa0/1 interface in the source network is displayed by default (172.16.1.1). Enter the IP address of the R1 Loopback 1 interface in the Destination Network field (**172.20.1.1**), and click **Continue** to begin the debugging process.

If the debug is successful, you should see an Information window indicating that troubleshooting was successful and the tunnel is up.

Step 2: Ping from PC-C to the R1 Lo1 interface at 172.20.1.1 to generate some interesting traffic.

Step 3: Issue the show crypto isakmp sa command on R3 to view the security association created.

Step 4: Issue the show crypto ipsec sa command on R1 to see how many packets have been received from R3 and decrypted by R1.

Part 6: Secure Network Switches (Chapter 6)

Note: Not all security features in this part of the lab will be configured on all switches, although they normally would be in a production network.

Task 1: Configure Passwords and a Login Banner on S1.

Step 1: Configure the enable secret password.

Use an enable secret password of **ciscoenapa55**.

Step 2: Encrypt plaintext passwords.

Step 3: Configure the console and vty lines.

a. Configure a console password of **ciscoconpa55** and enable login. Set the **exec-timeout** value to log out after five (**5**) minutes of inactivity. Prevent console messages from interrupting command entry.

b. Configure a vty lines password of **ciscovtypa55** and enable login. Set the **exec-timeout** value to log out after five (**5**) minutes of inactivity.

Step 4: Configure a login warning banner.

Configure a warning to unauthorized users with a MOTD banner that says **"Unauthorized access strictly prohibited!"**.

Step 5: Disable HTTP access.

HTTP access to the switch is enabled by default. To prevent HTTP access, disable the HTTP server and HTTP secure server.

Task 2: Secure Access Ports on S1.

Step 1: Disable trunking access ports that are in use.

On S1, configure port F0/6 as access mode only.

Step 2: Enable PortFast access ports that are in use.

PortFast is configured on access ports that connect to a workstation or server to enable the port to forward traffic more quickly.

Enable PortFast on the S1 Fa0/6 access port.

Step 3: Enable BPDU guard access ports that are in use.

Enable BPDU guard on the F0/6 access port.

Task 3: Configure Port Security and Disable Unused Ports.

Step 1: Configure basic port security for the S1 access port.

Shut down user access ports that are in use on S1 and enable basic default port security. This sets the maximum MAC addresses to 1 and the violation action to shut down. Use the **sticky** option to allow the secure MAC address that is dynamically learned on a port to the switch running configuration. Re-enable the access port to which port security was applied.

Step 2: Disable unused ports on S1.

As a further security measure, disable any ports not being used on each switch.

Ports Fa0/1 and Fa0/6 are used on switch S1. Shut down the remaining Fast Ethernet ports and the two Gigabit Ethernet ports.

Step 3: Save the running configuration to the startup configuration for each switch.

Part 7: Configure ASA Basic Settings and Firewall (Chapter 9)

Task 1: Prepare the ASA for ASDM Access.

Step 1: Clear the previous ASA configuration settings.

a. Use the **write erase** command to remove the **startup-config** file from flash memory.

b. Use the **reload** command to restart the ASA.

Step 2: Bypass Setup Mode and configure the ASDM VLAN interfaces using the CLI.

a. When prompted to preconfigure the firewall through interactive prompts (Setup mode), respond with **no**.

b. Enter privileged EXEC mode. The password should be blank (no password) at this point.

c. Enter global configuration mode. Respond with **no** to the prompt to enable anonymous reporting.

d. The VLAN 1 logical interface will be used by PC-B to access ASDM on ASA physical interface E0/1. Configure interface **VLAN 1** and name it **inside**. The Security Level should be automatically set to the highest level of 100. Specify IP address **192.168.10.1** and subnet mask **255.255.255.0**.

e. Enable physical interface E0/1 and verify the E0/1 and VLAN 1 interface status. The status and protocol for interface E0/1 and VLAN 1 should be up/up.

f. Preconfigure interface VLAN 2 and name it **outside**, add physical interface E0/0 to **VLAN 2**, and bring up the **E0/0** interface. You will assign the IP address using ASDM.

g. Test connectivity to the ASA by pinging from PC-B to ASA interface VLAN 1 IP address **192.168.1.1**. The pings should be successful.

Step 3: Configure and verify access to the ASA from the inside network.

a. Use the **http** command to configure the ASA to accept HTTPS connections and to allow access to ASDM from any host on the inside network 192.168.10.0/24.

b. Open a browser on PC-B and test the HTTPS access to the ASA by entering **https://192.168.1.1**.

c. From the ASDM Welcome page, click **Run ASDM**. When prompted for a username and password, leave them blank and click **OK**.

Task 2: Configure Basic ASA Settings Using the ASDM Startup Wizard.

Step 1: Access the Configuration menu and launch the Startup wizard.

At the top left of the screen, click **Configuration** > **Launch Startup wizard**.

Step 2: Configure the hostname, domain name, and the enable password.

a. On the first Startup wizard screen, select the **Modify Existing Configuration** option.

b. On the Startup Wizard Step 2 screen, configure the ASA hostname **CCNAS-ASA** and domain name **ccnasecurity.com**. Change the enable mode password from blank (no password) to **ciscoenapa55**.

Step 3: Configure the outside VLAN interfaces.

a. On the Startup Wizard Step 3 screen – Interface Selection, do not change the current settings; these were previously defined using the CLI.

b. On the Startup Wizard Step 4 screen – Switch Port Allocation, verify that port **Ethernet1** is in Inside VLAN 1 and that port Ethernet0 is in Outside VLAN 2.

c. On the Startup Wizard Step 5 screen – Interface IP Address Configuration, enter an Outside IP address of **209.165.200.10** and Mask **255.255.255.248**.

Step 4: Configure DHCP, address translation, and administrative access.

a. On the Startup Wizard Step 6 screen – DHCP Server, select **Enable DHCP server on the Inside Interface** and specify a starting IP address of **192.168.1.5** and ending IP address of **192.168.1.30**. Enter the DNS Server 1 address of **10.3.3.3** and **ccnasecurity.com** for the domain name. Do **NOT** check the box to enable Autoconfiguration from Interface.

b. On the Startup Wizard Step 7 screen – Address Translation (NAT/PAT), configure the ASA to **Use Port Address Translation (PAT)** and select the **Use the IP address of the outside interface** option.

c. On the Startup Wizard Step 8 screen – Administrative Access, HTTPS/ASDM access is currently configured for hosts on inside network 192.168.10.0/24. Add **Telnet** access to the ASA for the inside network **192.168.1.0** with a subnet mask of **255.255.255.0**. Add **SSH** access to the ASA from host **172.16.1.3** on the **outside** network.

d. Finish the wizard and deliver the commands to the ASA.

    Note: ASDM may hang after delivering the configuration changes to the ASA. If this happens, close ASDM and, on the PC Desktop, double-click the **ASDM on 192.168.1.1** icon to restart ASDM. When prompted, leave **Username** blank and enter **ciscoenapa55** as the password.

Step 5: Test Telnet access to the ASA.

a. From a command prompt or GUI Telnet client on PC-B, Telnet to the ASA inside interface at IP address **192.168.1.1**.

b. Log in to the ASA using the default login password of **cisco**. Enter privileged EXEC mode and provide the password **ciscoenapa55**. Exit the Telnet session by using the **quit** command.

Task 3: Configuring ASA Settings from the ASDM Configuration Menu.

Step 1: Set the ASA date and time.

At the **Configuration > Device Setup** screen, click **System Time > Clock**, set the time zone, current date and time, and apply the commands to the ASA.

Step 2: Configure a static default route for the ASA.

a. At the **Configuration > Device Setup** screen, click **Routing > Static Routes**. Add a static route for the **outside** interface, specify **Any** for the network object and a Gateway IP of **209.165.200.9** (R1 Fa0/0). Apply the commands to the ASA.

b. On the ASDM **Tools** menu, select **Ping**, and enter the IP address of router R1 S0/0/0 (**10.10.10.1**). The ping should succeed.

Step 3: Test access to an external website from PC-B.

Open a browser on PC-B and enter the IP address of the R1 S0/0/0 interface (**10.10.10.1**) to simulate access to an external website. The R1 HTTP server was enabled in Part 2. You should be prompted with a user authentication login dialog box from the R1 GUI device manager. Exit the browser.

Note: You will be unable to ping from PC-B to R1 S0/0/0, because the default ASA application inspection policy does not permit ICMP from the internal network.

Step 4: Configure AAA for SSH client access.

a. At the **Configuration > Device Management** screen, click **Users/AAA > User Accounts > Add**. Create a new user named **admin** with a password of **cisco123**. Allow this user **Full access** (ASDM, SSH, Telnet, and console) and set the privilege level to **15**. Apply the command to the ASA.

b. At the **Configuration** > **Device Management** screen, click **Users/AAA** > **AAA Access**. On the Authentication tab, require authentication for **HTTP/ASDM**, **SSH**, and **Telnet** connections, and specify the **LOCAL** server group for each connection type. Click **Apply** to send the commands to the ASA.

   Note: The next action you attempt within ASDM will require you to log in as **admin** with password **cisco123**.

c. From PC-C, open an SSH client and attempt to access the ASA outside interface at **209.165.200.10**. You should be able to establish the connection. When prompted to log in, enter username **admin** and password **cisco123**.

d. After logging in to the ASA using SSH, enter the **enable** command and provide the password **ciscoenapa55**. Issue the **show run** command to display the current configuration you have created using ASDM.

e. Connect to the ASA inside interface from a PC-B via Telnet using IP address 192.168.1.1.

Part 8: Configuring a DMZ, Static NAT, and ACLs (Chapter 9)

In Part 7, you configured address translation using PAT for the inside network. In this part, you will create a DMZ on the ASA, configure static NAT to a DMZ server, and apply ACLs to control access to the server.

To accommodate the addition of a DMZ and a web server, you will use another address from the ISP range assigned, 209.165.200.8/29 (.8-.15). Router R1 Fa0/0 and the ASA outside interface already use 209.165.200.9 and .10, respectively. You will use public address **209.165.200.11** and static NAT to provide address translation access to the server.

Step 1: Configure the DMZ interface VLAN 3 on the ASA.

a. Configure DMZ VLAN 3, which is where the public access web server will reside. Assign it IP address **192.168.2.1/24**, name it **dmz**, and assign it a security level of **70**.

   Note: If you are working with the ASA 5505 base license, you will see the error message shown in the output below. The ASA 5505 Base license allows for the creation of up to three named VLAN interfaces. However, you must disable communication between the third interface and one of the other interfaces using the **no forward** command. This is not an issue if the ASA has a Security Plus license, which allows 20 named VLANs.

   Because the server does not need to initiate communication with the inside users, disable forwarding to interface VLAN 1.

b. Assign ASA physical interface **E0/2** to DMZ **VLAN 3** and enable the interface.

c. Display the status for all ASA interfaces using the **show interface ip brief** command.

d. Display the information for the Layer 3 VLAN interfaces using the **show ip address** command.

e. Display the VLANs and port assignments on the ASA using the **show switch vlan** command.

Step 2: Configure static NAT to the DMZ server using a network object.

Configure a network object named **dmz-server** and assign it the static IP address of the DMZ server (**192.168.2.3**). While in object definition mode, use the **nat** command to specify that this object is used to translate a DMZ address to an outside address using static NAT and specify a public translated address of **209.165.200.11**.

Step 3: Configure an ACL to allow access to the DMZ server from the Internet.

Configure a named access list **OUTSIDE-DMZ** that permits any IP protocol from any external host to the internal IP address of the DMZ server. Apply the access list to the ASA **outside** interface in the **in** direction.

Note: Unlike IOS ACLs, the ASA ACL **permit** statement must permit access to the internal private DMZ address. External hosts access the server using its public static NAT address, and the ASA translates it to the internal host IP address and applies the ACL.

You can modify this ACL to allow only services that you want to expose to external hosts, such as web (HTTP) or file transfer (FTP).

Step 4: Test access to the DMZ server.

a. Create a loopback 0 interface on Internet router R2 representing an external host. Assign Lo0 IP address **172.30.1.1** and a mask of **255.255.255.0**. Ping the DMZ server public address from R2 using the loopback interface as the source of the ping. The pings should be successful.

b. Clear the NAT counters using the **clear nat counters** command.

c. Ping from PC-C to the DMZ server at the public address **209.165.200.11**. The pings should be successful.

d. Issue the **show nat** and **show xlate** commands on the ASA to see the effect of the pings. Both the PAT (inside to outside) and static NAT (dmz to outside) policies are shown.

Note: Pings from inside to outside are translated hits. Pings from outside host PC-C to the DMZ are considered untranslated hits.

Note: The flag is "s" indicating a static translation.

e. Because the ASA inside interface (**VLAN 1**) is set to a security level of 100 (the highest) and the DMZ interface (**VLAN 3**) is set to 70, you can also access the DMZ server from a host on the inside network. The ASA acts like a router between the two networks. Ping the DMZ server (**PC-A**) internal address (**192.168.2.3**) from inside network host PC-B (**192.168.1.X**). The pings should be successful due to the interface security level and the fact that ICMP is being inspected on the inside interface by the global inspection policy. The pings from PC-B to PC-A do not affect the NAT translation counts, because both PC-B and PC-A are behind the firewall and no translation takes place.

f. The DMZ server cannot ping PC-B on the inside network, because the DMZ interface VLAN 3 has a lower security level and the fact that, when the VLAN 3 interface was created, it was necessary to specify the **no forward** command. Try to ping from the DMZ server PC-A to PC-B at IP address 192.168.1.X. The pings should be unsuccessful.

g. Use the **show run** command to display the configuration for VLAN 3.

Note: An access list can be applied to the inside interface to control the type of access to be permitted or denied to the DMZ server from inside hosts.

Part 9: Configure ASA Clientless SSL VPN Remote Access (Chapter 9)

Step 1: Start the VPN wizard.

On PC-B, on the ASDM main menu, click **Wizards** > **VPN Wizards** > **Clientless SSL VPN wizard**. The SSL VPN wizard Clientless SSL VPN Connection screen displays.

Step 2: Configure the SSL VPN user interface.

On the SSL VPN Interface screen, configure **VPN-Con-Prof** as the Connection Profile Name, and specify **outside** as the interface to which outside users will connect.

Step 3: Configure AAA user authentication.

On the User Authentication screen, click **Authenticate Using the Local User Database**, enter the username **VPNuser** with a password of **remote**. Click **Add** to create the new user.

Step 4: Configure the VPN group policy.

On the Group Policy screen, create a new group policy named **VPN-Grp-Pol**.

Step 5: Configure the bookmark list.

a. From the Clientless Connections Only – Bookmark List screen, click **Manage** to create an HTTP server bookmark in the bookmark list. In the Configure GUI Customization Objects window, click **Add** to open the Add Bookmark List window. Name the list **WebServer-XX**, where *XX* is your initials.

b. Add a new Bookmark with **Web Mail** as the Bookmark Title. Enter the server destination IP address of PC-B **192.168.1.3** (simulating a web server).

Step 6: Verify VPN access from the remote host.

a. Open the browser on PC-C and enter the login URL for the SSL VPN into the address field (**https://209.165.200.10**). Use secure HTTP (HTTPS) as SSL is required to connect to the ASA.

b. The Login window should appear. Enter the previously configured username **VPNuser** and password **remote**, and click **Logon** to continue.

Step 7: Access the web portal window.

After the user authenticates, the ASA SSL web portal webpage will be displayed, listing the various bookmarks previously assigned to the profile. If the Bookmark points to a valid server IP address or hostname that has HTTP web services installed and functional, the outside user can access the server from the ASA portal.

Note: In this lab, the web mail server is not installed on PC-B.

Router Interface Summary Table

Router Interface Summary				
Router Model	**Ethernet Interface #1**	**Ethernet Interface #2**	**Serial Interface #1**	**Serial Interface #2**
1700	Fast Ethernet 0 (Fa0)	Fast Ethernet 1 (Fa1)	Serial 0 (S0)	Serial 1 (S1)
1800	Fast Ethernet 0/0 (Fa0/0)	Fast Ethernet 0/1 (Fa0/1)	Serial 0/0/0 (S0/0/0)	Serial 0/0/1 (S0/0/1)
1900	Gigabit Ethernet 0/0 (G0/0)	Gigabit Ethernet 0/1 (G0/1)	Serial 0/0/0 (S0/0/0)	Serial 0/0/1 (S0/0/1)
2801	Fast Ethernet 0/0 (Fa0/0)	Fast Ethernet 0/1 (Fa0/1)	Serial 0/1/0 (S0/1/0)	Serial 0/1/1 (S0/1/1)
2811	Fast Ethernet 0/0 (Fa0/0)	Fast Ethernet 0/1 (Fa0/1)	Serial 0/0/0 (S0/0/0)	Serial 0/0/1 (S0/0/1)
2900	Gigabit Ethernet 0/0 (G0/0)	Gigabit Ethernet 0/1 (G0/1)	Serial 0/0/0 (S0/0/0)	Serial 0/0/1 (S0/0/1)

Note: To find out how the router is configured, look at the interfaces to identify the type of router and how many interfaces the router has. There is no way to effectively list all the combinations of configurations for each router class. This table includes identifiers for the possible combinations of Ethernet and Serial interfaces in the device. The table does not include any other type of interface, even though a specific router may contain one. An example of this might be an ISDN BRI interface. The string in parenthesis is the legal abbreviation that can be used in Cisco IOS commands to represent the interface.